Letters from Egypt

Letters from Egypt

An Englishwoman on the Nile, 1862–69

LUCIE DUFF GORDON

ELAND
London

This edition of the letters first published by R. Brimley Johnson in 1902, from earlier editions by John Murray dated 1865 and 1875

This edition, with its additions, published by Eland Publishing Ltd
61 Exmouth Market, London EC1R 4QL in 2021

ISBN 978 1 78060 038 3
A full CIP record for this book is available from the British Library

Cover image: *A Lady Receiving Visitors (The Reception)*, 1873
by John Frederick Lewis (1804–76) from the Yale Center
for British Art, Paul Mellon Collection

Text set in Great Britain by James Morris
Printed in Spain by GraphyCems, Navarra

Contents

List of Illustrations

Publisher's Note

LUCIE DUFF GORDON contracted tuberculosis sometime in the 1850s, and by 1861 her doctors feared for her life should she face another damp, English winter. After trying South Africa for one season (her lungs were not impressed), she travelled to Egypt to see how she would fare there. Her eldest daughter, Janet, had just married and moved to Alexandria, so it meant that she could at least be close to one of her 'chicks'. The hot, dry climate of Luxor, right in the centre of Egypt, gave her seven more years of life.

It was obvious to the lucky recipients of these vivid and sympathetic reports of life on the Nile – mainly her mother and her husband – that Lucie's letters deserved publication. Lucie Duff Gordon's *Letters from Egypt 1863–65* first appeared in 1865, edited back in London by her mother Sarah Austin. They were received with great acclaim and reprinted twice before the end of the year. Six years after Lucie's death in 1869, her daughter, Janet Ross, put together a second volume of her mother's letters, published in 1875 as *Last Letters from Egypt*. In 1902 Janet married the two books together, added a personal memoir, an introduction by George Meredith and re-edited the text. In 1969, Lucie's great-grandson, Gordon Waterfield, produced an 'enlarged centenary edition'. His lengthy footnotes were informed by his own 1937 biography, *Lucie Duff Gordon in England, South Africa and Egypt*, but his scholarship occasionally stifles Lucie's quick wit. Having read both editions back-to-back, it is obvious that Janet did a very fine job in cutting back on family matters to create a tighter portrait of Egypt.

So we have opted to reproduce Janet Ross's 1902 edition here, divested of the literary barnacles – the prefaces, introductions, notes and memoirs – that have clustered around it and keep the reader at bay.

While reading her captivating prose, you may wish to refer to the notes at the end of the book which help make sense of Lucie's references to matters both English and Egyptian. And once finished, you may well want to know more about Lucie herself, so we have commissioned a biographical afterword, which is informed by all this material, and also by Katherine Frank's 1994 biography, *Lucie Duff Gordon: A Passage to Egypt.*

Letters from Egypt

To Mrs. Austin

GRAND CAIRO,
Tuesday, November 11, 1862.

DEAREST MUTTER,

I write to you out of the real Arabian Nights. Well may the Prophet (whose name be exalted) smile when he looks on Cairo. It is a golden existence, all sunshine and poetry, and, *I* must add, kindness and civility. I came up last Thursday by railway with the American Consul-General, a charming person, and had to stay at this horrid Shepheard's Hotel.* But I do little but sleep here. Hekekian Bey, a learned old Armenian, takes care of me every day, and the American Vice-Consul is my sacrifice. I went on Sunday to his child's christening, and heard Sakna, the 'Restorer of Hearts.' She is wonderfully like Rachel,* and her singing is *hinreisend* from expression and passion. Mr. Wilkinson (the Consul) is a Levantine, and his wife Armenian, so they had a grand fantasia; people feasted all over the house and in the street. Arab music *schmetterte*, women yelled the *zaghareet*, black servants served sweetmeats, pipes, and coffee, and behaved as if they belonged to the company, and I was strongly under the impression that I was at Nurreddin's wedding with the Vizier's daughter. Yesterday I went to Heliopolis with Hekekian Bey and his wife, and visited an Armenian country lady close by.

My servant Omar turns out a jewel. He has *déterré* an excellent boat for the Nile voyage, and I am to be mistress of a captain, a mate, eight men and a cabin boy for £25 a month. I went to Boulak, the port of Cairo, and saw various boats, and admired the way in which the English travellers pay for their insolence and caprices. Similar boats cost people with dragomans £50 to £65. But, then, 'I shall lick the fellows,' etc., is what I hear all round. The dragoman, I conclude, pockets the difference. The owner of the boat, Sid Achmet el-Berberi, asked £30, whereupon I touched my breast, mouth and eyes, and stated through Omar that I was not, like other Ingeleez, made of money, but would give £20. He then showed another boat at £20, very much worse, and I departed (with fresh civilities) and looked at others, and saw two more for £20; but neither was clean, and neither had a little boat for landing. Meanwhile Sid Achmet came after me and explained that, if I was not like other Ingeleez in money, I likewise differed in politeness, and had refrained from abuse, etc., etc., and I should have the boat for £25. It was so very excellent in all fittings, and so much larger, that I thought it would make a great difference in health, so I said if he would go before the American Vice-Consul (who is looked on as a sharp hand) and would promise all he said to me before him, it should be well.

Mr. Thayer, the American Consul-General, gives me letters to every consular agent depending on him; and two Coptic merchants whom I met at the fantasia have already begged me to 'honour their houses.' I rather think the poor agents, who are all Armenians and Copts, will think I am the republic in person. The weather has been all this time like a splendid English August, and I hope I shall get rid of my cough in time, but it has been very bad. There is no cold at night here as at the Cape, but it is nothing like so clear and bright.

Omar took Sally sightseeing* all day while I was away, into several mosques; in one he begged her to wait a minute while he said a prayer. They compare notes about their respective countries and are great friends; but he is put out at my not having provided her with a husband long ago, as is one's duty towards a 'female servant,' which almost always here means a slave.

Of all the falsehoods I have heard about the East, that about women being old hags at thirty is the biggest. Among the poor fellah women it may be true enough, but not nearly as much as in Germany; and I have now seen a considerable number of Levantine ladies looking very handsome, or at least comely, till fifty. Sakna, the Arab Grisi,* is fifty-five—an ugly face, I am told (she was veiled and one only saw the eyes and glimpses of her mouth when she drank water), but the figure of a leopard, all grace and beauty, and a splendid voice of its kind, harsh but thrilling like Malibran's. I guessed her about thirty, or perhaps thirty-five. When she improvised, the finesse and grace of her whole *Wesen* were ravishing. I was on the point of shouting out 'Wallah!'* as heartily as the natives. The eight younger Halmeh (*i.e.*, learned women, which the English call Almeh and think is an improper word) were ugly and screeched. Sakna was treated with great consideration and quite as a friend by the Armenian ladies with whom she talked between her songs. She is a Muslimeh and very rich and charitable; she gets £50 for a night's singing at least.

It would be very easy to learn colloquial Arabic, as they all speak with such perfect distinctness that one can follow the sentences and catch the words one knows as they are repeated. I think I know forty or fifty words already, besides my 'salaam aleikum' and 'backsheesh.'

The reverse of the brilliant side of the medal is sad enough: deserted palaces, and crowded hovels scarce good enough for pigstyes. 'One day man see his dinner, and one other day none at all,' as Omar observes; and the children are shocking from bad food, dirt and overwork, but the little pot-bellied, blear-eyed wretches grow up into noble young men and women under all their difficulties. The faces are all sad and rather what the Scotch call 'dour,' not *méchant* at all, but harsh, like their voices. All the melody is in walk and gesture; they are as graceful as cats, and the women have exactly the 'breasts like pomegranates' of their poetry. A tall Bedaween woman came up to us in the field yesterday to shake hands and look at us. She wore a white sackcloth shift and veil, *und weiter nichts*, and asked Mrs. Hekekian a good many questions about me, looked at my face and hands, but took no notice of my rather smart gown which the village women admired so much, shook hands again with the air of a princess, wished me health and happiness, and strode off across the graveyard like a stately ghost. She was on a journey all alone, and somehow it looked very solemn and affecting to see her walking away towards the desert in the setting sun like Hagar.* All is so Scriptural in the country here. Sally called out in the railroad, 'There is Boaz,* sitting in the cornfield'; and so it was, and there he has sat for how many thousand years,—and Sakna sang just like Miriam in one war-song.

Wednesday.—My contract was drawn up and signed by the American Vice-Consul to-day, and my Reis* kissed my hand in due form, after which I went to the bazaar to buy the needful pots and pans. The transaction lasted an hour. The copper is so much per oka, the workmanship so much; every article is weighed by a sworn weigher and a ticket sent with it. More Arabian Nights. The shopkeeper compares notes with me about numerals, and is as much amused as I. He treats me to coffee and a pipe from a neighbouring shop while Omar eloquently depreciates the goods and offers half the value. A water-seller offers a brass cup of water; I drink, and give the huge sum of twopence, and he distributes the contents of his skin to the crowd (there always is a crowd) in my honour. It seems I have done a pious action. Finally a boy is called to carry the *batterie de cuisine*, while Omar brandishes a gigantic kettle which he has picked up a little bruised for four shillings. The boy has a donkey which I mount astride *à l'Arabe*, while the boy carries all the copper things on his head. We are rather a grand procession, and quite enjoy the fury of the dragomans and other leeches who hang on the English at such independent proceedings, and Omar gets reviled for spoiling the trade by being cook, dragoman, and all in one.

I went this morning with Hekekian Bey* to the two earliest mosques. The Touloun is exquisite—noble, simple, and what ornament there is is the most delicate lacework and embossing in stone and wood. This Arab architecture is even more lovely than our Gothic. The Touloun is now a vast poorhouse, a nest of paupers. I went into three of their lodgings. Several Turkish families were in a large square room neatly divided into little partitions with old mats hung on ropes. In each were as many bits of carpet, mat and patchwork as the poor owner could collect, and a small chest and a little brick cooking-place in one corner of the room with three earthern pipkins for I don't know how many people;—that was all—they possess no sort of furniture, but all was scrupulously clean and no bad smell whatever. A little boy seized my hand and showed where he slept, ate and cooked with the most expressive pantomime. As there were women, Hekekian could not come in, but when I came out an old man told us they received three loaves (cakes as big as a sailor's biscuit), four piastres a month—*i.e.*, eightpence per adult—a suit of clothes a year, and on festive occasions lentil soup. Such is the almshouse here. A little crowd belonging to the house had collected, and I gave sixpence to an old man, who transferred it to the first old man to be *divided* among them all, ten or twelve people at least, mostly blind or lame. The poverty wrings my heart. We took leave with salaams and politeness like the best society, and then turned into an Arab hut stuck against the lovely arches. I stooped low under the door, and several women crowded in. This was still poorer, for there were no mats or rags of carpet, a still worse cooking-place, a sort of dog-kennel piled up of loose stones to sleep in, which contained a small chest and the print of human forms on the stone floor. It was, however, quite free from dust, and perfectly sweet. I gave the young woman who had led me in sixpence, and here the difference between Turk and Arab appeared. The division of this created a perfect storm of noise, and we left the five or six Arab women outshrieking a whole rookery. I ought to say that no one begged at all.

Friday.—I went to-day on a donkey to a mosque in the bazaar, of what we call Arabesque style, like the Alhambra, very handsome. The Kibleh* was very beautiful, and as I was admiring it Omar pulled a lemon out of his breast and smeared it on the porphyry pillar on one side of the arch, and then entreated me to lick it. It cures all diseases. The old man who showed the mosque pulled eagerly at my arm to make me perform this absurd ceremony, and I thought I should have been forced to do it. The base of the pillar was clogged with lemon-juice. I then went to the tombs of the Khalìfah;* one of the great ones had such arches and such wondrous cupolas but all in ruins. There are scores of these noble buildings, any one of which is a treasure, falling to decay. The next, strange to say, was in perfect repair. I got off the donkey, and Omar fidgeted and hesitated a little and consulted with a woman who had the key. As there were no overshoes I pulled my boots off, and was rewarded by seeing the footprints of Mohammed on two black stones, and a lovely little mosque, a sort of *Sainte Chapelle*. Omar prayed with ardent fervour and went out backwards, saluting the Prophet aloud. To my surprise the woman was highly pleased with sixpence, and did not ask for more. When I remarked this, Omar said that no Frank had ever been inside to his knowledge. A mosque-keeper of the sterner sex would not have let me in. I returned home through endless streets and squares of Moslem tombs, those of the Memlooks among them. It was very striking; and it was getting so dark that I thought of Nurreddin Bey, and wondered if a Jinn would take me anywhere if I took up my night's lodging in one of the comfortable little cupola-covered buildings.

My Coptic friend has just called in to say that his brother expects me at Kenneh. I find nothing but civility and a desire to please. My boat is the *Zint el Bachreyn*,* and I carry the English flag and a small American distinguishing pennant as a signal to my consular agents. We sail next Wednesday. Good-bye for the present, dearest Mutter.

To Sir Alexander Duff Gordon

BOAT OFF EMBABEH,
November 21, 1862.

DEAREST ALICK,

We embarked yesterday, and after the fashion of Eastern caravans are abiding to-day at a village opposite Cairo; it is Friday, and therefore would be improper and unlucky to set out on our journey. The scenes on the river are wonderfully diverting and curious, so much life and movement. But the boatmen are sophisticated; my crew have all sported new white drawers in honour of the Sitti Ingleezee's supposed modesty—of course compensation will be expected. Poor fellows! they are very well mannered and quiet in their rags and misery, and their queer little humming song is rather pretty, 'Eyah Mohammad, eyah Mohammad,' *ad infinitum*, except when an energetic man cries 'Yallah!'—*i.e.*, 'O God!'—which means 'go it' in everyday life. Omar is gone to fetch one or two more 'unconsidered trifles,' and I have been explaining the defects to be remedied in the cabin door, broken window, etc., to my Reis with the help of six words of Arabic and dumb show, which they understand and answer with wonderful quickness.

The air on the river is certainly quite celestial—totally unlike the damp, chilly feeling of the hotel and Frank quarter of Cairo. The Isbekeeyeh, or public garden, where all the Franks live, was a lake, I believe, and is still very damp.

I shall go up to the second Cataract as fast as possible, and return back at leisure. Hekekian Bey came to take leave yesterday, and lent me several books; pray tell Senior what a kindness his introduction was. It would have been rather dismal in Cairo—if one could be dismal there—without a soul to speak to. I was sorry to know no Turks or Arabs, and have no opportunity of seeing any but the tradesman of whom I bought my stores but that was very amusing. The young man of whom I bought my *finjaans* was so handsome, elegant and melancholy that I know he was the lover of the Sultan's favourite slave. How I wish you were here to enjoy all this, so new, so beautiful, and yet so familiar, life—and you would like the people, poor things! they are complete children, but amiable children.

I went into the village here, where I was a curiosity, and some women took me into their houses and showed me their sleeping-place, cookery, poultry, etc.; and a man followed me to keep off the children, but no backsheesh was asked for, which showed that Europeans were rare there. The utter destitution is terrible to see, though in this climate of course it matters less, but the much-talked-of dirt is simply utter poverty. The poor souls are as clean as Nile mud and water will make their bodies, and they have not a second shirt, or any bed but dried mud.

Give my love to my darlings, and don't be uneasy if you don't get letters. My cough has been better now for five days without a bad return of it, so I hope it is really better; it is the first reprieve for so long. The sun is so hot, a regular broil, November 21, and all doors and windows open in the cabin—a delicious breeze.

To Mrs. Austin

FESHN,
Monday, November 30, 1862.

DEAREST MUTTER,

I have now been enjoying this most delightful way of life for ten days, and am certainly much better. I begin to eat and sleep again, and cough less. My crew are a great amusement to me. They are mostly men from near the first Cataract above Assouan, sleek-skinned, gentle, patient, merry black fellows. The little black Reis is the very picture of good-nature and full of fun, 'chaffing' the girls as we pass the villages, and always smiling. The steersman is of lighter complexion, also very cheery, but decidedly pious. He prays five times a day and utters ejaculations to the apostle Rusool continually. He hurt his ankle on one leg and his instep on the other with a rusty nail, and they festered. I dressed them with poultices, and then with lint and strapping, with perfect success, to the great admiration of all hands, and he announced how much better he felt, 'Alhamdulillah, kieth-el-hairack khateer ya Sitti' (Praise be to God and thanks without end O Lady), and everyone echoed, 'kieth-el-hairack khateer.' The most important person is the 'weled'—boy—Achmet. The most merry, clever, omnipresent little rascal, with an ugly little pug face, a shape like an antique Cupid, liberally displayed, and a skin of dark brown velvet. His voice, shrill and clear, is always heard foremost; he cooks for the crew, he jumps overboard with the rope and gives advice on all occasions, grinds the coffee with the end of a stick in a mortar, which he holds between his feet, and uses the same large stick to walk proudly before me, brandishing it if I go ashore for a minute, and ordering everybody out of the way. 'Ya Achmet!' resounds all day whenever anybody wants anything, and the 'weled' is always ready and able. My favourite is Osman, a tall, long-limbed black who seems to have stepped out of a hieroglyphical drawing, shirt, skull-cap and all. He has only those two garments, and how anyone contrives to look so inconceivably 'neat and respectable' (as Sally truly remarked) in that costume is a mystery. He is always at work, always cheerful, but rather silent—in short, the able seaman and steady, respectable 'hand' *par excellence*. Then we have El Zankalonee from near Cairo, an old fellow of white complexion and a valuable person, an inexhaustible teller of stories at night and always *en train*, full of jokes and remarkable for a dry humour much relished by the crew. I wish I understood the stories, which sound delightful, all about Sultans and Efreets, with effective 'points,' at which all hands exclaim 'Mashallah!' or 'Ah!' (as long as you can drawl it). The jokes, perhaps, I may as well be ignorant of. There is a certain Shereef who does nothing but laugh and work and be obliging; helps Omar with one hand and Sally with the other, and looks like a great innocent black child. The rest of the dozen are of various colours, sizes and ages, some quite old, but all very quiet and well-behaved.

We have had either dead calm or contrary wind all the time and the men have worked very hard at the tow-rope. On Friday I proclaimed a halt in the afternoon at a village at prayer-time for the pious Muslims to go to the mosque; this gave great satisfaction, though only five went, Reis, steersman, Zankalonee and two old men. The up-river men never pray at all, and Osman occupied himself by buying salt out of another boat and stowing it away to take up to his family, as it is terribly dear high up the river. At Benisouef we halted to buy meat and bread, it is *comme qui dirait* an assize town, there is one butcher who kills one sheep a day. I walked about the streets escorted by Omar in front and two sailors with huge staves behind, and created a sensation accordingly. It is a dull little country town with a wretched palace of Said Pasha. On Sunday we halted at Bibbeh, where I caught sight of a large Coptic church and sallied forth to see whether they would let me in. The road lay past the house of the headman of the village, and there 'in the gate' sat a patriarch, surrounded by his servants and his cattle. Over the gateway were crosses and queer constellations of dots, more like Mithraic symbols than anything Christian, but Girgis was a Copt, though the chosen head of the Muslim village. He rose as I came up, stepped out and salaamed, then took my hand and said I must go into his house before I saw the church and enter the hareem. His old mother, who looked a hundred, and his pretty wife, were very friendly; but, as I had to leave Omar at the door, our talk soon came to an end, and Girgis took me out into the divan, without the sacred precincts of the hareem. Of course we had pipes and coffee, and he pressed me to stay some days, to eat with him every day and to accept all his house contained. I took the milk he offered, and asked him to visit me in the boat, saying I must return before sunset when it gets cold, as I was ill. The house was a curious specimen of a wealthy man's house—I could not describe it if I tried, but I felt I was acting a passage of the Old Testament. We went to the church, which outside looked like nine beehives in a box. Inside, the nine domes resting on square pillars were very handsome. Girgis was putting it into thorough repair at his own expense, and it will cost a good deal, I think, to repair and renew the fine old wood panelling of such minute and intricate workmanship. The church is divided by three screens; one in front of the eastern three domes is impervious and conceals the holy of holies. He opened the horseshoe door for me to look in, but explained that no Hareem might cross the threshold. All was in confusion owing to the repairs which were actively going on without the slightest regard to Sunday; but he took up a large bundle, kissed it, and showed it me. What it contained I cannot guess, and I scrupled to inquire through a Muslim interpreter. To the right of this sanctum is the tomb of a Muslim saint! enclosed under the adjoining dome. Here we went in and Girgis kissed the tomb on one side while Omar salaamed it on the other—a pleasant sight. They were much more particular about our shoes than in the mosques. Omar wanted to tie handkerchiefs over my boots like at Cairo, but the priest objected and made me take them off and march about in the brick and mortar rubbish in my stockings. I wished to hear the service, but it was not till sunset, and, as far as I could make out, not different on Sunday to other days. The Hareems are behind the screen furthest removed from the holy screen, behind a third screen where also was the font, locked up and shaped like a Muslim tomb in little. (Hareem is used here just like the German *Frauenzimmer*, to mean a respectable woman. Girgis spoke of me to Omar as 'Hareem.') The Copts have but one wife, but they shut her up much closer than the Arabs. The children were sweetly pretty, so unlike the Arab brats, and the men very good-looking. They did not seem to acknowledge me at all as a *co-religionnaire*, and asked whether we of the English religion did not marry our brothers and sisters.

The priest then asked me to drink coffee at his house close by, and there I 'sat in the gate'—*i.e.*, in a large sort of den raised 2 feet from the ground and matted, to the left of the gate. A crowd of Copts collected and squatted about, and we were joined by the mason who was repairing the church, a fine, burly, rough-bearded old Mussulman, who told how the Sheykh buried in the church of Bibbeh had appeared to him three nights running at Cairo and ordered him to leave his work and go to Bibbeh and mend his church, and how he came and offered to do so without pay if the Copts would find the materials. He spoke with evident pride, as one who had received a Divine command, and the Copts all confirmed the story and everyone was highly gratified by the miracle. I asked Omar if he thought it was all true, and he had no doubt of it. The mason he knew to be a respectable man in full work, and Girgis added that he had tried to get a man to come for years for the purpose without success. It is not often that a dead saint contrives to be equally agreeable to Christians and Mussulmans, and here was the staunch old 'true believer' working away in the sanctuary which they would not allow an English fellow-Christian to enter.

Whilst we sat hearing all these wonders, the sheep and cattle pushed in between us, coming home at eve. The venerable old priest looked so like Father Abraham, and the whole scene was so pastoral and Biblical that I felt quite as if my wish was fulfilled to live a little a few thousands of years ago. They wanted me to stay many days, and then Girgis said I must stop at Feshn where he had a fine house and garden, and he would go on horseback and meet me there, and would give me a whole troop of Fellaheen to pull the boat up quick. Omar's eyes twinkled with fun as he translated this, and said he knew the Sitt would cry out, as she always did about the Fellaheen, as if she were hurt herself. He told Girgis that the English customs did not allow people to work without pay, which evidently seemed very absurd to the whole party.

GEBEL SHEYK EMBARAK,
Thursday.

I stopped last night at Feshn, but finding this morning that my Coptic friends were not expected till the afternoon, I would not spend the whole day, and came on still against wind and stream. If I could speak Arabic I should have enjoyed a few days with Girgis and his family immensely, to learn their *Ansichten* a little; but Omar's English is too imperfect to get beyond elementary subjects. The thing that strikes me most is the tolerant spirit that I see everywhere. They say 'Ah! it is your custom,' and express no sort of condemnation, and Muslims and Christians appear perfectly good friends, as my story of Bibbeh goes to prove. I have yet to see the much-talked-of fanaticism, at present I have not met with a symptom of it. There were thirteen Copt families at Bibbeh and a considerable Muslim population, who had elected Girgis their headman and kissed his hand very heartily as our procession moved through the streets. Omar said he was a very good man and much liked.

The villages look like slight elevations in the mud banks cut into square shapes. The best houses have neither paint, whitewash, plaster, bricks nor windows, nor any visible roofs. They don't give one the notion of human dwellings at all at first, but soon the eye gets used to the absence of all that constitutes a house in Europe, the impression of wretchedness wears off, and one sees how picturesque they are, with palm-trees and tall pigeon-houses, and here and there the dome over a saint's tomb. The men at work on the river-banks are exactly the same colour as the Nile mud, with just the warmer hue of the blood circulating beneath the skin. Prometheus has just formed them out of the universal material at hand, and the sun breathed life into them. Poor fellows—even the boatmen, ragged crew as they are—say 'Ah, Fellaheen!' with a contemptuous pity when they see me watch the villagers at work.

The other day four huge barges passed us towed by a steamer and crammed with hundreds of the poor souls torn from their homes to work at the Isthmus of Suez,* or some palace of the Pasha's, for a nominal piastre a day, and find their own bread and water and cloak. One of my crew, Andrasool, a black savage whose function is always to jump overboard whenever the rope gets entangled or anything is wanted, recognised some relations of his from a village close to Assouan. There was much shouting and poor Andrasool looked very mournful all day. It may be his turn next. Some of the crew disloyally remarked that they were sure the men there wished they were working for a Sitti Ingleez, as Andrasool told them he was. Think too what splendid pay it must be that the boat-owner can give out of £25 a month to twelve men, after taking his own profits, the interest of money being enormous.

When I call my crew black, don't think of negroes. They are elegantly-shaped Arabs and all gentlemen in manners, and the black is transparent, with amber *reflets* under it in the sunshine; a negro looks *blue* beside them. I have learned a great deal that is curious from Omar's confidences, who tells me his family affairs and talks about the women of his family, which he would not to a man. He refused to speak to his brother, a very grand dragoman, who was with the Prince of Wales, and who came up to us in the hotel at Cairo and addressed Omar, who turned his back on him.

I asked the reason, and Omar told me how his brother had a wife, 'An old wife, been with him long time, very good wife.' She had had three children—all dead. All at once the dragoman, who is much older than Omar, declared he would divorce her and marry a young woman. Omar said, 'No, don't do that; keep her in your house as head of your home, and take one of your two black slave girls as your Hareem.' But the other insisted, and married a young Turkish wife; whereupon Omar took his poor old sister-in-law to live with him and his own young wife, and cut his grand brother dead. See how characteristic!—the urging his brother to take the young slave girl 'as his Hareem,' like a respectable man—that would have been all right; but what he did was 'not good.' I'll trouble you (as Mrs. Grote used to say) to settle these questions to everyone's satisfaction. I own Omar seemed to me to take a view against which I had nothing to say. His account of his other brother, a confectioner's household with two wives, was very curious. He and they, with his wife and sister-in-law, all live together, and one of the brother's wives has six children—three sleep with their own mother and three with their *other* mother—and all is quite harmonious.

SIOUT,
December 10.

I could not send a letter from Minieh, where we stopped, and I visited a sugar manufactory and a gentlemanly Turk, who superintended the district, the Moudir. I heard a boy singing a *Zikr* (the ninety-nine attributes of God) to a set of dervishes in a mosque, and I think I never heard anything more beautiful and affecting. Ordinary Arab singing is harsh and nasal, but it can be wonderfully moving. Since we left Minieh we have suffered dreadfully from the cold; the chickens died of it, and the Arabs look blue and pinched. Of course it is *my weather* and there never was such cold and such incessant contrary winds known. To-day was better, and Wassef, a Copt here, lent me his superb donkey to go up to the tomb in the mountain.

The tomb is a mere cavern, so defaced, but the view of beautiful Siout standing in the midst of a loop of the Nile was ravishing. A green deeper and brighter than England, graceful minarets in crowds, a picturesque bridge, gardens, palm-trees, then the river beyond it, the barren yellow cliffs as a frame all around that. At our feet a woman was being carried to the grave, and the boys' voices rang out the Koran full and clear as the long procession—first white turbans and then black veils and robes—wound along. It is all a dream to me. You can't think what an odd effect it is to take up an English book and read it and then look up and hear the men cry, 'Yah Mohammad.' 'Bless thee, Bottom, how art thou translated;' it is the reverse of all one's former life when one sat in England and read of the East. '*Und nun sitz ich mitten drein*' in the real, true Arabian Nights, and don't know whether 'I be I as I suppose I be' or not.

Tell Alick the news, for I have not written to any but you. I do so long for my Rainie. The little Copt girls are like her, only pale; but they don't let you admire them for fear of the evil-eye.

To Sir Alexander Duff Gordon

THEBES,*
December 20, 1862.

DEAR ALICK,

I have had a long, dawdling voyage up here, but enjoyed it much, and have seen and heard many curious things. I only stop here for letters and shall go on at once to Wady Halfeh, as the weather is very cold still, and I shall be better able to enjoy the ruins when I return about a month hence, and shall certainly prefer the tropics now. I can't describe the kindness of the Copts. The men I met at a party in Cairo wrote to all their friends and relations to be civil to me. Wassef's attentions consisted first in lending me his superb donkey and accompanying me about all day. Next morning arrived a procession headed by his clerk, a gentlemanly young Copt, and consisting of five black memlooks carrying a live sheep, a huge basket of the most delicious bread, a pile of cricket-balls of creamy butter, a large copper caldron of milk and a cage of poultry. I was confounded, and tried to give a good baksheesh to the clerk, but he utterly declined. At Girgeh one Mishrehgi was waiting for me, and was in despair because he had only time to get a few hundred eggs, two turkeys, a heap of butter and a can of milk. At Keneh one Issa (Jesus) also lent a donkey, and sent me three boxes of delicious Mecca dates, which Omar thought stingy. Such attentions are agreeable here where good food is not to be had except as a gift. They all made me promise to see them again on my return and dine at their houses, and Wassef wanted to make a fantasia and have dancing girls. How you would love the Arab women in the country villages. I wandered off the other day alone, while the men were mending the rudder, and fell in with a troop of them carrying water-jars—such sweet, graceful beings, all smiles and grace. One beautiful woman pointed to the village and made signs of eating and took my hand to lead me. I went with her, admiring them as they walked. Omar came running after and wondered I was not afraid. I laughed, and said they were much too pretty and kindly-looking to frighten anyone, which amused them immensely when he told them so. They all wanted me to go and eat in their houses, and I had a great mind to it, but the wind was fair and the boat waiting, so I bid my beautiful friends farewell. They asked if we wanted anything—milk or eggs—for they would give it with pleasure, it was not their custom to sell things, they said, I offered a bit of money to a little naked child, but his mother would not let him take it. I shall never forget the sweet, engaging creatures at that little village, or the dignified politeness of an old weaver whose loom I walked in to look at, and who also wished to 'set a piece of bread before me.' It is the true poetical pastoral life of the Bible in the villages where the English have not been, and happily they don't land at the little places. Thebes has become an English watering-place. There are now nine boats lying here, and the great object is to *do the Nile* as fast as possible. It is a race up to Wady Halfeh or Assouan. I have gained so much during this month that I hope the remaining three will do real good, as the weather will improve with the new year they tell me. All the English stay here and 'make Christmas,' as Omar calls it, but I shall go on and do my devotions with the Copts at Esneh or Edfou. I found that their seeming disinclination to let one attend their service arose from an idea that we English would not recognise them as Christians. I wrote a curious story of a miracle to my mother, I find that I was wrong about the saint being a Mussulman (and so is Murray); he is no less than Mar Girghis, our own St. George himself. Why he selected a Mussulman mason I suppose he best knows.

In a week I shall be in Nubia. Some year we must all make this voyage; you would revel in it. Kiss my darlings for me.

To Sir Alexander Duff Gordon

THEBES,
February 11, 1863.

DEAREST ALICK,

On arriving here last night I found one letter from you, dated December 10, and have received nothing else. Pray write again forthwith to Cairo where I hope to stay some weeks. A clever old dragoman I met at Philæ offers to lend me furniture for a lodging or a tent for the desert, and when I hesitated he said he was very well off and it was not his business to sell things, but only to be paid for his services by rich people, and that if I did not accept it as he meant it he should be quite hurt. This is what I have met with from everything Arab—nothing but kindness and politeness. I shall say farewell to Egypt with real feeling; among other things, it will be quite a pang to part with Omar who has been my shadow all this time and for whom I have quite an affection, he is so thoroughly good and amiable.

I am really much better I hope and believe, though only within the last week or two. We have had the coldest winter ever known in Nubia, such bitter north-east winds, but when the wind by great favour did not blow, the weather was heavenly. If the millennium really does come I shall take a good bit of mine on the Nile. At Assouan I had been strolling about in that most poetically melancholy spot, the granite quarry of old Egypt and burial-place of Muslim martyrs, and as I came homewards along the bank a party of slave merchants, who had just loaded their goods for Senaar from the boat on the camels, asked me to dinner, and, oh! how delicious it felt to sit on a mat among the camels and strange bales of goods and eat the hot tough bread, sour milk and dates, offered with such stately courtesy. We got quite intimate over our leather cup of sherbet (brown sugar and water), and the handsome jet-black men, with features as beautiful as those of the young Bacchus, described the distant lands in a way which would have charmed Herodotus. They proposed to me to join them, 'they had food enough,' and Omar and I were equally inclined to go. It is of no use to talk of the ruins; everybody has said, I suppose, all that can be said, but Philæ surpassed my expectations. No wonder the Arab legends of Ans el Wogood are so romantic, and Abou Simbel and many more. The scribbling of names is quite infamous, beautiful paintings are defaced by Tomkins and Hobson, but worst of all Prince Pückler Muskau* has engraved his and his *Ordenskreuz* in huge letters on the naked breast of that august and pathetic giant who sits at Abou Simbel.* I wish someone would kick him for his profanity.

I have eaten many odd things with odd people in queer places, dined in a respectable Nubian family (the castor-oil was trying), been to a Nubian wedding—such a dance I saw. Made friends with a man much looked up to in his place (Kalabshee—notorious for cutting throats), inasmuch as he had killed several intrusive tax-gatherers and recruiting officers. He was very gentlemanly and kind and carried me up a place so steep I could not have reached it. Just below the cataract—by-the-by going up is nothing but noise and shouting, but coming down is fine fun—*Fantasia khateer* as my excellent little Nubian pilot said. My sailors all prayed away manfully and were horribly frightened. I confess my pulse quickened, but I don't think it was fear. Well, below the cataract I stopped for a religious fête, and went to a holy tomb with the darweesh, so extraordinarily handsome and graceful—the true *feingemacht* noble Bedaween type. He took care of me through the crowd, who never had seen a Frank woman before and crowded fearfully, and pushed the true believers unmercifully to make way for me. He was particularly pleased at my not being afraid of Arabs; I laughed, and asked if he was afraid of us. 'Oh no! he would like to come to England; when there he would work to eat and drink, and then sit and sleep in the church.' I was positively ashamed to tell my religious friend that with us the 'house of God' is not the house of the poor stranger. I asked him to eat with me but he was holding a preliminary Ramadan (it begins next week), and could not; but he brought his handsome sister, who was richly dressed, and begged me to visit him and eat of his bread, cheese and milk. Such is the treatment one finds if one leaves the highroad and the backsheesh-hunting parasites. There are plenty of 'gentlemen' barefooted and clad in a shirt and cloak ready to pay attentions which you may return with a civil look and greeting, and if you offer a cup of coffee and a seat on the floor you give great pleasure, still more if you eat the dourah and dates, or bread and sour milk with an appetite.

At Koom Ombo we met a Rifaee darweesh* with his basket of tame snakes. After a little talk he proposed to initiate me, and so we sat down and held hands like people marrying. Omar sat behind me and repeated the words as my 'Wakeel,' then the Rifaee twisted a cobra round our joined hands and requested me to spit on it, he did the same and I was pronounced safe and enveloped in snakes. My sailors groaned and Omar shuddered as the snakes put out their tongues—the darweesh and I smiled at each other like Roman augurs. I need not say the creatures were toothless.

It is worth going to Nubia to see the girls. Up to twelve or thirteen they are neatly dressed in a bead necklace and a leather fringe 4 inches wide round the loins, and anything so absolutely perfect as their shapes or so sweetly innocent as their look can't be conceived. My pilot's little girl came in the dress mentioned before carrying a present of cooked fish on her head and some fresh eggs; she was four years old and so *klug*. I gave her a captain's biscuit and some figs, and the little pet sat with her little legs tucked under her, and ate it so *manierlich* and was so long over it, and wrapped up some more white biscuit to take home in a little rag of a veil so carefully. I longed to steal her, she was such a darling. Two beautiful young Nubian women visited me in my boat, with hair in little plaits finished off with lumps of yellow clay burnished like golden tags, soft, deep bronze skins, and lips and eyes fit for Isis and Hathor. Their very dress and ornaments were the same as those represented in the tombs, and I felt inclined to ask them how many thousand years old they were. In their house I sat on an ancient Egyptian couch with the semicircular head-rest, and drank out of crockery which looked antique, and they brought a present of dates in a basket such as you may see in the British Museum. They are dressed in drapery like Greek statues, and are as perfect, but have hard, bold faces, and, though far handsomer, lack the charm of the Arab women; and the men, except at Kalabshee and those from far up the country, are not such gentlemen as the Arabs.

Everyone is cursing the French here. Forty thousand men always at work at the Suez Canal at starvation-point, does not endear them to the Arabs. There is great excitement as to what the new Pasha will do. If he ceases to give forced labour, the Canal, I suppose, must be given up. Well, I must leave off and send my letter to Mustapha Aga to forward. I shall stay here ten days or so, and then return slowly to Cairo on March 10, the last day of Ramadan. I will stay a short time at Cairo, and then take a small boat and drop down to Alexandria and see Janet. How I did wish for my darling Rainie to play with Achmet in the boat and see the pretty Nubian boys and girls. I have seen and heard so much, that like M. de Conti *je voudrais être levé pour l'aller dire*. I long to bore you with traveller's tales. Pray write soon.

Omar wanted to hear all that 'the gentleman' said about 'weled and bint' (boy and girl), and was quite delighted to hear of Maurice's good report at school, he thinks that the 'Abou el welàd' (father of the children—you, to wit) will send a sheep to the 'fikee' who teaches him. I have learned a new code of propriety altogether—*célà a du bon et du mauvais*, like ours. When I said 'my husband' Omar blushed and gently corrected me; when my donkey fell in the streets he cried with vexation, and on my mentioning the fall to Hekekian Bey he was quite indignant. 'Why you say it, ma'am? that shame'—a *faux pas* in fact. On the other hand they mention all that belongs to the production of children with perfect satisfaction and pleasure. A very pleasing, modest and handsome Nubian young woman, wishing to give me the best present she could think of, brought me a mat of her own making, and which had been her marriage-bed. It was a gift both friendly and honourable, and I treasure it accordingly. Omar gave me a description of his own marriage, appealing to my sympathy about the distress of absence from his wife. I intimated that English people were not accustomed to some words and might be shocked, on which he said, 'Of course I not speak of my Hareem to English gentleman, but to good Lady can speak it.'

Good-bye, dear Alick, no, that is improper: I must say 'O my Lord' or 'Abou Maurice.'

To Mrs. Austin

A few miles below Girgeh,
March 7, 1863.

Dearest Mutter,

I was so glad to find from your letter (which Janet sent me to Thebes by a steamer) that mine from Siout had reached you safely. First and foremost I am wonderfully better. In Cairo the winter has been terribly cold and damp, as the Coptic priest told me yesterday at Girgeh. So I don't repent the expense of the boat for *j'en ai pour mon argent*—I am *all* the money better and really think of getting well. Now that I know the ways of this country a little, which Herodotus truly says is like no other, I see that I might have gone and lived at Thebes or at Keneh or Assouan on next to nothing, but then how could I know it? The English have raised a mirage of false wants and extravagance which the servants of the country of course, some from interest and others from mere ignorance, do their best to keep up. As soon as I had succeeded in really persuading Omar that I was not as rich as a Pasha and had no wish to be thought so, he immediately turned over a new leaf as to what must be had and said 'Oh, if I could have thought an English lady would have eaten and lived and done the least like Arab people, I might have hired a house at Keneh for you, and we might have gone up in a clean passenger boat, but I thought no English could bear it.' At Cairo, where we shall be, Inshallaha, on the 19th, Omar will get a lodging and borrow a few mattresses and a table and chair and, as he says, 'keep the money in our pockets instead of giving it to the hotel.' I hope Alick got my letter from Thebes, and that he told you that I had dined with 'the blameless Ethiopians.' I have seen all the temples in Nubia and down as far as I have come, and nine of the tombs at Thebes. Some are wonderfully beautiful—Abou Simbel, Kalabshee, Koom Ombo—a little temple at El Kab, lovely—three tombs at Thebes and most of all Abydos; Edfou and Dendera are the most perfect, Edfou quite perfect, but far less beautiful. But the most lovely object my eyes ever saw is the island of Philæ. It gives one quite the supernatural feeling of Claude's best landscapes, only not the least like them—*ganz anders*. The Arabs say that Ans el Wogood, the most beautiful of men, built it for his most beautiful beloved, and there they lived in perfect beauty and happiness all alone. If the weather had not been so cold while I was there I should have lived in the temple, in a chamber sculptured with the mystery of Osiris' burial and resurrection. Omar cleaned it out and meant to move my things there for a few days, but it was too cold to sleep in a room without a door. The winds have been extraordinarily cold this year, and are so still. We have had very little of the fine warm weather, and really been pinched with cold most of the time. On the shore away from the river would be much better for invalids.

Mustapha Aga, the consular agent at Thebes, has offered me a house of his, up among the tombs in the finest air, if ever I want it. He was very kind and hospitable indeed to all the English there. I went into his hareem, and liked his wife's manners very much. It was charming to see that she henpecked her handsome old husband completely. They had fine children and his boy, about thirteen or so, rode and played Jereed one day when Abdallah Pasha had ordered the people of the neighbourhood to do it for General Parker. I never saw so beautiful a performance. The old General and I were quite excited, and he tried it to the great amusement of the Sheykh el Beled. Some young Englishmen were rather grand about it, but declined mounting the horses and trying a throw. The Sheykh and young Hassan and then old Mustapha wheeled round and round like beautiful hawks, and caught the palm-sticks thrown at them as they dashed round. It was superb, and the horses were good, though the saddles and bridles were rags and ends of rope, and the men mere tatterdemalions. A little below Thebes I stopped, and walked inland to Koos to see a noble old mosque falling to ruin. No English had ever been there and we were surrounded by a crowd in the bazaar. Instantly five or six tall fellows with long sticks improvised themselves our body-guard and kept the people off, who *du reste* were perfectly civil and only curious to see such strange 'Hareem,' and after seeing us well out of the town evaporated as quietly as they came without a word. I gave about ten-pence to buy oil, as it is Ramadan and the mosque ought to be lighted, and the old servant of the mosque kindly promised me full justice at the Day of Judgment, as I was one of those Nasranee of whom the Lord Mohammed said that they are not proud and wish well to the Muslimeen. The Pasha had confiscated all the lands belonging to the mosque, and allowed 300 piastres—not £2 a month—for all expenses; of course the noble old building with its beautiful carving and arabesque mouldings must fall down. There was a smaller one beside it, where he declared that anciently forty girls lived unmarried and recited the Koran—Muslim nuns, in fact. I intend to ask the Alim, for whom I have a letter from Mustapha, about such an anomaly.

Some way above Bellianeh Omar asked eagerly leave to stop the boat as a great Sheyk had called to us, and we should inevitably have some disaster if we disobeyed. So we stopped and Omar said, 'come and see the Sheyk, ma'am.' I walked off and presently found about thirty people, including all my own men, sitting on the ground round St. Simon Stylites—without the column. A hideous old man like Polyphemus, utterly naked, with the skin of a rhinoceros all cracked with the weather, sat there, and had sat day and night, summer and winter, motionless for twenty years. He never prays, he never washes, he does not keep Ramadan, and yet he is a saint. Of course I expected a good hearty curse from such a man, but he was delighted with my visit, asked me to sit down, ordered his servant to bring me sugar-cane, asked my name and tried to repeat it over and over again, and was quite talkative and full of jokes and compliments, and took no notice of anyone else. Omar and my crew smiled and nodded, and all congratulated me heartily. Such a distinction proves my own excellence (as the Sheyk knows all people's thoughts), and is sure to be followed by good fortune. Finally Omar proposed to say the Fathah in which all joined except the Sheykh, who looked rather bored by the interruption, and desired us not to go so soon, unless I were in a hurry. A party of Bedaween came up on camels with presents for the holy man, but he took no notice of them, and went on questioning Omar about me, and answering my questions. What struck me was the total absence of any sanctimonious air about the old fellow, he was quite worldly and jocose; I suppose he knew that his position was secure, and thought his dirt and nakedness proved his holiness enough. Omar then recited the Fathah again, and we rose and gave the servants a few foddahs—the saint takes no notice of this part of the proceeding—but he asked me to send him twice my hand full of rice for his dinner, an honour so great that there was a murmur of congratulation through the whole assembly. I asked Omar how a man could be a saint who neglected all the duties of a Muslim, and I found that he fully believed that Sheykh Seleem could be in two places at once, that while he sits there on the shore he is also at Mecca, performing every sacred function and dressed all in green. 'Many people have seen him there, ma'am, quite true.'

From Bellianeh we rode on pack-donkeys without bridles to Abydos, six miles through the most beautiful crops ever seen. The absence of weeds and blight is wonderful, and the green of Egypt, where it is green, would make English green look black. Beautiful cattle, sheep and camels were eating the delicious clover, while their owners camped there in reed huts during the time the crops are growing. Such a lovely scene, all sweetness and plenty. We ate our bread and dates in Osiris' temple, and a woman offered us buffalo milk on our way home, which we drank warm out of the huge earthen pan it had been milked in. At Girgeh I found my former friend Mishregi absent, but his servants told some of his friends of my arrival, and about seven or eight big black turbans soon gathered in the boat. A darling little Coptic boy came with his father and wanted a '*kitaab*' (book) to write in, so I made one with paper and the cover of my old pocket-book, and gave him a pencil. I also bethought me of showing him 'pickys' in a book, which was so glorious a novelty that he wanted to go with me to my town, 'Beled Ingleez,' where more such books were to be found.

SIOUT,
March 9.

I found here letters from Alick, telling me of dear Lord Lansdowne's death.* Of course I know that his time was come, but the thought that I shall never see his face again, that all that kindness and affection is gone out of my life, is a great blow. No friend could leave such a blank to me as that old and faithful one, though the death of younger ones might be more tragic; but so many things seem gone with him into the grave. Many indeed will mourn that kind, wise, steadfast man—*Antiqua fides*. No one nowadays will be so noble with such unconsciousness and simplicity. I have bought two Coptic turbans to make a black dress out of. I thought I should like to wear it for him—here, where 'compliment' is out of the question.

I also found a letter from Janet, who has been very ill; the account was so bad that I have telegraphed to hear how she is, and shall go at once to Alexandria if she is not better. If she is I shall hold to my plan and see Beni Hassan and the Pyramids on my way to Cairo. I found my kind friend the Copt Wassef kinder than ever. He went off to telegraph to Alexandria for me, and showed so much feeling and real kindness that I was quite touched.

I was grieved to hear that you had been ill again, dearest Mutter. The best is that I feel so much better that I think I may come home again without fear; I still have an irritable cough, but it has begun to have lucid intervals, and is far less frequent. I can walk four or five miles and my appetite is good. All this in spite of really cold weather in a boat where nothing shuts within two fingers' breadths. I long to be again with my own people.

Please send this to Alick, to whom I will write again from Cairo.

To Sir Alexander Duff Gordon

March 10, 1863.

'If in the street I led thee, dearest,
Though the veil hid thy face divine,
They who beheld thy graceful motion
Would stagger as though drunk with wine.

Nay, e'en the holy Sheykh, while praying
For guidance in the narrow way,
Must needs leave off, and on the traces
Of thine enchanting footsteps stray.

O ye who go down in the boats to Dumyat,
Cross, I beseech ye, the stream to Budallah;
Seek my beloved, and beg that she will not
Forget me, I pray and implore her by Allah.

'Fair as two moons is the face of my sweetheart,
And as to her neck and her bosom—Mashallah.
And unless to my love I am soon reunited
Death is my portion—I swear it by Allah.'

Thus sings Ali Asleemee, the most *debraillé* of my crew, a *hashshásh*, but a singer and a good fellow. The translation is not free, though the sentiments are. I merely rhymed Omar's literal word-for-word interpretation. The songs are all in a similar strain, except one funny one abusing the 'Sheykh el-Beled, may the fleas bite him.' Horrid imprecation! as I know to my cost, for after visiting the Coptic monks at Girgeh I came home to the boat with myriads. Sally said she felt like Rameses the Great, so tremendous was the slaughter of the active enemy.

I had written the first page just as I got to Siout and was stopped by bad news of Janet; but now all is right again, and I am to meet her in Cairo, and she proposes a jaunt to Suez and to Damietta. I have got a superb illumination to-night, improvised by Omar in honour of the Prince of Wales's marriage, and consequently am writing with flaring candles, my lantern being on duty at the masthead, and the men are singing an epithalamium and beating the tarabookeh as loud as they can.

You will have seen my letter to my mother, and heard how much better I am for the glorious air of Nubia and the high up-country. Already we are returning into misty weather. I dined and spent the day with Wassef and his Hareem, such an amiable, kindly household. I was charmed with their manner to each other, to the slaves and family. The slaves (all Muslims) told Omar what an excellent master they had. He had meant to make a dance-fantasia, but as I had not good news it was countermanded. Poor

Wassef ate his boiled beans rather ruefully, while his wife and I had an excellent dinner, she being excused fasting on account of a coming baby. The Copt fast is no joke, neither butter, milk, eggs nor fish being allowed for fifty-five days. They made Sally dine with us, and Omar was admitted to wait and interpret. Wassef's younger brother waited on him as in the Bible, and his clerk, a nice young fellow, assisted. Black slaves brought the dishes in, and capital the food was. There was plenty of joking between the lady and Omar about Ramadan, which he had broken, and the Nasranee fast, and also about the number of wives allowed, the young clerk intimating that he rather liked that point in Islam. I have promised to spend ten or twelve days at their house if ever I go up the Nile again. I have also promised to send Wassef all particulars as to the expense, etc. of educating his boy in England, and to look after him and have him to our house in the holidays. I can't describe how anxiously kind these people were to me. One gets such a wonderful amount of sympathy and real hearty kindness here. A curious instance of the affinity of the British mind for prejudice is the way in which every Englishman I have seen scorns the Eastern Christians, and droll enough that sinners like Kinglake and I should be the only people to feel the tie of the 'common faith' (*vide* 'Eothen'). A very pious Scotch gentleman wondered that I could think of entering a Copt's house, adding that they were the publicans (tax-gatherers) of this country, which is partly true. I felt inclined to mention that better company than he or I had dined with publicans, and even sinners.

The Copts are evidently the ancient Egyptians. The slightly aquiline nose and long eye are the very same as the profiles of the tombs and temples, and also like the very earliest Byzantine pictures; *du reste*, the face is handsome, but generally sallow and rather inclined to puffiness, and the figure wants the grace of the Arabs. Nor has any Copt the thoroughbred, *distingué* look of the meanest man or woman of good Arab blood. Their feet are the long-toed, flattish foot of the Egyptian statue, while the Arab foot is classically perfect and you could put your hand under the instep.

The beauty of the Ababdeh, black, naked, and shaggy-haired, is quite marvellous. I never saw such delicate limbs and features, or such eyes and teeth.

CAIRO,
March 19.

After leaving Siout I caught cold. The worst of going up the Nile is that one must come down again and find horrid fogs, and cold nights with sultry days. So I did not attempt Sakhara and the Pyramids, but came a day before my appointed time to Cairo. Up here in the town it is much warmer and dryer, and my cough is better already. I found all your letters in many volumes, and was so excited over reading them that I could not sleep one moment last night, so excuse dulness, but I thought you'd like to know I was safe in Briggs' bank, and expecting Janet and Ross to-night.

To Mrs. Austin

CAIRO,
April 9, 1863.

DEAREST MUTTER,

I write to you because I know Janet is sure to write to Alick. I have had a very severe attack of bronchitis. As I seemed to be getting worse after Janet and Ross left for Alexandria, Omar very wisely sent for Hekekian Bey, who came at once bringing De Leo Bey, the surgeon-in-chief of the Pasha's troops, and also the doctor to the hareem. He has been most kind, coming two and three times a day at first. He won't take any fee, *sous prétexte* that he is *officier du Pasha*; I must send him a present from England. As to Hekekian Bey, he is absolutely the Good Samaritan, and these Orientals do their kindnesses with such an air of enjoyment to themselves that it seems quite a favour to let them wait upon one. Hekekian comes in every day with his handsome old face and a budget of news, all the gossip of the Sultan and his doings.* I shall always fancy the Good Samaritan in a tarboosh with a white beard and very long eyes. I am out of bed to-day for the second time, and waiting for a warm day to go out. Sally saw the illuminations last night; the Turkish bazaar she says was gorgeous. The Sultan and all his suite have not eaten bread here, all their food comes from Constantinople. To-morrow the Mahmaal goes*—think of my missing that sight! *C'est désclant.*

I have a black slave—a real one.* I looked at her little ears wondering they had not been bored for rings. She fancied I wished them bored (she was sitting on the floor close at my side), and in a minute she stood up and showed me her ear with a great pin through it: 'Is that well, lady?' the creature is eight years old. The shock nearly made me faint. What extremities of terror had reduced that little mind to such a state. She is very good and gentle, and sews quite nicely already. When she first came, she tells me, she thought I should eat her; now her one dread is that I should leave her behind. She sings a wild song of joy to Maurice's picture and about the little Sitt. She was sent from Khartoum as a present to Mr. Thayer, who has no woman-servant at all. He fetched me to look at her, and when I saw the terror-stricken creature being coarsely pulled about by his cook and groom, I said I would take her for the present. Sally teaches her, and she is very good; but now she has set her whole little black soul upon me. De Leo can give no opinion as to what I ought to do, as he knows little but Egypt, and thinks England rather like Norway, I fancy. Only don't let me be put in a dreadful mountain valley; I hear the drip, drip, drip of Eaux Bonnes in bad dreams still, when I am chilly and oppressed in my sleep. I'll write again soon, send this to Alick, please.

To Sir Alexander Duff Gordon

CAIRO,
April 13, 1863.

DEAREST ALICK,

You will have heard from my mother of my ill luck, falling sick again. The fact is that the spring in Egypt is very trying, and I came down the river a full month too soon. People do tell such lies about the heat. Today is the first warm day we have had; till now I have been shivering, and Sally too. I have been out twice, and saw the holy Mahmaal rest for its first station outside the town, it is a deeply affecting sight—all those men prepared to endure such hardship. They halt among the tombs of the Khalîfah, such a spot. Omar's eyes were full of tears and his voice shaking with emotion, as he talked about it and pointed out the Mahmaal and the Sheykh al-Gemel, who leads the sacred camel, naked to the waist with flowing hair. Muslim piety is so unlike what Europeans think it is, so full of tender emotions, so much more sentimental than we imagine—and it is wonderfully strong. I used to hear Omar praying outside my door while I was so ill, 'O God, make her better. O my God, let her sleep,' as naturally as we should say, 'I hope she'll have a good night.'

The Sultan's coming is a kind of riddle. No one knows what he wants. The Pasha has ordered all the women of the lower classes to keep indoors while he is here. Arab women are outspoken, and might shout out their grievances to the great Sultan.

April 15.—I continue to get better slowly, and in a few days will go down to Alexandria. Omar is gone to Boulak to inquire the cost of a boat, as I am not fond of the railroad, and have a good deal of heavy baggage, cooking utensils, etc., which the railway charges enormously for. The black slave girl, sent as a present to the American Consul-General, is as happy as possible, and sings quaint, soft little Kordofan songs all day. I hope you won't object to my bringing her home. She wails so terribly when Omar tells her she is not my slave, for fear I should leave her, and insists on being my slave. She wants to be a present to Rainie, the little Sitt, and laughs out so heartily at the thought of her. She is very quiet and gentle, poor little savage, and the utter slavishness of the poor little soul quite upsets me; she has no will of her own. Now she has taken to talking, and tells all her woes and how *batal* (bad) everyone was at Khartoum; and then she rubs her little black nose on my hand, and laughs so merrily, and says all is *quyis keteer* (very good) here, and she hugs herself with delight. I think Rainie will like her very much.

I am going to visit an old Muslim French painter's family. He has an Arab wife and grown-up daughters, and is a very agreeable old man with a store of Arab legends; I am going to persuade him to write them and let me translate them into English. The Sultan goes away to-day. Even water to drink has been brought from Constantinople; I heard that from Hekekian Bey, who formerly owned the eunuch who is now Kislar Aghasy to the Sultan himself. Hekekian had the honour of kissing his old slave's hand. If anyone tries to make you believe any bosh about civilisation in Egypt, laugh at it. The real life and the real people are exactly as described in the most veracious of books, the 'Thousand and One Nights'; the tyranny is the same, the people are not altered—and very charming people they are. If I could but speak the language I could get into Arab society here through two or three different people, and see more than many Europeans who have lived here all their lives. The Arabs are keenly alive to the least prejudice against them, but when they feel quite safe on that point they rather like the amusement of a stranger.

Omar devised a glorious scheme, if I were only well and strong, of putting me in a takterrawan and taking me to Mecca in the character of his mother, supposed to be a Turk. To a European man, of course, it would be impossible, but an enterprising woman might do it easily with a Muslim confederate. Fancy seeing the pilgrimage! In a few days I shall go down to Alexandria, if it makes me ill again I must return to Europe or go to Beyrout. I can't get a boat under £12; thus do the Arabs understand competition; the owner of boats said so few were wanted, times were bad on account of the railway, etc., he must have double what he used to charge. In vain Omar argued that that was not the way to get employment. 'Maleesh!' (Never mind!), and so I must go by rail. Is not that Eastern? Up the river, where there is no railroad, I might have had it at half that rate. All you have ever told me as most Spanish in Spain is in full vigour here, and also I am reminded of Ireland at every turn; the same causes produce the same effects.

To-day the Khamseen is blowing* and it is decidedly hot, quite unlike the heat at the Cape; this is close and gloomy, no sunshine. Altogether the climate is far less bright than I expected, very, very inferior to the Cape. Nevertheless, I heartily agree to the Arab saying: 'He who has drunk Nile water will ever long to drink it again'; and when a graceful woman in a blue shirt and veil lifts a huge jar from her shoulder and holds it to your lips with a hearty smile and welcome, it tastes doubly sweet. *Alhamdulillah!* Sally says all other water is like bad small-beer compared to sweet ale after the Nile water. When the Khamseen is over, Omar insists on my going to see the tree and the well where Sittina Mariam rested with Seyidna Issa in her arms during the flight into Egypt. It is venerated by Christian and Muslim alike, and is a great place for feasting and holiday-making out of doors, which the Arabs so dearly love. Do write and tell me what you wish me to do. If it were not that I cannot endure not to see you and the children, I would stay here and take a house at the Abbassieh in the desert; but I could not endure it. Nor can I endure this wandering life much longer. I must come home and die in peace if I don't get really better. Write to Alexandria next.

To Mr. Tom Taylor

CAIRO,
April 18, 1863.

MY DEAR TOM,

Your letter and Laura's were a great pleasure to me in this distant land. I could not answer before, as I have been very ill. But Samaritans came with oil and wine and comforted me. It had an odd, dreary effect to hear my friend Hekekian Bey, a learned old Armenian, and De Leo Bey, my doctor, discoursing Turkish at my bedside, while my faithful Omar cried and prayed *Yah Robbeena! Yah Saatir!* (O Lord! O Preserver!) 'don't let her die.'

Alick is quite right that I am in love with the Arabs' ways, and I have contrived to see and know more of family life than many Europeans who have lived here for years. When the Arabs feel that one really cares for them, they heartily return it. If I could only speak the language I could see anything. Cairo *is* the Arabian Nights; there is a little Frankish varnish here and there, but the government, the people—all is unchanged since that most veracious book was written. No words can describe the departure of the holy Mahmal and the pilgrims for Mecca. I spent half the day loitering about in the Bedaween tents admiring the glorious, free people. To see a Bedaween and his wife walk through the streets of Cairo is superb. Her hand resting on his shoulder, and scarcely deigning to cover her haughty face, she looks down on the Egyptian veiled woman who carries the heavy burden and walks behind her lord and master.

By no deed of my own have I become a slave-owner. The American Consul-General turned over to me a black girl of eight or nine, and in consequence of her reports the poor little black boy who is the slave and marmiton of the cook here has been entreating Omar to beg me to buy him and take him with me. It is touching to see the two poor little black things recounting their woes and comparing notes. I went yesterday to deposit my cooking things and boat furniture at my washerwoman's house. Seeing me arrive on my donkey, followed by a cargo of household goods, about eight or ten Arab women thronged round delighted at the idea that I was coming to live in their quarter, and offering me neighbourly services. Of course all rushed upstairs, and my old washerwoman was put to great expense in pipes and coffee. I think, as you, that I must have the 'black drop,' and that the Arabs see it, for I am always told that I am like them, with praises of my former good looks. 'You were beautiful Hareem once.' Nothing is more striking to me than the way in which one is constantly reminded of Herodotus. The Christianity and the Islam of this country are full of the ancient worship, and the sacred animals have all taken service with Muslim saints. At Minieh one reigns over crocodiles; higher up I saw the hole of Æsculapius' serpent at Gebel Sheykh Hereedee, and I fed the birds—as did Herodotus—who used to tear the cordage of boats which refused to feed them, and who are now the servants of Sheykh Naooneh, and still come on board by scores for the bread which no Reis dares refuse them. Bubastis' cats are still fed in the Cadi's court at public expense in Cairo, and behave with singular decorum when 'the servant of the cats' serves them their dinner. Among gods, Amun Ra, the sun-god and serpent-killer, calls himself Mar Girgis (St. George), and is worshipped by Christians and Muslims in the same churches, and Osiris holds his festivals as riotously as ever at Tanta in the Delta, under the name of Seyd el Bedawee. The *fellah* women offer sacrifices to the Nile, and walk round ancient statues in order to have children. The ceremonies at births and burials are not Muslim, but ancient Egyptian.

The Copts are far more close and reserved and backward than the Arabs, and they have been so repudiated by Europeans that they are doubly shy of us. The Europeans resent being called 'Nazranee' as a genteel Hebrew gentleman may shrink from 'Jew.' But I said boldly, '*Ana Nazraneeh. Alhamdulillah!*' (I am a Nazranee. Praise be to God), and found that it was much approved by the Muslims as well as the Copts. Curious things are to be seen here in religion—Muslims praying at the tomb of Mar Girgis (St. George) and the resting-places of Sittina Mariam and Seyidna Issa, and miracles, brand-new, of an equally mixed description.

If you have any power over any artists, send them to paint here. No words can describe either the picturesque beauty of Cairo or the splendid forms of the people in Upper Egypt, and above all in Nubia. I was in raptures at seeing how superb an animal man (and woman) really is. My donkey-girl at Thebes, dressed like a Greek statue—Ward es-Sham (the Rose of Syria)—was a feast to the eyes; and here, too, what grace and sweetness, and how good is a drink of Nile water out of an amphora held to your lips by a woman as graceful as she is kindly. 'May it benefit thee,' she says, smiling with all her beautiful teeth and eyes. '*Alhamdulillah*,' you reply; and it is worth thanking God for. The days of the beauty of Cairo are numbered. The mosques are falling to decay, the exquisite lattice windows rotting away and replaced by European glass and jalousies. Only the people and the Government remain unchanged. Read all the pretty paragraphs about civilisation here, and then say, Bosh!

If you know anyone coming here and wanting a good servant and dragoman, recommend my dear Omar Abou el-Haláweh of Alexandria. He has been my friend and companion, as well as my cook and general servant, now for six months, and we are very sad at our approaching separation. I am to spend a day in his house with his young wife at Alexandria, and to eat his bread. He sadly wants to go with me to Europe and to see my children. Sally, I think, is almost as fond of the Arabs as I am, and very popular. My poor ragged crew were for ever calling out 'Yah Sara' for some assistance or other, hurt fingers or such calamities; and the quantity of doctoring I did was fearful. Sally was constantly wishing for you to see all manner of things and to sketch. What a yarn I have made!

To Mrs. Austin

ALEXANDRIA,
May 12, 1863.

DEAREST MUTTER,

I have been here a fortnight, but the climate disagrees so much with me that I am going back to Cairo at once by the advice of the doctor of the Suez Canal. I cannot shake off my cough here. Mr. Thayer kindly lends me his nice little bachelor house, and I take Omar back again for the job. It is very hot here, but with a sea-breeze which strikes me like ice; strong people enjoy it, but it gives even Janet cold in the head. She is very well, I think, and seems very happy. She is *Times* correspondent and does it very well.

I am terribly disappointed at not being as materially better as I had hoped I should be while in Upper Egypt. I cannot express the longing I have for home and my children, and how much I feel the sort of suspense it all causes to you and to Alick, and my desire to be with you.

One must come to the East to understand absolute equality. As there is no education and no reason why the donkey-boy who runs behind me may not become a great man, and as all Muslims are *ipso facto* equal; money and rank are looked on as mere accidents, and my *savoir vivre* was highly thought of because I sat down with Fellaheen and treated everyone as they treat each other. In Alexandria all that is changed. The European ideas and customs have extinguished the Arab altogether, and those who remain are not improved by the contact. Only the *Bedaween* preserve their haughty *nonchalance*. I found the Mograbee bazaar full of them when I went to buy a white cloak, and was amused at the way in which one splendid bronze figure, who lay on the shop-front, moved one leg to let me sit down. They got interested in my purchase, and assisted in making the bargain and wrapping the cloak round me Bedawee fashion, and they too complimented me on having 'the face of the Arab,' which means Bedaween. I wanted a little Arab dress for Rainie, but could not find one, as at her age none are worn in the desert.

I dined one day with Omar, or rather I ate at his house, for he would not eat with me. His sister-in-law cooked a most admirable dinner, and everyone was delighted. It was an interesting family circle. A very respectable elder brother a confectioner, whose elder wife was a black woman, a really remarkable person, who speaks Italian perfectly, and gave me a great deal of information and asked such intelligent questions. She ruled the house but had no children, so he had married a fair, gentle-looking Arab woman who had six children, and all lived in perfect harmony. Omar's wife is a tall, handsome girl of his own age, with very good manners. She had been outside the door of the close little court which constituted the house *once* since her marriage. I now begin to understand all about the *wesen* with the women. There is a good deal of chivalry in some respects, and in the respectable lower and middle classes the result is not so bad. I suspect that among the rich few are very happy. But I don't know them, or anything of the Turkish ways. I will go and see the black woman again and hear more, her conversation was really interesting.

To Sir Alexander Duff Gordon

ALEXANDRIA,
May 12, 1863.

DEAREST ALICK,

I only got your letter an hour ago, and the mail goes out at four. I enclose to you the letter I had written to my mother, so I need not repeat about my plans. Continue to write here, a letter comes as soon and safer. My general health is so much stronger and better—especially before I had this last severe attack—that I still hope, though it is a severe trial of patience not to throw it up and come home for good. It would be delightful to have you at Cairo now I have pots and pans and all needful for a house, but a carpet and a few mattresses, if you could camp with me *à l'Arabe*.

How you would revel in old Masr el-Kahira, peep up at lattice windows, gape like a *gasheem* (green one) in the bazaar, go wild over the mosques, laugh at portly Turks and dignified Sheykhs on their white donkeys, drink sherbet in the streets, ride wildly about on a donkey, peer under black veils at beautiful eyes and feel generally intoxicated! I am quite a good cicerone now of the glorious old city. Omar is in raptures at the idea that the Sidi el Kebir (the Great Master) might come, and still more if he brought the 'little master.'

He plans meeting you on the steamboat and bringing you to me, that I may kiss your hand first of all. Mashallah! How our hearts would be dilated!

To Mrs. Austin

MASR EL-KAHIRA, CAIRO,
May 21, 1863.

DEAREST MUTTER,

I came here on Saturday night. To-day is Wednesday, and I am already much better. I have attached an excellent donkey and his master, a delightful youth called Hassan, to my household for fifteen piastres (under two shillings) a day. They live at the door, and Hassan cleans the stairs and goes errands during the heat of the day, and I ride out very early, at six or seven, and again at five. The air is delicious now. It is very hot for a few hours, but not stifling, and the breeze does not chill one as it does at Alexandria. I live all day and all night with open windows, and plenty of fresh warm air is the best of remedies. I can do no better than stay here till the heat becomes too great. I left little Zeyneb at Alexandria with Janet's maid Ellen who quite loves her, and begged to keep her 'for company,' and also to help in their removal to the new house. She clung about me and made me promise to come back to her, but was content to stop with Ellen, whose affection she of course returns. It was pleasant to see her so happy, and how she relished being 'put to bed' with a kiss by Ellen or Sally. Her Turkish master, whom she pronounces to have been *batal* (bad), called her Salaam es-Sidi (the Peace of her Master); but she said that in her own village she used to be Zeyneb, and so we call her. She has grown fatter and, if possible, blacker. Mahbrooka (Good Fortune), the elder wife of Hegab, the confectioner, was much interested in her, as her fate had been the same. She was bought by an Italian who lived with her till his death, when she married Hegab. She is a pious Muslimeh, and invoked the intercession of Seyidna Mohammad for me when I told her I had no intention of baptizing Zeyneb by force, as had been done to her.

The fault of my lodging here is the noise. We are on the road from the railway and there is no quiet except in the few hot hours, when nothing is heard but the cool tinkle of the Sakka's brass cup as he sells water in the street, or perchance *erksoos* (liquorice-water), or caroub or raisin sherbet. The *erksoos* is rather bitter and very good. I drink it a good deal, for drink one must; a gulleh of water is soon gone. A gulleh is a wide-mouthed porous jar, and Nile water drunk out of it without the intervention of a glass is delicious. Omar goes to market every morning with a donkey—I went too, and was much amused—and cooks, and in the evening goes out with me if I want him. I told him I had recommended him highly, and hoped he would get good employment; but he declares that he will go with no one else so long as I come to Egypt, whatever the difference of wages may be. 'The bread I eat with you is sweet'—a pretty little unconscious antithesis to Dante. I have been advising his brother Hajjee Ali to start a hotel at Thebes for invalids, and he has already set about getting a house there; there is *one*. Next winter there will be steamers twice a week—to Assouan! Juvenal's distant Syene, where he died in banishment. My old washerwoman sent me a fervent entreaty through Omar that I would dine with her one day, since I had made Cairo delightful with my presence. If one will only devour these people's food, they are enchanted; they like that much better than a present. So I will honour her house some day. Good old Hannah, she is divorced for being too fat and old, and replaced by a young Turk whose family sponge on Hajjee Ali and are condescending. If I could afford it, I would have a sketch of a beloved old mosque of mine, falling to decay, and with three palm-trees growing in the middle of it. Indeed, I would have a book full, for all is exquisite, and alas, all is going. The old Copt quarter is *entamé*, and hideous, shabby French houses, like the one I live in, are being run up; and in this weather how much better would be the Arab courtyard, with its mastabah and fountain!

There is a quarrel now in the street; how they talk and gesticulate, and everybody puts in a word; a boy has upset a cake-seller's tray, '*Naal Abu'k!*' (Curses on your father) he claims six piastres damages, and everyone gives an opinion *pour ou contre*. We all look out of the window; my opposite neighbour, the pretty Armenian woman, leans out, and her diamond head-ornaments and earrings glitter as she laughs like a child. The Christian dyer is also very active in the row, which, like all Arab rows, ends in nothing; it evaporates in fine theatrical gestures and lots of talk. Curious! In the street they are so noisy, but get the same men in a coffee-shop or anywhere, and they are the quietest of mankind. Only one man speaks at a time, the rest listen, and never interrupt; twenty men don't make the noise of three Europeans.

Hekekian Bey is my near neighbour, and he comes in and we *fronder* the Government. His heart is sore with disinterested grief for the sufferings of the people. 'Don't they deserve to be decently governed, to be allowed a little happiness and prosperity? They are so docile, so contented; are they not a good people?' Those were his words as he was recounting some new iniquity. Of course half these acts are done under pretext of improving and civilising, and the Europeans applaud and say, 'Oh, but nothing could be done without forced labour,' and the poor Fellaheen are marched off in gangs like convicts, and their families starve, and (who'd have thought it) the population keeps diminishing. No wonder the cry is, 'Let the English Queen come and take us.' You see, I don't see things quite as Ross does, but mine is another *standpunkt*, and my heart is with the Arabs. I care less about opening up the trade with the Soudan and all the new railways, and I should like to see person and property safe, which no one's is here (Europeans, of course, excepted). Ismail Pasha got the Sultan to allow him to take 90,000 feddans of uncultivated land for himself as private property, very well, but the late Viceroy Said granted eight years ago certain uncultivated lands to a good many Turks, his *employés*, in hopes of founding a landed aristocracy and inducing them to spend their capital in cultivation. They did so, and now Ismail Pasha takes their improved land and gives them feddan for feddan of his new land, which will take five years to bring into cultivation, instead. He forces them to sign a *voluntary* deed of exchange, or they go off to Fazogloo, a hot Siberia whence none return. The Sultan also left a large sum of money for religious institutions and charities—Muslim, Jew, and Christian. None have received a foddah. It is true the Sultan and his suite plundered the Pasha and the people here; but from all I hear the Sultan really wishes to do good. What is wanted here is hands to till the ground, and wages are very high; food, of course, gets dearer, and the forced labour inflicts more suffering than before, and the population will decrease yet faster. This appears to me to be a state of things in which it is no use to say that public works must be made at any cost. The wealth will perhaps be increased, if meanwhile the people are not exterminated. Then, every new Pasha builds a huge new palace while those of his predecessors fall to ruin. Mehemet Ali's sons even cut down the trees of his beautiful botanical garden and planted beans there; so money is constantly wasted more than if it were thrown into the Nile, for then the Fellaheen would not have to spend their time, so much wanted for agriculture, in building hideous barrack-like so-called palaces. What chokes me is to hear English people talk of the stick being 'the only way to manage Arabs' as if anyone could doubt that it is the easiest way to manage any people where it can be used with impunity.

Sunday.—I went to a large unfinished new Coptic church this morning. Omar went with me up to the women's gallery, and was discreetly going back when he saw me in the right place, but the Coptic women began to talk to him and asked questions about me all the time I was looking down on the strange scene below. I believe they celebrate the ancient mysteries still. The clashing of cymbals, the chanting, a humming unlike any sound I ever heard, the strange yellow copes covered with stranger devices—it was *wunderlich*. At the end everyone went away, and I went down and took off my shoes to go and look at the church. While I was doing so a side-door opened and a procession entered. A priest dressed in the usual black robe and turban of all Copts carrying a trident-shaped sort of candlestick, another with cymbals, a lot of little boys, and two young ecclesiastics of some sort in the yellow satin copes (contrasting queerly with the familiar tarboosh of common life on their heads), these carried little babies and huge wax tapers, each a baby and a taper. They marched round and round three times, the cymbals going furiously, and chanting a jig tune. The dear little tiny boys marched just in front of the priest with such a pretty little solemn, consequential air. Then they all stopped in front of the sanctuary, and the priest untied a sort of broad-coloured tape which was round each of the babies, reciting something in Coptic all the time, and finally touched their foreheads and hands with water. This is a ceremony subsequent to baptism after I don't know how many days, but the priest ties and then unties the bands. Of what is this symbolical? *Je m'y perds*. Then an old man gave a little round cake of bread, with a cabalistic-looking pattern on it, both to Omar and to me, which was certainly baked for Isis. A lot of closely-veiled women stood on one side in the aisle, and among them the mothers of the babies who received them from the men in yellow copes at the end of the ceremony. One of these young men was very handsome, and as he stood looking down and smiling on the baby he held, with the light of the torch sharpening the lines of his features, would have made a lovely picture. The expression was sweeter than St. Vincent de Paul, because his smile told that he could have played with the baby as well as have prayed for it. In this country one gets to see how much more beautiful a perfectly natural expression is than any degree of the mystical expression of the best painters, and it is so refreshing that no one tries to look pious. The Muslim looks serious, and often warlike, as he stands at prayer. The Christian just keeps his everyday face. When the Muslim gets into a state of devotional frenzy he does not think of making a face, and it is quite tremendous. I don't think the Copt has any such ardours, but the scene this morning was all the more touching that no one was 'behaving him or herself' at all. A little acolyte peeped into the sacramental cup and swigged off the drops left in it with the most innocent air, and no one rebuked him, and the quite little children ran about in the sanctuary—up to seven they are privileged—and only they and the priests enter it. It is a pretty commentary on the words 'Suffer the little children,' etc.

I am more and more annoyed at not being able to ask questions for myself, as I don't like to ask through a Muslim and no Copts speak any foreign language, or very very few. Omar and Hassan had been at five this morning to the tomb of Sittina Zeyneb,* one of the daughters of the Prophet, to 'see her' (Sunday is her day of reception), and say the Fathah at her tomb. Next Friday the great Bairam begins and every Muslim eats a bit of meat at his richer neighbour's expense. It is the day on which the pilgrims go up the sacred mount near Mecca, to hear the sermon which terminates the Haj. Yesterday I went to call on pretty Mrs. Wilkinson, she is an Armenian of the Greek faith, and was gone to pray at the convent of Mar Girgis (St. George) to cure the pains a bad rheumatic fever has left in her hands. Evidently Mar Girgis is simply Ammon Ra, the God of the Sun and great serpent-slayer, who is still revered in Egypt by all sects, and Seyd el-Bedawee is as certainly one form of Osiris. His festivals, held twice a year at Tanta, still display the symbol of the Creator of all things. All is thus here—the women wail the dead, as on the old sculptures, all the ceremonies are pagan, and would shock an Indian Mussulman as much as his objection to eat with a Christian shocks an Arab. This country is a palimpsest, in which the Bible is written over Herodotus, and the Koran over that. In the towns the Koran is most visible, in the country Herodotus. I fancy it is most marked and most curious among the Copts, whose churches are shaped like the ancient temples, but they are so much less accessible than the Arabs that I know less of their customs.

Now I have filled such a long letter I hardly know if it is worth sending, and whether you will be amused by my commonplaces of Eastern life. I kill a sheep next Friday, and Omar will cook a stupendous dish for the poor Fellaheen who are lying about the railway-station, waiting to be taken to work somewhere. That is to be my Bairam, and Omar hopes for great benefit for me from the process.

To Sir Alexander Duff Gordon

CAIRO,
May 25, 1863.

DEAREST ALICK,

I have spun such a yarn to my mother that I shall make it serve for both. It may amuse you to see what impression Cairo makes. I ride along on my valiant donkey led by the stalwart Hassan and attended by Omar, and constantly say, 'Oh, if our master were here, how pleased he would be'—husband is not a correct word.

I went out to the tombs yesterday. Fancy that Omar witnessed the destruction of some sixty-eight or so of the most exquisite buildings—the tombs and mosques of the Arab Khaleefehs, which Said Pasha used to divert himself with bombarding for practice for his artillery. Omar was then in the boy corps of camel artillery, now disbanded. Thus the Pasha added the piquancy of sacrilege to barbarity.

The street and the neighbours would divert you. Opposite lives a Christian dyer who must be a seventh brother of the admirable barber. The same impertinence, loquacity, and love of meddling in everybody's business. I long to see him thrashed, though he is a constant comedy. My delightful servant, Omar Abou-el-Halláweh (the father of sweets)—his family are pastrycooks—is the type of all the amiable *jeune premiers* of the stories. I am privately of opinion that he is Bedr-ed-Deen Hassan, the more that he can make cream tarts and there is no pepper in them. Cream tarts are not very good, but lamb stuffed with pistachio nuts fulfils all one's dreams of excellence. The Arabs next door and the Levantines opposite are quiet enough, but how *do* they eat all the cucumbers they buy of the man who cries them every morning as 'fruit gathered by sweet girls in the garden with the early dew.'

The more I see of the back-slums of Cairo, the more in love I am with it. The oldest European towns are tame and regular in comparison, and the people are so pleasant. If you smile at anything that amuses you, you get the kindest, brightest smiles in return; they give hospitality with their faces, and if one brings out a few words, 'Mashallah! what Arabic the Sitt Ingleez speaks.' The Arabs are clever enough to understand the amusement of a stranger and to enter into it, and are amused in turn, and they are wonderfully unprejudiced. When Omar explains to me their views on various matters, he adds: 'The Arab people think so—I know not if right;' and the way in which the Arab merchants worked the electric telegraph, and the eagerness of the Fellaheen for steam-ploughs, are quite extraordinary. They are extremely clever and nice children, easily amused, easily roused into a fury which lasts five minutes and leaves no malice, and half the lying and cheating of which they are accused comes from misunderstanding and ignorance. When I first took Omar he was by way of 'ten pounds, twenty pounds,' being nothing for my dignity. But as soon as I told him that 'my master was a Bey who got £100 a month and no backsheesh,' he was as careful as if for himself. They see us come here and do what only their greatest Pashas do, hire a boat to ourselves, and, of course, think our wealth is boundless. The lying is mostly from fright. They dare not suggest a difference of opinion to a European, and lie to get out of scrapes which blind obedience has often got them into. As to the charges of shopkeepers, that is the custom, and the haggling a ceremony you must submit to. It is for the purchaser or employer to offer a price and fix wages—the reverse of Europe—and if you ask the price they ask something fabulous at random.

I hope to go home next month, as soon as it gets too hot here and is likely to be warm enough in England. I do so long to see the children again.

To Sir Alexander Duff Gordon

ALEXANDRIA,
October 19, 1863.

We had a wretched voyage, good weather, but such a *pétaudière* of a ship. I am competent to describe the horrors of the middle passage—hunger, suffocation, dirt, and such *canaille*, high and low, on board. The only gentleman was a poor Moor* going to Mecca (who stowed his wife and family in a spare boiler on deck). I saw him washing his children in the morning! '*Que c'est degoutant!*' was the cry of the French spectators. If an Arab washes he is a *sale cochon*—no wonder! A delicious man who sat near me on deck, when the sun came round to our side, growled between his clenched teeth: '*Voilà un tas d'intrigants a l'ombre tandis que le soleil me grille, moi*,' a good résumé of French politics, methinks. Well, on arriving at noon of Friday, I was consoled for all by seeing Janet in a boat looking as fresh and bright and merry as ever she could look. The heat has evidently not hurt her at all. Omar's joy was intense. He has had an offer of a place as messenger with the mails to Suez and back, £60 a year; and also his brother wanted him for Lady Herbert of Lea, who has engaged Hajjee Ali, and Ali promised high pay, but Omar said that he could not leave me. 'I think my God give her to me to take care of her, how then I leave her if she not well and not very rich? I can't speak to my God if I do bad things like that.' I am going to his house to-day to see the baby and Hajjee Hannah, who is just come down from Cairo. Omar is gone to try to get a dahabieh to go up the river, as I hear that the half-railway, half-steamer journey is dreadfully inconvenient and fatiguing, and the sight of the overflowing Nile is said to be magnificent, it is all over the land and eight miles of the railway gone. Omar kisses your hand and is charmed with the knife, but far more that my family should know his name and be satisfied with my servant.

I cannot live in Thayer's house because the march of civilisation has led a party of French and Wallachian women into the ground-floor thereof to instruct the ignorant Arabs in drinking, card-playing, and other vices. So I will consult Hajjee Hannah to-day; she may know of an empty house and would make divan cushions for me. Zeyneb is much grown and very active and intelligent, but a little louder and bolder than she was owing to the maids here wanting to christianise her, and taking her out unveiled, and letting her be among the men. However, she is as affectionate as ever, and delighted at the prospect of going with me. I have replaced the veil, and Sally has checked her tongue and scolded her sister Ellen for want of decorum, to the amazement of the latter. Janet has a darling Nubian boy. Oh dear! what an elegant person Omar seemed after the French 'gentleman,' and how noble was old Hamees's (Janet's doorkeeper) paternal but reverential blessing! It is a real comfort to live in a nation of truly well-bred people and to encounter kindness after the savage incivility of France.

Tuesday, October 20.

Omar has got a boat for £13, which is not more than the railway would cost now that half must be done by steamer and a bit on donkeys or on foot. Poor Hajjee Hannah was quite knocked up by the journey down; I shall take her up in my boat. Two and a half hours to sit grilling at noonday on the banks, and two miles to walk carrying one's own baggage is hard lines for a fat old woman. Everything is almost double in price owing to the cattle murrain and the high Nile. Such an inundation as this year was never known before. Does the blue God resent Speke's intrusion on his privacy? It will be a glorious sight, but the damage to crops, and even to the last year's stacks of grain and beans, is frightful. One sails among the palm-trees and over the submerged cotton-fields. Ismail Pasha has been very active, but, alas! his 'eye is bad,' and there have been as many calamities as under Pharaoh in his short reign. The cattle murrain is fearful, and is now beginning in Cairo and Upper Egypt. Ross reckons the loss at twelve millions sterling in cattle. The gazelles in the desert have it too, but not horses, asses or goats.

To Sir Alexander Duff Gordon

ALEXANDRIA,
October 26, 1863.

DEAREST ALICK,

I went to two hareems the other day with a little boy of Mustapha Aga's, and was much pleased. A very pleasant Turkish lady put out all her splendid bedding and dresses for me, and was most amiable. At another a superb Arab with most *grande dame* manners, dressed in white cotton and with unpainted face, received me statelily. Her house would drive you wild, such antique enamelled tiles covering the panels of the walls, all divided by carved woods, and such carved screens and galleries, all very old and rather dilapidated, but superb, and the lady worthy of the house. A bold-eyed slave girl with a baby put herself forward for admiration, and was ordered to bring coffee with such cool though polite imperiousness. One of our great ladies can't half crush a rival in comparison, she does it too coarsely. The quiet scorn of the pale-faced, black-haired Arab was beyond any English powers. Then it was fun to open the lattice and make me look out on the square, and to wonder what the neighbours would say at the sight of my face and European hat. She asked about my children and blessed them repeatedly, and took my hand very kindly in doing so, for fear I should think her envious and fear her eye—she had none.

Tuesday.—The post goes out to-morrow, and I have such a cold I must stay in bed and cannot write much. I go on Thursday and shall go to Briggs' house. Pray write to me at Cairo. Sally and I are both unwell and anxious to get up the river. I can't write more.

To Sir Alexander Duff Gordon

Kafr Zeyat,
October 31, 1863.

Dearest Alick,

We left Alexandria on Thursday about noon, and sailed with a fair wind along the Mahmoudieh Canal. My little boat flies like a bird, and my men are a capital set of fellows, bold and careful sailors. I have only seven in all, but they work well, and at a pinch Omar leaves the pots and pans and handles a rope or a pole manfully. We sailed all night and passed the locks at Atleh at four o'clock yesterday, and were greeted by old Nile tearing down like a torrent. The river is magnificent, 'seven men's height,' my Reis says, above its usual pitch; it has gone down five or six feet and left a sad scene of havoc on either side. However what the Nile takes he repays with threefold interest, they say. The women are at work rebuilding their mud huts, and the men repairing the dykes. A Frenchman told me he was on board a Pasha's steamer under M. de Lesseps' command, and they passed a flooded village where two hundred or so people stood on their roofs crying for help. Would you, could you, believe it that they passed on and left them to drown? None but an eyewitness could have made me believe such villainy.

All to-day we sailed in such heavenly weather—a sky like nothing but its most beautiful self. At the bend of the river just now we had a grand struggle to get round, and got entangled with a big timber boat. My crew got so vehement that I had to come out with an imperious request to everyone to bless the Prophet. Then the boat nearly pulled the men into the stream, and they pulled and hauled and struggled up to their waists in mud and water, and Omar brandished his pole and shouted 'Islam el Islam!' which gave a fresh spirit to the poor fellows, and round we came with a dash and caught the breeze again. Now we have put up for the night, and shall pass the railway-bridge to-morrow. The railway is all under water from here up to Tantah—eight miles—and in many places higher up.

To Sir Alexander Duff Gordon

CAIRO,
November 14, 1863.

Here I am at last in my old quarters at Thayer's house, after a tiresome negotiation with the Vice-Consul, who had taken possession and invented the story of women on the ground-floor. I was a week in Briggs' damp house, and too ill to write. The morning I arrived at Cairo I was seized with hæmorrhage, and had two days of it; however, since then I am better. I was very foolish to stay a fortnight in Alexandria.

The passage under the railway-bridge at Tantah (which is only opened once in two days) was most exciting and pretty. Such a scramble and dash of boats—two or three hundred at least. Old Zedan, the steersman, slid under the noses of the big boats with my little *Cangia* and through the gates before they were well open, and we saw the rush and confusion behind us at our ease, and headed the whole fleet for a few miles. Then we stuck, and Zedan raged; but we got off in an hour and again overtook and passed all. And then we saw the spectacle of devastation—whole villages gone, submerged and melted, mud to mud, and the people with their animals encamped on spits of sand or on the dykes in long rows of ragged makeshift tents, while we sailed over where they had lived. Cotton rotting in all directions and the dry tops crackling under the bows of the boat. When we stopped to buy milk, the poor woman exclaimed: 'Milk! from where? Do you want it out of my breasts?' However, she took our saucepan and went to get some from another family. No one refuses it if they have a drop left, for they all believe the murrain to be a punishment for churlishness to strangers—by whom committed no one can say. Nor would they fix a price, or take more than the old rate. But here everything has doubled in price.

Never did a present give such pleasure as Mme. De Leo's bracelet. De Leo came quite overflowing with gratitude at my having remembered such a trifle as his attending me and coming three times a day! He thinks me looking better, and advises me to stay on here till I feel it cold. Mr. Thayer's underling has been doing Levantine rogueries, selling the American protégé's claims to the Egyptian Government, and I witnessed a curious phase of Eastern life. Omar, when he found him in *my* house, went and ordered him out. I was ill in bed, and knew nothing till it was done, and when I asked Omar how he came to do it, he told me to be civil to him if I saw him as it was not for me to know what he was; that was his (Omar's) business. At the same time Mr. Thayer's servant sent him a telegram so insolent that it amounted to a kicking. Such is the Nemesis for being a rogue here. The servants know you, and let you feel it. I was quite 'flabbergasted' at Omar, who is so reverential to me and to the Rosses, and who I fancied trembled before every European, taking such a tone to a man in the position of a 'gentleman.' It is a fresh proof of the feeling of actual equality among men that lies at the bottom of such great inequality of position. Hekekian Bey has seen a Turkish Pasha's shins kicked by his own servants, who were cognisant of his misdeeds. Finally, on Thursday we got the keys of the house, and Omar came with two *ferashes* and shovelled out the Levantine dirt, and scoured and scrubbed; and on Friday afternoon (yesterday) we came in. Zeyneb has been very good ever since she has been with us, she will soon be a complete 'dragowoman,' for she is learning Arabic from Omar and English from us fast. In Janet's house she only heard a sort of 'lingua franca' of Greek, Italian, Nubian and English. She asked me 'How piccolo bint?' (How's the little girl?) a fine specimen of Alexandrian. Ross is here, and will dine with me to-night before starting by an express train which Ismail Pasha gives him.

On Thursday evening I rode to the Abbassieh, and met all the schoolboys going home for their Friday. Such a pretty sight! The little Turks on grand horses with velvet trappings and two or three sais running before them, and the Arab boys fetched—some by proud fathers on handsome donkeys, some by trusty servants on foot, some by poor mothers astride on shabby donkeys and taking up their darlings before them, some two and three on one donkey, and crowds on foot. Such a number of lovely faces—all dressed in white European-cut clothes and red tarbooshes.

Last night we had a wedding opposite. A pretty boy, about Maurice's size, or rather less, with a friend of his own size, dressed like him in a scarlet robe and turban, on each side, and surrounded by men carrying tapers and singing songs, and preceded by cressets flaring. He stepped along like Agag, very slowly and mincingly, and looked very shy and pretty. My poor Hassan (donkey-driver) is ill—I fear very ill. His father came with the donkey for me, and kept drawing his sleeve over his eyes and sighing so heavily. '*Yah Hassan meskeen! yah Hassan ibn!*' (Oh poor Hassan! oh Hassan my son!); and then, in a resigned tone, '*Allah kereem*' (God is merciful). I will go and see him this morning, and have a doctor to him 'by force,' as Omar says, if he is very bad. There is something heart-rending in the patient, helpless suffering of these people.

Sunday.—Abu Hassan reported his son so much better that I did not go after him, having several things to do, and Omar being deep in cooking a *festin de Balthazar* because Ross was to dine with me. The weather is delicious—much what we had at Bournemouth in summer—but there is a great deal of sickness, and I fear there will be more, from people burying dead cattle on their premises inside the town. It costs 100 *gersh* to bury one outside the town. All labour is rendered scarce, too, as well as food dear, and the streets are not cleaned and water hard to get. My *sakka* comes very irregularly, and makes quite a favour of supplying us with water. All this must tell heavily on the poor. Hekekian's wife had seventy head of cattle on her farm—one wretched bullock is left; and, of seven to water the house in Cairo, also one left, and that expected to die. I wonder what ill-conditioned fellow of a Moses is at the bottom of it. Hajjee Ali has just been here, and offers me his tents if I like to go up to Thebes and not live in a boat, so that I may not be dependent on getting a house there. He is engaged by Lady Herbert of Lea, so will not go to Syria this year and has all his tents to spare. I fancy I might be very comfortable among the tombs of the Kings or in the valley of Assaseef with good tents. It is never cold at all among the hills at Thebes—*au contraire*. On the sunny side of the valley you are broiled and stunned with heat in January, and in the shade it is heavenly. How I do wish you could come too, how you would enjoy it! I shall rather like the change from a boat life to a Bedawee one, with my own sheep and chickens and horse about the tent, and a small following of ragged retainers; moreover, it will be considerably cheaper, I think.

To Mrs. Austin

CAIRO,
November 21, 1863.

DEAREST MUTTER,

I shall stay on here till it gets colder, and then go up the Nile either in a steamer or a boat. The old father of my donkey-boy, Hassan, gave me a fine illustration of Arab feeling towards women to-day. I asked if Abd el-Kader* was coming here, as I had heard; he did not know, and asked me if he were not *Achul en-Benàt*, a brother of girls. I prosaically said I did not know if he had sisters. 'The Arabs, O lady, call that man a "brother of girls" to whom God has given a clean heart to love all women as his sisters, and strength and courage to fight for their protection.' Omar suggested a 'thorough gentleman' as the equivalent of Abou Hassan's title. Our European *galimatias* about the 'smiles of the fair,' etc., look very mean beside 'Achul en Benàt,' methinks. Moreover, they carry it into common life. Omar was telling me of some little family tribulations, showing that he is not a little henpecked. His wife wanted all his money. I asked how much she had of her own, as I knew she had property. 'Oh, ma'am! I can't speak of that, shame for me if I ask what money she got.' A man married at Alexandria, and took home the daily provisions for the first week; after that he neglected it for two days, and came home with a lemon in his hand. He asked for some dinner, and his wife placed the stool and the tray and the washing basin and napkin, and in the tray the lemon cut in quarters. 'Well, and the dinner?' 'Dinner! you want dinner? Where from? What man are you to want women when you don't keep them? I am going to the Cadi to be divorced from you;' and she did. The man must provide all necessaries for his Hareem, and if she has money or earns any she spends it in dress; if she makes him a skullcap or a handkerchief he must pay her for her work. *Tout n'est pas roses* for these Eastern tyrants, not to speak of the unbridled licence of tongue allowed to women and children. Zeyneb hectors Omar and I cannot persuade him to check her. 'How I say anything to it, that one child?' Of course, the children are insupportable, and, I fancy, the women little better.

A poor neighbour of mine lost his little boy yesterday, and came out in the streets, as usual, for sympathy. He stood under my window leaning his head against the wall, and sobbing and crying till, literally, his tears wetted the dust. He was too grieved to tear off his turban or to lament in form, but clasped his hands and cried, 'Yah weled, yah weled, yah weled' (O my boy, my boy). The bean-seller opposite shut his shop, the dyer took no notice but smoked his pipe. Some people passed on, but many stopped and stood round the poor man, saying nothing, but looking concerned. Two were well-dressed Copts on handsome donkeys, who dismounted, and all waited till he went home, when about twenty men accompanied him with a respectful air. How strange it seems to us to go out into the street and call on the passers-by to grieve with one! I was at the house of Hekekian Bey the other day when he received a parcel from his former slave, now the Sultan's chief eunuch. It contained a very fine photograph of the eunuch—whose face, though negro, is very intelligent and of charming expression—a present of illustrated English books, and some printed music composed by the Sultan, Abd el Aziz, himself. *O tempera! O mores!* one was a waltz. The very ugliest and scrubbiest of street dogs has adopted me—like the Irishman who wrote to Lord Lansdowne that he had selected him as his patron—and he guards the house and follows me in the street. He is rewarded with scraps, and Sally cost me a new tin mug by letting the dog drink out of the old one, which was used to scoop the water from the jars, forgetting that Omar and Zeyneb could not drink after the poor beast.

Monday.—I went yesterday to the port of Cairo, Boulak, to see Hassaneyn Effendi about boats. He was gone up the Nile, and I sat with his wife—a very nice Turkish woman who speaks English to perfection—and heard all sorts of curious things. I heard the whole story of an unhappy marriage made by Leyla, my hostess's sister, and much Cairo gossip. Like all Eastern ladies that I have seen she complains of indigestion, and said she knew she ought to go out more and to walk, but custom *e contra il nostro decoro*.

Mr. Thayer will be back in Egypt on December 15, so I shall embark about that time, as he may want his house here. It is now a little fresh in the early morning, but like fine English summer weather.

Tuesday.—Since I have been here my cough is nearly gone, and I am better for having good food again. Omar manages to get good mutton, and I have discovered that some of the Nile fish is excellent. The *abyad*, six or eight feet long and very fat, is delicious, and I am told there are still better; the eels are delicate and good too. Maurice might hook an *abyad*, but how would he land him? The worst is that everything is just double the price of last year, as, of course, no beef can be eaten at all, and the draught oxen being dead makes labour dear as well. The high Nile was a small misfortune compared to the murrain. There is a legend about it, of course. A certain Sheykh el-Beled (burgomaster) of some place—not mentioned—lost his cattle, and being rich defied God, said he did not care, and bought as many more; they died too, and he continued impenitent and defiant, and bought on till he was ruined, and now he is sinking into the earth bodily, though his friends dig and dig without ceasing night and day. It is curious how like the German legends the Arab ones are. All those about wasting bread wantonly are almost identical. If a bit is dirty, Omar carefully gives it to the dog; if clean, he keeps it in a drawer for making breadcrumbs for cutlets; not a bit must fall on the floor. In other things they are careless enough, but *das liebe Brod* is sacred—*vide* Grimms' *Deutsche Sagen*. I am constantly struck with resemblances to German customs. A Fellah wedding is very like the German *Bauern hochzeit* firing of guns and display of household goods, only on a camel instead of a cart. I have been trying to get a teacher of Arabic, but it is very hard to find one who knows any European language, and the consular dragoman asks four dollars a lesson. I must wait till I get to Thebes, where I think a certain young Said can teach me. Meanwhile I am beginning to understand rather more and to speak a very little. Please direct to me to Briggs and Co. at Cairo; if I am gone, the letters will follow up the river.

To Mrs. Ross

CAIRO,
December 1, 1863.

DEAREST JANET,

I should much like to go with Thayer if his times and seasons will suit mine; but I cannot wait indefinitely, still less come down the river before the end of April. But most likely the Pasha will give him a boat. It is getting cold here and I feel my throat sore to-day. I went to see Hassan yesterday, he is much better, but very weak and pale. It is such a nice family—old father, mother, and sister, all well-bred and pleasing like Hassan himself. He almost shrieked at hearing of your fall, and is most anxious to see you when you come here. Zeyneb, after behaving very well for three weeks, has turned quietly sullen and displays great religious intolerance. It would seem that the Berberi men have put it into her head that we are inferior beings, and she pretends not to be able to eat because she thinks everything is pig. Omar's eating the food does not convince her. As she evidently does not like us I will offer her to Mrs. Hekekian Bey, and if she does not do there, in a household of black Mussulman slaves, they must pass her on to a Turkish house. She is very clever and I am sorry, but to keep a sullen face about me is more than I can endure, as I have shown her every possible kindness. I think she despises Omar for his affection towards me. How much easier it is to instil the bad part of religion than the good; it is really a curious phenomenon in so young a child. She waits capitally at table, and can do most things, but she won't move if the fancy takes her except when ordered, and spends her time on the terrace. One thing is that the life is dull for a child, and I think she will be happier in a larger, more bustling house. I don't know whether, after the fearful example of Mrs. B., I can venture to travel up the Nile with such a *séducteur* as our dear Mr. Thayer. What do you think? Will gray hairs on my side and *mutual* bad lungs guarantee our international virtue; or will someone ask the Pater when he means to divorce me? Would it be considered that Yankeedoodle had 'stuck a feather in his cap' by leading a British matron and grandmother astray?

To Sir Alexander Duff Gordon

CAIRO,
December 2, 1863.

DEAREST ALICK,

It is beginning to be cold here, and I only await the results of my inquiries about possible houses at Thebes to hire a boat and depart. Yesterday I saw a camel go through the eye of a needle—

i.e., the low arched door of an enclosure; he must kneel and bow his head to creep through—and thus the rich man must humble himself. See how a false translation spoils a good metaphor, and turns a familiar simile into a ferociously communist sentiment. I expect Henry and Janet here in four or five days when her ancle allows her to travel. If I get a house at Thebes, I will only hire a boat up and dismiss it, and trust to Allah for my return. There are rumours of troubles at Jeddah, and a sort of expectation of fighting somewhere next spring; even here people are buying arms to a great extent, I think the gunsmiths' bazaar looks unusually lively. I do look forward to next November and your coming here; I know you would donkey-ride all day in a state of ecstasy. I never saw so good a servant as Omar and such a nice creature, so pleasant and good. When I hear and see what other people spend here in travelling and in living, and what bother they have, I say: 'May God favour Omar and his descendants.'

I stayed in bed yesterday for a cold, and my next-door neighbour, a Coptic merchant, kept me awake all night by auditing his accounts with his clerk. How would you like to chant your rows of figures? He had just bought lots of cotton, and I had to get into my door on Monday over a camel's back, the street being filled with bales.

[The house at Thebes of which my mother speaks in the following letter was built about 1815, over the ancient temple of Khem, by Mr. Salt, English Consul-General in Egypt. He was an archæologist and a student of hieroglyphics, and when Belzoni landed at Alexandria was struck by his ability, and sent him up to Thebes to superintend the removal of the great bust of Memnon, now in the British Museum. Belzoni, I believe, lived for some time in Mr. Salt's house, which afterwards became the property of the French Government, and was known as the *Maison de France*; it was pulled down in 1884 when the great temple of Luxor was excavated by M. Maspero. My late friend Miss A. B. Edwards wrote a description of his work in the *Illustrated London News*, from which I give a few extracts:

'Squatters settled upon the temple like a swarm of mason bees; and the extent of the mischief they perpetrated in the course of centuries may be gathered from the fact that they raised the level of the surrounding soil to such a height that the obelisks, the colossi, and the entrance pylon were buried to a depth of 40 feet, while inside the building the level of the native village was 50 feet above the original pavement. Seven months ago the first court contained not only the local mosque, but a labyrinthine maze of mud structures, numbering some thirty dwellings, and eighty strawsheds, besides yards, stables, and pigeon-towers, the whole being intersected by innumerable lanes and passages. Two large mansions—real mansions, spacious and, in Arab fashion, luxurious,—blocked the great Colonnade of Horembebi; while the second court, and all the open spaces and ruined parts of the upper end of the Temple, were encumbered by sheepfolds, goat-yards, poultry-yards, donkey-sheds, clusters of mud huts, refuse-heaps, and piles of broken pottery. Upon the roof of the portico there stood a large, rambling, ruinous old house, the property of the French Government, and known as the "Maison de France" …Within its walls the illustrious Champollion and his ally Rosellini lived and worked together in 1829, during part of their long sojourn at Thebes. Here the naval officers sent out by the French in 1831 to remove the obelisk which now stands in the Place de la Concorde took up their temporary quarters. And here, most interesting to English readers, Lady Duff Gordon lingered through some of her last winters, and wrote most of her delightful "Letters from Egypt." A little balcony with a broken veranda and a bit of lattice-work parapet, juts out above some mud walls at the end of the building. Upon that balcony she was wont to sit in the cool of the evening, watching the boats upon the river and the magical effect of the after-glow upon the Libyan mountains opposite. All these buildings—"Maison de France," stores, yards, etc. … are all swept away.']

To Sir Alexander Duff Gordon

CAIRO,
December 17, 1863.

DEAREST ALICK,

At last I hope I shall get off in a few days. I have had one delay and bother after another, chiefly caused by relying on the fine speeches of Mr. D. On applying straight to the French Consulate at Alexandria, Janet got me the loan of the *Maison de France* at Thebes at once. M. Mounier, the agent to Halim Pasha, is going up to Esneh, and will let me travel in the steamer which is to tow his dahabieh. It will be dirty, but will cost little and take me out of this dreadful cold weather in five or six days.

December 22.—I wrote the above five days ago, since when I have had to turn out of Thayer's house, as his new Vice-Consul wanted it, and am back at Briggs'. M. Mounier is waiting in frantic impatience to set off, and I ditto; but Ismail Pasha keeps him from day to day. The worry of depending on anyone in the East is beyond belief. Tell your mother that Lady Herbert is gone up the river; her son was much the better for Cairo. I saw Pietro, her courier, who is stupendously grand, he offered Omar £8 a month to go with them; you may imagine how Pietro despised his heathenish ignorance in preferring to stay with me for £3. It quite confirmed him in his contempt for the Arabs.

You would have laughed to hear me buying a carpet. I saw an old broker with one on his shoulder in the bazaar, and asked the price, 'eight napoleons'—then it was unfolded and spread in the street, to the great inconvenience of passers-by, just in front of a coffee-shop. I look at it superciliously, and say, 'Three hundred piastres, O uncle,' the poor old broker cries out in despair to the men sitting outside the coffee-shop: 'O Muslims, hear that and look at this excellent carpet. Three hundred piastres! By the faith, it is worth two thousand!' But the men take my part and one mildly says: 'I wonder that an old man as thou art should tell us that this lady, who is a traveller and a person of experience, values it at three hundred—thinkest thou we will give thee more?' Then another suggests that if the lady will consent to give four napoleons, he had better take them, and that settles it. Everybody gives an opinion here, and the price is fixed by a sort of improvised jury.

Christmas Day.—At last my departure is fixed. I embark to-morrow afternoon at Boulak, and we sail—or steam, rather—on Sunday morning early, and expect to reach Thebes in eight days. I heard a curious illustration of Arab manners to-day. I met Hassan, the janissary of the American Consulate, a very respectable, good man. He told me he had married another wife since last year—I asked what for. It was the widow of his brother who had always lived with him in the same house, and who died leaving two boys. She is neither young nor handsome, but he considered it his duty to provide for her and the children, and not to let her marry a stranger. So you see that polygamy is not always sensual indulgence, and a man may practise greater self-sacrifice so than by talking sentiment about deceased wives' sisters. Hassan has £3 a month, and two wives come expensive. I said, laughing, to Omar as we left him, that I did not think the two wives sounded very comfortable. 'Oh no! not comfortable at all for the man, but he take care of the women, that's what is proper—that is the good Mussulman.'

I shall have the company of a Turkish Effendi on my voyage—a Commissioner of Inland Revenue, in fact, going to look after the tax-gatherers in the Saeed. I wonder whether he will be civil. Sally is gone with some English servants out to the Virgin's tree, the great picnic frolic of Cairene Christians, and, indeed, of Muslimeen also at some seasons. Omar is gone to a *Khatmeh*—a reading of the Koran—at Hassan the donkey-boy's house. I was asked, but am afraid of the night air. A good deal of religious celebration goes on now, the middle of the month of Regeb, six weeks before Ramadan. I rather dread Ramadan as Omar is sure to be faint and ill, and everybody else cross during the first five days or so; then their stomachs get into training. The new passenger-steamers have been promised ever since the 6th, and will not now go till after the races—6th or 7th of next month. Fancy the Cairo races! It is growing dreadfully Cockney here, I must go to Timbuctoo: and we are to have a railway to Mecca, and take return tickets for the *Haj* from all parts of the world.

To Mrs. Austin

BOULAK, ON BOARD A RIVER STEAM-BOAT,
December 27, 1863.

DEAREST MUTTER,

After infinite delays and worries, we are at last on board, and shall sail to-morrow morning. After all was comfortably settled, Ismail Pasha sent for *all* the steamers up to Rhoda, near Minieh, and at the same time ordered a Turkish General to come up instantly somehow. So Latif Pasha, the head of the steamers, had to turn me out of the best cabin, and if I had not come myself, and taken rather forcible possession of the forecastle cabin, the servants of the Turkish General would not have allowed Omar to embark the baggage. He had been waiting all the morning in despair on the bank; but at four I arrived, and ordered the *hammals* to carry the goods into the forecabin, and walked on board myself, where the Arab captain pantomimically placed me in his right eye and on the top of his head. Once installed, this has become a hareem, and I may defy the Turkish Effendi with success. I have got a good-sized cabin with good, clean divans round three sides for Sally and myself. Omar will sleep on deck and cook where he can. A poor Turkish lady is to inhabit a sort of dusthole by the side of my cabin; if she seems decent, I will entertain her hospitably. There is no furniture of any sort but the divan, and we cook our own food, bring our own candles, jugs, basins, beds and everything. If Sally and I were not such complete Arabs we should think it very miserable; but as things stand this year we say, *Alhamdulillah* it is no worse! Luckily it is a very warm night, so we can make our arrangements unchilled. There is no door to the cabin, so we nail up an old plaid, and, as no one ever looks into a hareem, it is quite enough. All on board are Arabs—captain, engineer, and men. An English Sitt is a novelty, and the captain is unhappy that things are not *alla Franca* for me. We are to tow three dahabiehs—M. Mounier's, one belonging to the envoy from the Sultan of Darfour, and another. Three steamers were to have done it, but the Pasha had a fancy for all the boats, and so our poor little craft must do her best. Only fancy the Queen ordering all the river steamers up to Windsor!

At Minieh the Turkish General leaves us, and we shall have the boat to ourselves, so the captain has just been down to tell me. I should like to go with the gentlemen from Darfor, as you may suppose. See what strange combinations of people float on old Nile. Two Englishwomen, one French (Mme. Mounier), one Frenchman, Turks, Arabs, Negroes, Circassians, and men from Darfor, all in one party; perhaps the third boat contains some other strange element. The Turks are from Constantinople and can't speak Arabic, and make faces at the muddy river water, which, indeed, I would rather have filtered.

I hope to have letters from home to-morrow morning. Hassan, my faithful donkey-boy, will go to the post as soon as it is open and bring them down to Boulak. Darling Rainie sent me a card with a cock robin for Christmas; how terribly I miss her dear little face and talk! I am pretty well now; I only feel rather weaker than before and more easily tired. I send you a kind letter of Mme. Tastu's, who got her son to lend me the house at Thebes.

To Sir Alexander Duff Gordon

On board the steamer, near Siout,
Sunday, *January* 3, 1864.

Dearest Alick,

We left Cairo last Sunday morning, and a wonderfully queer company we were. I had been promised all the steamer to myself, but owing to Ismail Pasha's caprices our little steamer had to do the work of three—*i.e.*, to carry passengers, to tow M. Mounier's dahabieh, and to tow the oldest, dirtiest, queerest Nubian boat, in which the young son of the Sultan of Darfoor* and the Sultan's envoy, a handsome black of Dongola (not a negro), had visited Ismail Pasha. The best cabin was taken by a sulky old one-eyed Turkish Pasha, so I had the fore-cabin, luckily a large one, where I slept with Sally on one divan and I on the other, and Omar at my feet. He tried sleeping on deck, but the Pasha's Arnouts were too bad company,* and the captain begged me to 'cover my face' and let my servant sleep at my feet. Besides, there was a poor old asthmatic Turkish Effendi going to collect the taxes, and a lot of women in the engine-room, and children also. It would have been insupportable but for the hearty politeness of the Arab captain, a regular 'old salt,' and owing to his attention and care it was only very amusing.

At Benisouef, the first town above Cairo (seventy miles), we found no coals: the Pasha had been up and taken them all. So we kicked our heels on the bank all day, with the prospect of doing so for a week. The captain brought H.R.H. of Darfoor to visit me, and to beg me to make him hear reason about the delay, as I, being English, must know that a steamer could not go without coals. H.R.H. was a pretty imperious little nigger about eleven or twelve, dressed in a yellow silk kuftan and a scarlet burnous, who cut the good old captain short by saying, 'Why, she is a woman; she can't talk to me.' 'Wallah! wallah! what a way to talk to English Hareem!' shrieked the captain, who was about to lose his temper; but I had a happy idea and produced a box of French sweetmeats, which altered the young Prince's views at once. I asked if he had brothers. 'Who can count them? they are like mice.' He said that the Pasha had given him only a few presents, and was evidently not pleased. Some of his suite are the most formidable-looking wild beasts in human shape I ever beheld—bulldogs and wild-boars black as ink, red-eyed, and, ye gods! such jowls and throats and teeth!—others like monkeys, with arms down to their knees.

The Illyrian Arnouts on board our boat are revoltingly white—like fish or drowned people, no pink in the tallowy skin at all. There were Greeks also who left us at Minieh (second large town), and the old Pasha left this morning at Rodah. The captain at once ordered all my goods into the cabin he had left and turned out the Turkish Effendi, who wanted to stay and sleep with us. No impropriety! he said he was an old man and sick, and my company would be agreeable to him; then he said he was ashamed before the people to be turned out by an English woman. So I was civil and begged him to pass the day and to dine with me, and that set all right, and now after dinner he has gone off quite pleasantly to the fore-cabin and left me here. I have a stern-cabin, a saloon and an anteroom here, so we are comfortable enough—only the fleas! Never till now did I know what fleas could be; even Omar groaned and tossed in his sleep, and Sally and I woke every ten minutes. Perhaps this cabin may be better, some fleas may have landed in the beds of the Turks. I send a dish from my table every day henceforth to the captain; as I take the place of a Pasha it is part of my dignity to do so; and as I occupy the kitchen and burn the ship's coals, I may as well let the captain dine a little at my expense. In the day I go up and sit in his cabin on deck, and we talk as well as we can without an interpreter. The old fellow is sixty-seven, but does not look more than forty-five. He has just the air and manner of a seafaring-man with us, and has been wrecked four times—the last in the Black Sea during the Crimean War, when he was taken prisoner by the Russians and sent to Moscow for three years, until the peace. He has a charming boy of eleven with him, and he tells me he has twelve children in all, but only one wife, and is as strict a monogamist as Dr. Primrose, for he told me he should not marry again if she died, nor he believed would she. He is surprised at my gray hair.

There are a good many Copts on board too, of a rather low class and not pleasant. The Christian gentlemen are very pleasant, but the low are *low* indeed compared to the Muslimeen, and one gets a feeling of dirtiness about them to see them eat all among the coals, and then squat there and pull out their beads to pray without washing their hands even. It does look nasty when compared to the Muslim coming up clean washed, and standing erect and manly-looking to his prayers; besides they are coarse in their manners and conversation and have not the Arab respect for women. I only speak of the common people—not of educated Copts. The best fun was to hear the Greeks (one of whom spoke English) abusing the Copts—rogues, heretics, schismatics from the Greek Church, ignorant, rapacious, cunning, impudent, etc., etc. In short, they narrated the whole fable about their own sweet selves. I am quite surprised to see how well these men manage their work. The boat is quite as clean as an English boat as crowded could be kept, and the engine in beautiful order. The head-engineer, Achmet Effendi, and indeed all the crew and captain too, wear English clothes and use the universal 'All right, stop her—fooreh (full) speed, half speed—turn her head,' etc. I was delighted to hear 'All right—go ahead—*el-Fathah*' in one breath. Here we always say the *Fathah* (first chapter of the Koran, nearly identical with the Lord's Prayer) when starting on a journey, concluding a bargain, etc. The combination was very quaint. There are rats and fleas on board, but neither bugs nor cockroaches. Already the climate has changed, the air is sensibly drier and clearer and the weather much warmer, and we are not yet at Siout. I remarked last year that the climate changed most at Keneh, forty miles below Thebes. The banks are terribly broken and washed away by the inundation, and the Nile far higher even now than it was six weeks earlier last year.

At Benisouef, which used to be the great cattle place, not a buffalo was left, and we could not get a drop of milk. But since we left Minieh we see them again, and I hear the disease is not spreading up the river. Omar told me that the poor people at Benisouef were complaining of the drought and prospect of scarcity, as they could no longer water the land for want of oxen. I paid ten napoleons passage-money, and shall give four or five more as backsheesh, as I have given a good deal of trouble with all my luggage, beddings, furniture, provisions for four months, etc., and the boat's people have been more than civil, really kind and attentive to us; but a bad dahabieh would have cost forty, so I am greatly the gainer. Nothing can exceed the muddle, uncertainty and carelessness of the 'administration' at Cairo: no coals at the depots, boats announced to sail and dawdling on three weeks, no order and no care for anybody's convenience but the Pasha's own. But the subordinates on board the boats do their work perfectly well. We go only half as quickly as we ought because we have two very heavy dahabiehs in tow instead of one; but no time is lost, as long as the light lasts we go, and start again as soon as the moon rises. The people on board have promoted me in rank—and call me 'el-Ameereh,' an obsolete Arab title which the engineer thinks is the equivalent of 'Ladysheep,' as he calls it. 'Sitti,' he said, was the same as 'Meessees.' I don't know how he acquired his ideas on the subject of English precedence.

Omar has just come in with coffee, and begs me to give his best salaam to his big master and his little master and lady, and not to forget to tell them he is their servant and my memlook (slave) 'from one hand to the other' (the whole body). If we stay at all at Siout, I will ride a donkey up to Wassef's house, and leave this letter for him to send down with his next opportunity to Cairo. At Keneh we must try to find time to buy two filters and some gullehs (water-coolers); they are made there. At Thebes nothing can be got.

How I do wish you were here to enjoy all the new and strange sights! I am sure it would amuse you, and as the fleas don't bite you there would be no drawback. Janet sent me a photo of dear little Rainie; it is ugly, but very like the 'zuweyeh' (little one). Give her no end of kisses, and thank her for the cock robin, which pleased me quite as much as she thought it would.

To Sir Alexander Duff Gordon

Tuesday, January 5, 1864.

We left Siout this afternoon. The captain had announced that we should start at ten o'clock, so I did not go into the town, but sent

Omar to buy food and give my letter and best salaam to Wassef. But the men of Darfoor all went off declaring that they would stop, promising to cut off the captain's head if he went without them. Hassan Effendi, the Turk, was furious, and threatened to telegraph his complaints to Cairo if we did not go directly, and the poor captain was in a sad quandary. He appealed to me, peaceably sitting on the trunk of a palm-tree with some poor *fellaheen* (of whom more anon). I uttered the longest sentence I could compose in Arabic, to the effect that he was captain, and that while on the boat we were all bound to obey him. '*Mashallah!* one English Hareem is worth more than ten men for sense; these Ingeleez have only one word both for themselves and for other people: *doghree—doghree* (right is right); this Ameereh is ready to obey like a memlook, and when she has to command—whew!'—with a most expressive toss back of the head. The bank was crowded with poor *fellaheen* who had been taken for soldiers and sent to await the Pasha's arrival at Girgeh; three weeks they lay there, and were then sent down to Soohaj (the Pasha wanted to see them himself and pick out the men he liked); eight days more at Soohaj, then to Siout eight days more, and meanwhile Ismail Pasha has gone back to Cairo and the poor souls may wait indefinitely, for no one will venture to remind the Pasha of their trifling existence. *Wallah, wallah!*

While I was walking on the bank with M. and Mme. Mounier, a person came up and saluted them whose appearance puzzled me. Don't call me a Persian when I tell you it was an eccentric Bedawee young lady. She was eighteen or twenty at most, dressed like a young man, but small and feminine and rather pretty, except that one eye was blind. Her dress was handsome, and she had women's jewels, diamonds, etc., and a European watch and chain. Her manner was excellent, quite *ungenirt*, and not the least impudent or swaggering, and I was told—indeed, I could hear—that her language was beautiful, a thing much esteemed among Arabs. She is a virgin and fond of travelling and of men's society, being very clever, so she has her dromedary and goes about quite alone. No one seemed surprised, no one stared, and when I asked if it was *proper*, our captain was surprised. 'Why not? if she does not wish to marry, she can go alone; if she does, she can marry—what harm? She is a virgin and free.' She went to breakfast with the Mouniers on their boat (Mme. M. is Egyptian born, and both speak Arabic perfectly), and the young lady had many things to ask them, she said. She expressed her opinions pretty freely as far as I could understand her. Mme. Mounier had heard of her before, and said she was much respected and admired. M. Mounier had heard that she was a spy of the Pasha's, but the people on board the boat here say that the truth was that she went before Said Pasha herself to complain of some tyrannical Moodir who ground and imprisoned the *fellaheen*—a bold thing for a girl to do. To me she seems, anyhow, far the most curious thing I have yet seen.

The weather is already much warmer, it is nine in the evening, we are steaming along and I sit with the cabin window open. My cough is, of course, a great deal better. *Inshallah!* Above Keneh (about another 150 miles) it will go away. To-day, for the first time, I pulled my cloak over my head in the sun, it was so stinging hot—quite delicious, and it is the 5th of January. *Poveri voi* in the cold! Our captain was prisoner for three years at Moscow and at Bakshi Serai, and declares he never saw the sun at all—hard lines for an Egyptian. Do you remember the cigarettes you bought for me at Eaux Bonnes? Well, I gave them to the old Turkish Effendi, who is dreadfully asthmatic, and he is enchanted; of course five other people came to be cured directly. The rhubarb pills are a real comfort to travellers, for they can't do much harm, and inspire great confidence.

Luckily we left all the fleas behind in the fore-cabin, for the benefit of the poor old Turk, who, I hear, suffers severely. The divans were all brand-new, and the fleas came in the cotton stuffing, for there are no live things of any sort in the rest of the boat.

GIRGEH,
January 9, 1864.

We have put in here for the night. To-day we took on board three convicts in chains, two bound for Fazogloo, one for calumny and perjury, and one for manslaughter. Hard labour for life in that climate will soon dispose of them. The third is a petty thief from Keneh who has been a year in chains in the Custom-house of Alexandria, and is now being taken back to be shown in his own place in his chains. The *causes célèbres* of this country would be curious reading; they do their crimes so differently to us. If I can get hold of anyone who can relate a few cases well, I'll write them down. Omar has told me a few, but he may not know the details quite exactly.

I made further inquiries about the Bedawee lady, who is older than she looks, for she has travelled constantly for ten years. She is rich and much respected, and received in all the best houses, where she sits with the men all day and sleeps in the hareem. She has been in the interior of Africa and to Mecca, speaks Turkish, and M. Mounier says he found her extremely agreeable, full of interesting information about all the countries she had visited. As soon as I can talk I must try and find her out; she likes the company of Europeans.

Here is a contribution to folk-lore, new even to Lane I think.* When the coffee-seller lights his stove in the morning, he makes two cups of coffee of the best and nicely sugared, and pours them out all over the stove, saying, 'God bless or favour Sheykh Shadhilee and his descendants.' The blessing on the saint who invented coffee of course I knew, and often utter, but the libation is new to me. You see the ancient religion crops up even through the severe faith of Islam. If I could describe all the details of an Arab, and still more of a Coptic, wedding, you would think I was relating the mysteries of Isis. At one house I saw the bride's father looking pale and anxious, and Omar said, 'I think he wants to hold his stomach with both hands till the women tell him if his daughter makes his face white.' It was such a good phrase for the sinking at heart of anxiety. It certainly seems more reasonable that a woman's misconduct should blacken her father's face than her husband's. There are a good many things about hareem here which I am barbarian enough to think extremely good and rational. An old Turk of Cairo, who had been in Europe, was talking to an Englishman a short time ago, who politely chaffed him about Mussulman licence. The venerable Muslim replied, 'Pray, how many women have you, who are quite young, seen (that is the Eastern phrase) in your whole life?' The Englishman could not count—of course not. 'Well, young man, I am old, and was married at twelve, and I have seen in all my life seven women; four are dead, and three are happy and comfortable in my house. *Where are all yours?*' Hassaneyn Effendi heard the conversation, which passed in French, and was amused at the question.

I find that the criminal convicted of calumny accused, together with twenty-nine others not in custody, the Sheykh-el-Beled of his place of murdering his servant, and produced a basket full of bones as proof, but the Sheykh-el-Beled produced the living man, and his detractor gets hard labour for life. The proceeding is characteristic of the childish *ruses* of this country. I inquired whether the thief who was dragged in chains through the streets would be able to find work, and was told, 'Oh, certainly; is he not a poor man? For the sake of God everyone will be ready to help him.' An absolute uncertainty of justice naturally leads to this result. Our captain was quite shocked to hear that in my country we did not like to employ a returned convict.

LUXOR,
January 13, 1864.

We spent all the afternoon of Saturday at Keneh, where I dined with the English Consul, a worthy old Arab, who also invited our captain, and we all sat round his copper tray on the floor and ate with our fingers, the captain, who sat next me, picking out the best bits and feeding me and Sally with them. After dinner the French

Consul, a Copt, one Jesus Buktor, sent to invite me to a fantasia at his house, where I found the Mouniers, the Moudir, and some other Turks, and a disagreeable Italian, who stared at me as if I had been young and pretty, and put Omar into a great fury. I was glad to see the dancing-girls, but I liked old Seyyid Achmet's patriarchal ways much better than the tone of the Frenchified Copt. At first I thought the dancing queer and dull. One girl was very handsome, but cold and uninteresting; one who sang was also very pretty and engaging, and a dear little thing. But the dancing was contortions, more or less graceful, *very* wonderful as gymnastic feats, and no more. But the captain called out to one Latifeh, an ugly, clumsy-looking wench, to show the Sitt what she could do. And then it was revealed to me. The ugly girl started on her feet and became the 'serpent of old Nile,'—the head, shoulders and arms eagerly bent forward, waist in, and haunches advanced on the bent knees—the posture of a cobra about to spring. I could not call it *voluptuous* any more than Racine's *Phèdre*. It is *Venus toute entière à sa proie attachée*, and to me seemed tragic. It is far more realistic than the 'fandango,' and far less coquettish, because the thing represented is *au grande sérieux*, not travestied, *gazé*, or played with; and like all such things, the Arab men don't think it the least improper. Of course the girls don't commit any indecorums before European women, except the dance itself. Seyyid Achmet would have given me a fantasia, but he feared I might have men with me, and he had had a great annoyance with two Englishmen who wanted to make the girls dance naked, which they objected to, and he had to turn them out of his house after hospitably entertaining them.

Our procession home to the boat was very droll. Mme. Mounier could not ride an Arab saddle, so I lent her mine and *enfourché'd* my donkey, and away we went with men running with 'meshhaals' (fire-baskets on long poles) and lanterns, and the captain shouting out 'Full speed!' and such English phrases all the way—like a regular old salt as he is. We got here last night, and this morning Mustapha A'gha and the Nazir came down to conduct me up to my palace. I have such a big rambling house all over the top of the temple of

Khem. How I wish I had you and the chicks to fill it! We had about twenty *fellahs* to clean the dust of three years' accumulation, and my room looks quite handsome with carpets and a divan. Mustapha's little girl found her way here when she heard I was come, and it seemed quite pleasant to have her playing on the carpet with a dolly and some sugar-plums, and making a feast for dolly on a saucer, arranging the sugar-plums Arab fashion. She was monstrously pleased with Rainie's picture and kissed it. Such a quiet, nice little brown tot, and curiously like Rainie and walnut-juice.

The view all round my house is magnificent on every side, over the Nile in front facing north-west, and over a splendid range of green and distant orange buff hills to the south-east, where I have a spacious covered terrace. It is rough and dusty to the extreme, but will be very pleasant. Mustapha came in just now to offer me the loan of a horse, and to ask me to go to the mosque in a few nights to see the illumination in honour of a great Sheykh, a son of Sidi Hosseyn or Hassan. I asked whether my presence might not offend any Muslimeen, and he would not hear of such a thing. The sun set while he was here, and he asked if I objected to his praying in my presence, and went through his four *rekahs* very comfortably on my carpet. My next-door neighbour (across the courtyard all filled with antiquities) is a nice little Copt who looks like an antique statue himself. I shall *voisiner* with his family. He sent me coffee as soon as I arrived, and came to help. I am invited to El-Moutaneh, a few hours up the river, to visit the Mouniers, and to Keneh to visit Seyyid Achmet, and also the head of the merchants there who settled the price of a carpet for me in the bazaar, and seemed to like me. He was just one of those handsome, high-bred, elderly merchants with whom a story always begins in the Arabian Nights. When I can talk I will go and see a real Arab hareem. A very nice English couple, a man and his wife, gave me breakfast in their boat, and turned out to be business connections of Ross's, of the name of Arrowsmith; they were going to Assouan, and I shall see them on their way back. I asked Mustapha about the Arab young lady, and he spoke very highly of her, and is to let me know if she comes here and to offer hospitality from me: he did not know her name—she is called 'el *Hággeh*' (the Pilgrimess).

Thursday.—Now I am settled in my Theban palace, it seems more and more beautiful, and I am quite melancholy that you cannot be here to enjoy it. The house is very large and has good thick walls, the comfort of which we feel to-day for it blows a hurricane; but indoors it is not at all cold. I have glass windows and doors to some of the rooms. It is a lovely dwelling. Two funny little owls as big as my fist live in the wall under my window, and come up and peep in, walking on tip-toe, and looking inquisitive like the owls in the hieroglyphics; and a splendid horus (the sacred hawk) frequents my lofty balcony. Another of my contemplar gods I sacrilegiously killed last night, a whip snake. Omar is rather in consternation for fear it should be 'the snake of the house,' for Islam has not dethroned the *Dii lares et tutelares*.

I have been 'sapping' at the *Alif Bey* (A B C) to-day, under the direction of Sheykh Yussuf, a graceful, sweet-looking young man, with a dark brown face and such fine manners, in his *fellah* dress—a coarse brown woollen shirt, a *libdeh*, or felt skull-cap, and a common red shawl round his head and shoulders; writing the wrong way is very hard work. Some men came to mend the staircase, which had fallen in and which consists of huge solid blocks of stone. One crushed his thumb and I had to operate on it. It is extraordinary how these people bear pain; he never winced in the least, and went off thanking God and the lady quite cheerfully. Till to-day the weather has been quite heavenly; last night I sat with my window open, it was so warm. If only I had you all here! How Rainie would play in the temple, Maurice fish in the Nile, and you go about with your spectacles on your nose. I think you would discard Frangi dress and take to a brown shirt and a *libdeh*, and soon be as brown as any *fellah*. It was so curious to see Sheykh Yussuf blush from shyness when he came in first; it shows quite as much in the coffee-brown Arab skin as in the fairest European—quite unlike the much lighter-coloured mulatto or Malay, who never change colour at all. A photographer who is living here showed me photographs done high up the White Nile. One negro girl is so splendid that I must get him to do me a copy to send you. She is not perfect like the Nubians, but so superbly strong and majestic. If I can get hold of a handsome *fellahah* here, I'll get her photographed to show you in Europe what a woman's breast can be, for I never knew it before I came here—it is the most beautiful thing in the world. The dancing-girl I saw moved her breasts by some extraordinary muscular effort, first one and then the other; they were just like pomegranates and gloriously independent of stays or any support.

To Sir Alexander Duff Gordon

Wednesday, January 20, 1864.

I received your welcome letters of December 15 and 25 on Monday, to my great joy, but was much grieved to hear of Thomas's death, and still more so to hear from Janet that Thackeray and Mrs. Alison were dead. She died the morning I left Cairo, so her last act almost was to send sweetmeats to the boat after me on the evening before. Poor dear soul her sweetness and patience were very touching. We have had a week of piercing winds, and yesterday I stayed in bed, to the great surprise of Mustapha's little girl who came to see me. To-day was beautiful again, and I mounted old Mustapha's cob pony and jogged over his farm with him, and lunched on delicious sour cream and *fateereh* at a neighbouring village, to the great delight of the *fellaheen*. It was more Biblical than ever; the people were all relations of Mustapha's, and to see Sidi Omar, the head of the household, and the 'young men coming in from the field,' and the 'flocks and herds and camels and asses,' was like a beautiful dream. All these people are of high blood, and a sort of 'roll of Battle' is kept here for the genealogies of the noble Arabs who came in with Amr—the first Arab conqueror and lieutenant of Omar. Not one of these brown men, who do not own a second shirt, would give his brown daughter to the greatest Turkish Pasha. This country *noblesse* is more interesting to me by far than the town people, though Omar, who is quite a Cockney, and piques himself on being 'delicate,' turns up his nose at their beggarly pride, as Londoners used to do at bare-legged Highlanders. The air of perfect equality—except as to the respect due to the head of the clan—with which the villagers treated Mustapha, and which he fully returned, made it all seem so very gentlemanly. They are not so dazzled by a little show, and far more manly than the Cairenes. I am on visiting terms with all the 'county families' resident in Luxor already. The Názir (magistrate) is a very nice person, and my Sheykh Yussuf, who is of the highest blood (being descended from Abu-l-Hajjaj himself), is quite charming. There is an intelligent little German here as Austrian Consul, who draws nicely. I went into his house, and was startled by hearing a pretty Arab boy, his servant, inquire, '*Soll ich den Kaffee bringen?*' What next? They are all mad to learn languages, and Mustapha begs me and Sally to teach his little girl Zeyneb English.

Friday, 22*nd*.—Yesterday I rode over to Karnac, with Mustapha's *sais* running by my side. Glorious hot sun and delicious air. To hear the *sais* chatter away, his tongue running as fast as his feet, made me deeply envious of his lungs. Mustapha joined me, and pressed me to go to visit the Sheykh's tomb for the benefit of my health, as he and Sheykh Yussuf wished to say a *Fathah* for me; but I must not drink wine at dinner. I made a little difficulty on the score of difference of religion, but Sheykh Yussuf, who came up, said that he presumed I worshipped God, and not stones, and that sincere prayers were good anywhere. Clearly the bigotry would have been on my side if I had refused any longer. So in the evening I went with Mustapha. It was a very curious sight, the little dome illuminated with as much oil as the mosque could afford, and the tombs of Abu-l-Hajjaj and his three sons.* A magnificent old man, like Father Abraham himself, dressed in white, sat on a carpet at the foot of the tomb; he was the head of the family of Abu-l-Hajjaj. He made me sit by, and was extremely polite. Then came the Názir, the Kadee, a Turk travelling on Government business, and a few other gentlemen, who all sat down round us after kissing the hand of the old Sheykh. Everyone talked; in fact it was a *soirée* for the entertainment of the dead Sheykh. A party of men sat at the further end of the place, with their faces to the Kibleh, and played on a *taraboukeh* (sort of small drum stretched on earthenware which gives a peculiar sound), a tambourine without bells, and little tinkling cymbals fitting on thumb and fingers (crotales), and chanted songs in honour of Mohammed and verses from the Psalms of David. Every now and then one of our party left off talking, and prayed a little or counted his beads. The old Sheykh sent for coffee, and gave me the first cup—a wonderful concession. At last the Názir proposed a *Fathah* for me, which the whole group round me repeated aloud, and then each said to me, 'Our Lord God bless and give thee health and peace, to thee and thy family, and take thee back safe to thy master and thy children,' one adding *Ameen* and giving the salaam with the hand. I returned it, and said, 'Our Lord reward thee and all the people of kindness to strangers,' which was considered a very proper answer. After that we went away, and the worthy Názir walked home with me to take a pipe and a glass of sherbet, and enjoy a talk about his wife and eight children, who are all in Foum-el-Bachr', except two boys at school in Cairo. Government appointments are so precarious that it is not worth while to move them up here, as the expense would be too heavy on a salary of £15 a month, with the chance of recall any day. In Cairo or Lower Egypt it would be quite impossible for a Christian to enter a Sheykh's tomb at all—above all on his birthday festival and on the night of Friday.

Friday, January 29.—I have been too unwell to write all this week, but will finish this to-day to send off by Lady Herbert's boat. The last week has been very cold here, the thermometer at 59° and 60°, with a nipping wind and bright sun. I was obliged to keep my bed for three or four days, as of course a *palazzo* without doors or windows to speak of was very trying, though far better than a boat. Yesterday and to-day are much better, not really much warmer, but a different air.

The *moolid* (festival) of the Sheykh terminated last Saturday with a procession, in which the new cover of his tomb, and the ancient sacred boat, were carried on men's shoulders. It all seemed to have walked out of the royal tombs, only dusty and shabby instead of gorgeous. These festivals of the dead are such as Herodotus alludes to as held in honour of 'Him whose name he dares not mention—Him who sleeps in Philæ,' only the name is changed and the mummy is absent.

For a fortnight everyone who had a horse and could ride came and 'made fantasia' every afternoon for two hours before sunset; and very pretty it was. The people here show their good blood in their riding. On the last three days all strangers were entertained with bread and cooked meat at the expense of the Luxor people; every house killed a sheep and baked bread. As I could not do that for want of servants enough, I sent 100 piastres (12s.) to the servants of Abu-l-Hajjaj at the mosque to pay for the oil burnt at the tomb, etc. I was not well and in bed, but I hear that my gift gave immense satisfaction, and that I was again well prayed for. The Coptic Bishop came to see me, but he is a tipsy old monk and an impudent beggar. He sent for tea as he was ill, so I went to see him, and perceived that his disorder was arrakee. He has a very nice black slave, a Christian (Abyssinian, I think), who is a friend of Omar's, and who sent Omar a handsome dinner all ready cooked; among other things a chicken stuffed with green wheat was excellent. Omar constantly gets dinners sent him, a lot of bread, some dates and cooked fowls or pigeons, and *fateereh* with honey, all tied up hot in a cloth. I gave an old fellow a pill and dose some days ago, but his *dura ilia* took no notice, and he came for more, and got castor-oil. I have not seen him since, but his employer, *fellah* Omar, sent me a lot of delicious butter in return. I think it shows great intelligence in these people, how none of them will any longer consult an Arab *hakeem* if they can get a European to physic them. They now ask directly whether the Government doctors have been to Europe to learn *Hekmeh*, and if not they don't trust them—for poor 'savages' and 'heathens' *ce n'est pas si bête*. I had to interrupt my lessons from illness, but Sheykh Yussuf came again last night. I have mastered *Abba shedda o mus beteen—ibbi shedda o heftedeen*, etc. Oh dear, what must poor Arab children suffer in learning A B C! It is a terrible alphabet, and the *shekel* (points) are *désespérants*; but now I stick for want of a dictionary.

Mr. Arrowsmith kindly gave me Miss Martineau's book,* which I have begun. It is true as far as it goes, but there is the usual defect—the people are not real people, only part of the scenery to her, as to most Europeans. You may conceive how much we are naturalised when I tell you that I have received a serious offer of marriage for Sally. Mustapha A'gha has requested me to 'give her to him' for his eldest son Seyyid, a nice lad of nineteen or twenty at most. As Mustapha is the richest and most considerable person here, it shows that the Arabs draw no unfavourable conclusions as to our morals from the freedom of our manners. He said of course she would keep her own religion and her own customs. Seyyid is still in Alexandria, so it will be time to refuse when he returns. I said she was too old, but they think that no objection at all. She will have to say that her father would not allow it, for of course a handsome offer deserves a civil refusal. Sally's proposals would be quite an ethnological study; Mustapha asked what I should require as dowry for her. Fancy Sally as Hareem of the Sheykh-el-Beled of Luxor!

I am so charmed with my house that I begin seriously to contemplate staying here all the time. Cairo is so dear now, and so many dead cattle are buried there, that I think I should do better in this place. There is a huge hall, so large and cold now as to be uninhabitable, which in summer would be glorious. My dear old captain of steamer XII. would bring me up coffee and candles, and if I 'sap' and learn to talk to people, I shall have plenty of company.

The cattle disease has not extended above Minieh to any degree, and here there has not been a case. *Alhamdulillah!* Food is very good here, rather less than half Cairo prices even now; in summer it will be half that. Mustapha urges me to stay, and proposes a picnic of a few days over in the tombs with his Hareem as a diversion. I have got a photo, for a stereoscope, which I send you, of my two beloved, lovely palm-trees on the river-bank just above and looking over Philæ.

Hitherto my right side has been the bad one, but now one side is uneasy and the other impossible to lie on. It does not make one sleep pleasantly, and the loss of my good, sound sleep tries me, and so I don't seem well. We shall see what hot weather will do; if that fails I will give up the contest, and come home to see as much as I shall have time for of you and my chicks.

To Mrs. Austin

Sunday, February 7, 1864.

Dearest Mutter,

We have had our winter pretty sharp for three weeks, and everybody has had violent colds and coughs—the Arabs, I mean.

I have been a good deal ailing, but have escaped any violent cold altogether, and now the thermometer is up to 64°, and it feels very pleasant. In the sun it is always very hot, but that does not prevent the air from being keen, and chapping lips and noses, and even hands; it is curious how a temperature, which would be summer in England, makes one shiver at Thebes—*Alhamdulillah!* it is over now.

My poor Sheykh Yussuf is in great distress about his brother, also a young Sheykh (*i.e.*, one learned in theology and competent to preach in the mosque). Sheykh Mohammed is come home from studying in 'El-Azhar' at Cairo—I fear to die. I went with Sheykh Yussuf, at his desire, to see if I could help him, and found him gasping for breath and very, very ill. I gave him a little soothing medicine, and put mustard plasters on him, and as it relieved him, I went again and repeated them. All the family and a lot of neighbours crowded in to look on. There he lay in a dark little den with bare mud walls, worse off, to our ideas, than any pauper; but these people do not feel the want of comforts, and one learns to think it quite natural to sit with perfect gentlemen in places inferior to our cattle-sheds. I pulled some blankets up against the wall, and put my arm behind Sheykh Mohammed's back to make him rest while the poultices were on him, whereupon he laid his green turban on my shoulder, and presently held up his delicate brown face for a kiss like an affectionate child. As I kissed him, a very pious old moollah said *Bismillah* (In the name of God) with an approving nod, and Sheykh Mohammed's old father, a splendid old man in a green turban, thanked me with effusion, and prayed that my children might always find help and kindness. I suppose if I confessed to kissing a 'dirty Arab' in a 'hovel' the English travellers would execrate me; but it shows how much there is in 'Mussulman bigotry, unconquerable hatred, etc.,' for this family are Seyyids (descendants of the Prophet) and very pious. Sheykh Yussuf does not even smoke, and he preaches on Fridays. You would love these Saeedees, they are such thorough gentlemen. I rode over to the village a few days ago to see a farmer named Omar. Of course I had to eat, and the people were enchanted at my going alone, as they are used to see the English armed and guarded. Sidi Omar, however, insisted on accompanying me home, which is the civil thing here. He piled a whole stack of green fodder on his little nimble donkey, and hoisted himself atop of it without saddle or bridle (the fodder was for Mustapha A'gha), and we trotted home across the beautiful green barley-fields, to the amazement of some European young men out shooting. We did look a curious pair, certainly, with my English saddle and bridle, habit, hat and feather, on horseback, and Sidi Omar's brown shirt, brown legs and white turban, guiding his donkey with his chibouque. We were laughing very merrily, too, over my blundering Arabic.

Young Heathcote and Strutt called here, but were hurrying on up the river. I shall see more of them when they come down. Young Strutt is so like his mother I knew him in the street. I would like to give him a fantasia, but it is not proper for a woman to send for the dancing-girls, and as I am the friend of the Maōhn (police magistrate), the Kadee, and the respectable people here, I cannot do what is indecent in their eyes. It is quite enough that they approve my unveiled face, and my associating with men; that is 'my custom,' and they think no harm of it.

To-morrow or next day Ramadan begins at the first sight of the new moon. It is a great nuisance, because everybody is cross. Omar did not keep it last year, but this year he will, and if he spoils my dinners, who can blame him? There was a wedding close by here last night, and about ten o'clock all the women passed under my windows with crys of joy 'ez-zaghareet' down to the river. I find, on inquiry, that in Upper Egypt, as soon as the bridegroom has 'taken the face' of his bride, the women take her down to 'see the Nile.' They have not yet forgotten that the old god is the giver of increase, it seems.

I have been reading Miss Martineau's book; the descriptions are excellent, but she evidently knew and cared nothing about the people, and had the feeling of most English people here, that the difference of manners is a sort of impassable gulf, the truth being that their feelings and passions are just like our own. It is curious that all the old books of travels that I have read mention the natives of strange countries in a far more natural tone, and with far more attempt to discriminate character, than modern ones, *e.g.*, Niebuhr's Travels* here and in Arabia, Cook's Voyages, and many others. *Have* we grown so *very* civilised since a hundred years that outlandish people seem like mere puppets, and not like real human beings? Miss M.'s bigotry against Copts and Greeks is droll enough, compared to her very proper reverence for 'Him who sleeps in Philæ,' and her attack upon hareems outrageous; she implies that they are brothels. I must admit that I have not seen a Turkish hareem, and she apparently saw no other, and yet she fancies the morals of Turkey to be superior to those of Egypt. It is not possible for a woman to explain all the limitations to which ordinary people do subject themselves. Great men I know nothing of; but women can and do, without blame, sue their husbands-in-law for the full 'payment of debt,' and demand a divorce if they please in default. Very often a man marries a second wife out of duty to provide for a brother's widow and children, or the like. Of course licentious men act loosely as elsewhere. *Kulloolum Beni Adam* (we are all sons of Adam), as Sheykh Yussuf says constantly, 'bad-bad and good-good'; and modern travellers show strange ignorance in talking of foreign natives *in the lump*, as they nearly all do.

Monday.—I have just heard that poor Sheykh Mohammed died yesterday, and was, as usual, buried at once. I had not been well for a few days, and Sheykh Yussuf took care that I should not know of his brother's death. He went to Mustapha A'gha, and told him not to tell anyone in my house till I was better, because he knew 'what was in my stomach towards his family,' and feared I should be made worse by the news. And how often I have been advised not to meddle with sick Arabs, because they are sure to suspect a Christian of poisoning those who die! I do grieve for the graceful, handsome young creature and his old father. Omar was vexed at not knowing of his death, because he would have liked to help to carry him to the grave.

I have at last learned the alphabet in Arabic, and can write it quite tidily, but now I am in a fix for want of a dictionary, and have written to Hekekian Bey to buy me one in Cairo. Sheykh Yussuf knows not a word of English, and Omar can't read or write, and has no notion of grammar or of *word for word* interpretation, and it is very slow work. When I walk through the court of the mosque I give the customary coppers to the little boys who are spelling away loudly under the arcade, *Abba sheddeh o nusbeyteen*, *Ibbi sheddeh o heftedeen*, etc., with a keen sympathy with their difficulties and well-smudged tin slates. An additional evil is that the Arabic books printed in England, and at English presses here, require a 40-horse power microscope to distinguish a letter. The ciphering is like ours, but with other figures, and I felt very stupid when I discovered how I had reckoned Arab fashion from right to left all my life and never observed the fact. However, they 'cast down' a column of figures from top to bottom.

I am just called away by some poor men who want me to speak to the English travellers about shooting their pigeons.* It is very thoughtless, but it is in great measure the fault of the servants and dragomans who think they must not venture to tell their masters that pigeons are private property. I have a great mind to put a notice on the wall of my house about it. Here, where there are never less than eight or ten boats lying for full three months, the loss to the *fellaheen* is serious, and our Consul Mustapha A'gha is afraid to say anything. I have given my neighbours permission to call the pigeons mine, as they roost in flocks on my roof, and to go out and say that the Sitt objects to her poultry being shot, especially as I have had them shot off my balcony as they sat there.

I got a note from M. Mounier yesterday, inviting me to go and stay at El-Moutaneh, Halim Pasha's great estate, near Edfoo, and offering to send his dahabieh for me. I certainly will go as soon as the weather is decidedly hot. It is now very warm and pleasant. If I find Thebes too hot as summer advances I must drop down and return to Cairo, or try Suez, which I hear is excellent in summer—bracing desert air. But it is very tempting to stay here—a splendid cool house, food extremely cheap; about £1 a week for three of us for fish, bread, butter, meat, milk, eggs and vegetables; all grocery, of course, I brought with me; no trouble, rest and civil neighbours. I feel very disinclined to move unless I am baked out, and it takes a good deal to bake me. The only fear is the Khamaseen wind. I do not feel very well. I don't ail anything in particular; blood-spitting frequent, but very slight; much less cough; but I am so weak and good for nothing. I seldom feel able to go out or do more than sit in the balcony on one side or other of the house. I have no donkey here, the hired ones are so very bad and so dear; but I have written Mounier to try and get me one at El-Moutaneh and send it down in one of Halim Pasha's corn-boats. There is no comfort like a donkey always ready. If I have to send for Mustapha's horse, I feel lazy and fancy it is too much trouble unless I can go just when I want.

I have received a letter from Alexandria of January 8. What dreadful weather! We felt the ghost of it here in our three weeks of cold. Sometimes I feel as if I must go back to you all *coûte qui coûte*, but I know it would be no use to try it in the summer. I long for more news of you and my chicks.

To Mrs Ross

LUXOR,
Tuesday, February 8, 1864.

DEAREST CHILD,

I got your letter No. 3 about a week ago, and two others before it. I have been very lazy in writing, for it has been very cold (for Thebes), and I have been very seedy—no severe attack, but no strength at all. The last three or four days the weather has been warm, and I am beginning to feel better. I send this to Cairo by a clever, pleasant Mme. de Beaulaincourt, a daughter of Maréchal Castellane, who is here in one of the Pasha's steamers. She will call on you when she goes to Alexandria. I have been learning to write Arabic, and know my letters—no trifle, I assure you. My Sheykh is a perfect darling—the most graceful, high-bred young creature, and a Seyyid. These Saeedees are much nicer than the Lower Egypt people. They have good Arab blood in their veins, keep pedigrees, and are more manly and independent, and more liberal in religion.

Sheykh Yussuf took me into the tomb of his ancestor, Sheykh Abul Hajjaj, the great saint here, and all the company said a Fathah for my health. It was on the night of Friday, and during the moolid of the Sheykh. Omar was surprised at the proceeding, and a little afraid the dead Sheykh might be offended. My great friend is the Maōhn (police magistrate) here—a very kind, good man, much liked, I hear, by all except the Kadee, who was displeased at his giving the stick to a Mussulman for some wrong to a Copt. I am beginning to stammer out a little Arabic, but find it horribly difficult. The plurals are bewildering and the verbs quite heart-breaking. I have no books, which makes learning very slow work. I have written to Hekekian Bey to buy me a dictionary.

The house here is delightful—rather cold now, but will be perfect in hot weather—so airy and cheerful. I think I shall stay on here all the time the expense is nil, and it is very comfortable.

I have a friend in a farm in a neighbouring village, and am much amused at seeing country life. It cannot be rougher, as regards material comforts, in New Zealand or Central Africa, but there is no barbarism or lack of refinement in the manners of the people. M. Mounier has invited me to go and stay with them at El-Moutaneh, and offers to send his dahabieh for me. When it gets really hot I shall like the trip very much.

Pray, when you see Mme. Tastu, say civil things for me, and tell her how much I like the house. I think it wonderful that Omar cooked the dinner without being cross. I am sure I should swear if I had to cook for a heretic in Ramadan.

To Sir Alexander Duff Gordon

LUXOR,
February 12, 1864.

DEAREST ALICK,

We are in Ramadan now, and Omar really enjoys a good opportunity of 'making his soul.' He fasts and washes vigorously, prays his five times a day, goes to mosque on Fridays, and is quite merry over it, and ready to cook infidels' dinners with exemplary good-humour. It is a great merit in Muslims that they are not at all grumpy over their piety. The weather has set in since five or six days quite like paradise. I sit on my lofty balcony and drink the sweet northerly breeze, and look at the glorious mountain opposite, and think if only you and the chicks were here it would be 'the best o' life.' The beauty of Egypt grows on one, and I think it far more lovely this year than I did last. My great friend the Maōhn (he is *not* the Nazir, who is a fat little pig-eyed, jolly Turk) lives in a house which also has a superb view in another direction, and I often go and sit 'on the bench'—*i.e.*, the *mastabah* in front of his house—and do what little talk I can and see the people come with their grievances. I don't understand much of what goes on, as the *patois* is broad and doubles the difficulty, or I would send you a Theban police report; but the Maōhn is very pleasant in his manner to them, and they don't seem frightened. We have appointed a very small boy our *bowàb*, or porter—or, rather, he has appointed himself—and his assumption of dignity is quite delicious. He has provided himself with a huge staff, and he behaves like the most tremendous janissary. He is about Rainie's size, as sharp as a needle, and possesses the remains of a brown shirt and a ragged kitchen duster as turban. I am very fond of little Achmet, and like to see him doing *tableaux vivants* from Murillo with a plate of broken victuals. The children of this place have become so insufferable about *backsheesh* that I have complained to the Maōhn, and he will assemble a committee of parents and enforce better manners. It is only here and just where the English go. When I ride into the little villages I never hear the word, but am always offered milk to drink. I have taken it two or three times and not offered to pay, and the people always seem quite pleased.

Yesterday Sheykh Yussuf came again, the first time since his brother's death; he was evidently deeply affected, but spoke in the usual way, 'It is the will of God, we must all die,' etc. I wish you could see Sheykh Yussuf. I think he is the sweetest creature in look and manner I ever beheld—so refined and so simple, and with the animal grace of a gazelle. A high-bred Arab is as graceful as an Indian, but quite without the feline *Geschmeidigkeit* or the look of dissimulation; the eye is as clear and frank as a child's. Mr. Ruchl, the Austrian Consul here, who knows Egypt and Arabia well, tells me that he thinks many of them quite as good as they look, and said of Sheykh Yussuf, *Er ist so gemüthlich*. There is a German here deciphering hieroglyphics, Herr Dümmichen, a very agreeable man, but he has gone across the river to live at el-Kurneh. He has been through Ethiopia in search of temples and inscriptions. I am to go over and visit him, and see some of the tombs again in his company, which I shall enjoy, as a good interpreter is sadly wanted in those mysterious regions.

My chest is wonderfully better these last six or seven days. It is quite clear that downright heat is what does me good. Moreover, I have just heard from M. Mounier that a good donkey is *en route* in a boat from El-Moutaneh—he will cost me between £4 and £5 and will enable me to be about far more than I can by merely borrowing Mustapha's horse, about which I have scruples as he lends it to other lady travellers. Little Achmet will be my sais as well as my door-keeper, I suppose. I wish you would speak to Layard* in behalf of Mustapha A'gha. He has acted as English Consul here for something like thirty years, and he really is the slave of the travellers. He gives them dinners, mounts them, and does all the disagreeable business of wrangling with the reis and dragomans for them, makes himself a postmaster, takes care of their letters and sends them out to the boats, and does all manner of services for them, and lends his house for the infidels to pray in on Sundays when a clergyman is here. For this he has no remuneration at all, except such presents as the English see fit to make him, and I have seen enough to know that they are neither large nor always gracefully given. The old fellow at Keneh who has nothing to do gets regular pay, and I think Mustapha ought to have something; he is now old and rather infirm, and has to keep a clerk to help him; and at least, his expenses should be covered. Please say this to Layard from me as my message to him. Don't forget it, please, for Mustapha is a really kind friend to me at all times and in all ways.

February 14th.—Yesterday we had a dust-storm off the desert. It made my head heavy and made me feel languid, but did not affect my chest at all. To-day is a soft gray day; there was a little thunder this morning and a few, very few, drops of rain—hardly enough for even Herodotus to consider portentous. My donkey came down last night, and I tried him to-day, and he is very satisfactory though alarmingly small, as the real Egyptian donkey always is; the big ones are from the Hejaz. But it is wonderful how the little creatures run along under one as easy as possible, and they have no will of their own. I rode mine out to Karnac and back, and he did not seem to think me at all heavy. When they are overworked and overgalloped they become bad on the legs and easily fall, and all those for hire are quite stumped up, poor beasts—they are so willing and docile that everyone overdrives them.

To Mrs. Austin

LUXOR,
February 19, 1864.

DEAREST MUTTER,

I have only time for a few lines to go down by Mr. Strutt and Heathcote's boat to Cairo. They are very good specimens and quite recognised as 'belonging to the higher people,' because they 'do not make themselves big.' I received your letter of January 21 with little darling Rainie's three days ago.

I am better now that the weather is fine again. We had a whole day's rain (which Herodotus says is a portent here) and a hurricane from the south worthy of the Cape. I thought we should have been buried under the drifting sand. To-day is again heavenly. I saw Abd-el-Azeez, the chemist in Cairo; he seemed a very good fellow, and was a pupil of my old friend M. Chrevreul, and highly recommended by him. Here I am out of all European ideas. The Sheykh-el-Arab (of the Ababdeh tribe), who has a sort of town house here, has invited me out into the desert to the black tents, and I intend to pay a visit with old Mustapha A'gha. There is a Roman well in his yard with a ghoul in it. I can't get the story from Mustapha, who is ashamed of such superstitions, but I'll find it out. We had a fantasia at Mustapha's for young Strutt and Co., and a very good dancing-girl. Some dear old prosy English people made me laugh so. The lady wondered how the women here could wear clothes 'so different from English females—poor things!' but they were not *malveillants*, only pitying and wonderstruck—nothing astonished them so much as my salutations with Seleem Effendi, the Maōhn.

I begin to feel the time before me to be away from you all very long indeed, but I do think my best chance is a long spell of real heat. I have got through this winter without once catching cold at all to signify, and now the fine weather is come. I am writing in Arabic from Sheykh Yussuf's dictation the dear old story of the barber's brother with the basket of glass. The Arabs are so diverted at hearing that we all know the *Alf Leyleh o Leyleh*, the 'Thousand Nights and a Night.' The want of a dictionary with a teacher knowing no word of English is terrible. I don't know how I learn at all. The post is pretty quick up to here. I got your letter within three weeks, you see, but I get no newspapers; the post is all on foot and can't carry anything so heavy. One of my men of last year, Asgalani the steersman, has just been to see me; he says his journey was happier last year.

I hear that Phillips is coming to Cairo, and have written to him there to invite him up here to paint these handsome Saeedees. He could get up in a steamer as I did through Hassaneyn Effendi for a trifle. I wish you *could* come, but the heat here which gives me life would be quite *impossible* to you. The thermometer in the cold antechamber now is 67° where no sun ever comes, and the blaze of the sun is prodigious.

To Sir Alexander Duff Gordon

LUXOR,
February 26, 1864.

DEAREST ALICK,

I have just received your letter of the 3rd inst., and am glad to get such good tidings. You would be amused to see Omar bring me a letter and sit down on the floor till I tell him the family news, and then *Alhamdulillah*, we are so pleased, and he goes off to his pots and pans again. Lord and Lady Spencer are here, and his sister, in two boats. The English 'Milord,' extinct on the Continent, has revived in Egypt, and is greatly reverenced and usually much liked. 'These high English have mercy in their stomachs,' said one of my last year's sailors who came to kiss my hand—a pleasing fact in natural history! *Fee wahed Lord*, was little ragged Achmet's announcement of Lord Spencer—'Here's a Lord.' They are very pleasant people. I heard from Janet to-day of *ice* at Cairo and at Shoubra, and famine prices. I cannot attempt Cairo with meat at 1s. 3d. a pound, and will e'en stay here and grill at Thebes. Marry-come-up with your Thebes and savagery! What if we *do* wear ragged brown shirts? ''Tis manners makyth man,' and we defy you to show better breeding.

We are now in the full enjoyment of summer weather; there has been no cold for fully a fortnight, and I am getting better every day now. My cough has quite subsided, and the pain in the chest much diminished; if the heat does not overpower me I feel sure it will be very healing to my lungs. I sit out on my glorious balcony and drink the air from early morning till noon, when the sun comes upon it and drives me under cover. The thermometer has stood at 64° for a fortnight or three weeks, rising sometimes to 67°, but people in the boats tell me it is still cold at night on the river. Up here, only a stone's-throw from it, it is warm all night. I fear the loss of cattle has suspended irrigation to a fearful extent, and that the harvests of Lower Egypt of all kinds will be sadly scanty. The disease has not spread above Minieh, or very slightly; but, of course, cattle will rise in price here also. Already food is getting dearer here; meat is 4½ piastres—7d.—the *rötl* (a fraction less than a pound), and bread has risen considerably—I should say corn, for no bakers exist here. I pay a woman to grind and bake my wheat which I buy, and delicious bread it is. It is impossible to say how exactly like the early parts of the Bible every act of life is here, and how totally new it seems when one reads it here. Old Jacob's speech to Pharaoh really made me laugh (don't be shocked), because it is so exactly what a fellah says to a Pasha: 'Few and evil have been the days,' etc. (Jacob being a most prosperous man); but it is manners to say all that, and I feel quite kindly to Jacob, whom I used to think ungrateful and discontented; and when I go to Sidi Omar's farm, does he not say, 'Take now fine meal and bake cakes quickly,' and wants to kill a kid? *Fateereh* with plenty of butter is what the 'three men' who came to Abraham ate; and the way that Abraham's chief memlook, acting as Vakeel, manages Isaac's marriage with Rebekah! All the vulgarised associations with Puritanism and abominable little 'Scripture tales and pictures' peel off here, and the inimitably truthful representation of life and character—not a flattering one certainly—comes out, and it feels like Homer. Joseph's tears and his love for the brother born of the *same mother* is so perfect. Only one sees what a bad inferior race the Beni Israel were compared to the Beni Ishmael or to the Egyptians. Leviticus and Deuteronomy are so very heathenish compared to the law of the Koran, or to the early days of Abraham. Verily the ancient Jews were a foul nation, judging by the police regulations needful for them. Please don't make these remarks public, or I shall be burnt with Stanley and Colenso (unless I suffer Sheykh Yussuf to propose me El-Islam). He and M. de Rougé were here last evening, and we had an Arabic *soirée*. M. de Rougé speaks admirably, quite like an Alim, and it was charming to see Sheykh Yussuf's pretty look of grateful pleasure at finding himself treated like a gentleman and a scholar by two such eminent Europeans; for I (as a woman) am quite as surprising as even M. de Rougé's knowledge of hieroglyphics and Arabic *Fosseeha*. It is very interesting to see something of Arabs who have read and have the 'gentleman' ideas. His brother, the Imam, has lost his wife; he was married twenty-two years, and won't hear of taking another. I was struck with the sympathy he expressed with the English Sultana, as all the uneducated people say, 'Why doesn't she marry again?' It is curious how refinement brings out the same feelings under all 'dispensations.' I apologised to Yussuf for inadvertently returning the *Salaam aleykoum* (Peace be with thee), which he said to Omar, and which I, as an unbeliever, could not accept. He coloured crimson, touched my hand and kissed his own, quite distressed lest the distinction might wound me. When I think of a young parsonic prig at home I shudder at the difference. But Yussuf is superstitious; he told me how someone down the river cured his cattle with water poured over a *Mushaf* (a copy of the Koran), and has hinted at writing out a chapter for me to wear as a *hegab* (an amulet for my health). He is interested in the antiquities and in M. de Rougé's work, and is quite up to the connection between Ancient Egypt and the books of Moses, exaggerating the importance of *Seyidna Moussa*, of course.

If I go down to Cairo again I will get letters to some of the Alim there from Abd-el-Waris, the Imam here, and I shall see what no European but Lane has seen. I think things have altered since his day, and that men of that class would be less inaccessible than they were then; and then a woman who is old (Yussuf guessed me at sixty) and educated does not shock, and does interest them. All the Europeans here are traders, and only speak the vulgarest language, and don't care to know Arab gentlemen; if they see anything above their servants it is only Turks, or Arab merchants at times. Don't fancy that I can speak at all decently yet, but I understand a good deal, and stammer out a little.

To Mrs. Austin

Luxor,
March 1, 1864.

Dearest Mutter,

I think I shall have an opportunity of sending letters in a few days by a fast steamer, so I will begin one on the chance and send it by post if the steamer is delayed long. The glory of the climate now is beyond description, and I feel better every day. I go out early—at seven or eight o'clock—on my tiny black donkey, and come in to breakfast about ten, and go out again at four.

I want to photograph Yussuf for you. The feelings and prejudices and ideas of a cultivated Arab, as I get at them little by little, are curious beyond compare. It won't do to generalise from one man, of course, but even one gives some very new ideas. The most striking thing is the sweetness and delicacy of feeling—the horror of hurting anyone (this must be individual, of course: it is too good to be general). I apologised to him two days ago for inadvertently answering the *Salaam aleykoum*, which he, of course, said to Omar on coming in. Yesterday evening he walked in and startled me by a *Salaam aleykee* addressed to me; he had evidently been thinking it over whether he ought to say it to me, and come to the conclusion that it was not wrong. 'Surely it is well for all the creatures of God to speak peace (*Salaam*) to each other,' said he. Now, no uneducated Muslim would have arrived at such a conclusion. Omar would pray, work, lie, do anything for me—sacrifice money even; but I doubt whether he *could* utter *Salaam aleykoum* to any but a Muslim. I answered as I felt: 'Peace, oh my brother, and God bless thee!' It was almost as if a Catholic priest had felt impelled by charity to offer the communion to a heretic. I observed that the story of the barber was new to him, and asked if he did not know the 'Thousand and One Nights.' No; he studied only things of religion, no light amusements were proper for an Alim (elder of religion); *we* Europeans did not know that, of course, as *our* religion was to enjoy ourselves; but *he* must not make merry with diversions, or music, or droll stories. (See the mutual ignorance of all ascetics!) He has a little girl of six or seven, and teaches her to write and read; no one else, he believes, thinks of such a thing out of Cairo; there many of the daughters of the Alim learn—those who desire it. His wife died two years ago, and six months ago he married again a wife of twelve years old! (Sheykh Yussuf is thirty he tells me; he looks twenty-two or twenty-three.) What a stepmother and what a wife! He can repeat the whole Koran without a book, it takes twelve hours to do it. Has read the Towrát (old Testament) and the el-Aangeel (Gospels), of course, every Alim reads them. 'The words of Seyyidna Eesa are the true faith, but Christians have altered and corrupted their meaning. So we Muslims believe. We are all the children of God.' I ask if Muslims call themselves so, or only the slaves of God. ''Tis all one, children or slaves. Does not a good man care for both tenderly alike?' (Pray observe the Oriental feeling here. *Slave* is a term of affection, not contempt; and remember the Centurion's '*servant* (slave) whom he loved.') He had heard from Fodl Pasha how a cow was cured of the prevailing disease in Lower Egypt by water weighed against a *Mushaf* (copy of the Koran), and had no doubt it was true, Fodl Pasha had tried it. Yet he thinks the Arab doctors no use at all who use verses of the Koran.

M. de Rougé, the great *Egyptologue*, came here one evening; he speaks Arabic perfectly, and delighted Sheykh Yussuf, who was much interested in the translations of the hieroglyphics and anxious to know if he had found anything about *Moussa* (Moses) or *Yussuf* (Joseph). He looked pleased and grateful to be treated like a 'gentleman and scholar' by such an Alim as M. de Rougé and such a Sheykhah as myself. As he acts as clerk to Mustapha, our consular agent, and wears a shabby old brown shirt, or gown, and speaks no English, I dare say he not seldom encounters great slights (from sheer ignorance). He produced a bit of old Cufic MS. and consulted M. de R. as to its meaning—a pretty little bit of flattery in an Arab Alim to a Frenchman, to which the latter was not insensible, I saw. In answer to the invariable questions about all my family I once told him my father had been a great Alim of the Law, and that my mother had got ready his written books and put some lectures in order to be printed. He was amazed—first that I had a mother, as he told me he thought I was fifty or sixty, and immensely delighted at the idea. 'God has favoured your family with understanding and knowledge; I wish I could kiss the *Sheykhah* your mother's hand. May God favour her!' Maurice's portrait (as usual) he admired fervently, and said one saw his good qualities in his face—a compliment I could have fully returned, as he sat looking at the picture with affectionate eyes and praying, *sotto voce*, for *el gedda*, *el gemeel* (the youth, the beautiful), in the words of the *Fathah*, 'O give him guidance and let him not stray into the paths of the rejected!' Altogether, something in Sheykh Yussuf reminds me of Worsley: there is the same look of *Seelen reinheit*, with far less thought and intelligence; indeed little thought, of course, and an additional childlike innocence. I suppose some medieval monks may have had the same look, but no Catholic I have ever seen looks so peaceful or so unpretending. I see in him, like in all people who don't know what doubt means, that easy familiarity with religion. I hear him joke with Omar about Ramadan, and even about Omar's assiduous prayers, and he is a frequent and hearty laugher. I wonder whether this gives you any idea of a character new to you. It is so impossible to describe *manner*, which gives so much of the impression of novelty. My conclusion is the heretical one: that to dream of converting here is absurd, and, I will add, wrong. All that is wanted is general knowledge and education, and the religion will clear and develop itself. The elements are identical with those of Christianity, encumbered, as that has been, with asceticism and intolerance. On the other hand, the creed is simple and there are no priests, a decided advantage. I think the faith has remained wonderfully rational considering the extreme ignorance of those who hold it. I will add Sally's practical remark, that 'The prayers are a fine thing for lazy people; they must wash first, and the prayer is a capital drill.'

You would be amused to hear Sally when Omar does not wake in time to wash, pray, and eat before daybreak now in Ramadán. She knocks at his door and acts as Muezzin. 'Come, Omar, get up and pray and have your dinner' (the evening meal is 'breakfast,' the early morning one 'dinner'). Being a light sleeper she hears the Muezzin, which Omar often does not, and passes on the 'Prayers is better than sleep' in a prose version. Ramadán is a dreadful business; everybody is cross and lazy—no wonder! The camel-men quarrelled all day under my window yesterday, and I asked what it was all about. 'All about nothing; it is Ramadán with them,' said Omar laughing. 'I want to quarrel with someone myself; it is hot to-day, and thirsty weather.' Moreover, I think it injures the health of numbers permanently, but of course it is the thing of most importance in the eyes of the people; there are many who never pray at ordinary times, but few fail to keep Ramadán. It answers to the Scotch Sabbath, a comparison also borrowed from Sally.

Friday.—My friend Seleem Effendi has just been here talking about his own affairs and a good deal of theology. He is an immense talker, and I just put *eywas* (yes) and *là* (no) and *sahé* (very true), and learn manners and customs. He tells me he has just bought two black slave women, mother and daughter, from a Copt for about £35 the two. The mother is a good cook, and the daughter is 'for his bed,' as his wife does not like to leave Cairo and her boys at school there. It does give one a sort of start to hear a most respectable magistrate tell one such a domestic arrangement. He added that it would not interfere with the *Sittel Kebeer* (the great lady), the black girl being only a slave, and these people never think they have children enough. Moreover, he said he could not get on with his small pay without women to keep house, which is quite true here, and women are not respectable in a man's house on other terms. Seleem has a high reputation, and is said not to 'eat the people.' He is a hot Mussulman, and held forth very much as a very superficial Unitarian might do, evidently feeling considerable contempt for the absurdities, as he thinks them, of the Copts (he was too civil to say Christians), but no hatred (and he is known to show no partiality), only he 'can't understand how people can believe such nonsense.' He is a good specimen of the good, honest, steady-going man-of-the-world Muslim, a strong contrast to the tender piety of dear Sheykh Yussuf, who has all the feelings which we call Christian charity in the highest degree, and whose face is like that of 'the beloved disciple,' but who has no inclination for doctrinal harangues like worthy Seleem. There is a very general idea among the Arabs that Christians hate the Muslims; they attribute to us the old Crusading spirit. It is only lately that Omar has let us see him at prayer, for fear of being ridiculed, but now he is sure that is not so, I often find him praying in the room where Sally sits at work, which is a clean, quiet place. Yussuf went and joined him there yesterday evening, and prayed with him, and gave him some religious instruction quite undisturbed by Sally and her needlework, and I am continually complimented on *not hating* the Muslims. Yussuf promises me letters to some Alim in Cairo when I go there again, that I may be shown the Azhar (the great college). Omar had told him that I refused to go with a janissary from the Consul for fear of giving offence to any very strict Muslims, which astonished him much. He says his friends shall dress me in their women's clothes and take me in. I asked whether as a concealment of my religion, and he said no, only there were 'thousands' of young men, and it would be 'more delicate' that they should not stare and talk about my face.

Seleem told me a very pretty grammatical quibble about 'son' and 'prophet' (apropos of Christ) on a verse in the Gospel, depending on the reduplicative sign ّ (*sheddeh*) over one letter; he was just as put out when I reminded him that it was written in Greek, as our amateur theologians are if you say the Bible was not originally composed in English. However, I told him that many Christians in England, Germany, and America did not believe that Seyyidna Eesa was God, but only the greatest of prophets and teachers, and that I was myself of that opinion. He at once declared that that was sufficient, that all such had 'received guidance,' and were not 'among the rejected'; how could they be, since such Christians only believed the teaching of Eesa, which was true, and not the falsifications of the priests and bishops (the bishops always 'catch it,' as schoolboys say). I was curious to hear whether on the strength of this he would let out any further intolerance against the Copts, but he said far less and far less bitterly than I have heard from Unitarians, and debited the usual most commonplace, common-sense kind of arguments on the subject. I fancy it would not be very palatable to many Unitarians, to be claimed *mir nichts dir nichts* as followers of *el-Islam*; but if people really wish to convert in the sense of improving, that door is open, and no other.

Monday, 7th.—The steamer is come down already and will, I suppose, go on to-morrow, so I must finish this letter to go by it. I have not received any letter for some time, and am anxiously expecting the post. We have now settled into quite warm weather ways, no more going out at mid-day. It is now broiling, and I have been watching eight tall fine blacks swimming and capering about, their skins shining like otters' fur when wet. They belong to a *gelláab*—a slave-dealer's boat. The beautiful thing is to see the men and boys at work among the green corn, the men half naked and the boys wholly so; in the sun their brown skins look just like dark clouded amber—semi-transparent, so fine are they.

I rejoice to say that on Wednesday is Bairam, and to-morrow Ramadan 'dies.' Omar is very thin and yellow and headachy, and everyone is cross. How I wish I were going, instead of my letter, to see you all, but it is evident that this heat is the thing that does me good, if anything will.

To Sir Alexander Duff Gordon

Luxor,
March 7, 1864.

Dearest Alick,

The real hot weather (speaking after the manner of the English) has begun, and the fine sun and clear air are delicious and reviving. My cough fades away, and my strength increases slowly. One can no longer go out in the middle of the day, and I mount my donkey early and late, with little Achmet trotting beside me. In the evenings comes my dear Sheykh Yussuf, and I blunder through an hour's dictation, and reading of the story of the Barber's fifth brother (he with the basket of glass). I presume that Yussuf likes me too, for I am constantly greeted with immense cordiality by graceful men in green turbans, belonging, like him, to the holy family of Sheykh Abu-'l-Hajjaj. They inquire tenderly after my health, and pray for me, and hope I am going to stay among them.

You would be much struck here with the resemblance to Spain, I think. 'Cosas de España' is exactly the '*Shogl-el-Arab*,' and Don Fulano is the Arabic word *foolan* (such a one), as *Ojala* is *Inshallah* (please God). The music and dancing here, too, are Spanish, only 'more so' and much more.

March 10, 1864.—Yesterday was Bairam, and on Tuesday evening everybody who possessed a gun or a pistol banged away, every drum and taraboukeh was thumped, and all the children holloaed, *Ramadan Māt, Ramadan Māt* (Ramadan's dead) about the streets. At daybreak Omar went to the early prayer, a special ceremony of the day. There were crowds of people, so, as it was useless to pray and preach in the mosque, Sheykh Yussuf went out upon a hillock in the burying-ground, where they all prayed and he preached. Omar reported the sermon to me, as follows (it is all extempore): First Yussuf pointed to the graves, 'Where are all those people?' and to the ancient temples, 'Where are those who built them? Do not strangers from a far country take away their very corpses to wonder at? What did their splendour avail them? etc., etc. What then, O Muslims, *will* avail that you may be happy when that comes which will come for all? Truly God is just and will defraud no man, and He will reward you if you do what is right; and that is, to wrong no man, neither in person, nor in his family, nor in his possessions. *Cease then to cheat one another, O men*, and to be greedy, and do not think that you can make amends by afterwards giving alms, or praying, or fasting, or giving gifts to the servants of the mosque. *Benefits come from God; it is enough for you if you do no injury to any man, and above all to any woman or little one*.' Of course it was much longer, but this was the substance, Omar tells me, and pretty sound morality too, methinks, and might be preached with advantage to a meeting of philanthropists in Exeter Hall. There is no predestination in *Islam*, and every man will be judged upon his actions. 'Even unbelievers God will not defraud,' says the Koran. Of course, a belief in meritorious works leads to the same sort of superstition as among Catholics, the endeavour to 'make one's soul' by alms, fastings, endowments, etc.; therefore Yussuf's stress upon doing no evil seems to me very remarkable, and really profound. After the sermon, all the company assembled rushed on him to kiss his head, and his hands and his feet, and mobbed him so fearfully that he had to lay about him with the wooden sword which is carried by the officiating Alim. He came to wish me the customary good wishes soon after, and looked very hot and tumbled, and laughed heartily about the awful kissing he had undergone. All the men embrace on meeting on the festival of Bairam.

The kitchen is full of cakes (ring-shaped) which my friends have sent me, just such as we see offered to the gods in the temples and tombs. I went to call on the Maōhn in the evening, and found a lot of people all dressed in their best. Half were Copts, among them a very pleasing young priest who carried on a religious discussion with Seleem Effendi, strange to say, with perfect good-humour on both sides. A Copt came up with his farm labourer, who had been beaten and the field robbed. The Copt stated the case in ten words, and the Maōhn sent off his cavass with him to apprehend the accused persons, who were to be tried at sunrise and beaten, if found guilty, and forced to make good the damage. General Hay called yesterday—a fine old, blue-eyed soldier. He found a lot of Fellaheen sitting with me, enjoying coffee and pipes hugely, and they were much gratified at our pressing them not to move or disturb themselves, when they all started up in dismay at the entrance of such a grand-looking Englishman and got off the carpet. So we told them that in our country the business of a farmer was looked upon as very respectable, and that the General would ask his farmers to sit and drink wine with him. '*Mashallah, taib kateer*' (It is the will of God, and most excellent), said old Omar, my fellah friend, and kissed his hand to General Hay quite affectionately. We English are certainly liked here. Seleem said yesterday evening that he had often had to do business with them, and found them always *doghri* (straight), men of one word and of no circumlocutions, 'and so unlike all the other Europeans, and especially the French!' The fact is that few but decent English come here, I fancy our scamps go to the colonies, whereas Egypt is the sink for all the iniquity of the South of Europe.

A worthy Copt here, one Todorus, took 'a piece of paper' for £20 for antiquities sold to an Englishman, and after the Englishman was gone, brought it to me to ask what sort of paper it was, and how he could get it changed, or was he, perhaps, to keep it till the gentleman sent him the money? It was a circular note, which I had difficulty in explaining, but I offered to send it to Cairo to Brigg's and get it cashed; as to when he would get the money I could not say, as they must wait for a safe hand to send gold by. I told him to put his name on the back of the note, and Todorus thought I wanted it *as a receipt* for the money which was yet to come, and was going cheerfully to write me a receipt for the £20 he was entrusting to me. Now a Copt is not at all green where his pocket is concerned, but they will take anything from the English. I do hope no swindler will find it out. Mr. Close told me that when his boat sank in the Cataract, and he remained half dressed on the rock, without a farthing, four men came and offered to lend him anything. While I was in England last year an Englishman to whom Omar acted as *laquais de place* went away owing him £7 for things bought. Omar had money enough to pay all the tradespeople, and kept it secret for fear any of the other Europeans should say, 'Shame for the English' and did not even tell his family. Luckily, the man sent the money by the next mail from Malta, and the Sheykh of the dragomans proclaimed it, and so Omar got it; but he would never have mentioned it else. This 'concealing of evil' is considered very meritorious, and where women are concerned positively a religious duty. *Le scandale est ce qui fait l'offense* is very much the notion in Egypt, and I believe that very forgiving husbands are commoner here than elsewhere. The whole idea is founded on the verse of the Koran, incessantly quoted, 'The woman is made for the man, but the man is made for the woman'; *ergo*, the obligations to chastity are equal; *ergo*, as the men find it difficult, they argue that the women do the same. I have never heard a woman's misconduct spoken of without a hundred excuses; perhaps her husband had slave girls, perhaps he was old or sick, or she didn't like him, or she couldn't help it. Violent love comes 'by the visitation of God,' as our juries say; the man or woman must satisfy it or die. A poor young fellow is now in the muristan (the madhouse) of Cairo owing to the beauty and sweet tongue of an English lady whose servant he was. How could he help it? God sent the calamity.

I often hear of Lady Ellenborough,* who is married to the Sheykh-el-Arab of Palmyra, and lives at Damascus. The Arabs think it inhuman of English ladies to avoid her. Perhaps she has repented; at all events, she is married and lives with her husband. I asked Omar if he would tell his brother if he saw his wife do anything wrong. (N.B.—He can't endure her.) 'Certainly not, I must cover her with my cloak.' I am told, also, that among the Arabs of the desert (the *real* Arabs), when a traveller, tired and wayworn, seeks their tents, it is the duty of his host, generally the Sheykh, to send him into the hareem, and leave him there three days, with full permission to do as he will after the women have bathed, and rubbed, and refreshed him. But then he must never speak of that Hareem; they are to him as his own, to be reverenced. If he spoke, the husband would kill him; but the Arab would never do it for a European, 'because all Europeans are so hard upon women,' and do not fear God and conceal their offences. If a dancing-girl repents, the most respectable man may and does marry her, and no one blames or laughs at him. I believe all this leads to a good deal of irregularity, but certainly the feeling is amiable. It is impossible to conceive how startling it is to a Christian to hear the rules of morality applied with perfect impartiality to both sexes, and to hear Arabs who know our manners talk of the English being 'jealous' and 'hard upon their women.' Any unchastity is wrong and *haram* (unlawful), but equally so in men and women. Seleem Effendi talked in this strain, and seemed to incline to greater indulgence to women on the score of their ignorance and weakness. Remember, I only speak of Arabs. I believe the Turkish ideas are different, as is their whole hareem system, and Egypt is not the rule for all Muslims.

Saturday, 12*th*.—I dined last night with Mustapha, who again had the dancing-girls for some Englishmen to see. Seleem Effendi got the doctor, who was of the party, to prescribe for him, and asked me to translate to him all about his old stomach as coolly as possible. He, as usual, sat by me on the divan, and during the pause in the dancing called 'el Maghribeeyeh,' the best dancer, to come and talk. She kissed my hand, sat on her heels before us, and at once laid aside the professional *galliardise* of manner, and talked very nicely in very good Arabic and with perfect propriety, more like a man than a woman; she seemed very intelligent. What a thing we should think it for a worshipful magistrate to call up a girl of that character to talk to a lady!

Yesterday we had a strange and unpleasant day's business. The evening before I had my pocket picked in Karnac by two men who hung about me, one to sell a bird, the other one of the regular 'loafers' who hang about the ruins to beg, and sell water or curiosities, and who are all a lazy, bad lot, of course. I went to Seleem, who wrote at once to the Sheykh-el-Beled of Karnac to say that we should go over next morning at eight o'clock to investigate the affair, and to desire him to apprehend the men. Next morning Seleem fetched me, and Mustapha came to represent English interests, and as we rode out of Luxor the Sheykh-el-Ababdeh joined us, with four of his tribe with their long guns, and a lot more with lances. He was a volunteer, and furious at the idea of a lady and a stranger being robbed. It is the first time it has happened here, and the desire to beat was so strong that I went to act as counsel for the prisoner. Everyone was peculiarly savage that it should have happened to me, a person well known to be so friendly to *el Muslimeen*. When we arrived we went into a square enclosure, with a sort of cloister on one side, spread with carpets where we sat, and the wretched fellows were brought in chains. To my horror, I found they had been beaten already. I remonstrated, 'What if you had beaten the wrong men?' '*Maleysh!* (Never mind!) we will beat the whole village until your purse is found.' I said to Mustapha, 'This won't do; you must stop this.' So Mustapha ordained, with the concurrence of the Maōhn, that the Sheykh-el-Beled and the *gefiyeh* (the keeper of the ruins) should pay me the value of the purse. As the people of Karnac are very troublesome in begging and worrying, I thought this would be a good lesson to the said Sheykh to keep better order, and I consented to receive the money, promising to return it and to give a napoleon over if the purse comes back with its contents (3½ napoleons). The

Sheykh-el-Ababdeh harangued the people on their ill-behaviour to Hareemát, called them *harámee* (rascals), and was very high and mighty to the Sheykh-el-Beled. Hereupon I went away to visit a Turkish lady in the village, leaving Mustapha to settle. After I was gone they beat eight or ten of the boys who had mobbed me, and begged with the two men. Mustapha, who does not like the stick, stayed to see that they were not hurt, and so far it will be a good lesson to them. He also had the two men sent over to the prison here, for fear the Sheykh-el-Beled should beat them again, and will keep them here for a time. So far so good, but my fear now is that innocent people will be squeezed to make up the money, if the men do not give up the purse. I have told Sheykh Yussuf to keep watch how things go, and if the men persist in the theft and don't return the purse, I shall give the money to those whom the Sheykh-el-Beled will assuredly squeeze, or else to the mosque of Karnac. I cannot pocket it, though I thought it quite right to exact the fine as a warning to the Karnac *mauvais sujets*. As we went home the Sheykh-el-Ababdeh (such a fine fellow he looks) came up and rode beside me, and said, 'I know you are a person of kindness; do not tell this story in this country. If Effendina (Ismail Pasha) comes to hear, he may "take a broom and sweep away the village."' I exclaimed in horror, and Mustapha joined at once in the request, and said, 'Do not tell anyone in Egypt. The Sheykh-el-Ababdeh is quite true; it might cost many lives.' The whole thing distressed me horribly. If I had not been there they would have beaten right and left, and if I had shown any desire to have anyone punished, evidently they would have half killed the two men. Mustapha behaved extremely well. He showed sense, decision, and more feelings of humanity than I at all expected of him. Pray do as I begged you, try to get him paid. Some of the Consuls in Cairo are barely civil, and old Mustapha has all the bother and work of the whole of the Nile boats (eighty-five this winter), and he is boundlessly kind and useful to the English, and a real protection against cheating, etc.

To Mr. Tom Taylor

March 16, 1864.

Dear Tom,

I cannot tell you how delighted I was to hear that all had gone well with Laura and your little daughter. *Mashallah!* God bless her! When I told Omar that a friend 'like my brother,' as Arabs say, had got a baby, he proposed to illuminate our house and fire off all the pistols in the premises. Pray give my kind love and best wishes to Laura.

I am living here a very quiet, dreamy sort of life in hot Thebes, visiting a little among my neighbours and learning a little Arabic from a most sweet, gentle young Sheykh who preaches on Fridays in the mosque of Luxor. I wish I could draw his soft brown face and graceful, brown-draped figure; but if I could, he is too devout I believe, to permit it. The police magistrate—el-Maōhn—Seleem Effendi, is also a great friend of mine, and the Kadee is civil, but a little scornful to heretical Hareem, I think. It is already very hot, and the few remaining traveller's dahabiehs are now here on their way down the river; after that I shall not see a white face for many months, except Sally's.

Sheykh Yussuf laughed so heartily over a print in an illustrated paper, from a picture of Hilton's, of Rebekah at the well, with the old *Vakeel* of Sidi Ibraheem (Abraham's chief servant) *kneeling* before the girl he was sent to fetch like an old fool without his turban, and Rebekah and the other girls in queer fancy dresses, and the camels with snouts like pigs. 'If the painter could not go to Es-Sham (Syria) to see how the Arab (Bedaween) really look,' said Sheykh Yussuf, 'why did he not paint a well in England with girls like English peasants? At least it would have looked natural to English people, and the *Vakeel* would not seem so like a *majnoon* (a madman) if he had taken off a hat.' I cordially agreed with Yussuf's art criticism. Fancy pictures of Eastern things are hopelessly absurd, and fancy poems too. I have got hold of a stray copy of Victor Hugo's '*Orientales*,' and I think I never laughed more in my life.

The corn is now full-sized here, but still green; in twenty days will be harvest, and I am to go to the harvest-home to a fellah friend of mine in a village a mile or two off. The crop is said to be unusually fine. Old Nile always pays back the damage he does when he rises so very high. The real disaster is the cattle disease, which still goes on, I hear, lower down. It has not at present spread above Minieh, but the destruction has been fearful.

I more and more feel the difficulty of quite understanding a people so unlike ourselves—the more I know them, I mean. One thing strikes me, that like children, they are not conscious of the great gulf which divides educated Europeans from themselves; at least, I believe it is so. We do not attempt to explain our ideas to them, but I cannot discover any such reticence in them. I wonder whether this has struck people who can talk fluently and know them better than I do? I find they appeal to my sympathy in trouble quite comfortably, and talk of religious and other feelings apparently as freely as to each other. In many respects they are more unprejudiced than we are, and very intelligent, and very good in many ways; and yet they seem so strangely childish, and I fancy I detect that impression even in Lane's book, though he does not say so.

If you write to me, dear Tom, please address me care of Briggs and Co., Cairo. I shall be so glad to hear of you and yours. Janet is going to England. I wish I were going too, but it is useless to keep trying a hopeless experiment. At present I am very comfortable in health as long as I do nothing and the weather is warm. I suffer little pain, only I feel weak and weary.

I have extensive practice in the doctoring line; bad eyes, of course, abound. My love to Watts, and give greetings to any other of my friends. I grieve over Thackeray much, and more over his girls' lonely sort of position.

I think you would enjoy, as I do, the peculiar sort of social equality which prevails here; it is the exact contrary of French *égalité*. There are the great and powerful people, much honoured (outwardly, at all events), but nobody has *inferiors*. A man comes in and kisses my hand, and sits down *off* the carpet out of respect; but he smokes his pipe, drinks his coffee, laughs, talks and asks questions as freely as if he were an Effendi or I were a fellahah; he is not my inferior, he is my poor brother. The servants in my friends' houses receive me with profound demonstrations of respect, and wait at dinner reverently, but they mix freely in the conversation, and take part in all amusements, music, dancing-girls, or reading of the Koran. Even the dancing-girl is not an outcast; she is free to talk to me, and it is highly irreligious to show any contempt or aversion. The rules of politeness are the same for all. The passer-by greets the one sitting still, or the one who comes into a room those who are already there, without distinction of rank. When I have greeted the men they always rise, but if I pass without, they take no notice of me. All this is very pleasant and graceful, though it is connected with much that is evil. The fact that any man may be a Bey or a Pasha to-morrow is not a good fact, for the promotion is more likely to fall on a bad slave than on a good or intelligent free man. Thus, the only honourable class are those who have nothing to hope from the great—I won't say anything to fear, for all have cause for that. Hence the high respectability and *gentility* of the merchants, who are the most independent of the Government. The English would be a little surprised at Arab judgments of them; they admire our veracity and honesty, and like us on the whole, but they blame the men for their conduct to women. They are shocked at the way Englishmen talk about Hareem among themselves, and think the English hard and unkind to their wives, and to women in general. English Hareemát is generally highly approved, and an Arab thinks himself a happy man if he can marry an English girl. I have had an offer for Sally from the chief man here for his son, proposing to allow her a free exercise of her religion and customs as a matter of course. I think the influence of foreigners is much more real and much more useful on the Arabs than on the Turks, though the latter show it more in dress, etc. But all the engineers and physicians are Arabs, and very good ones, too. Not a Turk has learnt anything practical, and the dragomans and servants employed by the English have learnt a strong appreciation of the value of a character for honesty, deserved or no; but many do deserve it. Compared to the couriers and *laquais de place* of Europe, these men stand very high. Omar has just run in to say a boat is going, so good-bye, and God bless you.

To Sir Alexander Duff Gordon

Luxor,
March 22, 1864.

Dearest Alick,

I am glad my letters amuse you. Sometimes I think they must breathe the unutterable dulness of Eastern life: not that it is dull to me, a curious spectator, but how the men with nothing to do can endure it is a wonder. I went yesterday to call on a Turk at Karnac; he is a gentlemanly man, the son of a former Moudir, who was murdered, I believe, for his cruelty and extortion. He has 1,000 feddans (acres, or a little more) of land, and lives in a mud house, larger but no better than any fellahs, with two wives and the brother of one of them. He leaves the farm to his fellaheen altogether, I fancy. There was one book, a Turkish one; I could not read the title-page, and he did not tell me what it was. In short, there was no means of killing time but the narghile, no horse, no gun, nothing, and yet they did not seem bored. The two women are always clamorous for my visits, and very noisy and school-girlish, but apparently excellent friends and very good-natured. The gentleman gave me a *kufyeh* (thick head kerchief for the sun), so I took the ladies a bit of silk I happened to have. You never heard anything like his raptures over Maurice's portrait, '*Mashallah, Mashallah, Wallahy zay el ward*' (It is the will of God, and by God he is like a rose). But I can't 'cotton to' the Turks. I always feel that they secretly dislike us European women, though they profess huge admiration and pay *personal* compliments, which an Arab very seldom attempts. I heard Seleem Effendi and Omar discussing English ladies one day lately while I was inside the curtain with Seleem's slave girl, and they did not know I heard them. Omar described Janet, and was of the opinion that a man who was married to her could want nothing more. 'By my soul, she rides like a Bedawee, she shoots with the gun and pistol, and rows the boat; she speaks many languages, works with the needle like an Efreet, and to see her hands run over the teeth of the music-box (keys of piano) amazes the mind, while her singing gladdens the soul. How then should her husband ever desire the coffee-shop? *Wallahy!* she can always amuse him at home. And as to my lady, the thing is not that she does not know. When I feel my stomach tightened, I go to the divan and say to her, "Do you want anything, a pipe, or sherbet, or so and so?" and I talk till she lays down her book and talks to me, and I question her and amuse my mind, and, by God! if I were a rich man and could marry one English Hareem like that I would stand before her and serve her like her memlook. You see I am only this lady's servant, and I have not once sat in the coffee-shop because of the sweetness of her tongue. Is it not therefore true that the man who can marry such Hareem is rich more than with money?' Seleem seemed disposed to think a little more of looks, though he quite agreed with all Omar's enthusiasm, and asked if Janet were beautiful. Omar answered with decorous vagueness that she was a 'moon,' but declined mentioning her hair, eyes, etc. (it is a liberty to describe a woman minutely). I nearly laughed out at hearing Omar relate his manœuvres to make me 'amuse his mind'; it seems I am in no danger of being discharged for being dull.

The weather has set in so hot that I have shifted my quarters out of my fine room to the south-west into one with only three sides looking over a lovely green view to the north-east, with a huge sort of solid veranda, as large as the room itself, on the open side; thus I live in the open air altogether. The bats and the swallows are quite sociable; I hope the serpents and scorpions will be more reserved. '*El Khamaseen*' (the fifty) has begun, and the wind is enough to mix up heaven and earth, but it is not distressing like the Cape south-easter, and, though hot, not choking like the Khamseen in Cairo and

Alexandria. Mohammed brought me a handful of the new wheat just now. Think of harvest in March and April! These winds are as good for the crops here as a 'nice steady rain' is in England. It is not necessary to water so much when the wind blows strong. As I rode through the green fields along the dyke, a little boy sang as he turned round on the musically-creaking Sakìah (the water-wheel turned by an ox) the one eternal Sakìah tune—the words are *ad libitum*, and my little friend chanted 'Turn oh Sakìah to the right and turn to the left—who will take care of me if my father dies? Turn oh Sakìah, etc., pour water for the figs and the grass and for the watermelons. Turn oh Sakìah!' Nothing is so pathetic as that Sakìah song.

I passed the house of the Sheykh-el-Ababdeh, who called out to me to take coffee. The moon was splendid and the scene was lovely. The handsome black-brown Sheykh in dark robes and white turban, Omar in a graceful white gown and red turban, and the wild Ababdeh in all manner of dingy white rags, and with every kind of uncouth weapon, spears, matchlocks, etc., in every kind of wild and graceful attitude, with their long black ringlets and bare heads, a few little black-brown children quite naked and shaped like Cupids. And there we sat and looked so romantic and talked quite like ladies and gentlemen about the merits of Sakna and Almás, the two great rival women-singers of Cairo. I think the Sheykh wished to display his experiences of fashionable life.

The Copts are now fasting and cross. They fast fifty-five days for Lent; no meat, fish, eggs, or milk, no exception for Sundays, no food till after twelve at noon, and no intercourse with the hareem. The only comfort is lots of arrak, and what a Copt can carry decently is an unknown quantity; one seldom sees them drunk, but they imbibe awful quantities. They offer me wine and arrak always, and can't think why I don't drink it. I believe they suspect my Christianity in consequence of my preference for Nile water. As to that, though, they scorn all heretics, *i.e.*, all Christians but themselves and the Abyssinians, more than they do the Muslims, and dislike them more; the procession of the Holy Ghost question divides us with the Gulf of Jehannum. The gardener of this house is a Copt, such a nice fellow, and he and Omar chaff one another about religion with the utmost good humour; indeed they are seldom touchy with the Moslems. There is a pretty little man called Michaïl, a Copt, vakeel to M. Mounier. I wish I could draw him to show a perfect specimen of the ancient Egyptian race; his blood must be quite unmixed. He came here yesterday to speak to Ali Bey, the Moudir of Keneh, who was visiting me (a splendid handsome Turk he is); so little Michaïl crept in to mention his business under my protection, and a few more followed, till Ali Bey got tired of holding a durbar in my divan and went away to his boat. You see the people think the *courbash* is not quite so handy with an English spectator. The other day Mustapha A'gha got Ali Bey to do a little job for him—to let the people in the Gezeereh (the island), which is Mustapha's property, work at a canal there instead of at the canal higher up for the Pasha. Very well, but down comes the Nazir (the Moudir's *sub.*), and courbashes the whole Gezeereh, not Mustapha, of course, but the poor *fellaheen* who were doing his corvée instead of the Pasha's by the Moudir's order. I went to the Gezeereh and thought that Moses was at work again and had killed a firstborn in every house by the crying and wailing, when up came two fellows and showed me their bloody feet, which their wives were crying over like for a death, *Shorghl el Mizr*—things of Egypt—like *Cosas de España*.

Wednesday.—Last night I bored Sheykh Yussuf with Antara and Abou-Zeyd, maintaining the greater valour of Antara who slew 10,000 for the love of Ibla; you know Antara. Yussuf looks down on such profanities, and replied, 'What are Antara and Abou-Zeyd compared to the combats of our Lord Moses with Og and other infidels of might, and what is the love of Antara for Ibla compared to that of our Lord Solomon for Balkees (Queen of Sheba), or their beauty and attractiveness to that of our Lord Joseph?' And then he related the combat of *Seyyidna Mousa* with Og; and I thought, 'hear O ye Puritans, and give ear O ye Methodists, and learn how religion and romance are one to those whose manners and ideas are the manners and ideas of the Bible, and how Moses was not at all a crop-eared Puritan, but a gallant warrior!' There is the

Homeric element in the religion here, the Prophet is a hero like Achilles, and like him directed by God—Allah instead of Athene. He fights, prays, teaches, makes love, and is truly a *man*, not an abstraction; and as to wonderful events, instead of telling one to 'gulp them down without looking' (as children are told with a nasty dose, and as we are told about Genesis, etc.) they believe them and delight in them, and tell them to amuse people. Such a piece of deep-disguised scepticism as *Credo quia impossibile* would find no favour here; 'What is impossible to God?' settles everything. In short, Mohammed has somehow left the stamp of romance on the religion, or else it is in the blood of the people, though the Koran is prosy and 'common-sensical' compared to the Old Testament. I used to think Arabs intensely prosaic till I could understand a little of their language, but now I can trace the genealogy of Don Quixote straight up to some Sheykh-el-Arab.

A fine, handsome woman with a lovely baby came to me the other day. I played with the baby, and gave it a cotton handkerchief for its head. The woman came again yesterday to bring me a little milk and some salad as a present, and to tell my fortune with date stones. I laughed, and so she contented herself with telling Omar about his family, which he believed implicitly. She is a clever woman evidently, and a great sibyl here. No doubt she has faith in her own predictions. She told Mme. Mounier (who is a Levantine) that she would never have a child, and was forbidden the house accordingly, and the prophecy has 'come true.' Superstition is wonderfully infectious here. The fact is that the Arabs are so intensely impressionable, and so cowardly about inspiring any ill-will, that if a man looks askance at them it is enough to make them ill, and as calamities are not infrequent, there is always some mishap ready to be laid to the charge of somebody's 'eye.' Omar would fain have had me say nothing about the theft of my purse, for fear the Karnac people should hate me and give me the eye. A part of the boasting about property, etc., is politeness, so that one may not be supposed to be envious of one's neighbours' nice things. My Sakka (water carrier) admired my bracelet yesterday, as he was watering the verandah floor, and instantly told me of all the gold necklaces and earrings he had bought for his wife and daughters, that I might not be uneasy and fear his envious eye. He is such a good fellow. For two shillings a month he brings up eight or ten huge skins of water from the river a day, and never begs or complains, always merry and civil. I shall enlarge his backsheesh. There are a lot of camels who sleep in the yard under my verandah; they are pretty and smell nice, but they growl and swear at night abominably. I wish I could draw you an Egyptian farm-yard, men, women and cattle; but what no one can draw is the amber light, so brilliant and so soft, not like the Cape diamond sunshine at all, but equally beautiful, hotter and less dazzling. There is no glare in Egypt like in the South of France, and, I suppose, in Italy.

Thursday.—I went yesterday afternoon to the island again to see the crops, and show Sally my friend farmer Omar's house and Mustapha's village. Of course we had to eat, and did not come home till the moon had long risen. Mustapha's brother Abdurachman walked about with us, such a noble-looking man, tall, spare, dignified and active, grey-bearded and hard-featured, but as lithe and bright-eyed as a boy, scorning any conveyance but his own feet, and quite dry while we 'ran down.' He was like Boaz, the wealthy gentleman peasant—nothing except the Biblical characters gave any idea of the rich *fellah*. We sat and drank new milk in a 'lodge in a garden of cucumbers' (the 'lodge' is a neat hut of palm branches), and saw the moon rise over the mountains and light up everything like a softer sun. Here you see all colours as well by moonlight as by day; hence it does not look as brilliant as the Cape moon, or even as I have seen in Paris, where it throws sharp black shadows and white light. The night here is a tender, subdued, dreamy sort of enchanted-looking day. My Turkish acquaintance from Karnac has just been here; he boasted of his house in Damascus, and invited me to go with him after the harvest here, also of his beautiful wife in Syria, and then begged me not to mention her to his wives here.

It is very hot now; what will it be in June? It is now 86° in my shady room at noon; it will be hotter at two or three. But the mornings and evenings are delicious. I am shedding my clothes by degrees; stockings are unbearable. Meanwhile my cough is almost gone, and the pain is quite gone. I feel much stronger, too; the horrible feeling of exhaustion has left me; I suppose I must have salamander blood in my body to be made lively by such heat. Sally is quite well; she does not seem at all the worse at present.

Saturday.—This will go to-morrow by some travellers, the last winter swallows. We went together yesterday to the Tombs of the Kings on the opposite bank. The mountains were red-hot, and the sun went down into Amenti all on fire. We met Mr. Dümmichen, the German, who is living in the temple of Dayr el-Bahree, translating inscriptions, and went down Belzoni's tomb. Mr. Dümmichen translated a great many things for us which were very curious, and I think I was more struck with the beauty of the drawing of the figures than last year. The face of the Goddess of the Western shore, Amenti, Athor, or Hecate, is ravishing as she welcomes the King to her regions; death was never painted so lovely. The road is a long and most wild one—truly through the valley of the shadow of death—not an insect nor a bird. Our moonlight ride home was beyond belief beautiful. The Arabs who followed us were immensely amused at hearing me interpret between German and English, and at my speaking Arabic; they asked if I was dragoman of all the languages in the world. One of them had droll theories about 'Amellica' (America), as they pronounce it always. Was the King very powerful that the country was called '*Al Melekeh*' (the Kings)? I said, 'No: all are Kings there: you would be a King like the rest.' My friend disapproved utterly: 'If all are Kings they must all be taking away every man the other's money'—a delightful idea of the kingly vocation.

When we landed on the opposite shore, I told little Achmet to go back in the ferry-boat, in which he had brought me over my donkey; a quarter of an hour after I saw him by my side. The guide asked why he had not gone as I told him. 'Who would take care of the lady?' the monkey is Rainie's size. Of course he got tired, and on the way home I told him to jump up behind me *en croupe* after the

Fellah fashion. I thought the Arabs would never have done laughing and saying *Wallah* and *Mashallah*. Sheykh Yussuf talked about the excavations, and is shocked at the way the mummies are kicked about. One boy told him they were not Muslims as an excuse, and he rebuked him severely, and told him it was *haraam* (accursed) to do so to the children of Adam. He says they have learned it very much of Mariette Bey, but I suspect it was always so with the fellaheen. To-day a tremendous wind is blowing; excellent for the corn. At Mustapha's farm they are preparing for the harvest, baking bread and selecting a young bull to be killed for the reapers. It is not hot to-day; only 84° in a cool room. The dust is horrid with this high wind; everything is gritty, and it obscures the sun. I am desired to eat a raw onion every day during the Khamseen for health and prosperity. This too must be a remnant of ancient Egypt. How I do long to see you and the children. Sometimes I feel rather down-hearted, but it is no good to say all that. And I am much better and stronger. I stood a long ride and some scrambling quite well last evening.

To Sir Alexander Duff Gordon

LUXOR,
April 6, 1864.

DEAREST ALICK,

I received yours of March 10 two days ago; also one from Hekekian Bey, much advising me to stay here the summer and get my disease 'evaporated.' Since I last wrote the great heat abated, and we now have 76° to 80°, with strong north breezes up the river—glorious weather—neither too hot nor chilly at any time. Last evening I went out to the threshing-floor to see the stately oxen treading out the corn, and supped there with Abdurachman on roasted corn, sour cream, and eggs, and saw the reapers take their wages, each a bundle of wheat according to the work he had done—the most lovely sight.

The graceful, half-naked, brown figures loaded with sheaves; some had earned so much that their mothers or wives had to help to carry it, and little fawn-like, stark-naked boys trudged off, so proud of their little bundles of wheat or of *hummuz* (a sort of vetch much eaten both green and roasted). The *sakka* (water-carrier), who has brought water for the men, gets a handful from each, and drives home his donkey with empty waterskins and a heavy load of wheat, and the barber who has shaved all these brown heads on credit this year past gets his pay, and everyone is cheerful and happy in their gentle, quiet way; here is no beer to make men sweaty and noisy and vulgar; the harvest is the most exquisite pastoral you can conceive. The men work seven hours in the day (*i.e.*, eight, with half-hours to rest and eat), and seven more during the night; they go home at sunset to dinner, and sleep a bit, and then to work again—these 'lazy Arabs'! The man who drives the oxen on the threshing-floor gets a measure and a half for his day and night's work, of threshed corn, I mean. As soon as the wheat, barley, *addas* (lentils) and *hummuz* are cut, we shall sow *dourrah* of two kinds, common maize and Egyptian, and plant sugar-cane, and later cotton. The people work very hard, but here they eat well, and being paid in corn they get the advantage of the high price of corn this year.

I told you how my purse had been stolen and the proceedings thereanent. Well, Mustapha asked me several times what I wished to be done with the thief, who spent twenty-one days here in irons. With my absurd English ideas of justice I refused to interfere at all, and Omar and I had quite a tiff because he wished me to say, 'Oh, poor man, let him go; I leave the affair to God.' I thought Omar absurd, but it was I who was wrong. The authorities concluded that it would oblige me very much if the poor devil were punished with a 'rigour beyond the law,' and had not Sheykh Yussuf come and explained the nature of the proceedings, the man would have been sent up to the mines in Fazogloo *for life*, out of civility to me, by the Moudir of Keneh, Ali Bey. There was no alternative between my 'forgiving him for the love of God' or sending him to a certain death by a climate insupportable to these people. Mustapha and Co. tried hard to prevent Sheykh Yussuf from speaking to me, for fear I should be angry and complain at Cairo, if my vengeance were not wreaked on the thief, but he said he knew me better, and brought the *procès verbal* to show me. Fancy my dismay! I went to Seleem Effendi and to the Kádee with Sheykh Yussuf, and begged the man might be let go, and not sent to Keneh at all. Having settled this, I said that I had thought it right that the people of Karnac should pay the money I had lost, as a fine for their bad conduct to strangers, but that I did not require it for the sake of the money, which I would accordingly give to the poor of Luxor in the mosque and in the church (great applause from the crowd). I asked how many were Muslimeen and how many Nazranee, in order to divide the three napoleons and a half, according to the numbers. Sheykh Yussuf awarded one napoleon to the church, two to the mosque, and the half to the water-drinking place—the *Sebeel*—which was also applauded. I then said, 'Shall we send the money to the bishop?' but a respectable elderly Copt said, '*Maleysh!* (never mind) better give it all to Sheykh Yussuf; he will send the bread to the church.' Then the Cadi made me a fine speech, and said I had behaved like a great *Emeereh*, and one that feared God; and Sheykh Yussuf said he knew the English had mercy in their stomachs, and that I especially had Mussulman feelings (as we say, Christian charity). Did you ever hear of such a state of administration of justice. Of course, sympathy here, as in Ireland, is mostly with the 'poor man' in prison—'in trouble,' as we say. I find that accordingly a vast number of disputes are settled by private arbitration, and Yussuf is constantly sent for to decide between contending parties, who abide by his decision rather than go to law; or else five or six respectable men are called upon to form a sort of amateur jury, and to settle the matter. In criminal cases, if the prosecutor is powerful, he has it all his own way; if the prisoner can bribe high, he is apt to get off. All the appealing to my compassion was quite *en règle*. Another trait of Egypt.

The other day we found all our water-jars empty and our house unsprinkled. On enquiry it turned out that the *sakkas* had all run away, carrying with them their families and goods, and were gone no one knew whither, in consequence of some 'persons having authority,' one, a Turkish *cawass* (policeman), having forced them to fetch water for building purposes at so low a price that they could not bear it. My poor *sakka* is gone without a whole month's pay—two shillings!—the highest pay by far given in Luxor. I am interested in another story. I hear that a plucky woman here has been to Keneh, and threatened the Moudir that she will go to Cairo and complain to Effendina himself of the unfair drafting for soldiers—her only son taken, while others have bribed off. She'll walk in this heat all the way, unless she succeeds in frightening the Moudir, which, as she is of the more spirited sex in this country, she may possibly do. You see these Saeedes are a bit less patient than Lower Egyptians. The *sakkas* can strike, and a woman can face a Moudir.

You would be amused at the bazaar here. There is a barber, and on Tuesdays some beads, calico, and tobacco are sold. The only artisan is—a jeweller! We spin and weave our own brown woollen garments, and have no other wants, but gold necklaces and nose and earrings are indispensable. It is the safest way of hoarding, and happily combines saving with ostentation. Can you imagine a house without beds, chairs, tables, cups, glasses, knives—in short, with nothing but an oven, a few pipkins and water-jars, and a couple of wooden spoons, and some mats to sleep on? And yet people are happy and quite civilised who live so. An Arab cook, with his fingers and one cooking-pot, will serve you an excellent dinner quite miraculously. The simplification of life possible in such a climate is not conceivable unless one has seen it. The Turkish ladies whom I visit at Karnac have very little more. They are very fond of me, and always want me to stay and sleep, but how could I sleep in my clothes on a mat-divan, poor spoiled European that I am? But they pity and wonder far more at the absence of my 'master.' I made a bad slip of the tongue and said 'my husband' before Abdul Rafiah, the master of the house. The ladies laughed and blushed tremendously, and I felt very awkward, but they turned the tables on me in a few minutes by some questions they asked quite coolly.

I hardly know what I shall have to do. If the heat does not turn out overpowering, I shall stay here; if I cannot bear it, I must go down the river. I asked Omar if he could bear a summer here, so dull for a young man fond of a little coffee-shop and gossip, for that, if he could not, he might go down for a time and join me again, as I could manage with some man here. He absolutely cried, kissed my hands, and declared he was never so happy as with me, and he could not rest if he thought I had not all I wanted. 'I am your *memlook*, not your servant—your *memlook*.' I really believe that these people sometimes love their English masters better than their own people. Omar certainly has shown the greatest fondness for me on all occasions.

To Mrs. Ross

LUXOR,
April 7, 1864.

DEAREST JANET,

I have continued very fairly well. We had great heat ten days ago; now it is quite cool. Harvesting is going on, and never did I see in any dream so lovely a sight as the whole process. An acquaintance of mine, one Abdurachman, is Boaz, and as I sat with him on the threshing-floor and ate roasted corn, I felt quite puzzled as to whether I were really alive or only existing in imagination in the Book of Ruth. It is such a *kief* that one enjoys under the palm-trees, with such a scene. The harvest is magnificent here; I never saw such crops. There is no cattle disease, but a good deal of sickness among the people; I have to practise very extensively, and often feel very anxious, as I cannot refuse to go to the poor souls and give them medicine, with sore misgivings all the while. Fancy that Hekekian Bey can't get me an Arabic dictionary in Cairo. I must send to London, I suppose, which seems hardly worth while. I wish you could see my teacher, Sheykh Yussuf. I never before saw a pious person amiable and good like him. He is intensely devout, and not at all bigoted—a difficult combination; and, moreover, he is lovely to behold, and has the prettiest and merriest laugh possible. It is quite curious to see the mixture of a sort of learning with utter ignorance and great superstition, and such perfect high-breeding and beauty of character. It is exactly like associating with St. John.

I want dreadfully to be able to draw, or to photograph. The group at the Sheykh-el-Ababdeh's last night was ravishing, all but my ugly hat and self. The black ringlets and dirty white drapery and obsolete weapons—the graceful splendid Sheykh 'black but beautiful' like the Shulamite—I thought of Antar and Abou Zeyd.

Give my salaam to Mme. Tastu and ask her whether I may stay on here, or if I go down stream during the heat whether I may return next winter, in which case I might leave some of my goods. Hekekian strongly advises me to remain here, and thinks the heat will be good. I will try; 88° seemed to agree with me wonderfully, my cough is much better.

To Sir Alexander Duff Gordon

LUXOR,
April 14, 1864.

DEAREST ALICK,

I have but this moment received your letter of the 18th March, which went after Janet, who was hunting at Tel-el-Kebir. We have had a tremendous Khamseen wind, and now a strong north wind quite fresh and cool. The thermometer was 92° during the Khamseen, but it did me no harm. Luckily I am very well for I am worked hard, as a strange epidemic has broken out, and I am the *Hakeemeh* (doctress) of Luxor. The *Hakeem* Pasha from Cairo came up and frightened the people, telling them it was catching, and Yussuf forgot his religion so far as to beg me not to be all day in the people's huts; but

Omar and I despised the danger, I feeling sure it was not infectious, and Omar saying *Min Allah*. The people get stoppage of the bowels and die in eight days unless they are physicked; all who have sent for me in time have recovered. *Alhamdulillah*, that I can help the poor souls. It is harvest, and the hard work, and the spell of intense heat, and the green corn, beans, etc., which they eat, brings on the sickness. Then the Copts are fasting from all animal food, and full of green beans and salad, and green corn. Mustapha tried to persuade me not to give physick, for fear those who died should pass for being poisoned, but both Omar and I are sure it is only to excuse his own selfishness. Omar is an excellent assistant. The bishop tried to make money by hinting that if I forbade my patients to fast, I might pay for their indulgence. One poor, peevish little man refused the chicken-broth, and told me that we Europeans had *our* heaven in *this* world; Omar let out *kelb* (dog), but I stopped him, and said, 'Oh, my brother, God has made the Christians of England unlike those of Egypt, and surely will condemn neither of us on that account; mayest thou find a better heaven hereafter than I now enjoy here.' Omar threw his arms round me and said, 'Oh, thou good one, surely our Lord will reward thee for acting thus with the meekness of a Muslimeh, and kissing the hand of him who strikes thy face.' (See how each religion claims humility.) Suleyman was not pleased at his fellow-christian's display of charity. It does seem strange that the Copts of the lower class will not give us the blessing, or thank God for our health like the Muslimeen. Most of my patients are Christians, and some are very nice people indeed. The people here have named me Sittee (Lady) *Noor-ala-Noor*. A poor woman whose only child, a young man, I was happy enough to cure when dreadfully ill, kissed my feet and asked by what name to pray for me. I told her my name meant *Noor* (light—*lux*), but as that was one of the names of God I could not use it. 'Thy name is *Noor-ala-Noor*,' said a man who was in the room. That means something like 'God is upon thy mind,' or 'light from the light,' and *Noor-ala-Noor* it remains; a combination of one of the names of God is quite proper, like Abdallah, Abdurachman, etc. I begged some medicines from a Countess Braniscki, who went down the other day; when all is gone I don't know what I shall do. I am going to try to make castor oil; I don't know how, but I shall try, and Omar fancies he can manage it. The cattle disease has also broken out desperately up in Esneh, and we see the dead beasts float down all day. Of course we shall soon have it here.

Sunday, April 17.—The epidemic seems to be over, but there is still a great deal of gastric fever, etc., about. The *hakeem* from Keneh has just been here—such a pleasing, clever young man, speaking Italian perfectly, and French extremely well. He is the son of some fellah of Lower Egypt, sent to study at Pisa, and has not lost the Arab gentility and elegance by a *Frenghi* education. We fraternised greatly, and the young *hakeem* was delighted at my love for his people, and my high opinion of their intelligence. He is now gone to inspect the sick, and is to see me again and give me directions. He was very unhappy that he could not supply me with medicines; none are to be bought above Cairo, except from the hospital doctors, who sell the medicines of the Government, as the Italian at Siout did. But Ali Effendi is too honest for that. The old bishop paid me a visit of three and a half hours yesterday, and *pour me tirer une carotte* he sent me a loaf of sugar, so I must send a present 'for the church' to be consumed in raki. The old party was not very sober, and asked for wine. I coolly told him it was *haraam* (forbidden) to us to drink during the day—only with our dinner. I never will give the Christians drink here, and now they have left off pressing me to drink spirits at their houses. The bishop offered to alter the hour of prayer for me, and to let me into the *Heykel* (where women must not go) on Good Friday, which will be eighteen days hence. All of which I refused, and said I would go on the roof of the church and look down through the window with the other *Hareemat*. Omar kissed the bishop's hand, and I said: 'What! do *you* kiss his hand like a Copt?' 'Oh yes, he is an old man, and a servant of my God, but dreadful dirty,' added Omar; and it was too true. His presence diffused a fearful monastic odour of sanctity. A Bishop must be a monk, as priests are married.

Monday.—To-day Ali Effendi-*el-Hakeem* came to tell me how he had been to try to see my patients and failed; all the families declared they were well and would not let him in. Such is the deep distrust of everything to do with the Government. They all waited till he was gone away, and then came again to me with their ailments. I scolded, and they all said, '*Wallah, ya Sitt, ya Emeereh*; that is the *Hakeem* Pasha, and he would send us off to hospital at Keneh, and then they would poison us; by thy eyes do not be angry with us, or leave off from having compassion on us on this account.' I said, 'Ali Effendi is an Arab and a Muslim and an *Emeer* (gentleman), and he gave me good advice, and would have given more,' etc. No use at all. He is the Government doctor, and they had rather die, and will swallow anything from *el-Sittee Noor-ala-Noor*. Here is a pretty state of things.

I gave Sheykh Yussuf £4 for three months' daily lessons last night, and had quite a contest to force it upon him. 'It is not for money, oh Lady;' and he coloured crimson. He had been about with Ali Effendi, but could not get the people to see him. The Copts, I find, *have* a religious prejudice against him, and, indeed, against all heretics. They consider themselves and the Abyssinians as the only true believers. If they acknowledge *us* as brethren, it is for money. I speak only of the low class, and of the priests; of course the educated merchants are very different. I had two priests and two deacons, and the mother of one, here to-day for physic for the woman. She was very pretty and pleasing; miserably reduced and weak from the long fast. I told her she must eat meat and drink a little wine, and take cold baths, and gave her quinine. She will take the wine and the quinine, but neither eat nor wash. The Bishop tells them they will die if they break the fast, and half the Christians are ill from it. One of the priests spoke a little English; he fabricates false antiques very cleverly, and is tolerably sharp; but, Oh *mon Dieu*, it is enough to make one turn Muslim to compare these greasy rogues with such high-minded charitable *shurafa* (noblemen) as Abd-el-Waris and Sheykh Yussuf. A sweet little Copt boy who is very ill will be killed by the stupid bigotry about the fast. My friend Suleyman is much put out, and backs my exhortations to the sick to break it. He is a capital fellow, and very intelligent, and he and Omar are like brothers; it is the priests who do all they can to keep alive religious prejudice. *Alhamdulillah*, they are only partially successful. Mohammed has just heard that seventy-five head of cattle are dead at El-Moutaneh. Here only a few have died as yet, and Ali Effendi thinks the disease less virulent than in Lower Egypt. I hope he is right; but dead beasts float down the river all day long.

To turn to something more amusing—but please don't tell it—such a joke against my gray hairs. I have had a proposal, or at least an attempt at one. A very handsome Sheykh-el-Arab (*Bedawee*) was here for a bit, and asked Omar whether I were a widow or divorced, as in either case he would send a *dellaleh* (marriage brokeress) to me. Omar told him that would never do. I had a husband in England; besides, I was not young, had a married daughter, my hair was gray, etc. The Sheykh swore he didn't care; I could dye my hair and get a divorce; that I was not like stupid modern women, but like an ancient Arab *Emeereh*, and worthy of Antar or Abou Zeyd—a woman for whom men killed each other or themselves—and he would pay all he could afford as my dowry. Omar came in in fits of laughter at the idea, and the difficulty he had had in stopping the *dellaleh's* visit. He told the Sheykh I should certainly beat her I should be so offended. The disregard of differences of age here on marriage is very strange. My adorer was not more than thirty, I am sure. Don't tell people, my dear Alick; it is so very absurd; I should be 'ashamed before the people.'

Saturday, April 23.—Alhamdulillah! the sickness is going off. I have just heard Suleyman's report as follows: Hassan Abou-Achmet kisses the Emeereh's feet, and the bullets have cleaned his stomach six times, and he has said the *Fathah* for the Lady. The two little girls who had diarrhœa are well. The Christian dyer has vomited his powder and wants another. The mother of the Christian cook who married the priest's sister has got dysentery. The hareem of Mustapha Abou-Abeyd has two children with bad eyes. The Bishop had a quarrel, and scolded and fell down, and cannot speak or move;

I must go to him. The young-deacon's jaundice is better. The slave girl of Kursheed A'gha is sick, and Kursheed is sitting at her head in tears; the women say I must go to her, too. Kursheed is a fine young Turk, and very good to his *Hareemat*. That is all; Suleyman has nothing on earth to do, and brings me a daily report; he likes the gossip and the importance.

The reis of a cargo-boat brought me up your Lafontaine, and some papers and books from Hekekian Bey. Sheykh Yussuf is going down to Cairo, to try to get back some of the lands which Mahommed Ali took away from the mosques and the Ulema without compensation. He asked me whether Ross would speak for him to Effendina! What are the Muslimeen coming to? As soon as I can read enough he offers to read in the Koran with me—a most unusual proceeding, as the 'noble Koran' is not generally put into the hands of heretics; but my 'charity to the people in sickness' is looked upon by Abd-el-Waris the Imam, and by Yussuf, as a proof that I have 'received direction,' and am of those Christians of whom *Seyyidna* Mohammed (upon whose name be peace) has said 'that they have no pride, that they rival each other in good works, and that God will increase their reward.' There is no *arrière pensée* of conversion that they think hopeless, but charity covers all sins with Muslimeen. Next Friday is the *Djuma el-Kebeer* (Good Friday) with the Copts, and the prayers are in the daytime, so I shall go to the church. Next moon is the great Bairam, *el-Eed el-Kebeer* (the great festival), with the Muslimeen—the commemoration of the sacrifice of Isaac or Ishmael (commentators are uncertain which)—and Omar will kill a sheep for the poor for the benefit of his baby, according to custom. I have at length compassed the destruction of mine enemy, though he has not written a book. A fanatical Christian dog (quadruped), belonging to the Coptic family who live on the opposite side of the yard, hated me with such virulent intensity that, not content with barking at me all day, he howled at me all night, even after I had put out the lantern and he could not see me in bed. Sentence of death has been recorded against him, as he could not be beaten into toleration. Michaïl, his master's son, has just come down from El-Moutaneh, where he is *vakeel* to M. Mounier. He gives a fearful account of the sickness there among men and cattle—eight and ten deaths a day; here we have had only four a day, at the worst, in a population of (I guess) some 2,000. The Mouniers have put themselves in quarantine, and allow no one to approach their house, as Mustapha wanted me to do. One hundred and fifty head of cattle have died at El-Moutaneh; here only a few calves are dead, but as yet no full-grown beasts, and the people are healthy again. I really think I did some service by not showing any fear, and Omar behaved manfully. By-the-by, will you find out whether a *passaporto*, as they call it, a paper granting British protection, can be granted in England. It is the object of Omar's highest ambition to belong as much as possible to the English, and feel safe from being forced to serve a Turk. If it can be done by any coaxing and jobbing, pray do it, for Omar deserves any service I can render him in return for all his devotion and fidelity. Someone tried to put it into his head that it was *haraam* to be too fond of us heretics and be faithful, but he consulted Sheykh Yussuf, who promised him a reward hereafter for good conduct to me, and who told me of it as a good joke, adding that he was *raghil ameen*, the highest praise for fidelity, the sobriquet of the Prophet. Do not be surprised at my lack of conscience in desiring to benefit my own follower *in qualunque modo*; justice is not of Eastern growth, and *Europeo* is 'your only wear,' and here it is only base not to stick by one's friends. Omar kisses the hands of the *Sidi-el-Kebeer* (the great master), and desires his best salaam to the little master and the little lady, whose servant he is. He asks if I, too, do not kiss Iskender Bey's hand in my letter, as I ought to do as his Hareem, or whether 'I make myself big before my master,' like some French ladies he has seen? I tell him I will do so if Iskender Bey will get him his *warak* (paper), whereupon he picks up the hem of my gown and kisses that, and I civilly expostulate on such condescension to a woman. Yussuf is quite puzzled about European women, and a little shocked at the want of respect to their husbands they display. I told him that the outward respect shown to us by our men was *our veil*, and explained how superficial the difference was. He fancied that the law gave us the upper hand. Omar reports yesterday's sermon 'on toleration,' it appears. Yussuf took the text of 'Thou shalt love thy brother as thyself, and never act towards him but as thou wouldest he should act towards thee.' I forget chapter and verse; but it seems he took the bull by the horns and declared *all men* to be brothers, not Muslimeen only, and desired his congregation to look at the good deeds of others and not at their erroneous faith, for God is all-knowing (*i.e.*, He only knows the heart), and if they saw aught amiss to remember that the best man need say *Astafer Allah* (I beg pardon of God) seven times a day.

I wish the English could know how unpleasant and mischievous their manner of talking to their servants about religion is. Omar confided to me how bad it felt to be questioned, and then to see the Englishman laugh or put up his lip and say nothing. 'I don't want to talk about his religion at all, but if he talks about mine he ought to speak of his own, too. You, my Lady, say, when I tell you things, that is the same with us, or that is different, or good, or not good in your mind, and that is the proper way, not to look like thinking "all nonsense."'

ESNEH,
Saturday, April 30.

On Thursday evening as I was dreamily sitting on my divan, who should walk in but Arthur Taylor, on his way, all alone in a big dahabieh, to Edfou. So I offered to go too, whereupon he said he would go on to Assouan and see Philæ as he had company, and we went off to Mustapha to make a bargain with his Reis for it; thus then here we are at Esneh. I embarked on Wednesday evening, and we have been two days *en route*. Yesterday we had the thermometer at 110; I was the only person awake all day in the boat. Omar, after cooking, lay panting at my feet on the deck. Arthur went fairly to bed in the cabin; ditto Sally. All the crew slept on the deck. Omar cooked amphibiously, bathing between every meal. The silence of noon with the *white heat* glowing on the river which flowed like liquid tin, and the silent Nubian rough boats floating down without a ripple, was magnificent and really awful. Not a breath of wind as we lay under the lofty bank. The Nile is not quite so low, and I see a very different scene from last year. People think us crazy to go up to Assouan in May, but I do enjoy it, and I really wanted to forget all the sickness and sorrow in which I have taken part. When I went to Mustapha's he said Sheykh Yussuf was ill, and I said 'Then I won't go.' But Yussuf came in with a sick headache only. Mustapha repeated my words to him, and never did I see such a lovely expression in a human face as that with which Yussuf said *Eh, ya Sitt!* Mustapha laughed, and told him to thank me, and Yussuf turned to me and said, in a low voice, 'my sister does not need thanks, save from God.' Fancy a Shereef, one of the Ulema, calling a *Frengeeyeh* 'sister'! His pretty little girl came in and played with me, and he offered her to me for Maurice. I cured Kursheed's Abyssinian slave-girl. You would have laughed to see him obeying my directions, and wiping his eyes on his gold-embroidered sleeve. And then the Coptic priest came for me for his wife who was ill. He was in a great quandary, because, if she died, he, as a priest, could never marry again, as he loudly lamented before her; but he was truly grieved, and I was very happy to leave her convalescent.

Verily we are sorely visited. The dead cattle float down by thousands. M. Mounier buried a thousand at El-Moutaneh alone, and lost forty men. I would not have left Luxor, but there were no new cases for four days before, and the worst had been over for full ten days. Two or three poor people brought me new bread and vegetables to the boat when they saw me going, and Yussuf came down and sat with us all the evening, and looked quite sad. Omar asked him why, and he said it made him think how it would seem when '*Inshallah* should be well and should leave my place empty at Luxor and go back with the blessing of God to my own place and to my own people.' Whereupon Omar grew quite sentimental too, and nearly cried. I don't know how Arthur would have managed without us, for he had come with two Frenchmen who had proper servants and who left the boat at Girgeh, and he has a wretched little dirty idiotic Coptic tailor as a servant, who can't even sew on a button. It is becoming quite a calamity about servants here. Arthur tells me that men, not fit to light Omar's pipe, asked him £10 a month in Cairo and would not take less, and he gives his Copt £4. I really feel as if I were cheating Omar to let him stay on for £3; but if I say anything he kisses my hand and tells me 'not to be cross.'

I have letters from Yussuf to people at Assouan. If I want anything I am to call on the Kadee. We have a very excellent boat and a good crew, and are very comfortable. When the Luxor folk heard the 'son of my uncle' was come, they thought it must be my husband. I was diverted at Omar's propriety. He pointed out to Mustapha and Yussuf how *he* was to sleep in the cabin between Arthur's and mine, which was considered quite satisfactory apparently, and it was looked upon as very proper of Omar to have arranged it so, as he had been sent to put the boat in order. Arthur has been all along the Suez Canal, and seen a great many curious things. The Delta must be very unlike Upper Egypt from all he tells me. The little troop of pilgrims for Mecca left Luxor about ten days ago. It was a pretty and touching sight. Three camels, five donkeys, and about thirty men and women, several with babies on their shoulders, all uttering the *zaghareet* (cry of joy). They were to walk to Koseir (eight days' journey with good camels), babies and all. It is the happiest day of their lives, they say, when they have scraped together money enough to make the *hajj*.

This minute a poor man is weeping beside our boat over a pretty heifer decked with many *hegabs* (amulets), which have not availed against the sickness. It is heart-rending to see the poor beasts and their unfortunate owners. Some dancing girls came to the boat just now for cigars which Arthur had promised them, and to ask after their friend el Maghribeeyeh, the good dancer at Luxor, whom they said was very ill. Omar did not know at all about her, and the girls seemed much distressed. They were both very pretty, one an Abyssinian. I must leave off to send this to the post; it will cost a fortune, but you won't grudge it.

To Sir Alexander Duff Gordon

LUXOR,
May 15, 1864,
Day before Eed-el-Kebir
(*Bairam*).

DEAREST ALICK,

We returned to Luxor the evening before last just after dark. The salute which Omar fired with your old horse-pistols brought down a lot of people, and there was a chorus of *Alhamdulilah Salaameh ya Sitt*, and such a kissing of hands, and 'Welcome home to your place' and 'We have tasted your absence and found it bitter,' etc., etc. Mustapha came with letters for me, and Yussuf beaming with smiles, and Mahommed with new bread made of new wheat, and Suleyman with flowers, and little Achmet rushing in wildly to kiss hands. When the welcome had subsided, Yussuf, who stayed to tea, told me all the cattle were dead. Mustapha lost thirty-four, and has three left; and poor farmer Omar lost all—forty head. The distress in Upper Egypt will now be fearful. Within six weeks *all* our cattle are dead. They are threshing the corn with donkeys, and men are turning the sakiahs (water-wheels) and drawing the ploughs, and dying by scores of overwork and want of food in many places. The whole agriculture depended on the oxen, and they are all dead. At El-Moutaneh and the nine villages round Halim Pasha's estate 24,000 head have died; four beasts were left when we were there three days ago.

We spent two days and nights at Philæ and *Wallahy!* it was hot. The basalt rocks which enclose the river all round the island were burning. Sally and I slept in the Osiris chamber, on the roof of the temple, on our air-beds. Omar lay across the doorway to guard us, and Arthur and his Copt, with the well-bred sailor Ramadan, were sent to bivouac on the Pylon. Ramadan took the hareem under his special and most respectful charge, and waited on us devotedly, but never raised his eyes to our faces, or spoke till spoken to. Philæ is six or seven miles from Assouan, and we went on donkeys through the beautiful Shellaleeh (the village of the cataract), and the noble place of tombs of Assouan. Great was the amazement of everyone at seeing Europeans so out of season; we were like swallows in January to them. I could not sleep for the heat in the room, and threw on an *abbayeh* (cloak) and went and lay on the parapet of the temple. What a night! What a lovely view! The stars gave as much light as the moon in Europe, and all but the cataract was still as death and glowing hot, and the palm-trees were more graceful and dreamy than ever. Then Omar woke, and came and sat at my feet, and rubbed them, and sang a song of a Turkish slave. I said, 'Do not rub my feet, oh brother—that is not fit for thee' (because it is below the dignity of a free Muslim altogether to touch shoes or feet), but he sang in his song, 'The slave of the Turk may be set free by money, but how shall one be ransomed who has been paid for by kind actions and sweet words?' Then the day broke deep crimson, and I went down and bathed in the Nile, and saw the girls on the island opposite in their summer fashions, consisting of a leathern fringe round their slender hips—divinely graceful—bearing huge saucer-shaped baskets of corn on their stately young heads; and I went up and sat at the end of the colonnade looking up into Ethiopia, and dreamed dreams of 'Him who sleeps in Philæ,' until the great Amun Ra kissed my northern face too hotly, and drove me into the temple to breakfast, and coffee, and pipes, and *kief*. And in the evening three little naked Nubians rowed us about for two or three hours on the glorious river in a boat made of thousands of bits of wood, each a foot long; and between whiles they jumped overboard and disappeared, and came up on the other side of the boat. Assouan was full of Turkish soldiers, who came and took away our donkeys, and stared at our faces most irreligiously. I did not go on shore at Kom Ombos or El Kab, only at Edfou, where we spent the day in the temple; and at Esneh, where we tried to buy sugar, tobacco, etc., and found nothing at all, though Esneh is a *chef-lieu*, with a Moudir. It is only in winter that anything is to be got for the travellers. We had to ask the Nazir in Edfou to *order* a man to sell us charcoal. People do without sugar, and smoke green tobacco, and eat beans, etc., etc. Soon we must do likewise, for our stores are nearly exhausted.

We stopped at El-Moutaneh, and had a good dinner in the Mouniers' handsome house, and they gave me a loaf of sugar. Mme. Mounier described Rachel's stay with them for three months at Luxor, in my house, where they then lived. She hated it so, that on embarking to leave she turned back and spat on the ground, and cursed the place inhabited by savages, where she had been *ennuyée a mort*. Mme. Mounier fully sympathised with her, and thought no *femme aimable* could live with Arabs, who are not at all *galants*. She is Levantine, and, I believe, half Arab herself, but hates the life here, and hates the Muslims. As I write this I laugh to think of *galanterie* and *Arab* in one sentence, and glance at 'my brother' Yussuf, who is sleeping on a mat, quite overcome with the Simoom* (which is blowing) and the fast which he is keeping to-day, as the eve of the *Eed-el-Kebir* (great festival). This is the coolest place in the village. The glass is only 95½° now (eleven a.m.) in the darkened divan. The Kádee, and the Maōhn, and Yussuf came together to visit me, and when the others left he lay down to sleep. Omar is sleeping in the passage, and Sally in her room. I alone don't sleep—but the Simoom is terrible. Arthur runs about all day, sight-seeing and drawing, and does not suffer at all from the heat. I can't walk now, as the sand blisters my feet.

Tuesday, May 17.—Yesterday the Simoom was awful, and last night I slept on the terrace, and was very hot. To-day the north wind sprang up at noon and revived us, though it is still 102° in my divan. My old 'great-grandfather' has come in for a pipe and coffee; he was Belzoni's guide, and his eldest child was born seven days before the French under Bonaparte marched into Luxor. He is superbly handsome and erect, and very talkative, but only remembers old times, and takes me for Mme. Belzoni. He is grandfather to Mahommed, the guard of this house, and great-grandfather to my little Achmet. His grandsons have married him to a tidy old woman to take care of him; he calls me 'My lady grand-daughter,' and Omar he calls 'Mustapha,' and we salute him as 'grandfather.' I wish I could paint him; he is so grand to look at. Old Mustapha had a son born yesterday—his tenth child. I must go and wish him joy, after which I will go to Arthur's boat and have a bathe; the sailors rig me out a capital awning. We had a good boat, and a capital crew; one man Mahommed, called Alatee (the singer), sang beautifully, to my great delight, and all were excellent fellows, quiet and obliging; only his servant was a lazy beast, dirty and conceited—a Copt, spoiled by an Italian education and Greek associates, thinking himself very grand because he was a Christian. I wondered at the patience and good-nature with which Omar did all his work and endured all his insolence. There was one stupendous row at Assouan, however. The men had rigged out a sort of tent for me to bathe in over the side of the boat, and Ramadan caught the Copt trying to peep in, and half strangled him. Omar called him 'dog,' and asked him if he was an infidel, and Macarius told him I was a Christian woman, and not *his Hareem*. Omar lost his temper, and appealed to the old reis and all the sailors, 'O Muslims, ought not I to cut his throat if he had defiled the noble person of the lady with his pig's eyes? God forgive me for mentioning her in such a manner.' Then they all cursed him for a pig and an infidel, and threatened to put him ashore and leave him for his vile conduct towards noble *Hareem*. Omar sobbed with passion, saying that I was to him like the 'back of his mother,' and how 'dare Macarius take my name in his dirty mouth,' etc. The Copt tried to complain of being beaten afterwards, but I signified to him that he had better hold his tongue, for that I understood Arabic, upon which he sneaked off.

To Mrs. Austin

LUXOR,
Monday, *May* 23, 1864.

DEAREST MUTTER,

I meant to have written to you by Arthur Taylor, who left for Cairo yesterday morning, but the Simoom made me so stupid that I could hardly finish a letter to Alick. So I begin one to-day to recount the wonders of the season here. I went over to Mustapha's island to spend the day in the tent, or rather the hut, of dourrah-stalks and palm-branches, which he has erected there for the threshing and winnowing. He had invited me and 'his worship' the Maōhn to a picnic. Only imagine that it *rained*! all day, a gentle slight rain, but enough to wet all the desert. I laughed and said I had brought English weather, but the Maōhn shook his head and opined that we were suffering the anger of God. Rain in summer-time was quite a terror. However, we consoled ourselves, and Mustapha called a nice little boy to recite the 'noble Koran' for our amusement, and out of compliment to me he selected the chapter of the family of Amran (the history of Jesus), and recited it with marvellous readiness and accuracy. A very pleasant-mannered man of the Shourafa of Gurneh came and joined us, and was delighted because I sent away a pipe which Abdurachman brought me (it is highly improper to smoke while the Koran is being read or recited). He thanked me for the respect, and I told him I knew he would not smoke in a church, or while I prayed; why should I? It rather annoys me to find that they always expect from us irreverence to their religion which they would on no account be guilty of to ours. The little boy was a *fellah*, the child of my friend Omar, who has lost all his cattle, but who came as pleasant and smiling as ever to kiss my hand and wait upon me. After that the Maōhn read the second chapter, 'the Cow,' in a rather nasal, quavering chant. I perceived that no one present understood any of it, except just a few words here and there—not much more than I could follow myself from having read the translation. I think it is not any nearer spoken Arabic than Latin is to Italian. After this, Mustapha, the Maōhn, Omar, Sally and I, sat down round the dinner-tray, and had a very good dinner of lamb, fowls and vegetables, such as bahmias and melucheeah, both of the mallow order, and both excellent cooked with meat; rice, stewed apricots (mish-mish), with nuts and raisins in it, and cucumbers and water-melons strewed the ground. One eats all *durcheinander* with bread and fingers, and a spoon for the rice, and green limes to squeeze over one's own bits for sauce. We were very merry, if not very witty, and the Maōhn declared, '*Wallahi!* the English are fortunate in their customs, and in the enjoyment of the society of learned and excellent *Hareemat*;' and Omar, lying on the rushes, said: 'This is the happiness of the Arab. Green trees, sweet water, and a kind face, make the "garden"' (paradise), an Arab saying. The Maōhn joked him as to how a 'child of Cairo' could endure *fellah* life. I was looking at the heaps of wheat and thinking of Ruth, when I started to hear the soft Egyptian lips utter the very words which the Egyptian girl spake more than a thousand years ago: 'Behold my mother! where she stays I stay, and where she goes I will go; her family is my family, and if it pleaseth God, nothing but the Separator of friends (death) shall divide me from her.' I really could not speak, so I kissed the top of Omar's turban, Arab fashion, and the Maōhn blessed him quite solemnly, and said: 'God reward thee, my son; thou hast honoured thy lady greatly before thy people, and she has honoured thee, and ye are an example of masters and servants, and of kindness and fidelity;' and the brown labourers who were lounging about said: 'Verily, it is true, and God be praised for people of excellent conduct.' I never expected to feel like Naomi, and possibly many English people might only think Omar's unconscious repetition of Ruth's words rather absurd, but to me they sounded in perfect harmony with the life and ways of this country and these people, who are so full of tender and affectionate feelings, when they have not been crushed out of them. It is not humbug; I have seen their actions. Because they use grand compliments, Europeans think they are never sincere, but the compliments are not meant to deceive, they only profess to be forms. Why do the English talk of the beautiful sentiment of the Bible and pretend to feel it so much, and when they come and see the same life before them they ridicule it.

Tuesday.—We have a family quarrel going on. Mohammed's wife, a girl of eighteen or so, wanted to go home on Bairam day for her mother to wash her head and unplait her hair. Mohammed told her not to leave him on that day, and to send for a woman to do it for her; whereupon she cut off her hair, and Mohammed, in a passion, told her to 'cover her face' (that is equivalent to a divorce) and take her baby and go home to her father's house. Ever since he has been mooning about the yard and in and out of the kitchen very glum and silent. This morning I went into the kitchen and found Omar cooking with a little baby in his arms, and giving it sugar. 'Why what is that?' say I. 'Oh don't say anything. I sent Achmet to fetch Mohammed's baby, and when he comes here he will see it, and then in talking I can say so and so, and how the man must be good to the *Hareem*, and what this poor, small girl do when she big enough to ask for her father.' In short, Omar wants to exercise his diplomacy in making up the quarrel. After writing this I heard Mohammed's low, quiet voice, and Omar's boyish laugh, and then silence, and went to see the baby and its father. My kitchen was a pretty scene. Mohammed, in his ample brown robes and white turban, lay asleep on the floor with the baby's tiny pale face and little eyelids stained with kohl against his coffee-brown cheek, both fast asleep, baby in her father's arms. Omar leant against the *fournaise* in his house-dress, a white shirt open at the throat and white drawers reaching to the knees, with the red tarboosh and red and yellow *kufyeh* (silk handkerchief) round it turban-wise, contemplating them with his great, soft eyes. The two young men made an excellent contrast between Upper and Lower Egypt. Mohammed is the true Arab type—coffee-brown, thin, spare, sharp-featured, elegant hands and feet, bright glittering small eyes and angular jaw—not a handsome Arab, but *bien charactérisé*. Omar, the colour of new boxwood or old ivory, pale, with eyes like a cow, full lips, full chin and short nose, not the least negro, but perfectly Egyptian, the eyes wide apart—unlike the Arab—moustache like a woman's eyebrow, curly brown hair, bad hands and feet and not well made, but graceful in movement and still more in countenance, very inferior in beauty to the pure Arab blood which prevails here, but most sweet in expression. He is a true *Akh-ul-Benât* (brother of girls), and truly chivalrous to *Hareem*. How astonished Europeans would be to hear Omar's real opinion of their conduct to women. He mentioned some Englishman who had divorced his wife and made her frailty public. You should have seen him spit on the floor in abhorrence. Here it is quite blackguard not to forfeit the money and take all the blame in a divorce.

Friday.—We have had better weather again, easterly wind and pretty cool, and I am losing the cough and languor which the damp of the Simoom brought me. Sheykh Yussuf has just come back from Keneh, whither he and the Kadee went on their donkeys for some law business. He took our saddle bags at Omar's request, and brought us back a few pounds of sugar and some rice and tobacco (isn't it like Fielding's novels?). It is two days' journey, so they slept in the mosque at Koos half way. I told Yussuf how Suleyman's child has the smallpox and how Mohammed only said it was *Min Allah* (from God) when I suggested that his baby should be vaccinated at once. Yussuf called him in and said: 'Oh man, when thou wouldst build a house dost thou throw the bricks in a heap on the ground and say the building thereof is from God, or dost thou use the brains and hands which God has given thee, and then pray to Him to bless thy work? In all things do the best of thy understanding and means, and then say *Min Allah*, for the end is with Him!' There is not a pin to choose in fatalism here between Muslim and Christian, the lazy, like Mohammed and Suleyman (one Arab the other Copt), say *Min Allah* or any form of dawdle you please; but the true Muslim doctrine is just what Yussuf laid down—'do all you can and be resigned to whatever be the result.' *Fais ce que dois advienne qui pourra* is good doctrine. In fact, I am very much puzzled to discover the slightest difference between Christian and Muslim morality or belief—if you exclude certain dogmas—and in fact, very little is felt here. No one attempts to apply different standards of morals or of piety to a Muslim and a Copt. East and West is the difference, not Muslim and Christian. As to that difference I could tell volumes. Are they worse? Are they better? Both and neither. I am, perhaps, not quite impartial, because I am *sympathique* to the Arabs and they to me, and I am inclined to be 'kind' to their virtues if not 'blind' to their faults, which are visible to the most inexperienced traveller.

You see all our own familiar 'bunkum' (excuse the vulgarity) falls so flat on their ears, bravado about 'honour,' 'veracity,' etc., etc., they look blank and bored at. The schoolboy morality as set forth by Maurice is current here among grown men. Of course we tell lies to Pashas and Beys, why shouldn't we? But shall I call in that ragged sailor and give him an order to bring me up £500 in cash from Cairo when he happens to come? It would not be an unusual proceeding. I sleep every night in a *makaab* (sort of verandah) open to all Luxor, and haven't a door that has a lock. They bother me for backsheesh; but oh how poor they are, and how rich must be a woman whose very servants drink sugar to their coffee! and who lives in the *Kasr* (palace) and is respectfully visited by Ali Bey—and, come to that, Ali Bey would like a present even better than the poorest fellah, who also loves to give one. When I know, as I now do thoroughly, all Omar's complete integrity—without any sort of mention of it—his self-denial in going ragged and shabby to save his money for his wife and child (a very great trial to a good-looking young Arab), and the equally unostentatious love he has shown to me, and the delicacy and real nobleness of feeling which come out so oddly in the midst of sayings which, to our ideas, seem very shabby and time-serving, very often I wonder if there be anything as good in the civilised West. And as Sally most justly says, 'All their goodness is quite their own. God knows there is no one to teach anything but harm!'

Tuesday.—Two poor fellows have just come home from the Suez Canal work with gastric fever, I think. I hope it won't spread. The wife of one said to me yesterday, 'Are there more *Sittat* (ladies) like you in your village?' 'Wallah,' said I, 'there are many better, and good doctors, Alhamdullillah!' 'Alhamdullillah,' said she, 'then the poor people don't want you so much, and by God you must stay here for *we* can't do without you, so write to your family to say so, and don't go away and leave us.'

Thursday, June 2.—A steamer has just arrived which will take this letter, so I can only say good-bye, my dearest Mutter, and God bless you. I continue very fairly well. The epidemic here is all but over; but my medical fame has spread so, that the poor souls come twenty miles (from Koos) for physic. The constant phrase of 'Oh our sister, God hath sent thee to look to us!' is so sad. *Such* a little help is a wonder to my poor fellaheen. It is not so hot as it was I think, except at night, and I now sleep half the night outside the house. The cattle are all dead; perhaps five are left in all Luxor. *Allah kereem!* (God is merciful) said fellah Omar, 'I have one left from fifty-four.' The grain is unthreshed, and butter three shillings a pound! We get nothing here but by post; no papers, no nothing. I suppose the high Nile will bring up boats. Now the river is down at its lowest, and now I really know how Egyptians live.

To Sir Alexander Duff Gordon

LUXOR,
Sunday, June 12, 1864.

DEAREST ALICK,

Three letters have I received from you within a few days, for the post of the Saeed is not that of the Medes and Persians. I have had an abominable toothache, which quite floored me, and was aggravated by the Oriental custom, namely, that all the *beau monde* of Thebes *would* come and sit with me, and suggest remedies, and look into my mouth, and make quite a business of my tooth. Sheykh Yussuf laid two fingers on my cheek and recited verses from the Koran, I regret to say with no effect, except that while his fingers touched me the pain ceased. I find he *is* celebrated for soothing headaches and other nervous pains, and I daresay is an unconscious mesmeriser. The other day our poor Maōhn was terrified by a communication from Ali Bey (Moudir of Keneh) to the effect that he had heard from Alexandria that someone had reported that the dead cattle had lain about the streets of Luxor and that the place was pestilential. The British mind at once suggested a counter-statement, to be signed by the most respectable inhabitants. So the Cadi drew it up, and came and read it to me, and took my deposition and witnessed my signature, and the Maōhn went his way rejoicing, in that 'the words of the Englishwoman' would utterly defeat Ali Bey. The truth was that the worthy Maōhn worked really hard, and superintended the horrible dead cattle business in person, which is some risk and very unpleasant. To dispose of three or four hundred dead oxen every day with a limited number of labourers is no trifle, and if a travelling Englishman smells one a mile off he calls us 'lazy Arabs.' The beasts could not be buried deep enough, but all were carried a mile off from the village. I wish some of the dilettanti who stop their noses at us in our trouble had to see or to do what I have seen and done.

June 17.—We have had four or five days of such fearful heat with a Simoom that I have been quite knocked up, and literally could not write. Besides, I sit in the dark all day, and am now writing so—and at night go out and sit in the verandah, and can't have candles because of the insects. I sleep outside till about six a.m., and then go indoors till dark again. This fortnight is the hottest time. To-day the drop falls into the Nile at its source, and it will now rise fast and cool the country. It has risen one cubit, and the water is green; next month it will be blood colour. My cough has been a little troublesome again, I suppose from the Simoom. The tooth does not ache now. *Alhamdulillah!* for I rather dreaded the *muzeyinn* (barber) with his *tongs*, who is the sole dentist here. I was amused the other day by the entrance of my friend the Maōhn, attended by Osman Effendi and his cawass and pipe-bearer, and bearing a saucer in his hand, wearing the look, half sheepish, half cocky, with which elderly gentlemen in all countries announce what he did, *i.e.*, that his black slave-girl was three months with child and longed for olives, so the respectable magistrate had trotted all over the bazaar and to the Greek corn-dealers to buy some, but for no money were they to be had, so he hoped I might have some and forgive the request, as I, of course, knew that a man must beg or even steal for a woman under these circumstances. I called Omar and said, 'I trust there are olives for the honourable

Hareem of Seleem Effendi—they are needed there.' Omar instantly understood the case, and 'Praise be to God a few are left; I was about to stuff the pigeons for dinner with them; how lucky I had not done it.' And then we belaboured Seleem with compliments. 'Please God the child will be fortunate to thee,' say I. Omar says, 'Sweeten my mouth, oh Effendim, for did I not tell thee God would give thee good out of this affair when thou boughtest her?' While we were thus rejoicing over the possible little mulatto, I thought how shocked a white Christian gentleman of our Colonies would be at our conduct to make all this fuss about a black girl—'*he* give her sixpence' (under the same circumstances I mean) 'he'd see her d---d first,' and my heart warmed to the kind old Muslim sinner (?) as he took his saucer of olives and walked with them openly in his hand along the street. Now the black girl is free, and can only leave Seleem's house by her own good will and probably after a time she will marry and he will pay the expenses. A man can't sell his slave after he has made known that she is with child by him, and it would be considered unmanly to detain her if she should wish to go. The child will be added to the other eight who fill the Maōhn's quiver in Cairo and will be exactly as well looked on and have equal rights if he is as black as a coal.

A most quaint little half-black boy a year and a half old has taken a fancy to me and comes and sits for hours gazing at me and then dances to amuse me. He is Mahommed our guard's son by a jet-black slave of his and is brown-black and very pretty. He wears a bit of iron wire in one ear and iron rings round his ankles, and that is all—and when he comes up little Achmet, who is his uncle, 'makes him fit to be seen' by emptying a pitcher of water over his head to rinse off the dust in which of course he has been rolling—that is equivalent to a clean pinafore. You would want to buy little Said I know, he is so pretty and so jolly. He dances and sings and jabbers baby Arabic and then sits like a quaint little idol cross-legged quite still for hours.

I am now writing in the kitchen, which is the coolest place where there is any light at all. Omar is diligently spelling words of six letters, with the wooden spoon in his hand and a cigarette in his mouth, and Sally is lying on her back on the floor. I won't describe our costume. It is now two months since I have worn stockings, and I think you would wonder at the fellaha who 'owns you,' so deep a brown are my face, hands and feet. One of the sailors in Arthur's boat said: 'See how the sun of the Arabs loves her; he has kissed her so hotly that she can't go home among English people.'

June 18.—I went last night to look at Karnac by moonlight. The giant columns were overpowering. I never saw anything so solemn. On our way back we met the Sheykh-el-Beled, who ordered me an escort of ten men home. Fancy me on my humble donkey, guarded most superfluously by ten tall fellows, with oh! such spears and venerable matchlocks. At Mustapha's house we found a party seated before the door, and joined it. There was a tremendous Sheykh-el-Islam from Tunis, a Maghribee, seated on a carpet in state receiving homage. I don't think he liked the heretical woman at all. Even the Maōhn did not dare to be as 'politeful' as usual to me, but took the seat above me, which I had respectfully left vacant next to the holy man. Mustapha was in a stew, afraid not to do the respectful to me, and fussing after the Sheykh. Then Yussuf came fresh from the river, where he had bathed and prayed, and then you saw the real gentleman. He salaamed the great Sheykh, who motioned to him to sit before him, but Yussuf quietly came round and sat *below* me on the mat, leaned his elbow on my cushion, and made more demonstration of regard for me than ever, and when I went came and helped me on my donkey. The holy Sheykh went away to pray, and Mustapha hinted to Yussuf to go with him, but he only smiled, and did not stir; he had prayed an hour before down at the Nile. It was as if a poor curate had devoted himself to a rank papist under the eye of a scowling Shaftesbury Bishop. Then came Osman Effendi, a young Turk, with a poor devil accused in a distant village of stealing a letter with money in it addressed to a Greek money-lender. The discussion was quite general, the man, of course, denying all. But the Nazir had sent word to beat him. Then Omar burst out, 'What a shame to beat a poor man on the mere word of a Greek money-lender who eats the people; the Nazir shouldn't help him.' There was a Greek present who scowled at Omar, and the Turk gaped at him in horror. Yussuf said, with his quiet smile, 'My brother, thou art talking English,' with a glance at me; and we all laughed, and I said, 'Many thanks for the compliment.' All the village is in good spirits; the Nile is rising fast, and a star of most fortunate character has made its appearance, so Yussuf tells me, and portends a good year and an end to our afflictions. I am much better to-day, and I think I too feel the rising Nile; it puts new life into all things. The last fortnight or three weeks have been very trying with the Simoom and intense heat. I suppose I look better for the people here are for ever praising God about my amended looks. I am too hot, and it is too dark to write more.

To Sir Alexander Duff Gordon

LUXOR,
June 26, 1864.

DEAREST ALICK,

I have just paid a singular visit to a political *detenu* or exile rather. Last night Mustapha came in with a man in great grief who said his boy was very ill on board a cangia just come from Cairo and going to Assouan. The watchman on the river-bank had told him that there was an English Sitt 'who would not turn her face from anyone in trouble' and advised him to come to me for medicine, so he went to Mustapha and begged him to bring him to me, and to beg the cawass (policeman) in charge of El-Bedrawee (who was being sent to Fazoghlou in banishment) to wait a few hours. The cawass (may he not suffer for his humanity) consented. He described his boy's symptoms and I gave him a dose of castor oil and said I would go to the boat in the morning. The poor fellow was a Cairo merchant but living at Khartoum, he poured out his sorrow in true Eastern style. 'Oh my boy, and I have none but he, and how shall I come before his mother, a Habbesheeyeh, oh Lady, and tell her "thy son is dead"?' So I said, '*Allah kereem ya Seedee*, and *Inshallah tayib*,' etc., etc., and went this morning early to the boat. It was a regular old Arab cangia lumbered up with corn, sacks of matting, a live sheep, etc., and there I found a sweet graceful boy of fifteen or so in a high fever. His father said he had visited a certain Pasha on the way and evidently meant that he had been poisoned or had the evil eye. I assured him it was only the epidemic and asked why he had not sent for the doctor at Keneh. The old story! He was afraid, 'God knows what a government doctor might do to the boy.' Then Omar came in and stood before El-Bedrawee and said, 'Oh my master, why do we see thee thus? Mashallah, I once ate of thy bread when I was of the soldiers of Said Pasha, and I saw thy riches and thy greatness, and what has God decreed against thee?' So El-Bedrawee who is (or was) one of the wealthiest men of Lower Egypt and lived at Tantah, related how Effendina (Ismail Pasha) sent for him to go to Cairo to the Citadel to transact some business, and how he rode his horse up to the Citadel and went in, and there the Pasha at once ordered a cawass to take him down to the Nile and on board a common cargo boat and to go with him and take him to Fazoghlou. Letters were given to the cawass to deliver to every Moudir on the way, and another despatched by hand to the Governor of Fazoghlou with orders concerning El-Bedrawee. He begged leave to see his son once more before starting, or any of his family. 'No, he must go at once and see no one.' But luckily a fellah, one of his relations had come after him to Cairo and had £700 in his girdle; he followed El-Bedrawee to the Citadel and saw him being walked off by the cawass and followed him to the river and on board the boat and gave him the £700 which he had in his girdle. The various Moudirs had been civil to him, and friends in various places had given him clothes and food. He had not got a chain round his neck or fetters, and was allowed to go ashore with the cawass, for he had just been to the tomb of Abou-l-Hajjaj and had told that dead Sheykh all his affliction and promised, if he came back safe, to come every year to his *moolid* (festival) and pay the whole expenses (*i.e.* feed all comers). Mustapha wanted him to dine with him and me, but the cawass could not allow it, so Mustapha sent him a fine sheep and some bread, fruit, etc. I made him a present of some quinine, rhubarb pills, and sulphate of zinc for eye lotion. Here you know we all go upon a more than English presumption and believe every prisoner to be innocent and a victim—as he gets no trial he *never* can be proved guilty—besides poor old El-Bedrawee declared he had not the faintest idea what he was accused of or how he had offended Effendina.

I listened to all this in extreme amazement, and he said, 'Ah! I know you English manage things very differently; I have heard all about your excellent justice.'

He was a stout, dignified-looking fair man, like a Turk, but talking broad Lower Egypt fellah talk, so that I could not understand him, and had to get Mustapha and Omar to repeat his words. His father was an Arab, and his mother a Circassian slave, which gave the fair skin and reddish beard. He must be over fifty, fat and not healthy; of course he is *meant* to die up in Fazoghlou, especially going at this season. He owns (or owned, for God knows who has it now) 12,000 feddans of fine land between Tantah and Samanhoud, and was enormously rich. He consulted me a great deal about his health, and I gave him certainly very good advice. I cannot write in a letter which I know you will show what drugs a Turkish doctor had furnished him with to 'strengthen' him in the trying climate of Fazoghlou. I wonder was it intended to kill him or only given in ignorance of the laws of health equal to his own?

After a while the pretty boy became better and recovered consciousness, and his poor father, who had been helping me with trembling hands and swimming eyes, cried for joy, and said, 'By God the most high, if ever I find any of the English, poor or sick or afflicted up in Fazoghlou, I will make them know that I Abu Mahommed never saw a face like the pale face of the English lady bent over my sick boy.' And then El-Bedrawee and his fellah kinsman, and all the crew blessed me and the Captain, and the cawass said it was time to sail. So I gave directions and medicine to Abu Mahommed, and kissed the pretty boy and went out. El-Bedrawee followed me up the bank, and said he had a request to make—would I pray for him in his distress. I said, 'I am not of the Muslimeen,' but both he and Mustapha said, *Maleysh* (never mind), for that it was quite certain I was not of the *Mushkireen*, as they hate the Muslimeen and their deeds are evil—but blessed be God, many of the English begin to repent of their evil, and to love the Muslims and abound in kind actions. So we parted in much kindness. It was a strange feeling to me to stand on the bank and see the queer savage-looking boat glide away up the stream, bound to such far more savage lands, and to be exchanging kind farewells quite in a homely manner with such utter 'aliens in blood and faith.' 'God keep thee Lady, God keep thee Mustapha.' Mustapha and I walked home very sad about poor El-Bedrawee.

Friday, *July* 7.—It has been so 'awfully' hot that I have not had pluck to go on with my letter, or indeed to do anything but lie on a mat in the passage with a minimum of clothes quite indescribable in English. *Alhamdulilah!* laughs Omar, 'that I see the clever English people do just like the lazy Arabs.' The worst is not the positive heat, which has not been above 104° and as low as 96° at night, but the horrible storms of hot wind and dust which are apt to come on at night and prevent one's even lying down till twelve or one o'clock. Thebes is bad in the height of summer on account of its expanse of desert, and sand and dust. The Nile is pouring down now gloriously, and *really* red as blood—more crimson than a Herefordshire lane—and in the distance the reflection of the pure blue sky makes it deep violet. It had risen five cubits a week ago; we shall soon have it all over the land here. It is a beautiful and inspiriting sight to see the noble old stream as young and vigorous as ever. No wonder the Egyptians worshipped the Nile: there is nothing like it. We have had all the plagues of Egypt this year, only the lice are commuted for bugs, and the frogs for mice; the former have eaten me and the latter have eaten my clothes. We are so ragged! Omar has one shirt left, and has to sleep without and wash it every night. The dust, the drenching perspiration, and the hard-fisted washing of Mahommed's slave-women destroys everything.

Mustapha intends to give you a grand *fantasia* if you come, and to have the best dancing girls down from Esneh for you; but I am consternated to hear that you can't come till December. I hoped you would have arrived in Cairo early in November, and spent a month there with me, and come up the river in the middle of December when Cairo gets very cold.

I remain very well in general health, but my cough has been troublesome again. I do not feel at all like breathing cold damp air again. This depresses me very much as you may suppose. You will have to divorce me, and I must marry some respectable Kadee. I have been too 'lazy Arab,' as Omar calls it, to go on with my Arabic lessons, and Yussuf has been very busy with law business connected with the land and the crops. Every harvest brings a fresh settling of the land. Wheat is selling at £1 the ardeb here *on the threshing-floor*, and barley at one hundred and sixteen piastres; I saw some Nubians pay Mustapha that. He is in comic perplexity about saying *Alhamdulillah* about such enormous gains—you see it is rather awkward for a Muslim to thank God for dear bread—so he compounds by very lavish almsgiving. He gave all his fellaheen clothes the other day—forty calico shirts and drawers. Do you remember my describing an Arab *emancipirtes Fraülein* at Siout? Well, the other day I saw as I thought a nice-looking lad of sixteen selling corn to my opposite neighbour, a Copt. It was a girl. Her father had no son and is infirm, so she works in the field for him, and dresses and does like a man. She looked very modest and was quieter in her manner than the veiled women often are.

I am so glad to hear such good accounts of my Rainie and Maurice. I can hardly bear to think of another year without seeing them. However it is fortunate for me that 'my lines have fallen in pleasant places,' so long a time at the Cape or any Colony would have become intolerable. Best love to Janet, I really can't write, it's too hot and dusty. Omar desires his salaam to his great master and to that gazelle Sittee Ross.

To Sir Alexander Duff Gordon

LUXOR,
August 13, 1864.

DEAREST ALICK,

For the last month we have had a purgatory of hot wind and dust, such as I never saw—impossible to stir out of the house. So in despair I have just engaged a return boat—a *Gelegenheit*—and am off to Cairo in a day or two, where I shall stop till *Inshallah!* you come to me. Can't you get leave to come at the beginning of November? Do try, that is the pleasant time in Cairo.

I am a 'stupid, lazy Arab' now, as Omar says, having lain on a mat in a dark stone passage for six weeks or so, but my chest is no worse—better I think, and my health has not suffered at all—only I am stupid and lazy. I had a pleasant visit lately from a great doctor from Mecca—a man so learned that he can read the Koran in seven different ways, he is also a physician of European *Hekmeh* (learning). Fancy my wonder when a great Alim in gorgeous Hegazee dress walked in and said: '*Madame, tout ce qu'on m'a dit de vous fait tellement l'éloge de votre cœur et de votre esprit que je me suis arreté pour tacher de me procurer le plaisir de votre connaissance!*' A lot of Luxor people came in to pay their respects to the great man, and he said to me that he hoped I had not been molested on account of religion, and if I had I must forgive it, as the people here were so very ignorant, and *barbarians were bigots everywhere*. I said, '*Wallahy*, the people of Luxor are my brothers!' and the Maōhn said, 'True, the fellaheen are like oxen, but not such swine as to insult the religion of a lady who has served God among them like this one. She risked her life every day.' 'And if she *had* died,' said the great theologian, 'her place was made ready among the martyrs of God, because she showed more love to her brothers than to herself!'

Now if this was humbug it was said in Arabic before eight or ten people, by a man of great religious authority.

Omar was *aux anges* to hear his Sitt spoken of 'in such a grand way for the religion.' I believe that a great change is taking place among the Ulema, that Islam is ceasing to be a mere party flag, just as occurred with Christianity, and that all the moral part is being more and more dwelt on. My great Alim also said I had practised the precepts of the Koran, and then laughed and added, 'I suppose I ought to say the Gospel, but what matters it, *el Hakh* (the truth) is one, whether spoken by Our Lord Jesus or by Our Lord Mahommed!' He asked me to go with him to Mecca next winter for my health, as it was so hot and dry there. I found he had fallen in with El-Bedrawee and the Khartoum merchant at Assouan. The little boy was well again, and I had been outrageously extolled by them. We are now sending off all the corn. I sat the other evening on Mustapha's doorstep and saw the Greeks piously and zealously attending to the divine command to spoil the Egyptians. Eight months ago a Greek bought up corn at 60 piastres the ardeb (he follows the Coptic tax-gatherer like a vulture after a crow), now wheat is at 170 piastres the ardeb here, and the fellah has paid 3½ *per cent. a month* besides. Reckon the profit! Two men I know are quite ruined, and have sold all they had. The cattle disease forced them to borrow at these ruinous rates, and now alas, the Nile is sadly lingering in its rise, and people are very anxious. Poor Egypt! or rather, poor Egyptians! Of course, I need not say that there is great improvidence in those who can be fleeced as they are fleeced. Mustapha's household is a pattern of muddling hospitality, and Mustapha is generous and mean by turns; but what chance have people like these, so utterly uncivilised and so isolated, against Europeans of unscrupulous characters.

I can't write more in the wind and dust. You shall hear again from Cairo.

To Sir Alexander Duff Gordon

CAIRO,
October 9, 1864.

DEAREST ALICK,

I have not written for a long time because I have had a fever. Now I am all right again, only weak. If you can come please bring the books in enclosed list for an American Egyptologist at Luxor—a friend of mine. My best love to Janet and my other chicks. I wish I could see my Maurice. Tell Janet that Hassan donkey boy, has married a girl of eleven, and Phillips that Hassan remembers him quite tenderly and is very proud of having had his 'face' drawn by him, 'certainly he was of the friends if not a brother of the Sitt, he so loved the things of the Arabs.' I went to the Hareem *soirée* at Hassan's before the wedding—at that event I was ill. My good doctor was up the river, and Hekekian Bey is in Italy, so I am very lonely here. The weather is bad, so very damp; I stream with perspiration more than in June at Luxor, and I don't like civilisation so very much. It keeps me awake at night in the grog shops and rings horrid bells and fights and quarrels in the street, and disturbs my Muslim nerves till I utter such epithets as *kelb* (dog) and *khanseer* (pig) against the Frangi, and wish I were in a 'beastly Arab' quarter.

To Mrs. Austin

CAIRO,
October 21, 1864.

DEAREST MUTTER,

I got your letter yesterday. I hope Alick got mine of two weeks ago before leaving, and told you I was better. I am still rather weak, however I ride my donkey and the weather has suddenly become gloriously dry and cool. I rather shiver with the thermometer at 79°—absurd is it not, but I got so used to real heat.

I never wrote about my leaving Luxor or my journey, for our voyage was quite tempestuous after the three first days and I fell ill as soon as I was in my house here. I hired the boat for six purses (£18) which had taken Greeks up to Assouan selling groceries and strong drinks, but the reis would not bring back their cargo of black slaves to dirty the boat and picked us up at Luxor. We sailed at daybreak having waited all one day because it was an unlucky day.

As I sat in the boat people kept coming to ask whether I was coming back very anxiously and bringing fresh bread, eggs and things as presents, and all the quality came to take leave and hope, *Inshallah*, I should soon 'come home to my village safe and bring the Master, please God, to see them,' and then to say the *Fattah* for a safe journey and my health. In the morning the balconies of my house were filled with such a group to see us sail—a party of wild Abab'deh with their long Arab guns and flowing hair, a Turk elegantly dressed, Mohammed in his decorous brown robes and snow-white turban, and several fellaheen. As the boat moved off the Abab'deh blazed away with their guns and Osman Effendi with a sort of blunderbuss, and as we dropped down the river there was a general firing; even Todoros (Theodore), the Coptic Mallim, popped off his American revolver. Omar keeping up a return with Alick's old horse pistols which are much admired here on account of the excessive noise they make.

Poor old Ismain, who always thought I was Mme. Belzoni and wanted to take me up to Abou Simbel to meet my husband, was in dire distress that he could not go with me to Cairo. He declared he was still *shedeed* (strong enough to take care of me and to fight). He is ninety-seven and only remembers fifty or sixty years ago and old wild times—a splendid old man, handsome and erect. I used to give him coffee and listen to his old stories which had won his heart. His grandson, the quiet, rather stately, Mohammed who is guard of the house I lived in, forgot all his Muslim dignity, broke down in the middle of his set speech and flung himself down and kissed and hugged my knees and cried. He had got some notion of impending ill-luck, I found, and was unhappy at our departure—and the backsheesh failed to console him. Sheykh Yussuf was to come with me, but a brother of his just wrote word that he was coming back from the Hejaz where he had been with the troops in which he is serving his time; I was very sorry to lose his company. Fancy how dreadfully irregular for one of the Ulema and a heretical woman to travel together. What would our bishops say to a parson who did such a thing? We had a lovely time on the river for three days, such moonlight nights, so soft and lovely; and we had a sailor who was as good as a professional singer, and who sang religious songs, which I observe excite people here far more than love songs. One which began 'Remove my sins from before thy sight Oh God' was really beautiful and touching, and I did not wonder at the tears which ran down Omar's face. A very pretty profane song was 'Keep the wind from me Oh Lord, I fear it will hurt me' (*wind* means *love*, which is like the Simoom) 'Alas! it has struck me and I am sick. Why do ye bring the physician? Oh physician put back thy medicine in the canister, for only he who has hurt can cure me.' The masculine pronoun is always used instead of *she* in poetry out of decorum—sometimes even in conversation.

October 23.—Yesterday I met a Saedee—a friend of the brother of the Sheykh of the wild Abab'deh, and as we stood handshaking and kissing our fingers in the road, some of the Anglo-Indian travellers passed and gazed with fierce disgust;* the handsome Hassan, being black, was such a flagrant case of a 'native.' Mutter dear, it is heart-breaking to see what we are sending to India now. The mail days are dreaded, we never know when some outrage may not excite 'Mussulman fanaticism.' The English tradesmen here complain as much as anyone, and I, who as the Kadee of Luxor said am 'not outside the family' (of Ishmael, I presume), hear what the Arabs really think. There are also crowds 'like lice' as one Mohammed said, of low Italians, French, etc., and I find my stalwart Hassan's broad shoulders no superfluous *porte-respect* in the Frangee quarter. Three times I have been followed and insolently stared at (*à mon age*)!! and once Hassan had to speak. Fancy how dreadful to Muslims! I hate the sight of a hat here now.

I can't write more now my eyes are weak still. Omar begs me to give you his best salaam and say, *Inshallah*, he will take great care of your daughter, which he most zealously and tenderly does.

To Mrs. Austin

On the Nile,
Friday, December 23, 1864.

Dearest Mutter,

Here I am again between Benisouef and Minieh, and already better for the clear air of the river and the tranquil boat life; I will send you my Christmas Salaam from Siout. While Alick was with me I had as much to do as I was able and could not write for there was much to see and talk about. I think he was amused but I fear he felt the Eastern life to be very poor and comfortless. I have got so used to having nothing that I had quite forgotten how it would seem to a stranger.

I am quite sorry to find how many of my letters must have been lost from Luxor; in future I shall trust the Arab post which certainly is safer than English travellers. I send you my long plaits by Alick, for I had my hair cut short as it took to falling out by handfuls after my fever, and moreover it is more convenient Turkish hareem fashion.

Please tell Dean Stanley how his old dragoman Mahommed Gazawee cried with pleasure when he told me he had seen Sheykh Stanley's sister on her way to India, and the 'little ladies' *knew his name* and shook hands with him, which evidently was worth far more than the backsheesh. I wondered who 'Sheykh' Stanley could be, and Mahommed (who is a darweesh and very pious) told me he was the *Gassis* (priest) who was *Imám* (spiritual guide) to the son of our Queen, 'and in truth,' said he, 'he is *really* a Sheykh and one who teaches the excellent things of religion, why he was kind even to his horse! and it is of the mercies of God to the English that such a one is the Imám of your Queen and Prince.' I said laughing, 'How dost thou, a darweesh among Muslims, talk thus of a Nazarene priest?' 'Truly oh Lady,' he answered, 'one who loveth all the creatures of God, him God loveth also, there is no doubt of that.' Is any one bigot enough to deny that Stanley has done more for real religion in the mind of that Muslim darweesh than if he had baptised a hundred savages out of one fanatical faith into another?

There is no hope of a good understanding with Orientals until Western Christians can bring themselves to recognise the common faith contained in the two religions, the *real* difference consists in all the class of notions and feelings (very important ones, no doubt) which we derive—not from the Gospels at all—but from Greece and Rome, and which of course are altogether wanting here.

Alick will tell you how curiously Omar illustrated the patriarchal feelings of the East by entirely dethroning me in favour of the 'Master.' 'That *our Master*, we all eat bread from his hand, and he work for *us*.' Omar and I were equal before *our Seedee*. He can sit at his ease at my feet, but when the Master comes in he must stand reverently, and gave me to understand that I too must be respectful.

I have got the boat of the American Mission at an outrageous price, £60, but I could get nothing under; the consolation is that the sailors profit, poor fellows, and get treble wages. My crew are all Nubians. Such a handsome reis and steersman—brothers—and there is a black boy, of fourteen or so, with legs and feet so sweetly beautiful as to be quite touching—at least I always feel those lovely round young innocent forms to be somehow affecting. Our old boat of last summer (Arthur Taylor's) is sailing in company with us, and stately old reis Mubharak hails me every morning with the Blessing of God and the Peace of the Prophet. Alee Kuptan, my steamboat captain will announce our advent at Thebes; he passed us to-day. This boat is a fine sailer, but iron built and therefore noisy, and not convenient. The crew encourage her with 'Get along, father of three,' because she has three sails, whereas two is the usual number. They are active good-humoured fellows—my men—but lack the Arab courtesy and *simpatico* ways, and then I don't understand their language which is pretty and sounds a little like Caffre, rather bird-like and sing-song, instead of the clattering guttural Arabic. I now speak pretty tolerably for a stranger, *i.e.* I can keep up a conversation, and understand all that is said to me much better than I can speak, and follow about half what people say to each other. When I see you, *Inshallah*, next summer I shall be a good scholar, I hope.

To Mrs. Austin

LUXOR,
January 2, 1865.

DEAREST MUTTER,

I posted a letter for you at Girgeh, as we passed Siout with a good wind, I hope you will get it. My crew worked as I never saw men work, they were paid to get to Luxor, and for eighteen days they never rested or slept day or night, and all the time were merry and pleasant. It shows what power of endurance these 'lazy Arabs' have when there is good money at the end of a job, instead of the favourite panacea of 'stick.'

We arrived at midnight and next morning my boat had the air of being pillaged. A crowd of laughing, chattering fellows ran off to the house laden with loose articles snatched up at random, loaves of sugar, pots and pans, books, cushions, all helter-skelter. I feared breakages, but all was housed safe and sound. The small boys of an age licensed to penetrate into the cabin, went off with the oddest cargoes of dressing things and the like—of backsheesh not one word. *Alhamdulillah salaameh!* 'Thank God thou art in peace,' and *Ya Sitt, Ya Emeereh*, till my head went round. Old Ismaeen fairly hugged me and little Achmet hung close to my side.

I went up to Mustapha's house while the unpacking took place and breakfasted there, and found letters from all of you, from you to darling Rainie, Sheykh Yussuf was charmed with her big writing and said he thought the news in that was the best of all.

The weather was intensely hot the first two days. Now it is heavenly, a fresh breeze and gorgeous sunshine. I brought two common Arab lanterns for the tomb of Abu-l-Hajjaj and his *moolid* is now going on. Omar took them and lighted them up and told me he found several people who called on the rest to say the *Fathah* for me. I was sitting out yesterday with the people on the sand looking at the men doing *fantasia* on horseback for the Sheykh, and a clever dragoman of the party was relating about the death of a young English girl whom he had served, and so *de fil en aiguille* we talked about the strangers buried here and how the bishop had extorted £100. I said, '*Maleysh* (never mind) the people have been hospitable to me alive and they will not cease if I die, but give me a tomb among the Arabs.' One old man said, 'May I not see thy day, oh Lady, and indeed thou shouldest be buried as a daughter of the Arabs, but we should fear the anger of thy Consul and thy family, but thou knowest that wherever thou art buried thou wilt assuredly lie in a Muslim grave.' 'How so?' said I. 'Why, when a bad Muslim dies the angels take him out of his tomb and put in one of the good from among the Christians in his place.' This is the popular expression of the doctrine that the good are sure of salvation. Omar chimed in at once, 'Certainly there is no doubt of it, and I know a story that happened in the days of Mahommed Ali Pasha which proves it.' We demanded the story and Omar began. 'There was once a very rich man of the Muslims so stingy that he grudged everybody even so much as a "bit of the paper inside the date" (Koran). When he was dying he said to his wife, "Go out and buy me a lump of pressed dates," and when she had brought it he bade her leave him alone. Thereupon he took all his gold out of his sash and spread it before him, and rolled it up two or three pieces at a time in the dates, and swallowed it piece after piece until only three were left, when his wife came in and saw what he was doing and snatched them from his hand. Presently after he fell back and died and was carried out to the burial place and laid in his tomb. When the Kadee's men came to put the seal on his property and found no money they said, "Oh woman, how is this? we know thy husband was a rich man and behold we find no money for his children and slaves or for thee." So the woman told what had happened, and the Kadee sent for three other of the Ulema, and they decided that after three days she should go herself to her husband's tomb and open it, and take the money from his stomach; meanwhile a guard was put over the tomb to keep away robbers. After three days therefore the woman went, and the men opened the tomb and said, "Go in O woman and take thy money." So the woman went down into the tomb alone. When there, instead of her husband's body she saw a box (coffin) of the boxes of the Christians, and when she opened it she saw the body of a young girl, adorned with many ornaments of gold necklaces, and bracelets, and a diamond *Kurs* on her head, and over all a veil of black muslin embroidered with gold. So the woman said within herself, "Behold I came for money and here it is, I will take it and conceal this business for fear of the Kadee." So she wrapped the whole in her *melayeh* (a blue checked cotton sheet worn as a cloak) and came out, and the men said "Hast thou done thy business?"' and she answered "Yes" and returned home.

'In a few days she gave the veil she had taken from the dead girl to a broker to sell for her in the bazaar, and the broker went and showed it to the people and was offered one hundred piastres. Now there sat in one of the shops of the merchants a great Ma-allim (Coptic clerk) belonging to the Pasha, and he saw the veil and said, "How much asketh thou?" and the broker said "Oh thine honour the clerk whatever thou wilt." "Take from me then five hundred piastres and bring the person that gave thee the veil to receive the money." So the broker fetched the woman and the Copt, who was a great man, called the police and said, "Take this woman and fetch my ass and we will go before the Pasha," and he rode in haste to the palace weeping and beating his breast, and went before the Pasha and said, "Behold this veil was buried a few days ago with my daughter who died unmarried, and I had none but her and I loved her like my eyes and would not take from her her ornaments, and this veil she worked herself and was very fond of it, and she was young and beautiful and just of the age to be married; and behold the Muslims go and rob the tombs of the Christians and if thou wilt suffer this we Christians will leave Egypt and go and live in some other country, O Effendina, for we cannot endure this abomination."

'Then the Pasha turned to the woman and said, "Woe to thee O woman, art thou a Muslimeh and doest such wickedness?" And the woman spoke and told all that had happened and how she sought money and finding gold had kept it. So the Pasha said, "Wait oh Ma-allim, and we will discover the truth of this matter," and he sent for the three Ulema who had desired that the tomb should be opened at the end of three days and told them the case; and they said, "Open now the tomb of the Christian damsel." And the Pasha sent his men to do so, and when they opened it behold it was full of fire, and within it lay the body of the wicked and avaricious Mussulman.' Thus it was manifest to all that on the night of terror the angels of God had done this thing, and had laid the innocent girl of the Christians among those who have received direction, and the evil Muslim among the rejected. Admire how rapidly legends arise here. This story which everybody declared was quite true is placed no longer ago than in Mahommed Ali Pasha's time.

There are hardly any travellers this year, instead of a hundred and fifty or more boats, perhaps twenty. A son of one of the Rothschilds, a boy of fourteen, has just gone up like a royal prince in one of the Pasha's steamers—all his expenses paid and crowds of attendants. 'All that honour to the money of the Jew,' said an old fellah to me with a tone of scorn which I could not but echo in my heart. He has turned out his dragoman—a respectable elderly man, very sick, and paid him his bare wages and the munificent sum of £5 to take him back to Cairo. On board there was a doctor and plenty of servants, and yet he abandons the man here on Mustapha's hands. I have brought Er-Rasheedee here (the sick man) as poor Mustapha is already overloaded with strangers. I am sorry the name of *Yahoodee* (Jew) should be made to stink yet more in the nostrils of the Arabs. I am very well, indeed my cough is almost gone and I can walk quite briskly and enjoy it. I think, dear Mutter, I am really better. I never felt the cold so little as this winter since my illness, the chilly mornings and nights don't seem to signify at all now, and the climate feels more delicious than ever.

Mr. Herbert, the painter, went back to Cairo from Farshoot below Keneh; so I have no 'Frangee' society at all. But Sheykh Yussuf and the Kadee drop in to tea very often and as they are agreeable men I am quite content with my company.

By the bye I will tell you about the tenure of land in Egypt which people are always disputing about, as the Kadee laid it down for me. The *whole* land belongs to the Sultan of Turkey, the Pasha being his vakeel (representative), nominally of course as we know. Thus there are no owners, only tenants paying from one hundred piastres tariff (£1) down to thirty piastres yearly per feddan (about an acre) according to the quality of the land, or the favour of the Pasha when granting it. This tenancy is hereditary to children only—not to collaterals or ascendants—and it may be sold, but in that case application must be made to the Government. If the owner or tenant dies childless the land reverts to the Sultan, *i.e.* to the Pasha, and *if the Pasha chooses to have any man's land he can take it from him on payment—or without.* Don't let any one tell you that I exaggerate; I have known it happen: I mean the *without*, and the man received feddan for feddan of desert, in return for his good land which he had tilled and watered.

To-morrow night is the great night of Sheykh Abu-l-Hajjaj's *moolid* and I am desired to go to the mosque for the benefit of my health, and that my friends may say a prayer for my children. The kind hearty welcome I found here has been a real pleasure, and every one was pleased because I was glad to come home to my *beled* (town), and they all thought it so nice of 'my master' to have come so far to see me because I was sick—all but one Turk, who clearly looked with pitying contempt on so much trouble taken about a sick old woman.

I have left my letter for a long while. You will not wonder—for after some ten days' fever, my poor guest Mohammed Er-Rasheedee died to-day. Two Prussian doctors gave me help for the last four days, but left last night. He sank to sleep quietly at noon with his hand in mine, a good old Muslim sat at his head on one side and I on the other. Omar stood at his head and his black boy Khayr at his feet. We had laid his face to the Kibleh and I spoke to him to see if he knew anything and when he nodded the three Muslims chanted the *Islamee La Illáhá*, etc., etc., while I closed his eyes. The 'respectable men' came in by degrees, took an inventory of his property which they delivered to me, and washed the body, and within an hour and a half we all went out to the burial place; I following among a troop of women who joined us to wail for 'the brother who had died far from his place.' The scene as we turned in between the broken colossi and the pylons of the temple to go to the mosque was over-powering. After the prayer in the mosque we went out to the graveyard, Muslims and Copts helping to carry the dead, and my Frankish hat in the midst of the veiled and wailing women; all so familiar and yet so strange. After the burial the Imám, Sheykh Abd-el-Waris, came and kissed me on the shoulders and the Shereef, a man of eighty, laid his hands on my shoulders and said, 'Fear not my daughter, neither all the days of thy life nor at the hour of thy death, for God is with thee.' I kissed the old man's hand and turned to go, but numberless men came and said 'A thousand thanks, O our sister, for what thou hast done for one among us,' and a great deal more. Now the solemn chanting of the *Fikees*, and the clear voice of the boy reciting the Koran in the room where the man died are ringing through the house. They will pass the night in prayer, and to-morrow there will be the prayer of deliverance in the mosque. Poor Khayr has just crept in to have a quiet cry—poor boy. He is in the inventory and to-morrow I must deliver him up to *les autorités* to be forwarded to Cairo with the rest of the property. He is very ugly with his black face wet and swollen, but he kisses my hand and calls me his mother quite 'natural like'—you see colour is no barrier here.

The weather is glorious this year, and in spite of some fatigue I am extremely well and strong, and have hardly any cough at all. I am so sorry that the young Rothschild was so hard to Er-Rasheedee and that his French doctor refused to come and see him. It makes bad blood naturally. However, the German doctors were most kind and helpful.

The festival of Abu-l-Hajjaj was quite a fine sight, not splendid at all—*au contraire*—but spirit-stirring; the flags of the Sheykh borne by his family chanting, and the men tearing about in mimic fight on horseback with their spears. My acquaintance of last year, Abd-el-Moutovil, the fanatical Sheykh from Tunis was there. At first he scowled at me. Then someone told him how Rothschild had left Er-Rasheedee, and he held forth about the hatred of all the unbelievers to the Muslims, and ended by asking where the sick man was. A quaint little smile twinkled in Sheykh Yussuf's soft eyes and he curled his silky moustache as he said demurely, 'Your Honour must go and visit him at the house of the English Lady.' I am bound to say that the Pharisee 'executed himself' handsomely, for in a few minutes he came up to me and took my hand and even hoped I would visit the tomb of Abu-l-Hajjaj with him!!

Since I wrote last I have been rather poorly—more cough, and most wearing sleeplessness. A poor young Englishman died here at the house of the Austrian Consular agent. I was too ill to go to him, but a kind, dear young Englishwoman, a Mrs. Walker, who was here with her family in a boat, sat up with him three nights and nursed him like a sister. A young American lay sick at the same time in the house, he is now gone down to Cairo, but I doubt whether he will reach it alive. The Englishman was buried on the first day of Ramadan where they bury strangers, on the site of a former Coptic church. Archdeacon Moore read the service; Omar and I spread my old flag over the bier, and Copts and Muslims helped to carry the poor stranger. It was a most impressive sight. The party of Europeans, all strangers to the dead but all deeply moved; the group of black-robed and turbaned Copts; the sailors from the boats; the gaily dressed dragomans; several brown-shirted fellaheen and the thick crowd of children—all the little

Abab'deh stark naked and all behaving so well, the expression on their little faces touched me most of all. As Muslims, Omar and the boatmen laid him down in the grave, and while the English prayer was read the sun went down in a glorious flood of light over the distant bend of the Nile. 'Had he a mother, he was young?' said an Abab'deh woman to me with tears in her eyes and pressing my hand in sympathy for that far-off mother of such a different race.

Passenger steamboats come now every fortnight, but I have had no letter for a month. I have no almanack and have lost count of European time—to-day is the 3 of Ramadan, that is all I know. The poor black slave was sent back from Keneh, God knows why—because he had no money and the Moudir could not 'eat off him' as he could off the money and property—he believes. He is a capital fellow, and in order to compensate me for what he eats he proposed to wash for me, and you would be amused to see Khayr with his coal-black face and filed teeth doing laundry-maid out in the yard. He fears the family will sell him and hopes he may fetch a good price for 'his boy'—only on the other hand he would so like me to buy him—and so his mind is disturbed. Meanwhile the having all my clothes washed clean is a great luxury.

The steamer is come and I must finish in haste. I have corrected the proofs. There is not much to alter, and though I regret several lost letters I can't replace them. I tried, but it felt like a forgery. Do you cut out and correct, dearest Mutter, you will do it much better than I.

To the Dowager Lady Duff Gordon

LUXOR,
January 8, 1865.

DEAR OLD LADY,

I received your kind letter in the midst of the drumming and piping and chanting and firing of guns and pistols and scampering of horses which constitute a religious festival in Egypt. The last day of the *moolid* of Abu-l-Hajjaj fell on the 1st January so you came to wish me 'May all the year be good to thee' as the people here were civil enough to do when I told them it was the first day of the *Frankish* year. (The *Christian* year here begins in September.)

I was very sorry to hear of poor Lady Theresa's (Lady Theresa Lewis) death. I feel as if I had no right to survive people whom I left well and strong when I came away so ill. As usual the air of Upper Egypt has revived me again, but I am still weak and thin, and hear many lamentations at my altered looks. However, '*Inshallah*, thou wilt soon be better.'

Why don't you make Alexander edit your letters from Spain? I am sure they would be far more amusing than mine can possibly be—for you *can* write letters and I never could. I wish I had Miss Berry's though I never did think her such a genius as most people, but her letters must be amusing from the time when they were written. Alexander will tell you how heavy the hand of Pharaoh is upon this poor people. 'My father scourged you with whips but I will scourge you with scorpions,' did not Rehoboam say so? or I forget which King of Judah. The distress here is frightful in all classes, and no man's life is safe.

Ali Bey Rheda told me the other day that Prince Arthur is coming here and that he was coming up with him after taking a Prince of Hohenzollern back to Cairo. There will be all the *fantasia* possible for him here. Every man that has a horse will gallop him to pieces in honour of the son of the Queen of the English, and not a charge of powder will be spared. If you see Layard tell him that Mustapha A'gha had the whole Koran read for his benefit at the tomb of Abu-l-Hajjaj besides innumerable *fathahs* which he said for him himself. He consulted me as to the propriety of sending Layard a backsheesh, but I declared that Layard was an Emeer of the Arabs and a giver, not a taker of backsheesh.

To Mrs. Austin

LUXOR,
January 9, 1865.

I gave Sheykh Yussuf your knife to cut his *kalem* (reed pen) with, and to his little girl the coral waistband clasp you gave me *as from you*. He was much pleased. I also brought the Shereef the psalms in Arabic to his great delight. The old man called on all 'our family' to say a *fathah* for their sister, after making us all laugh by shouting out '*Alhamdulillah!* here is our darling safe back again.'

I wish you could have seen me in the crowd at Keneh holding on to the Kadee's *farageeyeh* (a loose robe worn by the Ulema). He is the real original Kadee of the Thousand and One Nights. Did ever Kadee tow an Englishwoman round a Sheykh's tomb before? but I thought his determination to show the people that he considered a Christian not out of place in a Muslim holy place very edifying.

I find an exceedingly pleasant man here, an Abab'deh, a very great Sheykh from beyond Khartoum, a man of fifty I suppose, with manners like an English nobleman, simple and polite and very intelligent. He wants to take me to Khartoum for two months up and back, having a tent and a *takhterawan* (camel-litter) and to show me the Bishareen in the desert. We traced the route on my map which to my surprise he understood, and I found he had travelled into Zanzibar and knew of the existence of the Cape of Good Hope and the English colony there. He had also travelled in the Dinka and Shurook country where the men are seven feet and over high (Alexander saw a Dinka girl at Cairo three inches taller than himself!). He knows Madlle. Tiné* and says she is 'on everyone's head and in their eyes' where she has been. You may fancy that I find Sheykh Alee very good company.

To-day the sand in front of the house is thronged with all the poor people with their camels, of which the Government has made a new levy of eight camels to every thousand feddans. The poor beasts are sent off to transport troops in the Soudan, and not being used to the desert, they all die—at all events their owners never see one of them again. The discontent is growing stronger every day. Last week the people were cursing the Pasha in the streets of Assouan, and every one talks aloud of what they think.

January 11.—The whole place is in desolation, the men are being beaten, one because his camel is not good enough, another because its saddle is old and shabby, and the rest because they have not money enough to pay two months' food and the wages of one man, to every four camels, to be paid for the use of the Government beforehand. The *courbash* has been going on my neighbours' backs and feet all the morning. It is a new sensation too when a friend turns up his sleeve and shows the marks of the wooden handcuffs and the gall of the chain on his throat. The system of wholesale extortion and spoliation has reached a point beyond which it would be difficult to go. The story of Naboth's vineyard is repeated daily on the largest scale. I grieve for Abdallah-el-Habbashee and men of high position like him, sent to die by disease (or murder), in Fazoghou, but I grieve still more over the daily anguish of the poor fellaheen, who are forced to take the bread from the mouths of their starving families and to eat it while toiling for the private profit of one man. Egypt is one vast 'plantation' where the master works his slaves without even feeding them. From my window now I see the men limping about among the poor camels that are waiting for the Pasha's boats to take them, and the great heaps of maize which they are forced to bring for their food. I can tell you the tears such a sight brings to one's eyes are hot and bitter. These are no sentimental grievances; hunger, and pain, and labour without hope and without reward, and the constant bitterness of impotent resentment. To you all this must sound remote and almost fabulous. But try to imagine Farmer Smith's team driven off by the police and himself beaten till he delivered his hay, his oats and his farm-servant for the use of the Lord Lieutenant, and his two sons dragged in chains to work at railway embankments—and you will have some idea of my state of mind to-day. I fancy from the number of troops going up to Assouan that there is another rising among the blacks. Some of the black regiments revolted up in the Soudan last summer, and now I hear Shaheen Pasha is to be here in a day or two on his way up, and the camels are being sent off by hundreds from all the villages every day. But I am weary of telling, and you will sicken of hearing my constant lamentations.

Sheykh Hassan dropped in and dined with me yesterday and described his mother and her high-handed rule over him. It seems he had a 'jeunesse orageuse' and she defended him against his father's displeasure, but when the old Sheykh died she informed her son that if he ever again behaved in a manner unworthy of a Sheykh-el-Arab she would not live to see it. 'Now if my mother told me to jump into the river and drown I should say *hader* (ready), for I fear her exceedingly and love her above all people in the world, and have left everything in her hand.' He was good enough to tell me that I was the only woman he knew like his mother and that was why he loved me so much. I am to visit this Arab Deborah at the Abab'deh village two days ride from the first Cataract. She will come and meet me at the boat. Hassan was splendid when he said how he feared his mother exceedingly.

To my amazement to-day in walked the tremendous Alim from Tunis, Sheykh Abd-el-Moutovil, who used to look so black at me. He was very civil and pleasant and asked no end of questions about steam engines, and telegraphs and chemistry; especially whether it was true that the Europeans still fancied they could make gold. I said that no one had believed that for nearly two hundred years, and he said that the Arabs also knew it was 'a lie,' and he wondered to hear that Europeans, who were so clever, believed it. He had just been across the Nile to see the tombs of the Kings and of course 'improved the occasion' and uttered a number of the usual fine sayings about the vanity of human things. He told me I was the only Frank he had ever spoken to. I observed he did not say a word about religion, or use the usual pious phrases. By the bye, Sheykh Yussuf filled up my inkstand for me the other evening and in pouring the ink said 'Bismillah el-Rachman el-Racheem' (In the name of God, the merciful, the compassionate). I said 'I like that custom, it is good to remind us that ink may be a cruel poison or a good medicine.'

I am better, and have hardly any cough. The people here think it is owing to the intercession of Abu-l-Hajjaj who specially protects me. I was obliged to be wrapped in the green silk cover of his tomb when it was taken off to be carried in procession, partly for my health and general welfare, and as a sort of adoption into the family. I made a feeble resistance on the score of being a Nazraneeyeh, but was told 'Never fear, does not God know thee and the Sheykh also? no evil will come to thee on that account but good.' And I rather think that general goodwill and kindness is wholesome.

To Miss Austin

LUXOR,
February 7, 1865.

MY DEAREST CHARLEY,

I am tolerably well, but I am growing very homesick—or rather children-sick. As the time slips on I get more and more the feeling of all I am losing of my children. We have delicious weather here and have had all the time; there has been no cold at all this winter here.

M. Prévost Paradol* is here for a few days—a very pleasant man indeed, and a little good European talk is a very agreeable interlude to the Arab prosiness, or rather *enfantillage*, on the part of the women. I have sought about for shells and a few have been brought me from the Cataract, but of snails I can learn no tidings nor have I ever seen one, neither can I discover that there are any shells in the Nile mud. At the first Cataract they are found sticking to the rocks. The people here are very stupid about natural objects that are of no use to them. Like with the French small birds are all sparrows, and wild flowers there are none, and only about five varieties of trees in all Egypt.

This is a sad year—all the cattle are dead, the Nile is now as low as it was last July, and the song of the men watering with the *shadoofs* sounds sadly true as they chant *Ana ga-ahn*, etc.

'I am hungry, I am hungry for a piece of dourrah bread,' sings one, and the other chimes in, *Meskeen, meskeen* 'Poor man, poor man,' or else they sing a song about Seyyidna Iyoob 'Our master Job' and his patience. It is sadly appropriate now and rings on all sides as the *shadoofs* are greatly multiplied for lack of oxen to turn the *sakiahs* (waterwheels). All is terribly dear, and many are sick from sheer weakness owing to poor food; and then I hear fifty thousand are to be taken to work at the canal from Geezeh to Siout through the Fayoum. The only comfort is the enormous rise of wages, which however falls heavy on the rich. The sailors who got forty to fifty piastres five years ago now get three to five hundred piastres a month. So I fear I must give up my project of a dahabieh. If the new French Consul-General 'knows not Joseph' and turns me out, I am to live in a new house which Sheykh Yussuf is now building and of which he would give me the terrace and build three rooms on it for me. I wish I got better or worse, and could go home. I do get better, but *so* slowly, I cough a good deal at times, and I am very thin, but not so weak as I was or so breathless.

To Sir Alexander Duff Gordon

LUXOR,
February 7, 1865.

DEAREST ALICK,

I am enjoying a 'great indulgence of talk' with M. Prévost Paradol as heartily as any nigger. He is a delightful person. This evening he is coming with Arakel Bey, his Armenian companion, and I will invite a few Arabs to show him. I sent off the proofs yesterday per passenger steamer. I trust they will arrive safe. It is too disheartening about letters, so many are lost. I am dreadfully disappointed in my letters, I *really* don't think them good—you know I don't *blaguer* about my own performances. I am very glad people like my Cape letters which I forget—but honestly I don't think the Egyptian good. You know I don't 'pretend' if I think I have done something well and I was generally content with my translations, but I feel these all to be poor and what Maurice calls 'dry' when I know how curious and interesting and poetical the country really is.

I paid Fadil Pasha a visit on his boat, and it was just like the middle ages. In order to amuse me he called up a horrid little black boy of about four to do tricks like a dancing dog, which ended in a performance of the Mussulman prayer. The little beast was dressed in a Stamboulee dress of scarlet cloth.

All the Arab doctors come to see me now as they go up and down the river to give me help if I want it. Some are very pleasant men. Mourad Effendi speaks German exactly like a German. The old Sheykh-el-Beled of Erment who visits me whenever he comes here, and has the sweetest voice I ever heard, complained of the climate of Cairo. 'There is no sun there at all, it is no brighter or warmer than the moon.' What do you think our sun must be now you know Cairo. We have had a glorious winter, like the finest summer weather at home only so much finer.

Janet wishes to go with me if I go to Soden, I must make enquiries about the climate. Ross fears it is too cold for an Egyptian like me. I should enjoy to have all the family *au grand complet*. I will leave Luxor in May and get to you towards the latter part of June, if that pleases you, *Inshallah!*

To Mrs. Ross

LUXOR,
February 7, 1865.

DEAREST JANET,

It is quite heartrending about my letters. I have 'got the eye' evidently. The black slave of the poor dragoman who died in my house is here still, and like a dog that has lost his master has devoted himself to me. It seems nobody's business to take him away—as the Kadee did the money and the goods—and so it looks as if I should quietly inherit poor ugly Khayr. He is of a degree of ugliness quite transcendent, with teeth filed sharp 'in order to eat people' as he says, but the most good-humoured creature and a very fair laundry-maid. It is evidently no concern of mine to send him to be sold in Cairo, so I wait the event. If nobody ever claims him I shall keep him at whatever wages may seem fit, and he will subside into liberty. *Du reste*, the Maōhn here says he is legally entitled to his freedom. If the new French Consul-General will let me stay on here I will leave my furniture and come down straight to your hospitable roof in Alexandria *en route* for Europe. I fear my plan of a dahabieh of my own would be too expensive, the wages of common boatmen now are three napoleons a month. M. Prévost Paradol, whose company has been a real *bonne fortune* to me, will speak to the Consul-General. I know all Thebes would sign a round-robin in my favour if they only knew how, for I am very popular here, and the only *Hakeen*. I have effected some brilliant cures, and get lots of presents. Eggs, turkeys, etc., etc., it is quite a pleasure to see how the poor people instead of trying to sponge on one are anxious to make a return for kindness. I give nothing whatever but my physick. These country people are very good. A nice young Circassian Cawass sat up with a stranger, a dying Englishman, all night because I had doctored his wife. I have also a pupil, Mustapha's youngest boy, a sweet intelligent lad who is pining for an education. I wish he could go to England. He speaks English very well and reads and writes indifferently, but I never saw a boy so wild to learn. Is it difficult to get a boy into the Abbassieh college? as it is gratuitous I suppose it is. I quite grieve over little Achmet forced to dawdle away his time and his faculties here.

To Mrs. Austin

Luxor,
March 13, 1865.

Dearest Mutter,

I hope your mind has not been disturbed by any rumours of 'battle, murder and sudden death' up in our part of the world. A week ago we heard that a Prussian boat had been attacked, all on board murdered, and the boat burned; then that ten villages were in open revolt, and that Effendina (the Viceroy) himself had come up and 'taken a broom and swept them clean' *i.e.*—exterminated the inhabitants. The truth now appears to be that a crazy darweesh has made a disturbance—but I will tell it as I heard it. He did as his father likewise did thirty years ago, made himself *Ism* (name) by repeating one of the appellations of God, like *Ya Latif* three thousand times every night for three years which rendered him invulnerable. He then made friends with a Jinn who taught him many more tricks—among others, that practised in England by the Davenports of slipping out of any bonds. He then deluded the people of the desert by giving himself out as *El-Mahdi* (he who is to come with the Lord Jesus and to slay Antichrist at the end of the world), and proclaimed a revolt against the Turks. Three villages below Keneh—Gau, Rayanaeh and Bedeh took part in the disturbance, and Fodl Pasha came up with steamboats, burnt the villages, shot about one hundred men and devastated the fields. At first we heard one thousand were shot, now it is one hundred. The women and children will be distributed among other villages. The darweesh some say is killed, others that he is gone off into the desert with a body of bedaween and a few of the fellaheen from the three ravaged villages. Gau is a large place—as large, I think as Luxor. The darweesh is a native of Salamieh, a village close by here, and yesterday his brother, a very quiet man, and his father's father-in-law old Hajjee Sultan were carried off prisoners to Cairo, or Keneh, we don't know which. It seems that the boat robbed belonged to Greek traders, but no one was hurt, I believe, and no European boat has been molested.

Baron Kevenbrinck was here yesterday with his wife, and they saw all the sacking of the villages and said no resistance was offered by the people whom the soldiers shot down as they ran, and they saw the sheep etc. being driven off by the soldiers. You need be in no alarm about me. The darweesh and his followers could not pounce on us as we are eight good miles from the desert, *i.e.* the mountain, so we must have timely notice, and we have arranged that if they appear in the neighbourhood the women and children of the outlying huts should come into my house which is a regular fortress, and also any travellers in boats, and we muster little short of seven hundred men able to fight including Karnac, moreover Fodl Pasha and the troops are at Keneh only forty miles off.

Three English boats went down river to-day and one came up. The Kevenbrincks went up last night. I dined with them, she is very lively and pleasant. I nearly died of laughing to-day when little Achmet came for his lesson. He pronounced that he was sick of love for her. He played at cards with her yesterday afternoon and it seems lost his heart (he is twelve and quite a boyish boy, though a very clever one) and he said he was wishing to play a game for a kiss as the stake. He had put on a turban to-day, on the strength of his passion, to look like a man, and had neglected his dress otherwise because 'when young men are sick of love they always do so.' The fact is the Baroness was kind and amiable and tried to amuse him as she would have done to a white boy, hence Achmet's susceptible heart was 'on fire for her.' He also asked me if I had any medicine to make him white, I suppose to look lovely in her eyes. He little knows how very pretty he is with his brown face—as he sits cross-legged on the carpet at my feet in his white turban and blue shirt reading aloud—he was quite a picture. I have grown very fond of the little fellow, he is so eager to learn and to improve and so remarkably clever.

My little Achmet, who is donkey-boy and general little slave, the smallest slenderest quietest little creature, has implored me to take him with me to England. I wish Rainie could see him, she would be so 'arprized' at his dark brown little face, so *fein*, and with eyes like a dormouse. He is a true little Arab—can run all day in the heat, sleeps on the stones and eats anything—quick, gentle and noiseless and fiercely jealous. If I speak to any other boy he rushes at him and drives him away, and while black Khayr was in the house, he suffered martyrdom and the kitchen was a scene of incessant wrangle about the coffee. Khayr would bring me my coffee and Achmet resented the usurpation of his functions—of course quite hopelessly, as Khayr was a great stout black of eighteen and poor little Achmet not bigger than Rainie. I am really tempted to adopt the vigilant active little creature.

March 15.—Sheykh Yussuf returned from a visit to Salamieh last night. He tells me the darweesh Achmet et-Tayib is not dead, he believes that he is a mad fanatic and a communist. He wants to divide all property equally and to kill all the Ulema and destroy all theological teaching by learned men and to preach a sort of revelation or interpretation of the Koran of his own. 'He would break up your pretty clock,' said Yussuf, 'and give every man a broken wheel out of it, and so with all things.'

One of the dragomans here had been urging me to go down but Yussuf laughed at any idea of danger, he says the people here have fought the bedaween before and will not be attacked by such a handful as are out in the mountain now; *du reste* the Abu-l-Hajjajieh (family of Abu-l-Hajjaj) will 'put their seal' to it that I am their sister and answer for me with a man's life. It would be foolish to go down into whatever disturbance there may be alone in a small country boat and where I am not known. The Pasha himself we hear is at Girgeh with steamboats and soldiers, and if the slightest fear should arise steamers will be sent up to fetch all the Europeans. What I grieve over is the poor villagers whose little property is all confiscated, guilty and innocent alike, and many shot as they ran away. Hajjee Ali tells me privately that he believes the discontent against the Government is very deep and universal and that there will be an outbreak—but not yet. The Pasha's attempt to regulate the price of food by edicts has been very disastrous, and of course the present famine prices are laid to his charge—if a man will be omnipotent he must take the consequences when he fails. I don't believe in an outbreak—I think the people are too thoroughly accustomed to suffer and to obey, besides they have no means of communication, and the steamboats can run up and down and destroy them *en détail* in a country which is eight hundred miles long by from one to eight wide, and thinly peopled. Only Cairo could do anything, and everything is done to please the Cairenes at the expense of the fellaheen.

The great heat has begun these last three days. My cough is better and I am grown fatter again. The Nile is so low that I fancy that six weeks or two months hence I shall have to go down in two little boats—even now the dahabiehs keep sticking fast continually. I have promised some neighbours to bring back a little seed corn for them, some of the best English wheat without beard. All the wheat here is bearded and they have an ambition for some of ours. I long to bring them wheelbarrows and spades and pickaxes. The great folks get steamploughs, but the labourers work with their bare hands and a rush basket *pour tout potage*, and it takes six to do the work of one who has got good tools.

To Mrs. Ross

LUXOR,
March 25, 1865.

DEAREST JANET,

I hope you have not had visions of me plundered and massacred by the crazy darweesh who has caused the destruction of Gau and three other villages. I assure you we are quite quiet here and moreover have arranged matters for our defence if Achmet et Tayib should honour us with a visit. The heat has just set in, thermometer 89° to-day, of course I am much better, fatter and cough less.

Many thanks to Henry about Achmet Ibn-Mustapha, but his father is going to send him to England into Mr. Fowler's workshop, which will be a much better training I think. Mr. Fowler takes him without a premium most kindly. Lord Dudley will tell you what a splendid entertainment I gave him; I think he was quite frightened at the sight of the tray and the black fingers in the dishes.

The Abab'deh Sheykh and his handsome brother propose to take me to the moolid of Sheykh-el-Shadhilee (the coffee saint) in the desert to see all the wild Abab'deh and Bishareeyeh. It is very tempting, if I feel pretty well I must go I think and perhaps the change might do me good. They believe no European ever went to that festival. There are camel-races and a great show of pretty girls says the handsome Hassan. A fine young Circassian cawass here has volunteered to be my servant anywhere and to fight anybody for me because I have cured his pretty wife. You would love Kursheed with his clear blue eyes, fair face and brisk neat soldierly air. He has a Crimean medal and such a lot of daggers and pistols and is such a tremendous Muslim, but never-the-less he loves me and tells me all his affairs and how tiresome his wife's mother is. I tell him all wives' mothers always are, but he swears *Wallahi*, *Howagah* (Mr.) Ross don't say so, *Wallahi*, *Inshallah!*

To Sir Alexander Duff Gordon

LUXOR,
March 30, 1865.

DEAREST ALICK,

I have just received your letter of March 3 with one from Janet, which shows of how little moment the extermination of four villages is in this country, for she does not allude to our revolt and evidently has not heard of it.

In my last letter to Mutter I told how one Achmet et Tayib, a mad darweesh had raised a riot at Gau below Keneh and how a boat had been robbed and how we were all rather looking out for a *razzia* and determined to fight Achmet et Tayib and his followers. Then we called them *harámee* (wicked ones) and were rather blood-thirstily disposed towards them and resolved to keep order and protect our property. But now we say *nas messakeen* (poor people) and whisper to each other that God will not forget what the Pasha has done. The truth of course we shall never know. But I do know that one Pasha said he had hanged five hundred, and another that he had sent three hundred to Fazoghlou (*comme qui dirait Cayenne*) and all for the robbery of one Greek boat in which only the steersman was killed. I cannot make out that anything was done by the 'insurgents' beyond going out into the desert to listen to the darweesh's nonsense, and 'see a reed shaken by the wind;' the party that robbed the boat was, I am told, about forty strong. But the most horrid stories are current among the people of the atrocities committed on the wretched villagers by the soldiers. Not many were shot, they say, and they attempted no resistance, but the women and girls were outraged and murdered and the men hanged and the steamers loaded with plunder. The worst is that every one believes that the Europeans aid and abet, and all declare that the Copts were spared to please the *Frangees*. Mind I am not telling you *facts* only what the people are saying—in order to show you their feelings. One most respectable young man sat before me on the floor the other day and told me what he had heard from those who had come up the river. Horrible tales of the stench of the bodies which are left unburied by the Pasha's order—of women big with child ripped open, etc., etc. 'Thou knowest oh! our Lady, that we are people of peace in this place, and behold now if one madman should come and a few idle fellows go out to the mountain (desert) with him, Effendina will send his soldiers to destroy the place and spoil our poor little girls and hang us—is that right, oh Lady? and Achmet el-Berberi saw Europeans with hats in the steamer with Effendina and the soldiers. Truly in all the world none are miserable like us Arabs. The Turks beat us, and the Europeans hate us and say *quite right*. By God, we had better lay down our heads in the dust (die) and let the strangers take our land and grow cotton for themselves. As for me I am tired of this miserable life and of fearing for my poor little girls.'

Mahommed was really eloquent, and when he threw his *melayeh* over his face and sobbed, I am not ashamed to say that I cried too. I know very well that Mahommed was not quite wrong in what he says of the Europeans. I know the cruel old platitudes about governing Orientals by fear which the English pick up like mocking birds from the Turks. I know all about 'the stick' and 'vigour' and all that—but—'I sit among the people' and I know too that Mohammed feels just as John Smith or Tom Brown would feel in his place, and that men who were very savage against the rioters in the beginning, are now almost in a humour to rise against the Turks themselves just exactly as free-born Britons might be. There are even men of the class who have something to lose who express their disgust very freely.

I saw the steamer pass up to Fazoghlou but the prisoners were all below. The Sheykh of the Abab'deh here has had to send a party of his men to guard them through the desert. Altogether this year is miserable in Egypt. I have not once heard the *zaghareet*. Every one is anxious and depressed, and I fear hungry, the land is parched from the low Nile, the heat has set in six weeks earlier than usual, the animals are scarecrows for want of food, and now these horrid stories of bloodshed and cruelty and robbery (for the Pasha takes the lands of these villages for his own) have saddened every face. I think Hajjee Ali is right and that there will be more disturbances. If there are they will be caused by the cruelty and oppression at Gau and the three neighbouring villages. From Salamieh, two miles above Luxor, every man woman and child in any degree kin to Achmet et-Tayib has been taken in chains to Keneh and no one here expects to see one of them return alive. Some are remarkably good men, I hear, and I have heard men say 'if Hajjee Sultan is killed and all his family we will never do a good action any more, for we see it is of no use.'

There was a talk among the three or four Europeans here at the beginning of the rumours of a revolt of organising a defence among

Christians only. Conceive what a silly and gratuitous provocation! There was no religion in the business at all and of course the proper person to organise defence was the Maōhn, and he and Mustapha and others had planned using my house as a castle and defending that in case of a visit from the rioters. I have no doubt the true cause of the row is the usual one—hunger—the high price of food. It was like our Swing, or bread riots, nothing more and a very feeble affair too. It is curious to see the travellers' gay dahabiehs just as usual and the Europeans as far removed from all care or knowledge of the distresses as if they were at home. When I go and sit with the English I feel almost as if they were foreigners to me too, so completely am I now *Bint el-Beled* (daughter of the country) here.

I dined three days running with the Kevenbrincks and one day after dinner we sent for a lot of Arab Sheykhs to come for coffee—the two Abab'deh and a relation of theirs from Khartoum, the Sheykh of Karnac, one Mohammed a rich fellah, and we were joined by the A'gha of Halim Pasha's Hareem, and an ugly beast he is. The little Baroness won all hearts. She is a regular *vif argent* or as we say *Efreeteh* and to see the dark faces glittering with merry smiles as they watched her was very droll. I never saw a human being so thoroughly amused as the black Sheykh from the Soudan. Next day we dined at the Austrian agent's and the Baroness at last made the Maōhn dance a polka with her while the agent played the guitar. There were a lot of Copts about who nearly died of laughing and indeed so did I. Next day we had a capital dinner at Mustapha's, and the two Abab'deh Sheykhs, the Sheykh of Karnac, the Maōhn and Sheykh Yussuf dined with us. The Sheykh of Karnac gave a grand performance of eating like a Bedawee. I have heard you talk of *tripas elasticas* in Spain but *Wallahi!* anything like the performance of Sheykh Abdallah none but an eyewitness could believe. How he plucked off the lamb's head and handed it to me in token of the highest respect, and how the bones cracked beneath his fingers—how huge handfuls of everything were chucked right down his throat all scorching hot. I encouraged him of course, quoting the popular song about 'doing deeds that Antar did not' and we all grew quite uproarious. When Sheykh Abdallah asked for drink, I cried 'bring the *ballaree* (the big jar the women fetch water in) for the Sheykh,' and Sheykh Yussuf compared him to Samson and to Og, while I more profanely told how Antar broke the bones and threw them about. The little Baroness was delighted and only expressed herself hurt that no one had crammed anything into her mouth. I told the Maōhn her disappointment which caused more laughter as such a custom is unknown here, but he of course made no end of sweet speeches to her. After dinner she showed the Arabs how ladies curtsey to the Queen in England, and the Abab'deh acted the ceremonial of presentation at the court of Darfour, where you have to rub your nose in the dust at the King's feet. Then we went out with lanterns and torches and the Abab'deh did the sword dance for us. Two men with round shields and great straight swords do it. One dances a *pas seul* of challenge and defiance with prodigious leaps and pirouettes and Hah! Hahs! Then the other comes and a grand fight ensues. When the handsome Sheykh Hassan (whom you saw in Cairo) bounded out it really was heroic. All his attitudes were alike grand and graceful. They all wanted Sheykh Yussuf to play *el-Neboot* (single stick) and said he was the best man here at it, but his sister was not long dead and he could not. Hassan looks forward to Maurice's coming here to teach him 'the fighting of the English.' How Maurice would pound him!

On the fourth night I went to tea in Lord Hopetoun's boat and their sailors gave a grand *fantasia* excessively like a Christmas pantomime. One danced like a woman, and there was a regular pantaloon only 'more so,' and a sort of clown in sheepskin and a pink mask who was duly tumbled about, and who distributed *claques* freely with a huge wooden spoon. It was very good fun indeed, though it was quite as well that the ladies did not understand the dialogue, or that part of the dance which made the Maōhn roar with laughter. The Hopetouns had two handsome boats and were living like in May Fair. I am so used now to our poor shabby life that it makes quite a strange impression on me to see all that splendour—splendour which a year or two ago I should not even have remarked—and thus out of 'my inward consciousness' (as Germans say), many of the peculiarities and faults of the people of Egypt are explained to me and accounted for.

April 2.—It is so dreadfully hot and dusty that I shall rather hasten my departure if I can. The winds seem to have begun, and as all the land which last year was green is now desert and dry the dust is four times as bad. If I hear that Ross has bought and sent up a dahabieh I will wait for that, if not I will go in three weeks if I can.

To Mrs. Austin

LUXOR,
April 3, 1865.

DEAREST MUTTER,

I have just finished a letter to Alick to go by a steamer to-day. You will see it, so I will go on with the stories about the riots. Here is a thing happening within a few weeks and within sixty miles, and already the events assume a legendary character. Achmet et-Tayib is not dead and where the bullets hit him he shows little marks like burns. The affair began thus: A certain Copt had a Muslim slave-girl who could read the Koran and who served him. He wanted her to be his Hareem and she refused and went to Achmet et-Tayib who offered money for her to her master. He refused it and insisted on his rights, backed by the Government, and thereupon Achmet proclaimed a revolt and the people, tired of taxes and oppressions, said 'we will go with thee.' This is the only bit of religious legend connected with the business. But Achmet et-Tayib still sits in the Island, invisible to the Turkish soldiers who are still there.

Now for a little fact. The man who told me fourteen hundred had been beheaded was Hassan Sheykh of the Abab'deh who went to Gau to bring up the prisoners. The boat stopped a mile above Luxor, and my Mohammed, a most quiet respectable man and not at all a romancer went up in her to El-Moutaneh. I rode with him along the Island. When we came near the boat she went on as far as the point of the Island, and I turned back after only looking at her from the bank and smelling the smell of a slave-ship. It never occurred to me, I own, that the Bey on board had fled before a solitary woman on a donkey, but so it was. He told the Abab'deh Sheykh on board not to speak to me or to let me on board, and told the Captain to go a mile or two further. Mohammed heard all this. He found on board 'one hundred prisoners less two' (ninety-eight). Among them the Moudir of Souhaj, a Turk, in chains and wooden handcuffs like the rest. Mohammed took him some coffee and was civil to him. He says the poor creatures are dreadfully ill-used by the Abab'deh and the Nubians (Berberi) who guard them.

It is more curious than you can conceive to hear all the people say. It is just like going back four or five centuries at least, but with the heterogeneous element of steamers, electric telegraphs and the Bey's dread of the English lady's pen—at least Mohammed attributed his flight to fear of that weapon. It was quite clear that European eyes were dreaded, as the boat stopped three miles above Luxor and its dahabiehs, and had all its things carried that distance.

Yussuf and his uncle want to take me next year to Mecca, the good folks in Mecca would hardly look for a heretical face under the green veil of a *Shereefateh* of Abu-l-Hajjaj. The Hajjees (pilgrims) have just started from here to Cosseir with camels and donkeys, but most are on foot. They are in great numbers this year. The women chanted and drummed all night on the river bank, and it was fine to see fifty or sixty men in a line praying after their Imám with the red glow of the sunset behind them. The prayer in common is quite a drill and very stately to see. There are always quite as many women as men; one wonders how they stand the march and the hardships.

My little Achmet grows more pressing with me to take him. I will take him to Alexandria, I think, and leave him in Janet's house to learn more house service. He is a dear little boy and very useful. I don't suppose his brother will object and he has no parents. Achmet ibn-Mustapha also coaxes me to take him with me to Alexandria, and to try again to persuade his father to send him to England to Mr. Fowler. I wish most heartily I could. He is an uncommon child in every way, full of ardour to learn and do something, and yet childish and winning and full of fun. His pretty brown face is quite a pleasure to me. His remarks on the New Testament teach me as many things as I can teach him. The boy is pious and not at all ill taught, he is much pleased to find so little difference between the teaching of the Koran and the *Aangeel.* He wanted me, in case Omar did not go with me, to take him to serve me. Here there is no idea of its being derogatory for a gentleman's son to wait on one who teaches him, it is positively incumbent. He does all 'menial offices' for his mother, hands coffee, waits at table or helps Omar in anything if I have company, nor will he eat or smoke before me, or sit till I tell him—it is like service in the middle ages.

To Mrs. Ross

LUXOR,
April 3, 1865.

DEAREST JANET,

The weather has set in so horrid, as to dust, that I shall be glad to get away as soon as I can. If you have bought a dahabieh for me of course I will await its arrival. If not I will have two small boats from Keneh, whereby I shall avoid sticking in this very low water. Sheykh Hassan goes down in his boat in twenty days and urges me to travel under his escort, as of course the poor devils who are 'out on their keeping' after the Gau business have no means of living left but robbery, and Sheykh Hassan's party is good for seven or eight guns. You will laugh at my listening to such a cowardly proposition (on my part) but my friends here are rather bent upon it, and Hassan is a capital fellow. If therefore the dahabieh is *in rerum naturæ* and can start at once, well and good.

April 14.—The dahabieh sounds an excellent bargain to me and good for you also to get your people to Assouan first. Many thanks for the arrangement.

Your version of our massacre is quite curious to us here. I know very intimately the Sheykh-el-Arab who helped to catch the poor people and also a young Turk who stood by while Fadil Pasha had the men laid down by ten at a time and chopped with pioneers' axes. My Turkish friend (a very good-humoured young fellow) quite admired the affair and expressed a desire to do likewise to all the fellaheen in Egypt. I have seen with my own eyes a second boatload of prisoners. I wish to God the Pasha knew the deep exasperation which his subordinates are causing. I do not like to say all I hear. As to the Ulema, Kadees, Muftis, etc., I know many from towns and villages, and all say 'We are Muslims, but we should thank God to send Europeans to govern us,' the feeling is against the Government and the Turks up here—not against Christians. A Coptic friend of mine has lost all his uncle's family at Gau, all were shot down—Copt and Christian alike. As to Hajjee Sultan, who lies in chains at Keneh and his family up at Esneh, a better man never lived, nor one more liberal to Christians. Copts ate of his bread as freely as Muslims. He lies there because he is distantly related by marriage to Achmet et-Tayib, the real reason is because he is wealthy and some enemy covets his goods.

Ask M. Mounier what he knows. Perhaps I know even more of the feeling as I am almost adopted by the Abu-l-Hajjajeeah, and sit every evening with some party or another of decent men. I assure you I am in despair at all I see—and if the soldiers do come it will be worse than the cattle disease. Are not the cawasses bad enough? Do they not buy in the market at their own prices and beat the sakkas in sole payment for the skins of water? Who denies it here? Cairo is like Paris, things are kept sweet there, but up here—! Of course Effendina hears the 'smooth prophecies' of the tyrants whom he sends up river. When I wrote before I knew nothing certain but now I have eye-witnesses' testimony, and I say that the Pasha deceives or is deceived—I hope the latter. An order from him did stop the slaughter of women and children which Fadil Pasha was about to effect.

To turn to less wretched matters. I will come right down Alexandria with the boat, I shall rejoice to see you again.

Possibly the Abab'deh may come with me and I hope Sheykh Yussuf, 'my chaplain' as Arthur Taylor called him. We shall be quite a little fleet.

To Sir Alexander Duff Gordon

April, 1865.

Dearest Alexander,

Yesterday was the Bairam I rejoice to say and I have lots of physic to make up, for all the stomachs damaged by Ramadan.

I have persuaded Mr. Fowler the engineer who was with Lord Dudley to take my dear little pupil Achmet son of Ibn Mustapha to learn the business at Leeds instead of idling in his father's house here. I will give the child a letter to you in case he should go to London. He has been reading the gospels with me at his own desire. I refused till I had asked his father's consent, and Sheykh Yussuf who heard me begged me by all means to make him read it carefully so as to guard him against the heretical inventions he might be beset with among the English 'of the vulgar sort.' What a poser for a missionary!

I sent down the poor black lad with Arakel Bey. He took leave of me with his ugly face all blubbered like a sentimental hippopotamus. He said 'for himself, he wished to stay with me, but then what would his boy, his little master do—there was only a stepmother who would take all the money, and who else would work for the boy?' Little Achmet was charmed to see Khayr go, of whom he chose to be horribly jealous, and to be wroth at all he did for me. Now the Sheykh-el-Beled of Baidyeh has carried off my watchman, and the Christian Sheykh-el-Hara of our quarter of Luxor has taken the boy

Yussuf for the Canal. The former I successfully resisted and got back Mansoor, not indeed *incolumes* for *he* had been handcuffed and bastinadoed to make *me* pay 200 piastres, but he bore it like a man rather than ask me for the money and was thereupon surrendered. But the Copt will be a tougher business—he will want more money and be more resolved to get it. *Veremus*. I must I suppose go to the Nazir at the Canal—a Turk—and beg off my donkey boy.

I saw Hassan Sheykh-el-Abab'deh yesterday, who was loud in praise of your good looks and gracious manners. 'Mashallah, thy master is a sweet man, O Lady!'

Yesterday was Bairam, and lots of Hareem came in their best clothes to wish me a happy year and enjoyed themselves much with sweet cakes, coffee, and pipes. Kursheed's wife (whom I cured completely) looked very handsome. Kursheed is a Circassian, a fine young fellow much shot and hacked about and with a Crimean medal. He is cawass here and a great friend of mine. He says if I ever want a servant he will go with me anywhere and fight anybody—which I don't doubt in the least. He was a Turkish memlook and his condescension in wishing to serve a Christian woman is astounding. His fair face and clear blue eyes, and brisk, neat, soldier-like air contrast curiously with the brown fellaheen. He is like an Englishman only fairer and like them too fond of the courbash. What would you say if I appeared in Germany attended by a memlook with pistols, sword, dagger, carbine and courbash, and with a decided and imperious manner the very reverse of the Arab softness—and such a Muslim too—prays five times a day and extra fasts besides Ramadan. 'I beat my wife' said Kursheed, 'oh! I beat her well! she talked so, and I am like the English, I don't like too many words.' He was quite surprised that I said I was glad *my* master didn't dislike talking so much.

I was talking the other day with Yussuf about people trying to make converts and I said that eternal bêtise, 'Oh they mean well.' 'True, oh Lady! perhaps they do mean well, but God says in the Noble Koran that he who injures or torments those Christians whose conduct is not evil, merely on account of religion, shall never smell the fragrance of the Garden (paradise). Now when men begin to want to make others change their faith it is extremely hard for them *not* to injure or torment them and therefore I think it better to abstain altogether and to wish rather to see a Christian a good Christian and a Muslim a good Muslim.'

No wonder a most pious old Scotchman told me that the truth which undeniably existed in the Mussulman faith was the work of Satan and the Ulema his *meenesters*. My dear saint of a Yussuf a *meenester* of Satan! I really think I *have* learnt some 'Muslim humility' in that I endured the harangue, and accepted a two-penny tract quite mildly and politely and didn't argue at all. As his friend 'Satan' would have it, the Fikees were reading the Koran in the hall at Omar's expense who gave a Khatmeh that day, and Omar came in and politely offered him some sweet prepared for the occasion. I have been really amazed at several instances of English fanaticism this year. Why do people come to a Mussulman country with such bitter hatred 'in their stomachs' as I have seen three or four times. I feel quite hurt often at the way the people here thank me for what the poor at home would turn up their noses at. I think hardly a dragoman has been up the river since Rashedee died but has come to thank me as warmly as if I had done himself some great service—and many to give some little present. While the man was ill numbers of the fellaheen brought eggs, pigeons, etc. etc. even a turkey, and food is worth money now, not as it used to be. I am quite weary too of hearing 'Of all the Frangee I never saw one like thee.' Was no one ever at all humane before? For remember I give no money—only a little physic and civility. How the British cottagers would 'thank ye for nothing'—and how I wish my neighbours here could afford to do the same.

After much wrangling Mustapha has got back my boy Yussuf but the Christian Sheykh-el-Hara has made his brother pay £2 whereat Mohammed looks very rueful. Two hundred men are gone out of our village to the works and of course the poor Hareem have not bread to eat as the men had to take all they had with them. I send you a very pretty story like Tannhäuser.

There was once a man who loved a woman that lived in the same quarter. But she was true to her husband, and his love was hopeless, and he suffered greatly. One day as he lay on his carpet sick with love, one came to him and said, O, such-a-one, thy beloved has died even now, and they are carrying her out to the tomb. So the lover arose and followed the funeral, and hid himself near the tomb, and when all were gone he broke it open, and uncovered the face of his beloved, and looked upon her, and passion overcame him, and he took from the dead that which when living she had ever denied him.

But he went back to the city and to his house in great grief and anguish of mind, and his sin troubled him. So he went to a Kadee, very pious and learned in the noble Koran, and told him his case, and said, 'Oh my master the Kadee, can such a one as I obtain salvation and the forgiveness of God? I fear not.' And the Kadee gave him a staff of polished wood which he held in his hand, and said 'Who knoweth the mercy of God and his justice, but God alone—take then this staff and stick it in the sand beside the tomb where thou didst sin and leave it the night, and go next morning and come and tell me what thou shalt find, and may the Lord pardon thee, for thy sin is great.'

And the man went and did as the Kadee had desired, and went again at sunrise, and behold the staff had sprouted and was covered with leaves and fruit. And he returned and told the Kadee what had happened, and the Kadee replied, 'Praise be to God, the merciful, the compassionate.'

To Mrs. Austin

LUXOR,
April 29, 1865.

DEAREST MUTTER,

Since I wrote last I have received the box with the cheese quite fresh (and very good it tastes), and the various things. Nothing called forth such a shout of joy from me as your photo of the village pothouse. How green and fresh and tidy! Many Mashallah's have been uttered over the *beyt-el-fellaheen* (peasant's house) of England. The railings, especially, are a great marvel. I have also heard from Janet that Ross has bought me a boat for £200 which is to take four of his agents to Assouan and then come back for me. So all my business is settled, and, *Inshallah!* I shall depart in another three or four weeks.

The weather is quite cool and fresh again but the winds very violent and the dust pours over us like water from the dried up land, as well as from the Goomeh mountain. It is miserably uncomfortable, but my health is much better again—spite of all.

The Hakeem business goes on at a great rate. I think on an average I have four sick a day. Sometimes a dozen. A whole gipsy camp are great customers—the poor souls will bring all manner of gifts it goes to my heart to eat, but they can't bear to be refused. They are astounded to hear that people of their blood live in England and that I knew many of their customs—which are the same here.

Kursheed Agha came to take final leave being appointed to Keneh. He had been at Gau and had seen Fadil Pasha sit and make the soldiers lay sixty men down on their backs by ten at a time and *chop* them to death with the pioneers' axes. He estimated the people killed—men, women, and children at 1,600—but Mounier tells me it was over 2,000. Sheykh Hassan agreed exactly with Kursheed, only the Arab was full of horror and the Circassian full of exultation. His talk was exactly what we all once heard about 'Pandies,' and he looked and talked and laughed so like a fine young English soldier, that I was ashamed to call him the kelb (dog) which rose to my tongue, and I bestowed it on Fadil Pasha instead. I must also say in behalf of my own countrymen that they *had* provocation while here there was none. Poor Haggee Sultan lies in chains at Keneh. One of the best and kindest of men! I am to go and take secret messages to him, and money from certain men of religion to bribe the Moudir with. The Shurafa who have asked me to do this are from another place, as well as a few of the Abu-l-Hajjajieh. A very great Shereef indeed from lower Egypt, said to me the other day, 'Thou knowest if I am a Muslim or no. Well, I pray to the most Merciful to send us Europeans to govern us, and to deliver us from these wicked men.' We were all sitting after the funeral of one of the Shurafa and I was sitting between the Shereef of Luxor and the Imám—and this was said before thirty or forty men, all Shurafa. No one said 'No,' and many assented aloud.

The Shereef asked me to lend him the New Testament, it was a pretty copy and when he admired it I said, 'From me to thee, oh my master the Shereef, write in it as we do in remembrance of a friend—the gift of a Nazraneeyeh who loves the Muslimeen.' The old man kissed the book and said 'I will write moreover—to a Muslim who loves all such Christians'—and after this the old Sheykh of Abou Ali took me aside and asked me to go as messenger to Haggee Sultan for if one of them took the money it would be taken from them and the man get no good by it.

Soldiers are now to be quartered in the Saeed—a new plague worse than all the rest. Do not the cawasses already rob the poor enough? They fix their own price in the market and beat the sakkas as sole payment. What will the soldiers do? The taxes are being illegally levied on lands which are *sheragi*, *i.e.* totally unwatered by the last Nile and therefore exempt *by law*—and the people are driven to desperation. I feel sure there will be more troubles as soon as there arises any other demagogue like Achmet et-Tayib to incite the people and now every Arab sympathises with him. Janet has written me the Cairo version of the affair cooked for the European taste—and monstrous it is. The Pasha accuses some Sheykh of the Arabs of having gone from Upper Egypt to India to stir up the Mutiny against us! *Pourquoi pas* to conspire in Paris or London? It is too childish to talk of a poor Saeedee Arab going to a country of whose language and whereabouts he is totally ignorant, in order to conspire against people who never hurt him. You may suppose how Yussuf and I talk by ourselves of all these things. He urged me to try hard to get my husband here as Consul-General—assuming that he would feel as I do. I said, my master is not young, and to a just man the wrong of such a place would be a martyrdom. 'Truly thou hast said it, but it is a martyr we Arabs want; shall not the reward of him who suffers daily vexation for his brethren's sake be equal to that of him who dies in battle for the faith? If thou wert a man, I would say to thee, take the labour and sorrow upon thee, and thine own heart will repay thee.' He too said like the old Sheykh, 'I only pray for Europeans to rule us—now the fellaheen are really worse off than any slaves.' I am sick of telling of the daily oppressions and robberies. If a man has a sheep, the Moodir comes and eats it, if a tree, it goes to the Nazir's kitchen. My poor sakka is beaten by the cawasses in sole payment of his skins of water—and then people wonder my poor friends tell lies and bury their money.

I now know everybody in my village and the 'cunning women' have set up the theory that my eye is lucky; so I am asked to go and look at young brides, visit houses that are building, inspect cattle, etc. as a bringer of good luck—which gives me many a curious sight.

I went a few days ago to the wedding of handsome Sheykh Hassan the Abab'deh, who married the butcher's pretty little daughter. The group of women and girls lighted by the lantern which little Achmet carried up for me was the most striking thing I have seen. The bride—a lovely girl of ten or eleven all in scarlet, a tall dark slave of Hassan's blazing with gold and silver necklaces and bracelets, with long twisted locks of coal black hair and such glittering eyes and teeth, the wonderful wrinkled old women, and the pretty, wondering, yet fearless children were beyond description. The mother brought the bride up to me and unveiled her and asked me to let her kiss my hand, and to look at her, I said all the usual *Bismillah Mashallah's*, and after a time went to the men who were eating, all but Hassan who sat apart and who begged me to sit by him, and whispered anxious enquiries about his *aroosah's* looks. After a time he went to visit her and returned in half an hour very shy and covering his face and hand and kissed the hands of the chief guests. Then we all departed and the girl was taken to look at the Nile, and then to her husband's house. Last night he gave me a dinner—a very good dinner indeed, in his house which is equal to a very poor cattle shed at home. We were only five. Sheykh Yussuf, Omar, an elderly merchant and I. Hassan wanted to serve us but I made him sit.

The merchant, a well-bred man of the world who has enjoyed life and married wives everywhere—had arrived that day and found a daughter of his dead here. He said he felt very miserable—and everyone told him not to mind and consoled him oddly enough to English ideas. Then people told stories. Omar's was a good version of the man and wife who would not shut the door and agreed that the first to speak should do it—very funny indeed. Yussuf told a pretty tale of a Sultan who married a Bint el-Arab (daughter of the Bedawee) and how she would not live in his palace, and said she was no fellaha to dwell in houses, and scorned his silk clothes and sheep killed for her daily, and made him live in the desert with her. A black slave told a prosy tale about thieves—and the rest were more long than pointed.

Hassan's Arab feelings were hurt at the small quantity of meat set before me. (They can't kill a sheep now for an honoured guest.) But I told him no greater honour could be paid to us English than to let us eat lentils and onions like one of the family, so that we might not feel as strangers among them—which delighted all the party. After a time the merchant told us his heart was somewhat dilated—as a man might say his toothache had abated—and we said 'Praise be to God' all round.

A short time ago my poor friend the Maōhn had a terrible 'tile' fall on his head. His wife, two married daughters and nine miscellaneous children arrived on a sudden, and the poor man is now tasting the pleasures which Abraham once endured between Sarah and Hagar. I visited the ladies and found a very ancient Sarah and a daughter of wonderful beauty. A young man here—a Shereef—has asked me to open negotiations for a marriage for him with the Maōhn's grand daughter a little girl of eight—so you see how completely I am 'one of the family.'

My boat has not yet made its appearance. I am very well indeed now, in spite, or perhaps because of, the great heat. But there is a great deal of sickness—chiefly dysentery. I never get less than four new patients a day and my 'practice' has become quite a serious business. I spent all day on Friday in the Abab'deh quarters where Sheykh Hassan and his slave Rahmeh were both uncommonly ill. Both are 'all right' now. Rahmeh is the nicest negro I ever knew, and a very great friend of mine. He is a most excellent, honest, sincere man, and an Effendi (*i.e.* writes and reads) which is more than his master can do. He has seen all the queer people in the interior of Africa.

The Sheykh of the Bishareen—eight days' journey from Assouan has invited me and promises me all the meat and milk I can eat, they have nothing else. They live on a high mountain and are very fine handsome people. If only I were strong I could go to very odd places where Frangees are not. Read a very stupid novel (as a story) called '*le Secret du Bonheur*'—it gives the truest impression of the manners of Arabs that I have read—by Ernest Feydeau. According to his book *achouat* (we are brothers). The 'caressant' ways of Arabs are so well described.

It is the same here. The people come and pat and stroke me with their hands, and one corner of my brown abbaieh is faded with much kissing. I am hailed as *Sitt Betaana* 'Our own Lady,' and now the people are really enthusiastic because I refused the offer of some cawasses as a guard which a Bimbashee made me. As if I would have such fellows to help to bully my friends. The said Bimbashee (next in rank to a Bey) a coarse man like an Arnoout, stopped here a day and night and played his little Turkish game, telling me to beware—for the Ulema hated all Franks and set the people against us—and telling the Arabs that Christian Hakeems were all given to poison Muslims. So at night I dropped in at the Maōhn's with Sheykh Yussuf carrying my lantern—and was loudly hailed with a *Salaam Aleykee* from the old Shereef himself—who began praising the Gospel I had given him, and me at the same time. Yussuf had a little reed in his hand—the *kalem* for writing, about two feet long and of the size of a quill. I took it and showed it to the Bimbashee and said—'Behold the *neboot* wherewith we are all to be murdered by this Sheykh of the Religion.' The Bimbashee's bristly moustache bristled savagely, for he felt that the 'Arab dogs' and the Christian *khanzeereh* (feminine pig) were laughing at it together.

Another steam boat load of prisoners from Gau has just gone up. A little comfort is derived here from the news that, 'Praise be to God, Moussa Pasha (Governor of the Soudan) is dead and gone to Hell.' It must take no trifle to send him there judging by the quiet way in which Fadil Pasha is mentioned.

You will think me a complete rebel—but I may say to you what most people would think 'like my nonsense'—that one's pity becomes a perfect passion, when one *sits among the people*—as I do, and sees it all; least of all can I forgive those among Europeans and Christians who can help to 'break these bruised reeds.' However, in Cairo and more still in Alexandria, all is quite different. There, the same system which has been so successfully copied in France prevails. The capital is petted at the expense of the fellaheen. Prices are regulated in Cairo for meat and bread as they are or were in Paris, and the 'dangerous classes' enjoy all sorts of exemptions. Just like France! The Cairenes eat the bread and the fellaheen eat the stick.

The people here used to dislike Mounier who arrived poor and grew rich and powerful, but they all bless him now and say at El-Moutaneh a man eats his own meat and not the courbash of the Moudir—and Mounier has refused soldiers (as I refused them on my small account) and 'Please God,' he will never repent it. Yussuf says 'What the Turkish Government fears is not for *your* safety, but lest we should learn to love you too well,' and it is true. Here there is but one voice. 'Let the Franks come, let us have the laws of the Christians.'

In Cairo the Franks have dispelled this *douce illusion* and done the Turk's work as if they were paid for it. But here come only travellers who pay with money and not with stick—a degree of generosity not enough to be adored.

I perceive that I am a bore—but you will forgive my indignant sympathy with the kind people who treat me so well. Yussuf asked me to let the English papers know about the Gau business. An Alim ed Deen ul-Islam would fain call for help to the Times! Strange changes and signs of the times—these—are they not so?

I went to Church on Good Friday with the Copts. The scene was very striking—the priest dressed like a beautiful Crusader in white robes with crimson crosses. One thing has my hearty admiration. The few children who are taken to Church are allowed to play! Oh my poor little Protestant fellow Christians, can you conceive a religion so delightful as that which permits Peep-bo behind the curtain of the sanctuary! I saw little Butrus and Scendariah at it all church time—and the priest only patted their little heads as he carried the sacrament out to the Hareem. Fancy the parson kindly patting a noisy boy's head, instead of the beadle whacking him! I am entirely reconciled to the Coptic rules.

To Sir Alexander Duff Gordon

NILE BOAT, *URANIA*,
May, 1865.

Happy as I was in the prospect of seeing you all and miserable as poor Upper Egypt has become, I could not leave without a pang. Our Bairam was not gay. There was horse riding for Sheykh Gibreel (the cousin of Abu'l Haggag) and the scene was prettier than ever I saw. My old friend Yunis the Shereef insisted on showing me that at eighty-five he could still handle a horse and throw a Gereed 'for Sheykh Gibreel and the Lady' as he said. Then arrived the Mufettish of Zenia with his gay attendants and filled the little square in front of the Cadi's castellated house where we were sitting. The young Sheykh of Salamieh rode beautifully and there was some excellent Neboot play (sort of very severe quarterstaff peculiar to the Fellaheen).

Next day was the great dinner given by Mohammed and Mustapha outside Mohammed's house opposite Sheykh Gibreel's tomb—200 men ate at his gate. I went to see it and was of course asked to eat. 'Can one like thee eat the Melocheea of the Fellaheen?' So I joined a party of five round a little wooden tray, tucked up my sleeve and ate—dipping the bread into the Melocheea which is like very sloppy spinach but much nicer. Then came the master and his servants to deal the pieces of meat out of a great basket—sodden meat—and like Benjamin my piece was the largest, so I tore off a bit and handed it to each of my companions, who said 'God take thee safe and happy to thy place and thy children and bring thee back to us in safety to eat the meat of the festival together once more.'

The moon rose clear and bright behind the one tall palm tree that overhangs the tomb of Sheykh Gibreel. He is a saint of homely tastes and will not have a dome over him or a cover for his tomb, which is only surrounded by a wall breast-high, enclosing a small square bit of ground with the rough tomb on one side. At each corner was set up a flag, and a few dim lanterns hung overhead. The 200 men eating were quite noiseless—and as they rose, one by one washed their hands and went, the crowd melted away like a vision. But before all were gone, came the Bulook, or sub-magistrate—a Turkish Jack in office with the manners of a Zouave turned parish beadle. He began to sneer at the *melocheea* of the fellaheen and swore he could not eat it if he sat before it 1,000 years. Hereupon, Omar began to 'chaff' him. 'Eat, oh Bulook Pasha and if it swells thy belly the Lady will give thee of the physick of the English to clean thy stomach upwards and downwards of all thou hast eaten of the food of the fellaheen.' The Bulook is notorious for his exactions—his 'eating the people'—so there was a great laugh. Poor Omar was very ill next day—and every one thought the Bulook had given him the eye.

Then came the Mufettish in state to pay his *devoirs* to the Sheykh in the tomb. He came and talked to Mustapha and Yussuf and enumerated the people taken for the works, 200 from Luxor, 400 from Carnac, 310 from Zenia, 320 from Byadyeh, and 380 from Salamieh—a good deal more than half the adult men to go for sixty days leaving their fields uncultivated and their Hareem and children hungry—for they have to take all the food for themselves.

I rose sick at heart from the Mufettish's harsh voice, and went down to listen to the Moonsheeds chanting at the tomb and the Zikheers' strange sobbing, Allah, Allah.

I leaned on the mud wall watching the slender figures swaying in the moonlight, when a tall, handsome fellah came up in his brown shirt, felt *libdeh* (skull cap), with his blue cotton *melaya* tied up and full of dried bread on his back. The type of the Egyptian. He stood close beside me and prayed for his wife and children. 'Ask our God to pity them, O Sheykh, and to feed them while I am away. Thou knowest how my wife worked all night to bake all the wheat for me and that there is none left for her and the children.' He then turned to me and took my hand and went on, 'Thou knowest this lady, oh Sheykh Gibreel, take her happy and well to her place and bring her back to us—*el Fathah, yah Beshoosheh!*' and we said it together. I could have laid my head on Sheykh Gibreel's wall and howled. I thanked him as well as I could for caring about one like me while his own troubles were so heavy. I shall never forget that tall athletic figure and the gentle brown face, with the eleven days' moon of Zulheggeh, and the shadow of the palm tree. That was my farewell. 'The voice of the miserable is with thee, shall God not hear it?'

Next day Omar had a sharp attack of fever and was delirious—it lasted only two days but left him very weak and the anxiety and trouble was great—for my helping hands were as awkward as they were willing.

In a few days arrived the boat Urania. She is very nice indeed. A small saloon, two good berths—bath and cabinet, and very large *kasneh* (stern cabin). She is dirty, but will be extremely comfortable when cleaned and painted. On the 15th we sailed. Sheykh Yussuf went with me to Keneh, Mustapha and Seyd going by land—and one of Hajjee Sultan's disciples and several Luxor men were deck passengers. The Shereef gave me the bread and jars of butter for his grandsons in Gama'l Azhar, and came to see me off. We sat on the deck outside as there was a crowd to say good-bye and had a lot of Hareem in the cabin. The old Shereef made me sit down on the carpet close to him and then said 'we sit here like two lovers'—at eighty-five *even* an Arab and a Shereef may be '*gaillard*'—so I cried, 'Oh Shereef, what if Omar tells my master the secret thou hast let out—it is not well of thee.' There was a great laugh which ended in the Shereef saying 'no doubt thy master is of the best of the people, let us say the *Fathah* for him,' and he called on all the people '*El Fathah* for the master of the lady!' I hope it has benefited you to be prayed for at Luxor.

I had written so far and passed Minieh when I fell ill with pleurisy—I've lots more to tell of my journey but am too weak after two weeks in bed (and unable to lie down from suffocation)—but I am *much* better now. A man from the Azhar is reading the Koran for me outside—while another is gone with candles to Seyeedele Zeynet 'the fanatics!'

To Sir Alexander Duff Gordon

CAIRO,
June 16, 1865.

DEAREST ALICK,

I will go down to Alexandria in the boat and Omar will work at her. She wants a great deal of repairing I find, and his superintendence will save much money—besides he will do one man's work as he is a much better carpenter than most here having learnt of the English workmen on the railroad—but the Reis says the boat must come out of the water as her bottom is unsound. She is a splendid sailer I hear and remarkably comfortable. The beds in the *kasneh* would do for Jacob Omnium. So when you 'honour our house' you will be happy. The saloon is small, and the berths as usual. Also she is a very handsome shape—but she wants no end of repairs. So Omar is consoled at being left because he will 'save our money' a great deal by piecing sails, and cutting and contriving, and scraping and painting himself. Only he is afraid for me. However, *Allah Kereem*.

I have a very good Reis I think. The usual tight little black fellow from near Assouan—very neat and active and good tempered—the same cross steersman that we had up to Bedreshayn—but he knows his work well. We had contrary gales the whole way. My men worked all they possibly could, and pulled the rope all day and rowed all night, day after day—but we were twenty-eight days getting down.

I can't write any more.

To Mrs. Austin

ALEXANDRIA,
October 28, 1865.

I am truly grieved to hear of your wrist and to see your writing look cramped. I arrived here on Thursday after a splendid passage and was very comfortable on board. I found M. Olagnier waiting for me, and Omar, of course, and am *installé* at Ross's till my boat gets done which I am told will be in six days. She will be remarkably comfortable. Omar had caused a sort of divan with a roof and back to be constructed just outside the cabin-door where I always sat every evening, which will be the most delightful little nest one can conceive. I shall sit like a Pasha there.

My cough is still very harassing, but my chest less tight and painful, and I feel less utterly knocked down. The weather is beautiful here just now—warm and not nearly so damp as usual.

Lord Edward St. Maur was on board, he has much of his aunt's pleasantness. Also a very young Bombay Merchant—a Muslim who uttered not one syllable to any one but to me. His talk was just like that of a well-bred and intelligent young Englishman. I am glad to say that his views of the state of India were very encouraging—he seemed convinced that the natives were gradually working their way up to more influence, and said 'We shall have to thank you for a better form of government by far than any native one ever would have been'—he added, 'We Muslims have this advantage over the Hindus—that our religion is no barrier at all, socially or politically—between us and you—as theirs is. I mean it ought not to be when both faiths are cleared of superstition and fanaticism.' He spoke very highly of Sir Bartle Frere* but said 'I wish it were possible for more English *gentlemen* to come out to India.' He had been two years in England on mercantile business and was going back to his brother Ala-ed-deen much pleased with the English in England. It is one of the most comforting *Erscheinungen* I have seen coming from India—if that sort of good sense is pretty common among the very young men they certainly will work their way up.

I should like to see Bayley's article though I am quite sick of my book—it is very ungracious of me, but I can't help it.

To Mrs. Austin

ALEXANDRIA,
November 2, 1865.

DEAREST MUTTER,

The boat like all other things goes but slowly—however the weather here is unusually dry and fine.

I have just been to see my poor friend Sittee Zubeydeh, widow of Hassaneyn Effendi who died in England—and I am filled with admiration at her good sense and courage. She has determined to carry on her husband's business of letting boats herself, and to educate her children to the best of her power in habits of independence. I hope she will be successful, and receive the respect such rare conduct in a Turkish woman deserves from the English. I was much gratified to hear from her how kindly she had been treated in Glasgow. She said that nothing that could be done for her was left undone. She arrived this morning and I went to see her directly and was really astonished at all she said about her plans for herself and her children. Poor thing! it is a sad blow—for she and Hassaneyn were as thoroughly united as any Europeans could be.

I went afterwards to my boat, which I hope will be done in five or six days. I am extremely impatient to be off. She will be a most charming boat—both comfortable and pretty. The boom for the big sail is new—and I exclaimed, 'why you have broken the new boom and mended it with leather!' Omar had put on a *sham splice* to avert the evil eye from such a fine new piece of wood! Of course I dare not have the blemish renewed or *gare* the first puff of wind—besides it is too characteristic.

There is some cholera about again, I hear—ten deaths yesterday—so Olagnier tells me. I fancy the rush of Europeans back again, each bringing 'seven other devils worse than himself' is the cause of it.

I think I am beginning to improve a little; my cough has been terribly harassing especially at night—but the weather is very good, cool, and not damp.

To Mrs. Austin

CAIRO,
Monday, November 27, 1865.

DEAREST MUTTER,

I arrived here last night and found a whole heap of letters—and yours I will answer first. I had no heart to write any more from Alexandria where I was worried out of all courage and strength. At last after endless delays and vexations the dahabieh was *tant bien que mal* ready.

Talk of Arab dawdle! after what I went through—and now I have to wait here for fresh repairs, as we came up baling all the way and I fear cursing the Christian workmen who had bungled so shamefully.

However that is over, and I am much better as to my cough—indeed it is all but gone. Omar was very ill having had dysentery for two months, but he too is well again. He is very grateful for your kind mention of him and says, 'Send the Great Mother my best Salaam, and tell her her daughter's people are my people, and where she goes I will go too, and please God I will serve her rich or poor till "He who separates us" shall take me from her.' The words of Ruth came after all these centuries quite fresh from the soft Egyptian lips.

The 'He who separated us' I must explain to you. It is one of the attributes of God, *The Separator of Religions* implies toleration and friendship by attributing the two religions alike to God—and is never used towards one whose religion is not to be respected.

I have got a levee of former reis's, sailors, etc. some sick—but most come to talk.

The climate changes quite suddenly as one leaves the Delta, and here I sit at eight in the evening with open doors and windows.

I am so glad to hear of the great success of my dear Father's book, and to think of your courage in working at it still.

I suppose I shall be here a week longer as I have several jobs to do to my boat, and I shall try to get towed up so as to send back the boat as soon as possible in order to let her. Ali will give £80 a month for her if he gets a party of four to take up. I pay my Reis five napoleons a month while travelling and three while lying still. He is a good, active little fellow.

We were nearly smashed under the railway bridge by an iron barge—and *Wallah!* how the Reis of the bridge did whack the Reis of the barge. I thought it a sad loss of time, but Reis Ali and my Reis Mohammed seemed to look on the stick as the most effective way of extricating my anchor from the Pasha's rudder. My crew can't say 'Urania' so they sing 'go along, oh darling bride' *Arooset er-ralee*, as the little Sitt's best description, and 'Arooset er-ralee' will be the dahabieh's exoteric name—as '*El Beshoosheeh*' is my popular name.

To Mrs. Austin

Cairo,
December 5, 1865.

Dearest Mutter,

Alhamdulillah—now I am at rest. I have got all the boat in order. My captain, Reis Mohammed, is very satisfactory, and to-day we sail as soon as Omar comes back with the meat, etc. from market.

I received Meadow's review; I wish he had not said so much about me in it.

Mohammed Gazowee begs to give his best Salaam to Sheykh Stanley whom he longs to see again. He says that all the people said he was not a Christian, for he was not proud ever towards them as Christians are, but a real Sheykh, and that the Bedaween still talk of Sheykh Stanley and of his piety. The old half-witted jester of Luxor has found me out—he has wandered down here to see his eldest son who is serving in the army. He had brought a little boy with him, but is 'afraid for him' here, I don't know why, and has begged me to take the child up to his mother. These licensed *possenreisser* are like our fools in old times—but less witty than we fancy them to have been—thanks to Shakespeare, I suppose. Each district has one who attends all *moolids* and other gatherings of the people, and picks up a living. He tells me that the Turkish Názir of Zeneea has begun some business against our Kadee, Sheykh Ibraheem, and Sheykh Yussuf, accused them of something—he does not know what—*perhaps of being friends of Hajjee Sultan, or of stealing wood!!* If all the friends of Hajjee Sultan are to be prosecuted that will include the whole Saeed.

Of course I am anxious about my friends. All Haleem Pasha Oghdee's villages have been confiscated (those tributary to him for work) *sous prétexte* that he ill-used the people, *n.b.* he alone paid them—a bad example. Pharaoh is indeed laying intolerable burthens—not on the Israelites—but on the fellaheen.

Omar said of the great dinner to-day, 'I think all the food will taste of blood, it is the blood of the poor, and more *haram* than any pork or wine or blood of beasts.' Of course such sentiments are not to be repeated—but they are general. The *meneggets* who picked and made ten mattresses and fourteen cushions for me in half a day, were laughing and saying, 'for the Pasha's boat we work also, at so much a day and we should have done it in four days.' 'And for me if I paid by the day instead of by the piece, how long?' 'One day instead of half, O Lady, for fear thou shouldest say to us, you have finished in half a day and half the wages is enough for you.' That is the way in which all the work is done for *Effendeena*—no wonder his steamers don't pay.

I saw Ross yesterday—he tells me the Shereef of Mecca has sent him a horse.

To Sir Alexander Duff Gordon

THEBES,
From December 25, 1865, *to January* 3, 1866.

DEAREST ALICK,

I wish you all, 'may the year be good to thee' as we say here—and now for my history. We left Cairo on the 5th Decr. I was not well. No wind as usual, and we were a week getting to Benisonef, where the Stamboolee Greek lady who was so kind to me last summer in my illness came on board with a very well-bred Arab lady. I was in bed, and only stayed a few hours. On to Minieh another five or six days—walked about and saw the preparations for the Pasha's arrival. Nothing so flat as these affairs here. Not a creature went near the landing-place but his own servants, soldiers, and officials. I thought of the arrival of the smallest of German princes, which makes ten times the noise. Next on to Siout. Ill again, and did not land or see anyone. On to Girgeh, where we only stayed long enough to deliver money and presents which I had been begged to take for some old sailors of mine to their mothers and wives there.

Between Siout and Girgeh an Abyssinian slave lad came and wanted me to steal him; he said his master was a Copt and ill-used him, and the lady beat him. But Omar sagely observed to the sailors, who were very anxious to take him, that a bad master did not give his slave such good clothes and even a pair of shoes—*quel luxe!*—and that he made too much of his master being a Copt; no doubt he was a lazy fellow, and perhaps had run away with other property besides himself. Soon after I was sitting on the pointed prow of the boat with the Reis, who was sounding with his painted pole (*vide* antique sculptures and paintings), and the men towing, when suddenly something rose to the surface close to us: the men cried out *Beni Adam!* and the Reis prayed for the dead. It was a woman: the silver bracelets glittered on the arms raised and stiffened in the agony of death, the knees up and the beautiful Egyptian breasts floated above the water. I shall never forget the horrid sight. 'God have mercy on her,' prayed my men, and the Reis added to me, 'let us also pray for her father, poor man: you see, no robber has done this (on account of the bracelets). We are in the Saeed now, and most likely she has blackened her father's face, and he has been forced to strangle her, poor man.' I said 'Alas!' and the Reis continued, 'ah, yes, it is a heavy thing, but a man must whiten his face, poor man, poor man. God have mercy on him.' Such is Saeedee *point d'honneur*. However, it turned out she was drowned bathing.

Above Girgeh we stopped awhile at Dishné, a large village. I strolled up alone, *les mains dans les poches*, '*sicut meus est mos*:' and was soon accosted with an invitation to coffee and pipes in the strangers' place, a sort of room open on one side with a column in the middle, like two arches of a cloister, and which in all the villages is close to the mosque: two or three cloaks were pulled off and spread on the ground for me to sit on, and the milk which I asked for, instead of the village coffee, brought. In a minute a dozen men came and sat round, and asked as usual, 'Whence comest thou, and whither goest thou?' and my gloves, watch, rings, etc. were handed round and examined; the gloves always call forth many *Mashallah's*. I said, 'I come from the Frank country, and am going to my place near Abu'l Hajjaj.' Hereupon everyone touched my hand and said, 'Praise be to God that we have seen thee. Don't go on: stay here and take 100 feddans of land and remain here.' I laughed and asked, 'Should I wear the *zaboot* (brown shirt) and the *libdeh*, and work in the field, seeing there is no man with me?' There was much laughing, and then several stories of women who had farmed large properties well and successfully. Such undertakings on the part of women seem quite as common here as in Europe, and more common than in England.

I took leave of my new friends who had given me the first welcome home to the Saeed, and we went on to Keneh, which we reached early in the morning, and I found my well-known donkey-boys putting my saddle on. The father of one, and the two brothers of the other, were gone to work on the railway for sixty days' forced labour, taking their own bread, and the poor little fellows were left alone to take care of the Hareem. As soon as we reached the town, a couple of tall young soldiers in the Nizam uniform rushed after me, and greeted me in English; they were Luxor lads serving their time. Of course they attached themselves to us for the rest of the day. We then bought water jars (the *specialité* of Keneh); *gullehs* and *zees*—and I went on to the Kadee's house to leave a little string of beads, just to show that I had not forgotten the worthy Kadee's courtesy in bringing his little daughter to sit beside me at dinner when I went down the river last summer. I saw the Kadee giving audience to several people, so I sent in the beads and my salaam; but the jolly Kadee sallied forth into the street and 'fell upon my neck' with such ardour that my Frankish hat was sent rolling by contact with the turban of Islam. The Kadee of Keneh is the real original Kadee of our early days; sleek, rubicund, polite—a puisne judge and a dean rolled into one, combining the amenities of the law and the church—with an orthodox stomach and an orthodox turban, both round and stately. I was taken into the hareem, welcomed and regaled, and invited to the festival of Seyd Abd er-Racheem, the great saint of Keneh. I hesitated, and said there were great crowds, and some might be offended at my presence; but the Kadee declared 'by Him who separated us' that if any such ignorant persons were present it was high time they learnt better, and said that it was by no means unlawful for virtuous Christians, and such as neither hated nor scorned the Muslimeen, to profit by, or share in their prayers, and that I should sit before the Sheykh's tomb with him and the Mufti; and that *du reste*, they wished to give thanks for my safe arrival. Such a demonstration of tolerance was not to be resisted. So after going back to rest, and dine in the boat, I returned at nightfall into the town and went to the burial-place. The whole way was lighted up and thronged with the most motley crowd, and the usual mixture of holy and profane, which we know at the Catholic *fêtes* also; but more *prononcé* here. Dancing girls, glittering with gold brocade and coins, swaggered about among the brown-shirted fellaheen, and the profane singing of the *Alateeyeh* mingled with the songs in honour of the Arab prophet chanted by the Moonsheeds and the deep tones of the 'Allah, Allah' of the Zikeers. Rockets whizzed about and made the women screech, and a merry-go-round was in full swing. And now fancy me clinging to the skirts of the Cadi ul Islam (who did not wear a spencer, as the Methodist parson threatened his congregation he would do at the Day of Judgment) and pushing into the tomb of the Seyd Abd er-Racheem, through such a throng. No one seemed offended or even surprised. I suppose my face is so well known at Keneh. When my party had said a *Fattah* for me and another for my family, we retired to another *kubbeh*, where there was no tomb, and where we found the Mufti, and sat there all the evening over coffee and pipes and talk. I was questioned about English administration of justice, and made to describe the process of trial by jury. The Mufti is a very dignified gentlemanly man, and extremely kind and civil. The Kadee pressed me to stay next day and dine with him and the Mufti, but I said I had a lantern for Luxor, and I wanted to arrive before the *moolid* was over, and only three days remained. So the Kadee accompanied me back to the boat, looked at my maps, which pleased him very much, traced out the line of the railway as he had heard it, and had tea.

Next morning we had the first good wind, and bowled up to Luxor in one day, arriving just after sunset. Instantly the boat was filled. Of course Omar and the Reis at once organised a procession to take me and my lantern to the tomb of Abu-l-Hajjaj—it was the last night but one of his moolid. The lantern was borne on a pole between two of my sailors, and the rest, reinforced by men from a steamer which was there with a Prussian prince, sung and thumped the tarabookeh, and we all marched up after I had undergone every variety of salutation, from Sheykh Yussuf's embrace to the little boys' kissing of hands. The first thing I heard was the hearty voice of the old Shereef, who praised God that 'our darling' was safe back again, and then we all sat down for a talk; then more *Fattahs* were said for me, and for you, and for the children; and I went back to bed in my own boat. I found the guard of the French house had been taken off to Keneh to the works, after lying eight days in chains and wooden handcuffs for resisting, and claiming his rights as a French *protégé*. So we waited for his return, and for the keys which he had taken with him, in hopes that the Keneh authorities would not care to keep me out of the house. I wrote to the French Consular agent at Keneh, and to the Consul at Alexandria, and got him back the third day. What would you think in Europe to see me welcome with enthusiasm a servant just out of chains and handcuffs? At the very moment, too, that Mohammed and I were talking, a boat passed up the river with musick and singing on board. It was a Sheykh-el-Beled, of a place above Esneb, who had lain in prison three years in Cairo, and whose friends were making all the fantasia they could to celebrate the end of his misfortune, of disgrace, *il n'en est pas question*; and why should it? So many honest men go to prison that it is no presumption at all against a man.

The day after my arrival was the great and last day. The crowd was but little and not lively—times are too hard. But the riding was beautiful. Two young men from Hegaz performed wonderful feats.

I dined with the Maōhn, whose wife cooked me the best dinner I ever ate in this country, or almost anywhere. Marie, who was invited, rejoiced the kind old lady's heart by her Belgian appreciation of the excellent cookery. 'Eat, my daughter, eat,' and even I managed to give satisfaction. Such Bakloweh I never tasted. We removed to the house yesterday, and I have had company ever since.

One Sheykh Alee—a very agreeable man from beyond Khartoom, offers to take me up to Khartoom and back with a Takhterawan (camel litter) in company with Mustapha A'gha, Sheykh Yussuf and a troop of his own Abab'deh. It is a terrible temptation—but it would cost £50—so I refused. Sheykh Alee is so clever and well-bred that I should enjoy it much, and the climate at this season is delightful. He has been in the Denka country where the men are a cubit taller than Sheykh Hassan whom you know, and who enquires tenderly after you.

Now let me describe the state of things. From the Moudeeriat of Keneh only, 25,000 men are taken to work for sixty days without food or pay; each man must take his own basket, and each third man a hoe, not a basket. If you want to pay a substitute for a beloved or delicate son, it costs 1,000 piastres—600 at the lowest; and about 300 to 400 for his food. From Luxor only, 220 men are gone; of whom a third will very likely die of exposure to the cold and misery (the weather is unusually cold). That is to say that this little village, of at most 2,000 souls male and female (we don't usually count women, from decorum), will pay in labour at least £1,320 in sixty days. We have also already had eleven camels seized to go up to the Soudan; a camel is worth from £18 to £40.

Last year Mariette Bey made excavations at Gourneh forcing the people to work but promising payment at the rate of— Well, when he was gone the four Sheykhs of the village at Gourneh came to Mustapha and begged him to advance the money due from Government, for the people were starving. Mustapha agrees and gives above 300 purses—about £1,000 in *current* piastres on the understanding that he is to get the money from Government in *tariff*—and to keep the difference as his profit. If he cannot get it at all the fellaheen are to pay him back without interest. Of course at the rate at which money is here, his profit would be but small interest on the money unless he could get the money directly, and he has now waited six months in vain.

Abdallah the son of el-Habbeshee of Damankoor went up the river in chains to Fazoghlou a fortnight ago and Osman Bey ditto last week—El-Bedrawee is dead there, of course.

Shall I tell you what became of the hundred prisoners who were sent away after the Gau business? As they marched through the desert the Greek memlook looked at his list each morning, and said, 'Hoseyn, Achmet, Foolan (like the Spanish Don Fulano, Mr. so and so), you are free; take off his chains.' Well, the three or four men drop behind, where some arnouts strangle them out of sight. This is banishment to Fazoghlou. Do you remember *le citoyen est élargi* of the September massacres of Paris? Curious coincidence, is it not? Everyone is exasperated—the very Hareem talk of the government. It is in the air. I had not been five minutes in Keneh before I knew all this and much more. Of the end of Hajjee Sultan I will not speak till I have absolute certainty, but, I believe the proceeding was as I have described—set free in the desert and murdered by the way. I wish you to publish these facts, it is no secret to any but to those Europeans whose interests keep their eyes tightly shut, and they will soon have them opened. The blind rapacity of the present ruler will make him astonish the Franks some day, I think.

Wheat is now 400 piastres the ardeb up here; the little loaf, not quite so big as our penny roll, costs a piastre—about three-half-pence—and all in proportion. I need not say what the misery is. Remember that this is the second levy of 220 men within six months, each for sixty days, as well as the second seizure of camels; besides the conscription, which serves the same purpose, as the soldiers work on the Pasha's works. But in Cairo they are paid—and well paid.

It is curious how news travels here. The Luxor people knew the day I left Alexandria, and the day I left Cairo, long before I came. They say here that Abu-l-Hajjaj gave me his hand from Keneh, because he would not finish his moolid without me. I am supposed to be specially protected by him, as is proved by my health being so far better here than anywhere else.

By the bye, Sheykh Alee Abab'deh told me that all the villages *close* on the Nile escaped the cholera almost completely, whilst those who were half or a quarter of a mile inland were ravaged. At Keneh 250 a day died; at Luxor one child was supposed to have died of it, but I know he had diseased liver for a year or more. In the desert the Bishareen and Abab'deh suffered more than the people at Cairo, and you know the desert is usually the place of perfect health; but fresh Nile water seems to be *the* antidote. Sheykh Yussuf laid the mortality at Keneh to the canal water, which the poor people drink there. I believe the fact is as Sheykh Alee told me.

Now I will say good-bye, for I am tired, and will write anon to the rest. Let Mutter have this. I was very poorly till I got above Siout, and then gradually mended—constant blood spitting and great weakness and I am very thin, but, by the protection of Abu-l-Hajjaj I suppose I am already much better, and begin to eat again. I have not been out yet since the first day, having much to do in the house to get to rights. I felt very dreary on Christmas-day away from you all, and Omar's plum-pudding did not cheer me at all, as he hoped it would. He begs me to kiss your hand for him, and every one sends you salaam, and all lament that you are not the new Consul at Cairo.

Kiss my chicks, and love to you all. Janet, I hope is in Egypt ere this.

To Maurice Duff Gordon

LUXOR,
January 3, 1866.

MY DARLING MAURICE,

I was delighted to get your note, which arrived on New Year's day in the midst of the hubbub of the great festival in honour of the Saint of Luxor. I wish you could have seen two young Arabs (real Arabs from the Hedjaz, in Arabia) ride and play with spears and lances. I never saw anything like it—a man who played the tom-fool stood in the middle, and they galloped round and round him, with their spears crossed and the points resting on the ground, in so small a circle that his clothes whisked round with the wind of the horses' legs. Then they threw jereeds and caught them as they galloped: the beautiful thing was the perfect mastery of the horses: they were 'like water in their hands,' as Sheykh Hassan remarked. I perceived that I had never seen *real* horsemanship in my life before.

I am now in the 'palace' at Luxor with my dahabieh, 'Arooset er-Ralee' (the Darling Bride), under my windows; quite like a Pasha.

In coming up we had an alarm of robbers. Under the mountain called Gebel Foodah, we were entangled in shoals, owing to a change in the bed of the river, and forced to stay all night; and at three in the morning, the Reis sent in the boy to say he had seen a man creeping on all fours—would I fire my pistol? As my revolver had been stolen in Janet's house, I was obliged to beg him to receive any possible troop of armed robbers very civilly, and to let them take what they pleased. However, Omar blazed away with your father's old cavalry pistols (which had no bullets) and whether the robbers were frightened, or the man was only a wolf, we heard no more of the affair. My crew were horribly frightened, and kept awake till daybreak.

The last night before reaching Keneh, the town forty miles north of Luxor, my men held a grand fantasia on the bank. There was no wind, and we found a lot of old maize stalks; so there was a bonfire, and no end of drumming, singing and dancing. Even Omar relaxed his dignity so far as to dance the dance of the Alexandria young men; and very funny it all was. I laughed consumedly; especially at the modest airs and graces of a great lubberly fellow—one Hezayin, who acted the bride—in a representation of a Nubian wedding festivity. The new song of this year is very pretty—a declaration of love to a young Mohammed, sung to a very pretty tune. There is another, rather like the air of 'Di Provenza al mar' in the 'Traviata,' with extremely pretty words. As in England, every year has its new song, which all the boys sing about the streets.

I hope, darling, you are sapping this year, and intend to make up a bit for lost time. I hear you have lost no time in growing tall at all events—'ill weeds, etc.'—you know Omar desires all sorts of messages to you.

To Sir Alexander Duff Gordon

Monday, January 15, 1866.

Dearest Alick,

I hear that Mr. and Miss North* are to be here in a day or two. I hope you may have sent my saddle by them, for I want it sadly—mine is just possible for a donkey, but quite too broken for a horse.

Two great Sheykhs of Bishareen and Abab'deh came here and picked me up out walking alone. We went and sat in a field, and they begged me to communicate to the Queen of England that they would join her troops if she would invade Egypt. One laid my hand on his hand and said 'Thou hast 3,000 men in thy hand.' The other rules 10,000. They say there are 30,000 Arabs (bedaween) ready to join the English, for they fear that the Viceroy will try to work and rob them like the fellaheen, and if so they will fight to the last, or else go off into Syria. I was rather frightened—for them, I mean, and told them that our Queen could do nothing till 600 Sheykhs and 400 Ameers had talked in public—all whose talk was printed and read at Stambool and Cairo, and that they must not think of such a thing from our Queen, but if things became bad, it would be better for them to go off into Syria. I urged great caution upon them, and I need not repeat that to you, as the lives of thousands may be endangered. It might be interesting to be known in high places and in profound secret, as one of the indications of what is coming here.

If the saddle comes, as I hope, I may very likely go up to Assouan, and leave the boat and servants, and go into the desert for a few days to see the place of the Bishareen. They won't take anyone else: but you may be quite easy about me 'in the face' of a Sheykh-el-Arab. Handsome Sheykh Hassan, whom you saw at Cairo, will go with me. But if my saddle does not appear, I fear I should be too tired with riding a camel.

The little district of Koos, including Luxor, has been mulcted of camels, food for them and drivers, to the amount of 6,000 purses—last week—£18,000, *fact*. I cast up the account, and it tallied with what I got from a sub *employé*, nor is the discontent any longer whispered. Everyone talks aloud—and well they may.

To Mrs. Austin

Tuesday, 7 Ramadan.

DEAREST MUTTER,

I have just received your letter of Christmas-day, and am glad to answer it with a really amended report of myself. I had a very slight return a week ago, but for the last five or six days the daily flushing and fever has also ceased. I sent for one of the Arab doctors of the Azizeeyeh steamer to see Omar, and myself also, and he was very attentive, and took a note of medicines to send me from Cairo by a *confrère*: and when I offered a fee he said, 'God forbid—it is only our duty to do anything in the world for you.' Likewise a very nice Dr. Ingram saw some of my worst cases for me, and gave me good advice and help; but I want better books—Kesteven is very useful, as far as it goes, but I want something more *ausführlich* and scientific. Ramadan is a great trouble to me, though Sheykh Yussuf tells the people not to fast, if I forbid it: but many are ill from having begun it, and one fine old man of about fifty-five died of apoplexy on the fourth night. My Christian patient is obstinate, and fasts, in spite of me, and will, I think, seal his fate; he was so much better after the blistering and Dr. Ingram's mixture. I wish you could have seen a lad of eighteen or so, who came here to-day for medicine. I think I never saw such sweet frank, engaging manners, or ever heard any one express himself better: quite *une nature distinguée*, not the least handsome, but the most charming countenance and way of speaking.

My good friend the Maōhn spent the evening with me, and told me all the story of his marriage, though quite 'unfit to meet the virtuous eyes of British propriety—' as I read the other day in some paper apropos of I forget what—it will give you an idea of the feelings of a Muslim *honnête homme*, which Seleem is through and through. He knew his wife before he married her, she being twenty-five or twenty-six, and he a boy; she fell in love with him, and at seventeen he married her, and they have had ten children, all alive but two, and a splendid race they are. He told me how she courted him with glasses of sherbet and trays of sweetmeats, and how her mother proposed the marriage, and how she hesitated on account of the difference of age, but, of course, at last consented: all with the naïvest vanity in his own youthful attractions, and great extolling of her personal charms, and of her many virtues. When he was sent up here she would not, or could not, leave her children. On the Sitt's arrival his slave girl was arrogant, and refused to kiss her hand, and spoke saucily of her age, whereupon Seleem gave her in marriage to a black man and pays for her support, as long as she likes to suckle the child he (Seleem) had by her, which child will in due time return to his house. *Kurz*, the fundamental idea in it all, in the mind of an upright man, is, that if a man 'takes up' with a woman at all, he must make himself responsible for her before the world; and above all for the fate of any child he may have by her (you see the Prophet of the Arabs did not contemplate ladies *qui savent nager* so well in the troubled waters of life as we are now blessed with. I don't mean to say that many men are as scrupulous as my excellent friend Seleem, either here or even in our own moral society). All this was told with expressions quite incompatible with our manners, though not at all *leste*—and he expatiated on his wife's personal charms in a very quaint way; the good lady is now hard upon sixty and looks it fully; but he evidently is as fond of her as ever. As a curious trait of primitive manners, he told me of her piety and boundless hospitality; how when some friends came late one evening, unexpectedly, and there was only a bit of meat, she killed a sheep and cooked it for them with her own hands. And this is a Cairene lady, and quite a lady too, in manners and appearance. The day I dined there she was dressed in very ragged, old cotton clothes, but spotlessly clean; and she waited on me with a kind, motherly pleasure, that quite took away the awkwardness I felt at sitting down while she stood. In a few days she and her husband are to dine with me, a thing which no Arab couple ever did before (I mean dine out together), and the old lady was immensely amused at the idea. Omar will cook and all male visitors will be sent to the kitchen. Now that I understand all that is said to me, and a great deal of the general conversation, it is much more amusing. Seleem Effendi jokes me a great deal about my blunders, especially my lack of *politikeh*, the Greek word for what we should call flummery; and my saying *lazim* (you must, or rather *il faut*), instead of humble entreaties. I told him to teach me better, but he laughed heartily, and said, 'No, no, when you say *lazim*, it is *lazim*, and nobody wants the stick to force him to say *Hadr* (ready) O Sheykh-el-Arab, O Emeereh.'

Fancy my surprise the other day just when I was dictating letters to Sheykh Yussuf (letters of introduction for Ross's inspecting agent) with three or four other people here, in walked Miss North (Pop) whom I have not seen since she was a child. She and her father were going up the second cataract. She has done some sketches which, though rather unskilful, were absolutely true in colour and effect, and are the very first that I have seen that are so. I shall see something of them on their return. She seemed very pleasant. Mr. North looked rather horrified at the turbaned society in which he found himself. I suppose it did look odd to English eyes.

We have had three days of the south wind, which the 'Saturday Review' says I am not to call Samoom; and I was poorly, and kept in bed two days with a cold. Apropos, I will give you the Luxor contribution towards the further confusion of the Samoom (or Simoom) controversy. I told Sheykh Yussuf that an English newspaper, written by particularly clever people, said that I was wrong to call the bad wind here 'Samoom,' (it was in an article on Palgrave's book, I think). Sheykh Yussuf said, 'True, oh lady, no doubt those learned gentlemen' (politely saluting them with his hand) 'thought one such as thou shouldest have written classical Arabic (*Arabi fossieh*), and have called it "*al Daboor*;" nevertheless, it is proper to write it "Samoom," not, as some do "Simoom," which is the plural of *sim* (poison).' I shook my head, and said, I did not recollect *al Daboor*. Then my Reis, sitting at the door, offered his suggestion. 'Probably the English, who it is well known are a nation of sailors, use the name given to the land wind by *el-baharieh* (the boatmen), and call it *el-mereeseh*.' 'But,' said I, 'the clever gentlemen say that I am wrong altogether, and never can have seen a *real* Samoom, for that would have killed me in ten minutes.' Hereupon Sheykh Mohammed el-Abab'deh, who is not nearly so polished as his brother Hassan, burst into a regular bedawee roar of laughter, and said, 'Yah! do the *Ganassil* (Europeans) take thee for a rat, oh lady? Whoever heard of *el Beni Adam* (the children of Adam) dying of the wind? Men die of thirst quicker when the Samoom blows and they have no water. But no one ever died of the wind alone, except the rats—they do.' I give you the opinion of three 'representative men—' scholar, sailor, and bedawee; if that helps you to a solution of the controversy.

We have just had a scene, rather startling to notions about fatalism, etc. Owing to the importation of a good deal of cattle from the Soudan, there is an expectation of the prevalence of small-pox, and the village barbers are busy vaccinating in all directions to prevent the infection brought, either by the cattle or, more likely, by their drivers. Now, my maid had told me she had never been vaccinated, and I sent for Hajjee Mahmood to cut my hair and vaccinate her. To my utter amazement the girl, who had never shown any religious bigotry, and does not fast, or make any demonstrations, refused peremptorily. It appears that the priests and sisters appointed by the enlightened administration of Prussia instil into their pupils and penitents that vaccination is a 'tempting of God.' *Oh oui*, she said, *je sais bien que chez nous mes parents pouvaient recevoir un procès verbal, mais il vaut mieux cela que d'aller contre la volonté de Dieu. Si Dieu le veut, j'aurai la petite-vérole, et s'il ne veut pas, je ne l'aurai pas*. I scolded her pretty sharply, and said it was not only stupid, but selfish. 'But what can one do?' as Hajjee Mahmood said, with a pitying shake of his head; 'these Christians are so ignorant!' He blushed, and apologised to me, and said, 'It is not their fault; all this want of sense is from the priests who talk folly to them for money, and to keep them afraid before themselves. Poor things, *they* don't know the Word of God.—"Help thyself, oh my servant, and I will help thee."' This is the second contest I have had on this subject. Last year it was with a Copt, who was all *Allah kereem* and so on about his baby, with his child of four dying of small-pox. 'Oh, man,' said Sheykh Yussuf, 'if the wall against which I am now sitting were to shake above my head, should I fold my feet under me and say *Allah kereem*, or should I use the legs God has given me to escape from it?'

I had a visit the other day from a lady who, as I was informed, had been a harlot in Siout. She has repented, and married a converted Copt. They are a droll pair of penitents, so very smart in their dress and manner. But no one *se scandalise* at their antecedents—neither is it proper to repent in sackcloth and ashes, or to confess sins, except to God alone. You are not to *indulge* in telling them to others; it is an offence. Repent inwardly, and be ashamed to show it before the people—ask pardon of God only. A little of this would do no harm in Europe, methinks.

Here is a pretty story for you from the *Hadeth en-Nebbee* (sayings of the Prophet). 'Two prophets were sitting together, and discoursing of prayer and the difficulty of fixing the attention entirely on the act. One said to the other, "Not even for the duration of two *rekahs* (prayers ending with the prostration and *Allah akbar*) can a man fix his mind on God alone." The other said, "Nay, but I can do it!" "Say then two *rekahs*," replied the elder of the two; "I will give thee my cloak." Now he wore two cloaks—a new handsome red one and an old shabby blue one. The younger prophet rose, raised his hands to his head, said *Allah akbar*, and bent to the ground for his first *rekah*; as he rose again he thought "Will he give me the red cloak or the blue, I wonder?"' It is very stupid of me not to write down all the pretty stories I hear, but this one is a capital specimen of Arab wit. Some day I must bring over Omar with me, Inshallah, to England, and he will tell you stories like Scheherazade herself. A jolly Nubian Alim told me the other night how in his village no man ever eats meat, except on Bairam day: but one night a woman had a piece of meat given her by a traveller; she put it in the oven and went out. During her absence her husband came in and smelt it, and as it was just the time of the *eshé* (first prayers one hour after sunset), he ran up to the hill outside the village, and began to chaunt forth the *tekbeer* with all his might—*Allah akbar, Allah akbar*, etc. etc., till the people ran to see what was the matter. 'Why, to-day is Bairam,' says he. 'Where is thy witness, O man?' 'The meat in the oven—the meat in the oven.'

To Mrs. Austin

LUXOR,
February 15, 1866.

DEAREST MUTTER,

I have only time for a short letter to say that the cold weather is over and that I continue to improve, not very fast, but still very sensibly.

My young Frenchman turns out to be a M. Brune *grand prix de Rome*, an architect, and is a very nice fellow indeed, and a thorough gentleman. His odd awkward manner proved to be mere vexation at finding himself quartered *nolens volens* on a stranger, and a woman; but we have made great friends, and I have made him quite happy by telling him that he shall pay his share of the food. He was going to hurry off from shyness though he had begun a work here by which I fancy he hopes to get *Kudos*. I see he is poor and very properly proud. He goes out to the temple at sunrise, and returns to dinner at dark, and works well, and his drawings are very clever. In short, I am as much obliged to the French Consul for sending me such an intelligent man as I was vexed at first. An *homme sérieux* with an absorbing pursuit is always good company in the long run. Moreover M. Brune behaves like a perfect gentleman in every way. So *tout est pour le mieux.*

I am sorry to say that Marie has become so excessively bored, dissatisfied, and, she says, ill, that I am going to send her back rather than be worried so—and *damit hats eine ende* of European maids. Of course an ignorant girl *must* be bored to death here—a land of no amusements and no flirtation *is* unbearable. I shall borrow a slave of a friend here, an old black woman who is quite able and more than willing to serve me, and when I go down to Cairo I will get either a ci-devant slave or an elderly Arab woman. Dr. Patterson strongly advised me to do so last year. He had one who has been thirteen years his housekeeper, an old bedaweeyeh, I believe, and as I now am no longer looked upon as a foreigner, I shall be able to get a respectable Arab woman, a widow or a divorced woman of a certain age who will be too happy to have 'a good home,' as our maids say. I think I know one, a certain Fatoomeh, a widow with no children who does washing and needlework in Cairo. You need not be at all uneasy. I shall be taken good care of if I fall ill, much better than I should get from a European in a sulky frame of mind. Hajjee Ali has very kindly offered to take Marie down to Cairo and start her off to Alexandria, whence Ross's people can send her home. If she wants to stay in Alexandria and get placed by the nuns who piously exhorted her to extort ninety francs a month from me, so much the better for me. Ali refuses to take a penny from me for her journey—besides bringing me potatoes and all sorts of things: and if I remonstrate he says he and all his family and all they have is mine, in consequence of my treatment of his brother.

You will be amused and pleased to hear how Sheykh Yussuf was utterly puzzled and bewildered by the civilities he received from the travellers this year, till an American told Mustapha I had written a book which had made him (the American) wish well to the poor people of this country, and desire to behave more kindly to them than would have been the case before.

To-morrow is the smaller Bairam, and I shall have all the Hareem here to visit me.

Two such nice Englishmen called the other day and told me they lived in Hertford Street opposite Lady D. G.'s and saw Alexander go in and out, and met Maurice in the gardens. It gave me a terrible twinge of *Heimweh*, but I thought it so kind and pretty and *herzlich* of them to come and tell me how Alexander and Maurice looked as they went along the street.

To Mrs. Ross

February 22, 1866.

DEAREST JANET,

I received your letter of the 4th inst. yesterday. I am much distressed not to hear a better account of you. Why don't you go to Cairo for a time? Your experience of your German confirms me (if I needed it) in my resolution to have no more Europeans unless I should find one 'seasoned.' The nuisance is too great. I shall borrow a neighbour's slave for my stay here and take some one in Cairo. My dress will do very well in native hands.

I am at last getting really better again, I hope. We have had a cold winter, but not trying. There has not been much wind, and the weather has been very steady and clear. I wish I had Palgrave's book. Hajjee Ali was to bring up my box, but it had not arrived when he sailed. I will send down the old saddle whenever I can find a safe opportunity and have received the other.

Many thanks for all the various detachments of newspapers, which were a great solace. I wish you would give me your photo—large size—to hang up with Rainie and Maurice here and in the boat. Like the small one you gave me at Soden, you said you had some copies big.

My doctoring business has become quite formidable. I should like to sell my practice to any 'rising young surgeon.' It brings in a very fair income of vegetables, eggs, turkeys, pigeons, etc.

How is the Shereef of Mecca's horse? I ambition to ride that holy animal.

To Sir Alexander Duff Gordon

LUXOR,
February 22, 1866.

DEAREST ALICK,

The weather here is just beginning to get warm, and I of course to get better. There has been a good deal of nervous headache here this Ramadan. I had to attend the Kadee, and several more. My Turkish neighbour at Karnac has got a *shaitan* (devil), *i.e.* epileptic fits, and I was sent for to exorcise him, which I am endeavouring to do with nitrate of silver, etc.; but I fear imagination will kill him, so I advise him to go to Cairo, and leave the devil-haunted house. I have this minute killed the first snake of this year—a sign of summer.

I was so pleased to see two Mr. Watsons—your opposite neighbours—who said they saw you every morning go down the street—*ojala!* that I did so too! I liked Mr. and Mrs. Webb of Newstead Abbey very much; nice, hearty, pleasant, truly English people.

There have not been above twenty or thirty boats up this year—mostly Americans. There are some here now, very nice people, with four little children, who create quite an excitement in the place, and are 'mashallahed' no end. Their little fair faces do look very pretty here, and excite immense admiration.

Seyd has just come in to take my letter to the steamer which is now going down. So *addio*, dearest Alick. I am much better but still weakish, and very *triste* at my long separation.

To Sir Alexander Duff Gordon

Tuesday, March 6, 1866.

Dearest Alick,

I write to be ready for the last *down* steamer which will be here in a few days. Mr. and Miss North are here working hard at sketching, and M. Brune will take a place in their Dahabieh (my old Zint el Bahreyn), and leave me in six or seven days. I shall quite grieve to lose his company. If ever you or yours fall in with him, pray cultivate his acquaintance, he is very clever, very hard working, and a 'thorough-bred gentleman' as Omar declares. We are quite low-spirited at parting after a month spent together at Thebes.

I hear that Olagnier has a big house in Old Cairo and will lodge me. The Norths go to-day (Thursday) and M. Brune does not go with them as he intended, but will stay on and finish a good stroke of work and take his chance of a conveyance.

I spent yesterday out in Mustapha's tent among the bean gatherers, and will go again. I think it does me good and is not too long a ride. The weather has set in suddenly very hot, which rather tries everybody, but gloriously fine clear air. I hope you will get this, as old fat Hassan will take it to the office in Cairo himself—for the post is very insecure indeed. I have written very often, if you don't get my letters I suppose they interest the court of Pharaoh.

To Sir Alexander Duff Gordon

Thebes,
March 17, 1866.

Dearest Alick,

The high winds have begun with a vengeance and a great bore they are.

I went a few days ago out to Medarnoot, and lunched in Mustapha's tent, among his bean harvest. I was immensely amused by the man who went with me on to Medarnoot, one Sheriff, formerly an illustrious robber, now a watchman and very honest man. He rode a donkey, about the size of Stirling's wee pony, and I laughed, and said, 'The man should carry the ass.' No sooner said than done, Sheriff dismounted, or rather let his beast down from between his legs, shouldered the donkey, and ran on. His way of keeping awake is original; the nights are still cold, so he takes off all his clothes, rolls them up and lays them under his head, and the cold keeps him quite lively. I never saw so powerful, active and healthy an animal. He was full of stories how he had had 1,000 stripes of the courbash on his feet and 500 on his loins at one go. 'Why?' I asked. 'Why, I stuck a knife into a cawass who ordered me to carry water-melons; I said I was not his donkey; he called me worse: my blood got up, and so!—and the Pasha to whom the cawass belonged beat me. Oh, it was all right, and I did not say "ach" once, did I?' (addressing another). He clearly bore no malice, as he felt no shame. He has a grand romance about a city two days' journey from here, in the desert, which no one finds but by chance, after losing his way; and where the ground is strewed with valuable *anteekehs* (antiquities). I laughed, and said, 'Your father would have seen gold and jewels.' 'True,' said he, 'when I was young, men spit on a statue or the like, when they turned it up in digging, and now it is a fortune to find one.'

To Sir Alexander Duff Gordon

March 31, 1866.

DEAREST ALICK,

As for me I am much better again; the cough has subsided, I really think the Arab specific, camel's milk, has done me great good. I have mended ever since I took it. It has the merit of being quite delicious.

Yesterday I was much amused when I went for my afternoon's drink, to find Sheriff in a great taking at having been robbed by a woman, under his very nose. He saw her gathering hummuz from a field under his charge, and went to order her off, whereupon she coolly dropped the end of her *boordeh* which covered the head and shoulders, effectually preventing him from going near her; made up her bundle and walked off. His respect for the Hareem did not, however, induce him to refrain from strong language.

M. Brune has made very pretty drawings of the mosque here, both outside and in; it is a very good specimen of modern Arab architecture; and he won't believe it could be built without ground plan, elevations, etc., which amuses the people here, who build without any such inventions.

The harvest here is splendid this year, such beans and wheat, and prices have fallen considerably in both: but meat, butter, etc., remain very dear. My fame as a Hakeemeh has become far too great, and on market-days I have to shut up shop. Yesterday a very handsome woman came for medicine to make her beautiful, as her husband had married another who teazed her, and he rather neglected her. And a man offered me a camel load of wheat if I would read something over him and his wife to make them have children. I don't try to explain to them how very irrational they are but use the more intelligible argument that all such practices savour of the *Ebu er Rukkeh* (equivalent to black art), and are *haram* to the greatest extent; besides, I add, being 'all lies' into the bargain. The applicants for child-making and charm-reading are Copts or Muslims, quite in equal numbers, and appear alike indifferent as to what 'Book': but all but one have been women; the men are generally perfectly rational about medicine and diet.

I find there is a good deal of discontent among the Copts with regard to their priests and many of their old customs. Several young men have let out to me at a great rate about the folly of their fasts, and the badness and ignorance of their priests. I believe many turn Muslim from a real conviction that it is a better religion than their own, and not as I at first thought merely from interest; indeed, they seldom gain much by it, and often suffer tremendous persecution from their families; even they do not escape the rationalizing tendencies now abroad in Christendom. Then their early and indissoluble marriages are felt to be a hardship: a boy is married at eight years old, perhaps to his cousin aged seventeen (I know one here in that case), and when he grows up he wishes it had been let alone. A clever lad of seventeen propounded to me his dissatisfaction, and seemed to lean to Islam. I gave him an Arabic New Testament, and told him to read that first, and judge for himself whether he could not still conform to the Church of his own people, and inwardly believe and try to follow the Gospels. I told him it was what most Christians had to do, as every man could not make a sect for himself, while few could believe everything in any Church. I suppose I ought to have offered him the Thirty-nine Articles, and thus have made a Muslim of him out of hand. He pushed me a little hard about several matters, which he says he does not find in 'the Book': but on the whole he is well satisfied with my advice.

Coptic Palm Sunday, April 1.

We hear that Fadil Pasha received orders at Assouan to go up to Khartoum in Giaffar Pasha's place: it is a civil way of killing a fat old Turk, if it is true. He was here a week or two ago. My informant is one of my old crew who was in Fadil Pasha's boat.

I shall wait to get a woman-servant till I go to Cairo, the women here cannot iron or sew; so, meanwhile, the wife of Abd el-Kader does my washing, and Omar irons; and we get on capitally. Little Achmet waits, etc., and I think I am more comfortable so than if I had a maid,—it would be no use to buy a slave, as the trouble of teaching her would be greater than the work she would do for me.

My medical reputation has become far too great, and all my common drugs—Epsom salts, senna, aloes, rhubarb, quassia—run short. Especially do all the poor, tiresome, ugly old women adore me, and bore me with their aches and pains. They are always the doctor's greatest plague. The mark of confidence is that they now bring the sick children, which was never known before, I believe, in these parts. I am sure it would pay a European doctor to set up here;

the people would pay him a little, and there would be good profit from the boats in the winter. I got turkeys when they were worth six or eight shillings apiece in the market, and they were forced upon me by the fellaheen. I must seal up this for fear the boat should come; it will only pick up M. Brune and go on.

To Mrs. Ross

EED EL KEBEER,
Wednesday, *April*, 1866.

DEAREST JANET,

I had not heard a word of Henry's illness till Mr. Palgrave arrived* and told me, and also that he was better. Alhamdulillah! I only hope that you are not knocked up, my darling. I am not ill, but still feel unaccountably weak and listless. I don't cough much, and have got fatter on my *régime* of camel's milk,—so I hope I may get over the languor. The box has not made its appearance. What a clever fellow Mr. Palgrave is! I never knew such a hand at languages. The folks here are in admiration at his Arabic. I hope you will see M. Brune. I am sure you would like him. He is a very accomplished and gentlemanly man.

You have never told me your plans for this year or whether I shall find you when I go down. The last three days the great heat has begun and I am accordingly feeling better. I have just come home from the Bairam early prayer out in the burial-place, at which Palgrave also assisted. He is unwell, and tells me he leaves Luxor to-morrow morning. I shall stay on till I am too hot here, as evidently the summer suits me.

Many thanks for Miss Berry and for the wine, which makes a very pleasant change from the rather bad claret I have got. Palgrave's book I have read through hard, as he wished to take it back for you. It is very amusing.

If you come here next winter Mustapha hopes you will bring a saddle, and ride 'all his horses.' I think I could get you a very good horse from a certain Sheykh Abdallah here.

Well, I must say good-bye. *Kulloo sana intee tayib*, love to Henry.

To Mrs. Austin

BAIRAM,
April, 1866.

DEAREST MUTTER,

I write this to go down by Mr. Palgrave who leaves to-morrow. He has been with Mustapha Bey conducting an enquiry into Mustapha A'gha's business. Mariette Bey struck Mustapha, and I and some Americans took it ill and wrote a very strong complaint to our respective Consuls. Mariette denied the blow and the words 'liar, and son of a dog'—so the American and English Consuls sent up Palgrave as commissioner to enquire into the affair, and the Pasha sent Mustapha Bey with him. Palgrave is very amusing of course, and his knowledge of languages is wonderful, Sheykh Yussuf says few *Ulema* know as much of the literature and niceties of grammar and composition. Mustapha Bey is a darling; he knew several friends of mine, Hassan Effendi, Mustapha Bey Soubky, and others, so we were friends directly.

I have not yet got a woman-servant, but I don't miss it at all; little Achmet is very handy, Mahommed's slave girl washes, and Omar irons and cleans the house and does housemaid, and I have kept on the meek cook, Abd el-Kader, whom I took while the Frenchman was here. I had not the heart to send him away; he is such a *meskeen*. He was a smart travelling waiter, but his brother died, leaving a termagant widow with four children, and poor Abd el-Kader felt it his duty to bend his neck to the yoke, married her, and has two more children. He is a most worthy, sickly, terrified creature.

I have heard that a decent Copt here wants to sell a black woman owing to reverses of fortune, and that she might suit me. Sheykh Yussuf is to negotiate the affair and to see if the woman herself likes me for a mistress, and I am to have her on trial for a time, and if I like her and she me, Sheykh Yussuf will buy her with my money in his name. I own I have very little scruple about the matter, as I should consider her price as an advance of two or three years' wages and tear the paper of sale as soon as she had worked her price out, which I think would be a fair bargain. But I must see first whether Feltass (the Copt) really wants to sell her or only to get a larger price than is fair, in which case I will wait till I go to Cairo. Anything is better than importing a European who at once thinks one is at her mercy on account of the expense of the journey back.

I went out this morning to the early prayer of Bairam day, held in the burial-place. Mahmoud ibn-Mustapha preached, but the boys and the Hareem made such a noise behind us that I could not hear the sermon. The weather has set in hot these last days, and I am much the better. It seems strange that what makes others languid seems to strengthen me. I have been very weak and languid all the time, but the camel's milk has fattened me prodigiously, to Sherayeff's great delight; and the last hot days have begun to take away the miserable feeling of fatigue and languor.

Palgrave is not well at all, and his little black boy he fears will die, and several people in the steamer are ill, but in Luxor there is no sickness to speak of, only chronic old women, so old and ugly and *achy*, that I don't know what to do with them, except listen to their complaints, which begin, '*Ya ragleh*.' *Ragel* is man, so *ragleh* is the old German *Männin*, and is the civil way of addressing a Saeedee woman. To one old body I gave a powder wrapped up in a fragment of a *Saturday Review*. She came again and declared Mashallah! the *hegab* (charm) was a powerful one, for though she had not been able to wash off all the fine writing from the paper, even that little had done her a deal of good. I regret that I am unable to inform you what the subject of the article in the *Saturday* which had so drastic an effect.

Good-bye, dearest Mutter, I must go and take a sleep before the time of receiving the visits of to-day (the great festival). I was up before sunrise to see the prayer, so must have a siesta in a cool place. To-morrow morning early this will go. I hope you got a letter I sent ten days or so ago.

To Sir Alexander Duff Gordon

LUXOR,
May 10, 1866.

DEAREST ALICK,

The real summer heat—the *Shems el-Kebeer* (big sun) has fairly set in, and of course I am all the better. You would give my camel a good backsheesh if you saw how prodigiously fat I have grown on her milk; it beats codliver-oil hollow. You can drink a gallon without feeling it, it is so easy of digestion.

I have lent the dahabieh to Mustapha and to one or two more, to go to Keneh on business, and when she returns (which will be to-day) I shall make ready to depart too, and drop down stream. Omar wants me to go down to Damietta, to 'amuse my mind and dilate my stomach' a little; and I think of doing so.

Palgrave was here about a fortnight ago, on Mustapha's and Mariette's business. 'By God! this English way is wonderful,' said a witness, 'that English Bey questioned me till my stomach came out.' I loved Mustapha Bey, who was with him; such a nice, kind, gentle creature, and very intelligent and full of good sense. I rejoice to hear that he returns my liking, and has declared himself 'one of my darweeshes.' Talking of darweeshes reminds me of the Festival of Sheykh Gibrieel this year. I had forgotten the day, but in the evening some people came for me to go and eat some of the meat of the Sheykh, who is also a good patron of mine, they say; being a poor man's saint, and of a humble spirit, it is said he favours me. There was plenty of meat and *melocheea* and bread; and then *zikrs* of different kinds, and a *Gama el Fokara* (assembly of the poor). *Gama* is the true word for Mosque—*i.e.*, Meeting, which consists in a great circle of men seated thick on the ground, with two poets facing each other, who improvise religious verses. On this occasion the rule of the game was to end each stanza with a word having the sound of *wahed* (one), or *el Had* (the first). Thus one sung: 'Let a man take heed how he walks,' etc., etc.; and 'pray to God not to let him fall,' which sound like *Had*. And so they went on, each chanting a verse alternately. One gesticulated almost as much as an Italian and pronounced beautifully; the other was quiet, but had a nice voice, and altogether it was very pretty. At the end of each verse the people made a sort of chorus, which was sadly like the braying of asses. The *zikr* of the Edfoo men was very curious. Our people did it quietly, and the *moonsheed* sang very sweetly—indeed 'the song of the moonsheed is the sugar in the sherbet to the Zikkeer,' said a man who came up when it was over, streaming with perspiration and radiant with smiles. Some day I will write to you the whole '*grund Idee*' of a *zikr*, which is, in fact, an attempt to make present 'the communion of saints,' dead or living. As I write arrives the Arooset er-rallee, and my crew furl her big sail quite 'Bristol fashion.' My men have come together again, some from Nubia and some from the Delta; and I shall go down with my old lot.

Omar and Achmet have implored me not to take another maid at all; they say they live like Pashas now they have only the lady to please; that it will be a pleasure to 'lick my shoes clean,' whereas the boots of the *Cameriera* were intolerable. The feeling of the Arab servants towards European colleagues is a little like that of 'niggers' about 'mean whites'—mixed hatred, fear, and scorn. The two have done so well to make me comfortable that I have no possible reason for insisting on encumbering myself with 'an old man of the sea,' in the shape of a maid; and the difference in cost is immense. The one dish of my dinner is ample relish to their bread and beans, while the cooking for a maid, and her beer and wine, cost a great deal. Omar irons my clothes very tidily, and little Achmet cleans the house as nicely as possible. I own I am quite as much relieved by the absence of the 'civilised element' as my retainers are.

Did I describe the Coptic Good Friday? Imagine 450 *Rekahs* in church! I have seen many queer things, but nothing half so queer as the bobbing of the Copts.

I went the other day to the old church six or eight miles off, where they buried the poor old Bishop who died a week ago. Abu Khom, a Christian *shaheed* (martyr), is buried there. He appeared to Mustapha's father when lost in the desert, and took him safe home. On that occasion he was well mounted, and robed all in white, with a *litham* over his face. No one dares to steal anything near his tomb, not one ear of corn. He revealed himself long ago to one of the descendants of Abu-l-Hajjaj, and to this day every Copt who marries in Luxor gives a pair of fowls to the family of that Muslim in remembrance of Abu Khom.

I shall leave Luxor in five or six days—and write now to stop all letters in Cairo.

I don't know what to do with my sick; they come from forty miles off, and sometimes twenty or thirty people sleep outside the house. I dined with the Maōhn last night—'pot luck'—and was much pleased. The dear old lady was so vexed not to have a better dinner for me that she sent me a splendid tray of *baklaweh* this morning to make up for it.

To Maurice Duff Gordon

CAIRO,
June 22, 1866.

MAURICE MY DARLING,

I send you a Roman coin which a man gave me as a fee for medical attendance. I hope you will like it for your watch-chain. I made our Coptic goldsmith bore a hole in it. Why don't you write to me, you young rascal? I am now living in my boat, and I often wish for you here to donkey ride about with me. I can't write you a proper letter now as Omar is waiting to take this up to Mr. Palgrave with the drawings for your father. Omar desires his best salaam to you and to Rainie, and is very much disappointed that you are not coming out in the winter to go up to Luxor. We had a hurricane coming down the Nile, and a boat behind us sank. We only lost an anchor, and had to wait and have it fished up by the fishermen of a neighbouring village. In places the water was so shallow that the men had to push the boat over by main force, and all went into the river. The captain and I shouted out, *Islam el Islam*, equivalent to, 'Heave away, boys.' There are splendid illuminations about to take place here, because the Pasha has got leave to make his youngest boy his successor, and people are ordered to rejoice, which they do with much grumbling—it will cost something enormous.

To Mrs. Austin

Off Boulak, Cairo,
July 10, 1866.

Dearest Mutter,

I am much better again. My cold went off without a violent illness and I was only weak and nervous. I am very comfortable here, anchored off Boulak, with my Reis and one sailor who cleans and washes my clothes which Omar irons, as at Luxor, as he found the washerwomen here charged five francs a dozen for all small things and more for dresses. A bad *hashash* boy turned Achmet's head, who ran away for two days and spent a dollar in riotous living; he returned penitent, and got no fatted calf, but dry bread and a confiscation of his new clothes.

The heat, when I left Luxor, was prodigious. I was detained three days by the death of Sheykh Yussuf's poor little wife and baby (in childbirth) so I was forced to stay and eat the funeral feast, and be present at the *Khatmeh* (reading of the Koran on the third night), or it would not have seemed kind. The Kadee gave me a very curious prayer-book, the Guide of the Faithful, written in Darfour! in beautiful characters, and with very singular decorations, and in splendid binding. It contains the names of all the prophets and of the hundred appellations of Mohammed, and is therefore a powerful *hegab* or talisman. He requested me never to give it away and always to keep it with me. Such books cannot be bought with money at all. I also bought a most beautiful *hegab* of cornelian set in enamel, the verse of the throne splendidly engraved, and dated 250 years ago. I sent over by Palgrave to Alick M. Brune's lovely drawings of Luxor and Karnac, and to Maurice a gold coin which I received as a fee from an old Bedawee.

It was so hot that I could not face the ride up to Keneh, when all my friends there came to fetch me, nor could I go to Siout. I never felt such heat. At Benisouef I went to see our Maōhn's daughter married to another Maōhn there; it was a pleasant visit. The master of the house was out, and his mother and wife received me like one of the family; such a pretty woman and such darling children!—a pale, little slight girl of five, a sturdy boy of four, and a baby of one year old. The eager hospitality of the little creatures was quite touching. The little girl asked to have on her best frock, and then she stood before me and fanned me seriously and diligently, and asked every now and then, 'Shall I make thee a sherbet?' 'Shall I bring thee a coffee?' and then questions about grandpapa and grand-mamma, and Abd el-Hameed and Abd el-Fattah; while the boy sat on his heels before me and asked questions about my family in his baby talk, and assured me it was a good day to him, and wanted me to stay three days, and to sleep with them. Their father came in and gave each an ashara (10 foddahs, ½ piastre) which, after consulting together, they tied in the corner of my handkerchief; 'to spend on my journey.' The little girl took such care of my hat and gloves and shoes, all very strange garments to her, but politeness was stronger than curiosity with the little things. I breakfasted with them all next day, and found much cookery going on for me. I took a doll for my little friend Ayoosheh, and some sugar-plums for Mohammed, but they laid them aside in order to devote themselves to the stranger, and all quietly, and with no sort of show-off or obtrusiveness. Even the baby seemed to have the instinct of hospitality, and was full of smiles. It was all of a piece with the good old lady, their grandmother at Luxor, who wanted to wash my clothes for me herself, because I said the black slave of Mohammed washed badly. Remember that to do 'menial offices' for a guest is an honour and pleasure, and not derogatory at all here. The ladies cook for you, and say, 'I will cook my best for thee.' The worst is that they stuff one so. Little Ayoosheh asked after my children, and said, 'May God preserve them for thee! Tell thy little girl that Mohammed and I love her from afar off.' Whereupon Mohammed declared that in a few years, please God, when he should be *balal* (marriageable) he would marry her and live with me. When I went back to the boat the Effendi was ill with asthma, and I would not let him go with me in the heat (a polite man accompanies an honoured guest back to his house or boat, or tent). So the little boy volunteered, and we rode off on the Effendi's donkey, which I had to bestride, with Mohammed on the hump of the saddle before me. He was delighted with the boat, of course, and romped and played about till we sailed, when his slave took him home. Those children gave me a happy day with their earnest, gracious hospitality.

July 14th.—Since I wrote this, I have had the boat topsy-turvy, with a carpenter and a *menegget* (cushion-stuffer), and had not a corner even to write in. I am better, but still cough every morning. I am, however, much better, and have quite got over the nervous depression which made me feel unable and ashamed to write. My young carpenter—a Christian—half Syrian, half Copt, of the Greek rite, and altogether a Cairene—would have pleased you. He would not work on Sunday, but instead, came mounted on a splendid tall black donkey, and handsomely dressed, to pay me a visit, and go out with me for a ride. So he, I, and Omar went up to the Sittee (Lady) Zeyneb's mosque, to inquire for Mustapha Bey Soubky, the Hakeem

Pasha, whom I had known at Luxor. I was told by the porter of the mosque to seek him at the shop of a certain grocer, his particular friend, where he sits every evening. On going there we found the shop with its lid shut down (a shop is like a box laid on its side with the lid pulled up when open and dropped when shut; as big as a cobbler's stall in Europe). The young grocer was being married, and Mustapha Bey was ill. So I went to his house in the quarter—such narrow streets!—and was shown up by a young eunuch into the hareem, and found my old friend very poorly, but spent a pleasant evening with him, his young wife—a Georgian slave whom he had married,—his daughter by a former wife—whom he had married when he was fourteen, and the female dwarf buffoon of the Valideh Pasha (Ismail's mother) whose heart I won by rising to her, because she was so old and deformed. The other women laughed, but the little old dwarf liked it. She was a Circassian, and seemed clever. You see how the 'Thousand and One Nights' are quite true and real; how great Beys sit with grocers, and carpenters have no hesitation in offering civility to *naas omra* (noble people). This is what makes Arab society quite unintelligible and impossible to most Europeans.

My carpenter's boy was the son of a *moonsheed* (singer in the Mosque), and at night he used to sit and warble to us, with his little baby-voice, and little round, innocent face, the most violent love-songs. He was about eight years old, and sang with wonderful finish and precision, but no expression, until I asked him for a sacred song, which begins, 'I cannot sleep for longing for thee, O Full Moon' (the Prophet), and then the little chap warmed to his work, and the feeling came out.

Palgrave has left in my charge a little black boy of his, now at Luxor, where he left him very ill, with Mustapha A'gha. The child told me he was a *nyan-nyan* (cannibal), but he did not look ogreish. I have written to Mustapha to send him me by the first opportunity. Achmet has quite recovered his temper, and I do so much better without a maid that I shall remain so. The difference in expense is enormous, and the peace and quiet a still greater gain; no more grumbling and 'exigencies' and worry; Omar irons very fairly, and the sailor washes well enough, and I don't want toilette—anyhow, I would rather wear a sack than try the experiment again. An uneducated, coarse-minded European is too disturbing an element in the family life of Easterns; the sort of filial relation, at once familiar and reverential of servants to a master they like, is odious to English and still more to French servants. If I fall in with an Arab or Abyssinian woman to suit me I will take her; but of course it is rare; a raw slave can do nothing, nor can a fellaha, and a Cairo woman is bored to death up in the Saeed. As to care and attention, I want for nothing. Omar does everything well and with pride and pleasure, and is delighted at the saving of expense in wine, beer, meat, etc. etc. One feeds six or eight Arabs well with the money for one European.

While the carpenter, his boy, and two *meneggets* were here, a very moderate dish of vegetables, stewed with a pound of meat, was put before me, followed by a chicken or a pigeon for me alone. The stew was then set on the ground to all the men, and two loaves of a piastre each, to every one, a jar of water, and, *Alhamdulillah*, four men and two boys had dined handsomely. At breakfast a water-melon and another loaf a-piece, and a cup of coffee all round; and I pass for a true Arab in hospitality. Of course no European can live so, and they despise the Arabs for doing it, while the Arab servant is not flattered at seeing the European get all sorts of costly luxuries which he thinks unnecessary; besides he has to stand on the defensive, in order not to be made a drudge by his European fellow-servant, and despised for being one; and so he leaves undone all sorts of things which he does with alacrity when it is for 'the master' only. What Omar does now seems wonderful, but he says he feels like the Sultan now he has only me to please.

July 15*th*.—Last night came the two *meneggets* to pay a friendly visit, and sat and told stories; so I ordered coffee, and one took his sugar out of his pocket to put in his cup, which made me laugh inwardly. He told a fisherman, who stopped his boat alongside for a little conversation, the story of two fishermen, the one a Jew, the other a Muslim, who were partners in the time of the Arab Prophet (upon whom be blessing and peace!). The Jew, when he flung his nets called on the Prophet of the Jews, and hauled it up full of fish every time; then the Muslim called on our Master Mohammed etc., etc., and hauled up each time only stones, until the Jew said, 'Depart, O man, thou bringest us misfortune; shall I continue to take half thy stones, and give thee half my fish? Not so.' So the Muslim went to our Master Mohammed and said, 'Behold, I mention thy name when I cast my net, and I catch only stones and calamity. How is this?' But the blessed Prophet said to him, 'Because thy stomach is black inwardly, and thou thoughtest to sell thy fish at an unfair price, and to defraud thy partner and the people, while the Jew's heart was clean towards thee and the people, and therefore God listened to him rather than to thee.' I hope our fisherman was edified by this fine moral. I also had good stories from the chief diver of Cairo, who came to examine the bottom of my boat, and told me, in a whisper, a long tale of his grandfather's descent below the waters of the Nile, into the land of the people who lived there, and keep tame crocodiles to hunt fish for them. They gave him a sleeve-full of fishes' scales, and told him never to return, and not to tell about them: and when he got home the scales had turned to money. But most wonderful of all was Haggi Hannah's story of her own life, and the journey of Omar's mother carrying her old mother in a basket on her head from Damietta to Alexandria, and dragging Omar then a very little boy, by the hand. The energy of many women here is amazing.

The Nile is rising fast, and the *Bisheer* is come (the messenger who precedes the Hajj, and brings letters). *Bisheer* is 'good tidings,' to coin a word. Many hearts are lightened and many half-broken to-day. I shall go up to the Abassia to meet the Mahmal and see the Hajjees arrive.

Next Friday I must take my boat out of the water, or at least heel her over, to repair the bad places made at Alexandria. It seems I once cured a Reis of the Pasha's of dysentery at Minieh, and he has not forgotten it, though I had; so Reis Awad will give me a good place on the Pasha's bank, and lend ropes and levers which will save a deal of expense and trouble. I shall move out all the things and myself into a boat of Zubeydeh's for four or five days, and stay alongside to superintend my caulkers.

Miss Berry* *is* dull no doubt, but few books seem dull to me now, I can tell you, and I was much delighted with such a *pièce de résistance*. Miss Eden I don't wish for—that sort of theatre burlesque view of the customs of a strange country is inexpressibly tedious to one who is familiar with one akin to it. There is plenty of *real* fun to be had here, but that sort is only funny to cockneys. I want to read Baker's book very much. I am much pleased with Abd el-Kader's book which Dozon sent me, and want the original dreadfully for Sheykh Yussuf, to show him that he and I are supported by such an authority as the great Ameer in our notions about the real unity of the Faith. The book is a curious mixture of good sense and credulity—quite 'Arab of the Arabs.' I will write a paper on the popular beliefs of Egypt; it will be curious, I think. By the way, I see in the papers and reviews speculations as to some imaginary Mohammedan conspiracy, because of the very great number of pilgrims last year from all parts to Mecca. *C'est chercher midi à quatorze heures.* Last year the day of Abraham's sacrifice,—and therefore *the* day of the pilgrimage—(the sermon on Mount Arafat) fell on a Friday, and when that happens there is always a rush, owing to the popular notion that the *Hajj el-Gumma* (pilgrimage of the Friday) is seven times blessed, or even equivalent to making it seven times in ordinary years. As any beggar in the street could tell a man this, it may give you some notion of how absurdly people make theories out of nothing for want of a little commonsense.

The *Moolid en-Nebbee* (Festival of the Prophet) has just begun. I am to have a place in the great Derweesh's tent to see the Doseh.

The Nile is rising fast; we shall kill the poor little Luxor black lamb on the day of the opening of the canal, and have a *fantasia* at night; only I grieve for my little white pussy, who sleeps every night on Ablook's (the lamb's) woolly neck, and loves him dearly. Pussy ('Bish' is Arabic for puss) was the gift of a Coptic boy at Luxor, and is wondrous funny, and as much more active and lissom than a

European cat as an Arab is than an Englishman. She and Achmet and Ablook have fine games of romps. Omar has set his heart on an English signet ring with an oval stone to engrave his name on, here you know they sign papers with a signet, not with a pen. It must be *solid* to stand hard work.

Well, I must finish this endless letter. Here comes *such* a bouquet from the Pasha's garden (somebody's sister's son is servant to the chief eunuch and brings it to me), a great round of scarlet, surrounded with white and green and with tall reeds, on which are threaded single tube-rose flowers, rising out of it so as to figure a huge flower with white pistils. Arab gardeners beat French flower-girls in bouquets.

To Sir Alexander Duff Gordon

CAIRO,
July 17, 1866.

DEAREST ALICK,

I am perfectly comfortable now with my aquatic *ménage*. The Reis is very well behaved and steady and careful, and the sort of Caliban of a sailor is a very worthy savage. Omar of course is hardworked—what with going to market, cooking, cleaning, ironing, and generally keeping everything in nice order but he won't hear of a maid of any sort. No wonder!

A clever old Reis has just come and over-hauled the bottom of the boat, and says he can mend her without taking her out of the water. We shall see; it will be great luck if he can. As I am the river doctor, all the sailoring men are glad to do me a civility.

We have had the hottest of summers; it is now 98 in the cabin. I have felt very unwell, but my blue devils are quite gone, and I am altogether better. What a miserable war it is in Europe! I am most anxious for the next papers. Here it is money misery; the Pasha is something like bankrupt, and no one has had a day's pay these three months, even pensions of sixty piastres a month (seven shillings) to poor old female slaves of Mahommed Ali's are stopped.

August 4.—The heat is and has been something fearful: we are all panting and puffing. I can't think what Palgrave meant about my being tired of poor old Egypt; I am very happy and comfortable, only I felt rather weak and poorly this year, and sometimes, I suppose, rather *wacham*, as the Arabs say, after you and the children. The heat, too, has made me lazy—it is 110 in the cabin, and 96 at night.

I saw the *Moolid en-Nebbee* (Festival of the Prophet), and the wonderful *Dóseh* (treading); it is an awful sight; so many men drunk with religious ardour.* I also went to a Turkish Hareem, where my darweesh friends sent me; it is just like a tea-party at Hampton Court, only handsomer, not as to the ladies, but the clothes, furniture and jewels, and not a bit like the description in Mrs. Lott's most extraordinary book.* Nothing is so clean as a Turkish hareem, the furniture is Dutch as to cleanliness, and their persons only like themselves—but oh! how dull and *triste* it all seemed. One nice lady said to me, 'If I had a husband and children like thee, I would die a hundred times rather than leave them for an hour,' another envied me the power of going into the street and seeing the *Dóseh*. She had never seen it, and never would.

To-morrow Olagnier will dine and spend the night here, to see the cutting of the canal,* and the 'Bride of the Nile' on Monday morning. We shall sail up to old Cairo in the evening with the Bride's boat; also Hajjee Hannah is coming for the fantasia; after the high Nile we shall take the boat out and caulk her and then, if the excessive heat continues, I rather think of a month's jaunt to Beyrout just to freshen me up. Hajjee Ali is there, with all his travelling materials and tents, so I need only take Omar and a bath and carpet-bag. If the weather gets cool I shall stay in my boat. The heat is far more oppressive here than it was at Luxor two years ago; it is not so dry. The Viceroy is afraid of cholera, and worried the poor Hajjees this year with most useless quarantine. The *Mahmal* was smuggled into Cairo before sunrise, without the usual honours, and all sightseers and holiday makers disappointed, and all good Muslims deeply offended. The idea that the Pasha has turned Christian or even Jew is spreading fast; I hear it on all sides. The new firman illegitimatising so many of his children is of course just as agreeable to a sincere Moslem as a law sanctioning polygamy for our royal family would be with us.

To Sir Alexander Duff Gordon

OFF BOULAK,
August 20, 1866.

DEAREST ALICK,

Since I wrote I have had a bad bilious attack, which has of course aggravated my cough. Everyone has had the same, and most far worse than I, but I was very wretched and most shamefully cross. Omar said, 'That is not you but the sickness,' when I found fault with everything, and it was very true. I am still seedy. Also I am beyond measure exasperated about my boat. I went up to the *Ata el-Khalig* (cutting of the canal) to see the great sight of the 'Bride of the Nile,' a lovely spectacle; and on returning we all but sank. I got out into a boat of Zubeydeh's with all my goods, and we hauled up my boat, and found her bottom rotten from stem to stern. So here I am in the midst of wood merchants, sawyers, etc., etc., rebuilding her bottom. My Reis said he had 'carried her on his head all this time' but 'what could such a one as he say against the word of a Howagah, like Ross's storekeeper?' When the English cheat each other there remains nothing but to seek refuge with God. Omar buys the wood and superintends, together with the Reis, and the builders seem good workmen and fair-dealing. I pay day by day, and have a scribe to keep the accounts. If I get out of it for £150 I shall think Omar has done wonders, for every atom has to be new. I never saw anything so rotten afloat. If I had gone up the Cataract I should never have come down alive. It is a marvel we did not sink long ago.

Mahbrook, Palgrave's boy, has arrived, and turns out well. He is a stout lubberly boy, with infinite good humour, and not at all stupid, and laughs a good real nigger yahyah, which brings the fresh breezes and lilac mountains of the Cape before me when I hear it. When I tell him to do anything he does it with strenuous care, and then asks, *tayib?* (is it well) and if I say 'Yes' he goes off, as Omar says, 'like a cannon in Ladyship's face,' in a guffaw of satisfaction. Achmet, who is half his size, orders him about and teaches him, with an air of extreme dignity and says pityingly to me, 'You see, oh Lady, he is quite new, quite green.' Achmet, who had never seen a garment or any article of European life two years ago, is now a smart valet, with very distinct ideas of waiting at table, arranging my things etc. and cooks quite cleverly. Arab boys are amazing. I have promoted him to wages—one napoleon a month—so now he will keep his family. He is about a head taller than Rainie.

I intend to write a paper on the various festivals and customs of Copts and Muslims; but I must wait to see Abu Seyfeyn, near Luxor, the great Christian Saint, where all go to be cured of possession—all mad people. The Viceroy wages steady war against all festivals and customs. The *Mahmal* was burked this year, and the fair at Tantah forbidden. Then the Europeans spoil all; the Arabs no longer go to the *Ata el-Khalig*, and at the *Dóseh*, the Frangee carriages were like the Derby day. It is only up country that the real thing remains.

To-morrow my poor black sheep will be killed over the new prow of the boat; his blood 'straked' upon her, and his flesh sodden and eaten by all the workmen, to keep off the evil eye; and on the day she goes into the water, some *Fikees* will read the Koran in the cabin, and again there will be boiled mutton and bread. The Christian *Ma-allimeen* (skilled workmen) hold to the ceremony of the sheep quite as much as the others, and always do it over a new house, boat, mill, waterwheel etc.

Did I tell you Omar has another girl—about two months ago? His wife and babies are to come up from Alexandria to see him, for he will not leave me for a day, on account of my constantly being so ailing and weak. I hope if I die away from you all, you will do something for Omar for my sake, I cannot conceive what I should do without his faithful and loving care. I don't know why he is so devotedly fond of me, but he certainly does love me as he says 'like his mother,' and moreover as a very affectionate son loves his mother. How pleasant it would be if you could come—but please don't run any risks of fatigue or exposure to cold on your return. If you cannot come I shall go to Luxor early in October and send back the boat to let. I hear from Luxor that the people are all running away from the land, unable to pay triple taxes and eat bread: the ruin is universal. The poor Sheykhs el-Beled, who had the honour of dining with the Viceroy at Minieh have each had a squeeze politely administered. One poor devil I know had to 'make a present' of 50 purses.

How is my darling Rainie? I do so long for her earnest eyes at times, and wonder if I shall ever be able to get back to you all again. I fear that break down at Soden sent me down a great terrace. I have never lost the pain and the cough for a day since. I have not been out for an age, or seen anyone. Would you know the wife of your bosom in a pair of pink trousers and a Turkish *tob*? Such is my costume as I write. The woman who came to sew could not make a gown, so she made me a pair of trousers instead. Farewell, dearest, I dare hardly say how your hint of possibly coming has made me wish it, and yet I dread to persuade you. The great heat is quite over with the high Nile, and the air on the river fresh and cool—cold at night even.

To Sir Alexander Duff Gordon

Off Boulak
August 27, 1866.

Dearest Alick,

Your letter of the 18th has this moment arrived. I am very glad to hear you are so much better. I am still seedy-ish, but no worse.

Everybody is liver-sick this year, I give calomel and jalep all round—except to myself.

The last two or three days we have been in great tribulation about the boat. On Saturday all her ribs were finished, and the planking and caulking ready to be put on, when in the night up came the old Nile with a rush, and threatened to carry her off; but by the favour of Abu-l-Hajjaj and Sheykh el-Bostawee she was saved in this wise. You remember the tall old steersman who went with us to Bedreeshayn, and whom we thought so ill-conditioned; well, he was in charge of a dahabieh close by, and he called up all the Reises and steermen to help. 'Oh men of el-Bostawee, this is *our* boat (*i.e.* we are the servants of her owner) and she is in our faces;' and then he set the example, stripped and carried dust and hammered in piles all night, and by the morning she was surrounded by a dyke breast-high. The 'long-shore' men of Boulak were not a little surprised to see dignified Reises working for nothing like fellaheen. Meanwhile my three *Ma-allimeen*, the chief builder, caulker and foreman, had also stayed all night with Omar and my Reis, who worked like the rest, and the Sheykh of all the boat-builders went to visit one of my *Ma-allimeen*, who is his nephew, and hearing the case came down too at one in the morning and stayed till dawn. Then as the workmen passed, going to their respective jobs, he called them, and said, 'Come and finish this boat; it must be done by to-morrow night.' Some men who objected and said they were going to the Pasha's dockyard, got a beating *pro forma* and the end of it was that I found forty-six men under my boat working 'like Afreets and Shaitans,' when I went to see how all was going in the morning. The old Sheykh marked out a piece to each four men, and then said, 'If that is not done to-night, Oh dogs! to-morrow I'll put on the hat'—*i.e.* 'To-day I have beaten moderately, like an Arab, but to-morrow, please God, I'll beat like a Frank, and be mad with the stick.' *Kurz und gut*, the boat which yesterday morning was a skeleton, is now, at four p.m. to-day, finished, caulked, pitched and all capitally done; if the Nile carries off the dyke, she will float safe. The shore is covered with *débris* of other people's half-finished boats I believe. I owe the ardour of the *Ma-allims* and of the Sheykh of the builders to one of my absurd pieces of Arab civility. On the day when Omar killed poor Ablook, my black sheep, over the bows and 'straked' his blood upon them, the three *Ma-allimeen* came on board this boat to eat their dish, and I followed the old Arab fashion and ate out of the wooden dish with them and the Reis 'for luck,' or rather 'for a blessing' as we say here; and it seems that this gave immense satisfaction.

My Reis wept at the death of the black sheep, which used to follow him to the coffee-shop and the market, and 'was to him as a son,' he said, but he ate of him nevertheless. Omar surreptitiously picked out the best pieces for my dinner for three days, with his usual eye to economy; then lighted a fire of old wood, borrowed a cauldron of some darweeshes, cut up the sheep, added water and salt, onions and herbs, and boiled the sheep. Then the big washing copper (a large round flat tray, like a sponging bath) was filled with bread broken in pieces, over which the broth was slowly poured till the bread was soaked. Next came a layer of boiled rice, on the top of that the pieces of boiled meat, and over all was poured butter, vinegar and garlic boiled together. This is called a *Fettah*, and is the orthodox dish of darweeshes and given at all *Khatmehs* and other semi-religious, semi-festive, semi-charitable festivities. It is excellent and not expensive. I asked how many had eaten and was told one hundred and thirty men had 'blessed my hand.' I expended 160 piastres on bread, butter and vinegar, etc. and the sheep was worth two napoleons; three napoleons in all, or less—for I ate for two days of the mutton.

The three *Ma-allims* came on board this boat, as I said and ate; and it was fine to hear us—how polite we were. 'A bit more, oh *Ma-allim*?' 'Praise be to God, we have eaten well—we will return to our work'; 'By the Prophet, coffee and a pipe.' 'Truly thou art of the most noble people.' 'Oh *Ma-allim*, ye have honoured us and rejoiced us,' 'Verily this is a day white among days,' etc. A very clever Egyptian engineer, a pupil of Whitworth's, who is living in a boat alongside mine, was much amused, and said, 'Ah you know how to manage 'em.'

I have learnt the story of the two dead bodies that hitched in my anchor-chain some time ago. They were not Europeans as I thought, but Circassians—a young man and his mother. The mother used to take him to visit an officer's wife who had been brought up in the hareem of the Pasha's mother. The husband caught them, killed them, tied them together and flung them into the Nile near Rhoda, and gave himself into the hands of the police. All was of course hushed up. He goes to Fazoghlou; and I don't know what becomes of the slave-girl, his wife. These sort of things happen every day (as the bodies testify) among the Turks, but the Europeans never hear it. I heard it by a curious chance.

September 4.—My boat will soon be finished, and now will be as good as new. Omar has worked like a good one from daybreak till night, overlooking, buying all the materials, selling all the old wood and iron, etc., and has done capitally. I shall take a paper from my *Ma-allims* who are all first class men, to certify what they have done and that the boat is as good as new. Goodah Effendi has kindly looked at her several times for me and highly approves the work done. I never saw men do a better day's work than those at the boat. It is pretty to see the carpenter holding the wood with one hand and one foot while he saws it, sitting on the ground—just like the old frescoes. Do you remember the picture of boat-building in the tomb at Sakkara? Well, it is just the same; all done with the adze; but it is stout work they put into it, I can tell you.

If you do not come (and I do not like to press you, I fear the fatigue for you and the return to the cold winter) I shall go to Luxor in a month or so and send back the boat to let. I have a neighbour now, Goodah Effendi, an engineer, who studied and married in England. His wife is gone there with the children, and he is living in a boat close by; so he comes over of an evening very often, and I am glad of his company: he is a right good fellow and very intelligent.

My best love to all at home. I've got a log from the cedars of Lebanon, my Moslem carpenter who smoothed the broken end, swallowed the sawdust, because he believed 'Our Lady Mary' had sat under the tree with 'Our Lord Jesus.'

To Sir Alexander Duff Gordon

OFF BOULAK,
September 21, 1886.

I am better again now and go on very comfortably with my two little boys. Omar is from dawn till night at work at my boat, so I have only Mahbrook and Achmet, and you would wonder to see how well I am served. Achmet cooks a very good dinner, serves it and orders Mahbrook about. Sometimes I whistle and hear *hader* (ready) from the water and in tumbles Achmet, with the water running 'down his innocent nose' and looking just like a little bronze triton of a Renaissance fountain, with a blue shirt and white skull-cap added. Mahbrook is a big lubberly lad of the laugh-and-grow-fat breed, clumsy, but not stupid, and very good and docile. You would delight in his guffaws, and the merry games and hearty laughter of my *ménage* is very pleasant to me. Another boy swims over from Goodah's boat (his Achmet), and then there are games at piracy, and much stealing of red pots from the potter's boats. The joke is to snatch one under the owner's very nose, and swim off brandishing it, whereupon the boatman uses eloquent language, and the boys out-hector him, and everybody is much amused. I only hope Palgrave won't come back from Sookum Kaleh to fetch Mahbrook just as he has got clever—not at stealing jars, but in his work. He already washes my clothes very nicely indeed; his stout black arms are made for a washer-boy. Achmet looked forward with great eagerness to your coming. He is mad to go to England, and in his heart planned to ingratiate himself with you, and go as a 'general servant.' He is very little, if at all, bigger than a child of seven, but an Arab boy '*ne doute de rien*' and does serve admirably. What would an English respectable cook say to seeing 'two dishes and a sweet' cooked over a little old wood on a few bricks, by a baby in a blue shirt? and very well cooked too, and followed by incomparable coffee.

You will be pleased to hear that your capital story of the London cabman has its exact counterpart here. 'Oh gracious God, what aileth thee, oh Achmet my brother, and why is thy bosom contracted that thou hast not once said to me d—n thy father, or son of a dog or pig, as thou art used to do.'

Can't you save up your holidays and come for four months next winter with my Maurice? However perhaps you would be bored on the Nile. I don't know. People either enjoy it rapturously or are bored, I believe. I am glad to hear from Janet that you are well. I am much better. The carpenter will finish in the boat to-day, then the painter begins and in a week, Inshallah, I shall get back into her.

To Mrs. Austin

OFF BOULAK,
September 21, 1886.

DEAREST MUTTER,

I am a good deal better again; the weather is delightful, and the Nile in full flood, which makes the river scenery from the boat very beautiful. Alick made my mouth water with his descriptions of his rides with Janet about the dear old Surrey country, having her with him seems to have quite set him up. I have seen nothing and nobody but my 'next boat' neighbour, Goodah Effendi, as Omar has been at work all day in the boat, and I felt lazy and disinclined to go out alone. Big Hassan of the donkeys has grown too lazy to go about and I don't care to go alone with a small boy here. However I am out in the best of air all day and am very well off. My two little boys are very diverting and serve me very well. The news from Europe is to my ignorant ideas *désolant*, a *dégringolade back* into military despotism, which would have excited indignation with us in our fathers' days, I think. I get lots of newspapers from Ross, which afterwards go to an Arab grocer, who reads the *Times* and the *Saturday Review* in his shop in the bazaar! what next? The cargo of books which Alick and you sent will be most acceptable for winter consumption. If I were a painter I would take up the Moslem traditions of Joseph and Mary. He was not a white-bearded old gentleman at all you must know, but young, lovely and pure as Our Lady herself. They were cousins, brought up together; and she avoided the light conversation of other girls, and used to go to the well with her jar, hand in hand with Joseph carrying his. After the angel Gabriel had announced to her the will of God, and blown into her sleeve, whereby she conceived 'the Spirit of God,' Joseph saw her state with dismay, and resolved to kill her, as was his duty as her nearest male relation. He followed her, knife in hand, meaning always to kill her at the next tree, and each time his heart failed him, until they reached the well and the tree under which the Divine messenger stood once more and said, 'Fear not oh Joseph, the daughter of thy uncle bears within her Eesa, the Messiah, the Spirit of God.' Joseph married his cousin without fear. Is it not pretty? the two types of youthful purity and piety, standing hand in hand before the angel. I think a painter might make something out of the soft-eyed Syrian boy with his jar on his shoulder (hers on the head), and the grave, modest maiden who shrank from all profane company.

I now know all about Sheykh Seleem, and why he sits naked on the river bank; from very high authority—a great Sheykh to whom it has been revealed. He was entrusted with the care of some of the holy she camels, like that on which the Prophet rode to Jerusalem in one night, and which are invisible to all but the elect, and he lost one, and now he is God's prisoner till she is found.

A letter from aunt Charley all about her own and Rainie's country life, school feasts etc., made me quite cry, and brought before me—oh, how vividly—the difference between East and West, not quite *all* to the advantage of home however, though mostly. What is pleasant here is the primitive ways. Three times since I have been here lads of most respectable families of Luxor have come to ask hospitality, which consists in a place on the deck of the boat, and liberty to dip their bread in the common dish with my slave boy and Achmet. The bread they brought with them, 'bread and shelter' were not asked, as they slept *sub dio*. In England I must have refused the hospitality, on account of *gêne* and expense. The chief object to the lads was the respectability of being under my eye while away from their fathers, as a satisfaction to their families; and while they ate and slept like beggars, as we should say, they read their books and chatted with me, when I was out on the deck, on perfectly equal terms, only paying the respect proper to my age. I thought of the 'orphanages and institutions' and all the countless difficulties of that sort, and wondered whether something was not to be said for this absence of civilisation in knives, forks, beds, beer, and first and second tables above all. Of course climate has a good deal to do with the facility with which widows and orphans are absorbed here.

Goodbye dearest Mutter: to-day is post day, and Reis Mohammed is about to trudge into town in such a dazzling white turban and such a grand black robe. His first wife, whom he was going to divorce for want of children, has brought him a son, and we jeer him a little about what he may find in Luxor from the second, and wish him a couple of dozen.

To Sir Alexander Duff Gordon

CAIRO,
October 15, 1866.

DEAREST ALICK,

I have been back in my own boat four days, and most comfortable she is. I enlarged the saloon, and made a good writing table, and low easy divans instead of benches, and added a sort of pantry and sleeping cabin in front; so that Omar has not to come through the saloon to sleep; and I have all the hareem part to myself. Inside there is a good large stern cabin, and wash-closet and two small cabins with beds long enough even for you. Inshallah, you and Maurice will come next winter and go up the Nile and enjoy it with me. I intend to sail in ten days and to send back the 'Urania' to seek work for the winter. We had a very narrow escape of being flooded this year. I fear a deal of damage has been done to the dourrah and cotton crops. It was sad to see the villagers close by here trying to pull up a little green dourrah as the Nile slowly swallowed up the fields.

I was forced to flog Mabrook yesterday for smoking on the sly, a grave offence here on the part of a boy; it is considered disrespectful; so he was ordered, with much parade, to lie down, and Omar gave him two cuts with a rope's end, an apology for a flogging which would have made an Eton boy stare. The stick here is quite nominal, except in official hands. I can't say Mabrook seemed at all impressed, for he was laughing heartily with Omar in less than ten minutes; but the affair was conducted with as much solemnity as an execution.

'Sheykh' Stanley's friend, Gezawee, has married his negro slave to his own sister, on the plea that he was the best young man he knew. What would a Christian family say to such an arrangement?

My boat is beautifully buoyant now, and has come up by the bows in fine style. I have not sailed her yet, but have doubt she will 'walk well' as the Arabs say. Omar got £10 by the sale of old wood and nails, and also gave me 2000 piastres, nearly £12, which the workmen had given him as a sort of backsheesh. They all pay one, two or three piastres daily to any *wakeel* (agent) who superintends; that is his profit, and it is enormous at that rate. I said, 'Why did you not refuse it?' But Omar replied they had pay enough after that reduction, which is always made from them, and that in his opinion therefore, it came out of the master's pocket, and was 'cheatery.' How people have been talking nonsense about Jamaica *chez vous*. I have little doubt Eyre did quite right, and still less doubt that the niggers have had enough of the sort of provocation which I well know, to account for the outbreak. Baker's effusion is a very poor business. There may be blacks like tigers (and whites too in London for that matter). I myself have seen at least five sorts of blacks (negroes, not Arabs), more unlike each other than Swedes are unlike Spaniards; and many are just like ourselves. Of course they want governing with a strong hand, like all ignorant, childish creatures. But I am fully convinced that custom and education are the only real differences between one set of men and another, their inner nature is the same all the world over.

My Reis spoke such a pretty parable the other day that I must needs write it. A Coptic Reis stole some of my wood, which we got back by force and there was some reviling of the Nazarenes in consequence from Hoseyn and Ali; but Reis Mohammed said: 'Not so; Girgis is a thief, it is true, but many Christians are honest; and behold, all the people in the world are like soldiers, some wear red and some blue; some serve on foot, others on horseback, and some in ships; but all serve one Sultan, and each fights in the regiment in which the Sultan has placed him, and he who does his duty best is the best man, be his coat red or blue or black.' I said, 'Excellent words, oh Reis, and fit to be spoken from the best of pulpits.' It is surprising what happy sayings the people here hit upon; they cultivate talk for want of reading, and the consequence is great facility of narration and illustration. Everybody enforces his ideas like Christ, in parables. Hajjee Hannah told me two excellent fairy tales, which I will write for Rainie with some Bowdlerising, and several laughable stories, which I will leave unrecorded, as savouring too much of Boccaccio's manner, or that of the Queen of Navarre. I told Achmet to sweep the floor after dinner just now. He hesitated, and I called again: 'What manner is this, not to sweep when I bid thee?' 'By the most high God,' said the boy, 'my hand shall not sweep in thy boat after sunset, oh Lady; I would rather have it cut off than sweep thee out of thy property.' I found that you must not sweep at night, nor for three days after the departure of a guest whose return you desire, or of the master of the house. 'Thinkest thou that my brother would sweep away the dust of thy feet from the floors at Luxor,' continued Achmet, 'he would fear never to see thy fortunate face again.' If you don't want to see your visitor again you break a *gulleh* (water-jar) behind him as he leaves the house, and sweep away his footsteps.

What a canard your papers have in Europe about a constitution here. I won't write any politics, it is all too dreary; and Cairo gossip is odious, as you may judge by the productions of Mesdames Odouard and Lott. Only remember this, there is no law nor justice but the will, or rather the caprice, of one man. It is nearly impossible for any European to conceive such a state of things as really exists. Nothing but perfect familiarity with the governed, *i.e.* oppressed, class will teach it; however intimate a man may be with the rulers he will never fully take it in. I am *à l'index* here, and none of the people I know dare come to see me; Arab I mean. It was whispered in my ear in the street by a friend I met. Ismael Pasha's chief pleasure is gossip, and a certain number of persons, chiefly Europeans, furnish him with it daily, true or false. If the farce of the constitution ever should be acted here it will be superb. Something like the Consul going in state to ask the fellaheen what wages they got. I could tell you a little of the value of consular information; but what is the use? Europe is enchanted with the enlightened Pasha who has ruined this fine country.

I long so to see you and Rainie! I don't like to hope too much, but Inshallah, next year I shall see you all.

To Sir Alexander Duff Gordon

OFF BOULAK,
October 19, 1866.

I shall soon sail up the river. Yesterday Seyd Mustapha arrived, who says that the Greeks are all gone, and the poor Austrian at Thebes is dead, so I shall represent Europe in my single person from Siout to, I suppose, Khartoum.

You would delight in Mabrook; a man asked him the other day after his flogging, if he would not run away, to see what he would say as he alleged, I suspect he meant to steal and sell him. 'I run away, to eat lentils like you? when *my* Effendi gives me meat and bread every day, and *I eat such a lot*.' Is not that a delicious practical view of liberty? The creature's enjoyment of life is quite a pleasure to witness, and he really works very well and with great alacrity. If Palgrave claims him I think I must buy him.

I hear sad accounts from the Saeed: the new taxes and the new levies of soldiers are driving the people to despair and many are running away from the land, which will no longer feed them after paying all exactions, to join the Bedaween in the desert, which is just as if our peasantry turned gipsies. A man from Dishné visited me: the people there want me to settle in their village and offer me a voluntary *corvée* if I will buy land, so many men to work for me two days a month each, I haven't a conception why. It is a place about fifty miles below Luxor, a large agricultural village.

Omar's wife Mabrookah came here yesterday, a nice young woman, and the babies are fine children and very sweet-tempered. She told me that the lion's head, which I sent down to Alexandria to go to you, was in her room when a neighbour of hers, who had never had a child, saw it, and at once conceived. The old image worship survives in the belief, which is all over Egypt, that the 'Anteeks' (antiques) can cure barrenness. Mabrookah was of course very smartly dressed, and the reckless way in which Eastern women treat their fine clothes gives them a grand air, which no Parisian Duchess could hope to imitate—not that I think it a virtue mind you, but some vices are genteel.

Last night was a great Sheykh's fête, such drumming and singing, and ferrying across the river. The Nile is running down unusually fast, and I think I had better go soon, as the mud of Cairo is not so sweet as the mud of the upper land.

To Mrs. Austin

OFF BOULAK,
October 25, 1866.

DEAREST MUTTER,

I have got all ready, and shall sail on Saturday. My men have baked the bread, and received their wages to go to Luxor and bring the boat back to let. It is turning cold, but I feel none the worse for it, though I shall be glad to go. I've had a dreary, worrying time here, and am tired of hearing of all the meannesses and wickedness which constitute the *on dits* here. Not that I hear much, but there is nothing else. I shall be best at Luxor now the winter has set in so early. You would laugh at such winter when one sits out all day under an awning in English summer clothes, and wants only two blankets at night; but all is comparative *ici bas*, and I call it cold, and Mabrook ceases to consider his clothes such a grievance as they were to him at first, and takes kindly to a rough *capote* for the night. I have just been interrupted by my Reis and one of my men, who came in to display the gorgeous printed calico they have bought; one for his Luxor wife and the other for his betrothed up near Assouan. (The latter is about eight years old, and Hosein has dressed her and paid her expenses these five years, as is the custom up in that district.) The Reis has bought a silk head-kerchief for nine shillings, but that was in the marriage contract. So I must see, admire and wish good luck to the finery, and to the girls who are to wear it. Then we had a little talk about the prospects of letting the boat, and, Inshallah, making some money for *el gamma*, *i.e.*, 'all our company,' or 'all of us together.' The Reis hopes that the *Howagat* will not be too outrageous in their ways or given to use the stick, as the solution of every difficulty.

The young Shurafa of Abu-l-Hajjaj came from Gama'l Azhar to-day to bid me goodbye and bring their letters for Luxor. I asked them about the rumours that the Ulema are preaching against the Franks (which is always being said), but they had heard nothing of the sort, and said they had not heard of anything the Franks had done lately which would signify to the Muslims at all. It is not the Franks who press so many soldiers, or levy such heavy taxes three months in advance! I will soon write again. I feel rather like the wandering Jew and long for home and rest, without being dissatisfied with what I have and enjoy, God knows. If I *could* get better and come home next summer.

To Sir Alexander Duff Gordon

LUXOR,
November 21, 1866.

DEAREST ALICK,

I arrived here on the morning of the 11th. I am a beast not to have written, but I caught cold after four days and have really not been well, so forgive me, and I will narrate and not apologise. We came up best pace, as the boat is a flyer now, only fourteen days to Thebes, and to Keneh only eleven. Then we had bad winds, and my men pulled away at the rope, and sang about the *Reis el-Arousa* (bridegroom) going to his bride, and even Omar went and pulled the rope. We were all very merry, and played practical jokes on a rascal who wanted a pound to guide me to the tombs: we made him run miles, fetch innumerable donkeys, and then laughed at his beard. Such is boatmen fun. On arriving at Luxor I heard a *charivari* of voices, and knew I was 'at home,' by the shrill pipe of the little children, *el Sitt, el Sitt*. Visitors all day of course, at night comes up another dahabieh, great commotion, as it had been telegraphed from Cairo (which I knew before I left, and was to be stopped). So I coolly said, 'Oh Mustapha, the Indian saint (Walee) is in thine eye, seeing that an Indian is all as one with an Englishman.' 'How did I know there was an Indian and a Walee?' etc. Meanwhile the Walee had a bad thumb, and some one told his slave that there was a wonderful English doctress, so in the morning he sent for me, and I went inside the hareem. He was very friendly, and made me sit close beside him, told me he was fourth in descent from Abd el-Kader Gylamee of Bagdad, but his father settled at Hyderabad, where he has great estates. He said he was a Walee or saint, and would have it that I was in the path of the darweeshes; gave me medicine for my cough; asked me many questions, and finally gave me five dollars and asked if I wanted more? I thanked him heartily, kissed the money politely, and told him I was not poor enough to want it and would give it in his name to the poor of

Luxor, but that I would never forget that the Indian Sheykh had behaved like a brother to an English woman in a strange land. He then spoke in great praise of the 'laws of the English,' and said many more kind things to me, adding again, 'I tell thee thou art a Darweesh, and do not thou forget me.' Another Indian from Lahore, I believe the Sheykh's tailor, came to see me—an intelligent man, and a Syrian doctor; a manifest scamp. The people here said he was a *bahlawar* (rope-dancer). Well, the authorities detained the boat with fair words till orders came from Keneh to let them go up further. Meanwhile the Sheykh came out and performed some miracles, which I was not there to see, perfuming people's hands by touching them with his, and taking English sovereigns out of a pocketless jacket, and the doctor told wonders of him. Anyhow he spent £10 in one day here, and he is a regular darweesh. He and all the Hareem were poorly dressed and wore no ornaments whatever. I hope Seyd Abdurachman will come down safe again, but no one knows what the Government wants of him or why he is so watched. It is the first time I ever saw an Oriental travelling for pleasure. He had about ten or twelve in the hareem, among them his three little girls, and perhaps twenty men outside, Indians, and Arabs from Syria, I fancy.

Next day I moved into the old house, and found one end in ruins, owing to the high Nile and want of repair. However there is plenty more safe and comfortable. I settled all accounts with my men, and made an inventory in Arabic, which Sheykh Yussuf wrote for me, which we laughed over hugely. How to express a sauce-boat, a pie-dish, etc. in Arabic, was a poser. A genteel Effendi, who sat by, at last burst out in uncontrollable amazement; 'There is no God but God: is it possible that four or five Franks can use all these things to eat, drink and sleep on a journey?' (N.B. I fear the Franks will think the stock very scanty.) Whereupon master Achmet, with the swagger of one who has seen cities and men, held forth. 'Oh Effendim, that is nothing; Our Lady is almost like the children of the Arabs. One dish or two, a piece of bread, a few dates, and Peace, (as we say, there is an end of it). But thou shouldst see the merchants of Escandarieh, (Alexandria), three tablecloths, forty dishes, to each soul seven plates of all sorts, seven knives and seven forks and seven spoons, large and small, and seven different glasses for wine and beer and water.' 'It is the will of God,' replied the Effendi, rather put down: 'but,' he added, 'it must be a dreadful fatigue to them to eat their dinner.' Then came an impudent merchant who wanted to go down with his bales and five souls in my boat for nothing. But I said, 'Oh man, she is my property, and I will eat from her of thy money as of the money of the Franks.' Whereupon he offered £1, but was bundled out amid general reproaches for his avarice and want of shame. So all the company said a *Fattah* for the success of the voyage, and Reis Mohammed was exhorted to 'open his eyes,' and he should have a tarboosh if he did well.

Then I went to visit my kind friend the Maōhn's wife, and tell her all about her charming daughter and grandchildren. I was, of course, an hour in the streets salaaming, etc. '*Sheerafteenee Beledna*, thou hast honoured our country on all sides.' 'Blessings come with thee,' etc.

Everything is cheaper than last year, but there is no money to buy with, and the taxes have grown beyond bearing, as a fellah said, 'a man can't (we will express it "blow his nose," if you please; the real phrase was less parliamentary, and expressive of something at once *ventose* and valueless) without a cawass behind him to levy a tax on it.' The ha'porth of onions we buy in the market is taxed on the spot, and the fish which the man catches under my window. I paid a tax on buying charcoal, and another on having it weighed. People are terribly beaten to get next year's taxes out of them, which they have not the money to pay.

The Nubian M.P.'s passed the other day in three boats, towed by a steamer, very frightened and sullen. I fell in with some Egyptians on my way, and tried the European style of talk. 'Now you will help to govern the country, what a fine thing for you,' etc. I got such a look of rueful reproach. 'Laugh not thou at our beards O Effendim! God's mercy, what words are these? and who is there on the banks of the Nile who can say anything but *hader* (ready), with both hands on the head, and a salaam to the ground even to a Moudir; and thou talkest of speaking before Effendina! Art thou mad, Effendim?' Of all the vexations none are more trying than the distinctions which have been inflicted on the unlucky Sheykhs el-Beled. In fear and trembling they ate their Effendina's banquet and sadly paid the bill: and those who have had the *Nishan* (the order of the Mejeedee) have had to disburse fees whereat the Lord Chamberlain's staff's mouths might water, and now the wretched delegates to the Egyptian Chambers (God save the mark) are going down with their hearts in their shoes. The Nubians say that the Divan is to be held in the Citadel and that the road by which the Memlook Beys left it is not stopped up, though perhaps it goes underground nowadays.

November 27.—The first steamer full of travellers has just arrived, and with it the bother of the ladies all wanting my saddle. I forbade Mustapha to send for it, but they intimidate the poor old fellow, and he comes and kisses my hand not to get him into trouble with one old woman who says she is the relation of a Consul and a great lady in her own country. I am what Mrs. Grote called 'cake' enough to concede to Mustapha's fears what I had sworn to refuse henceforth. Last year five women on one steamer all sent for my saddle, besides other things—campstools, umbrellas, beer, etc., etc. This year I'll bolt the doors when I see a steamer coming. I hear the big people are so angry with the Indian saint because he treated them like dirt everywhere. One great man went with a Moudir to see him, and asked him to sell him a memlook (a young slave boy). The Indian, who had not spoken or saluted, burst forth, 'Be silent, thou wicked one! dost thou dare to ask me to sell thee a soul to take it with thee to hell?' Fancy the surprise of the 'distinguished' Turk. Never had he heard such language. The story has travelled all up the river and is of course much enjoyed.

Last night Sheykh Yussuf gave an entertainment, killed a sheep, and had a reading of the *Sirat er-Russoul* (Chapter on the Prophet). It was the night of the Prophet's great vision, and is a great night in Islam. I was sorry not to be well enough to go. Now that there is no Kadee here, Sheykh Yussuf has lots of business to settle; and he came to me and said, 'Expound to me the laws of marriage and inheritance of the Christians, that I may do no wrong in the affairs of the Copts, for they won't go and be settled by the priest out of the Gospels, and I can't find any laws, except about marriage in the Gospels.' I set him up with the text of the tribute money, and told him to judge according to his own laws, for that Christians had no laws other than those of the country they lived in. Poor Yussuf was sore perplexed about a divorce case. I refused to 'expound,' and told him all the learned in the law in England had not yet settled which text to follow.

Do you remember the German story of the lad who travelled *um das Grüseln zu lernen*? Well, I, who never *grüselte* before, had a touch of it a few evenings ago. I was sitting here quietly drinking tea, and four or five men were present, when a cat came to the door. I called 'biss, biss,' and offered milk, but pussy, after looking at us, ran away. 'Well dost thou, oh Lady,' said a quiet, sensible man, a merchant here, 'to be kind to the cat, for I dare say he gets little enough at home; *his* father, poor man, cannot cook for his children every day.' And then in an explanatory tone to the company, 'That is Alee Nasseeree's boy Yussuf—it must be Yussuf, because his fellow twin Ismaeen is with his mule at Negadeh.' *Mir grüselte*, I confess, not but what I have heard things almost as absurd from gentlemen and ladies in Europe; but an 'extravagance' in a *kuftan* has quite a different effect from one in a tail coat. 'What my butcher's boy who brings the meat—a cat?' I gasped. 'To be sure, and he knows well where to look for a bit of good cookery, you see. All twins go out as cats at night if they go to sleep hungry; and their own bodies lie at home like dead meanwhile, but no one must touch them, or they would die. When they grow up to ten or twelve they leave it off. Why your boy Achmet does it. Oh Achmet! do you go out as a cat at night?' 'No,' said Achmet tranquilly, 'I am not a twin—my sister's sons do.' I inquired if people were not afraid of such cats. 'No, there is no fear, they only eat a little of the cookery, but if you beat them they will tell their parents next day, "So-and-so beat me in his house last night," and show their bruises. No, they are not Afreets, they are *beni Adam* (sons of Adam), only twins do it, and if you give them a sort of onion broth and camel's milk the first thing when they are born, they don't do it at all.' Omar professed never to have heard of it, but I am sure he had, only he dreads being laughed at. One of the American missionaries told me something like it as belonging to the Copts, but it is entirely Egyptian, and common to both religions. I asked several Copts who assured me it was true, and told it just the same. Is it a remnant of the doctrine of transmigration? However the notion fully accounts for the horror the people feel at the idea of killing a cat.

A poor pilgrim from the black country was taken ill yesterday at a village six miles from here, he could speak only a few words of Arabic and begged to be carried to the Abab'deh. So the Sheykh el-Beled put him on a donkey and sent him and his little boy, and laid him in Sheykh Hassan's house. He called for Hassan and begged him to take care of the child, and to send him to an uncle somewhere in Cairo. Hassan said, 'Oh you will get well Inshallah, etc., and take the boy with you.' 'I cannot take him into the grave with me,' said the black pilgrim. Well in the night he died and the boy went to Hassan's mat and said, 'Oh Hassan, my father is dead.' So the two Sheykhs and several men got up and went and sat with the boy till dawn, because he refused to lie down or to leave his father's corpse. At daybreak he said, 'Take me now and sell me, and buy new cloth to dress my father for the tomb.' All the Abab'deh cried when they heard it, and Hassan went and bought the cloth, and some sweet stuff for the boy who remains with him. Such is death on the road in Egypt. I tell it as Hassan's slave told it to me, and somehow we all cried again at the poor little boy rising from his dead father's side to say, 'Come now sell me to dress my father for the tomb.' These strange black pilgrims always interest me. Many take four years to Mecca and home, and have children born to them on the road, and learn a few words of Arabic.

To Mrs. Ross

LUXOR,
December 5, 1866.

DEAREST JANET,

I write in answer to yours by the steamer, to go down by the same. I fancy I should be quite of your mind about Italy. I hate the return of Europe to

> 'The good old rule and ancient plan,
> That he should take who has the power,
> And he should keep who can.'

Nor can I be bullied into looking on 'might' as 'right.' Many thanks for the papers, I am anxious to hear about the Candia business. All my neighbours are sick at heart. The black boy Palgrave left with me is a very good lad, only he can't keep his clothes clean, never having been subject to that annoyance before. He has begun to be affectionate ever since I did not beat him for breaking my only looking-glass. I wish an absurd respect for public opinion did not compel him to wear a blue shirt and a tarboosh (his suit), I see it is misery to him. He is a very gentle cannibal.

I have been very unwell indeed and still am extremely weak, but I hope I am on the mend. A eunuch here who is a holy man tells me he saw my boat coming up heavily laden in his sleep, which indicates a 'good let.' I hope my reverend friend is right. If you sell any of your things when you leave Egypt let me have some blankets for the boat; if she is let to a friendly dragoman he will supply all deficiencies out of his own canteen, but if to one 'who knows not Joseph' I fear many things will be demanded by rightminded British travellers, which must be left to the Reis's discretion to buy for them. I hope all the *fattahs* said for the success of the 'Urania's' voyage will produce a due effect. Here we rely a good deal on the favour of Abu-l-Hajjaj in such matters. The *naïveté* with which people pray here for money is very amusing—though really I don't know why one shouldn't ask for one's daily sixpence as well as one's daily bread.

An idiot of a woman has written to me to get her a place as governess in an 'European or Arabian family in the neighbourhood of Thebes!' Considering she has been six years in Egypt as she says, she must be well fitted to teach. She had better learn to make *gilleh* and spin wool. The young Americans whom Mr. Hale sent were very nice. The Yankees are always the best bred and best educated travellers that I see here.

To Sir Alexander Duff Gordon

LUXOR,
December 31, 1886.

DEAREST ALICK,

I meant to have sent you a long yarn by a steamer which went the other day, but I have been in my bed. The weather set in colder than I ever felt it here, and I have been very unwell for some time. Dr. Osman Ibraheem (a friend of mine, an elderly man who studied in Paris in Mohammed Ali's time) wants me to spend the summer up here and take sand baths, *i.e.* bury myself up to the chin in the hot sand, and to get a Dongola slave to rub me. A most fascinating derweesh from Esneh gave me the same advice; he wanted me to go and live near him at Esneh, and let him treat me. I wish you could see Sheykh Seleem, he is a sort of remnant of the Memlook Beys—a Circassian—who has inherited his master's property up at Esneh, and married his master's daughter. The master was one of the Beys, also a slave inheriting from his master. Well after being a terrible *Shaitan* (devil) after drink, women, etc. Seleem has repented and become a man of pilgrimage and prayer and perpetual fasting; but he has retained the exquisite grace and charm of manner which must have made him irresistible in his *shaitan* days, and also the beautifully delicate style of dress—a dove-coloured cloth *sibbeh* over a pale blue silk *kuftan*, a turban like a snow-drift, under which flowed the silky fair hair and beard, and the dainty white hands under the long muslin shirt sleeve made a picture; and such a smile, and such ready graceful talk. Sheykh Yussuf brought him to me as a sort of doctor, and also to try and convert me on one point. Some Christians had made Yussuf quite miserable, by telling him of the doctrine that all unbaptised infants went to eternal fire; and as he knew that I had lost a child very young, it weighed on his mind that perhaps I fretted about this, and so he said he could not refrain from trying to convince me that God was not so cruel and unjust as the Nazarene priests represented Him, and that all infants whatsoever, as well as all ignorant persons, were to be saved. 'Would that I could take the cruel error out of the minds of all the hundreds and thousands of poor Christian mothers who must be tortured by it,' said he, 'and let them understand that their dead babies are with Him who sent and who took them.' I own I did not resent this interference with my orthodoxy, especially as it is the only one I ever knew Yussuf attempt.

Dr. Osman is a lecturer in the Cairo school of medicine, a Shereef, and eminently a gentleman. He came up in the passenger steamer and called on me and spent all his spare time with me. I liked him better than the bewitching derweesh Seleem; he is so like my old love Don Quixote. He was amazed and delighted at what he heard here about me. '*Ah Madame, on vous aime comme une sœur, et on vous respecte comme une reine; cela rejouit le cœur des honnêtes gens de voir tous les préjugés oubliés et détruits à ce point*.' We had no end of talk. Osman is the only Arab I know who has read a good deal of European literature and history and is able to draw comparisons. He said, '*Vous seule dans toute l'Egypte connaissez le peuple et comprenez ce qui se passe, tous les autres Européens ne savent absolument rien que les dehors; il n'y a que vous qui ayez inspiré la confiance qu'il faut pour connaître la vérité*.' Of course this is between ourselves, I tell you, but I don't want to boast of the kind thoughts people have of me, simply because I am decently civil to them.

In Egypt we are eaten up with taxes; there is not a penny left to anyone. The taxes for the whole year *eight months in advance* have been levied, as far as they can be beaten out of the miserable people. I saw one of the poor dancing girls the other day, (there are three in Luxor) and she told me how cruel the new tax on them is. It is left to the discretion of the official who farms it to make each woman pay according to her presumed gains, *i.e.* her good looks, and thus the poor women are exposed to all the caprices and extortions of the police. This last new tax has excited more disgust than any. 'We now know the name of our ruler,' said a fellah who had just heard of it, 'he is *Mawas* Pasha.' I won't translate—but it is a terrible epithet when uttered in a tone which gives it the true meaning, though in a general way the commonest word of abuse to a donkey, or a boy, or any other cattle. The wages of prostitution are unclean, and this tax renders all Government salaries unlawful according to strict law. The capitation tax too, which was remitted for three years on the pasha's accession to the people of Cairo, Alexandria, Damietta and Rascheed, is now called for. Omar will have to pay about £8 back tax, which he had fondly imagined himself excused from. You may conceive the distress this must cause among artisans, etc., who have spent their money and forgotten it, and feel cheated out of the blessings they then bestowed on the Pasha—as to that they will take out the change in curses.

There was a meeting here the other day of the Kadee, Sheykh el-Beled, and other notables to fix the amount of tax each man was to pay towards the increased police tax; and the old Shereef at the end spoke up, and said he had heard that one man had asked me to lend him money, and that he hoped such a thing would not happen again. Everyone knew I had had heavy expenses this year, and most likely had not much money; that my heart was soft, and that as everyone was in distress it would be 'breaking my head,' and in short that he should think it unmanly if anyone tried to trouble a lone woman with his troubles. I did offer one man £2 that he might not be forced to run away to the desert, but he refused it and said, 'I had better go at once and rob out there, and not turn rogue towards thee—never could I repay it.' The people are running away in all directions.

When the Moolid of the Sheykh came the whole family Abu-l-Hajjaj could only raise six hundred and twenty piastres among them to buy the buffalo cow, which by custom—strong as the laws of the Medes and Persians—must be killed for the strangers who come; and a buffalo cow is worth one thousand piastres. So the stout old Shereef (aged 87) took his staff and the six hundred and twenty piastres, and sallied forth to walk to Erment and see what God would send them; and a charitable woman in Erment did give a buffalo cow for the six hundred and twenty piastres, and he drove her home the twenty miles rejoicing.

There has been a burglary over at Gourneh, an unheard-of event. Some men broke into the house of the Coptic *gabit* (tax-gatherer) and stole the money-box containing about sixty purses—over £150. The *gabit* came to me sick with the fright which gave him jaundice, and about eight men are gone in chains to Keneh on suspicion. Hajjee Baba too, a Turkish cawass, is awfully bilious; he says he is 'sick from beating men, and it's no use, you can't coin money on their backs and feet when they haven't a para in the world.' Altogether everyone is gloomy, and many desperate. I never saw the aspect of a population so changed.

January 1, 1867. God bless you, dearest Alick, and grant you many good years more. I must finish this to go to-morrow by the steamer. I would give a great deal to see you again, but when will that be?

To Sir Alexander Duff Gordon

LUXOR,
January 12, 1867.

DEAREST ALICK,

Only two days ago I received letters from you of the 17 September and the 19 November. I wonder how many get lost and where? Janet gives me hopes of a visit of a few days in March and promises me a little terrier dog, whereat Omar is in raptures. I have made no plans at all, never having felt well enough to hope to be able to travel. The weather has changed for the better, and it is not at all old now; we shall see what the warmth does for me. You make my bowels yearn with your account of Rainie. If only we had Prince Achmet's carpet, and you could all come here for a few months.

We were greatly excited here last week; a boy was shot out in the sugar-cane field: he was with four Copts, and at first it looked ugly for the Copts. But the Maōhn tells me he is convinced they are innocent, and that they only prevaricated from fear—it was robbers shot the poor child. What struck and surprised me in the affair was the excessive horror and consternation it produced; the Maōhn had not had a murder in his district at all in eight years. The market-place was thronged with wailing women, Omar was sick all day, and the Maōhn pale and wretched. The horror of killing seems greater here than ever I saw it. Palgrave says the same of the Arabian Arabs in his book: it is not one's notion of Oriental feeling, but a murder in England is taken quite as a joke compared with the scene here. I fear there will be robberies, owing to the distress, and the numbers who are running away from the land unable to pay their taxes. Don't fear for me, for I have two watchmen in the house every night—the regular guard and an amateur, a man whose boy I took down to Cairo to study in Gama'l Azhar.

Palgrave has written to Ross wanting Mabrook back. I am very sorry, the more so as Mabrook is recalcitrant. 'I want to stay with thee, I don't want to go back to the Nazarene.' A boy who heard him said, 'but the Lady is a Nazarene too;' whereupon Mabrook slapped his face with great vigour. He will be troublesome if he does turn restive, and he is one who can only be managed by kindness. He is as good and quiet as possible with us, but the stubborn will is there and he is too ignorant to be reasoned with.

January 14.—To-day the four Copts have again changed their story, and after swearing that the robbers were strangers, have accused a man who has shot birds for me all this winter: and the poor devil is gone to Keneh in chains. The weather seems to have set in steadily for fine. I hope soon to get out, but my donkey has grown old and shaky and I am too weak to walk, so I sit in the balcony.

To Mrs. Austin

LUXOR,
January 14, 1867.

DEAREST MUTTER,

We have had a very cold winter and I have been constantly ailing, luckily the cough has transferred itself from the night to the day, and I get some good sleep. The last two days have been much warmer and I hope matters will mend. I am beginning to take cod-liver oil, as we can't find a milch camel anywhere.

My boat has been well let in Cairo and is expected here every day. The gentlemen shoot, and tell the crew not to row, and in short take it easy, and give them £2 in every place. Imagine what luxury for my crew. I shall have to dismiss the lot, they will be so spoilt. The English Consul-General came up in a steamer with Dr. Patterson and Mr. Francis. I dined with them one day; I wish you could have seen me carried in my armchair high up on the shoulders of four men, like a successful candidate, or more like one of the Pharaohs in an ancient bas-relief, preceded by torch bearers and other attendants and followers, my procession was quite regal. I wish I could show you a new friend of mine, Osman Ibraheem, who studied medicine five years in Paris. My heart warmed to him directly, because like most high-bred Arabs, he is so like Don Quixote—only Don Quixote quite in his senses. The sort of innocent sententiousness, and perfectly natural love of fine language and fine sentiments is unattainable to any European, except, I suppose, a Spaniard. It is quite unlike Italian fustian or French *sentiment*. I suppose to most Europeans it is ridiculous, but I used to cry when the carriers beat the most noble of all knights, when I was a little girl and read Don

Quixote; and now I felt as it were like Sancho, when I listened to Osman reciting bits of heroic poetry, or uttering 'wise saws' and 'modern instances,' with the peculiar mixture of strong sense of 'exultation' which stamps the great Don. I may not repeat all I heard from him of the state of things here, and the insults he had to endure—a Shereef and an educated man—from coarse Turkish Pashas; it was the carriers over again. He told me he had often cried like a woman, at night in his own room, at the miseries he was forced to witness and could do nothing to relieve; all the men I have particularly liked I find are more or less pupils of the Sheykh el-Bagooree now dead, who seems to have had a gift of inspiring honourable feeling. Our good Maōhn is one; he is no conjuror, but the honesty and goodness are heroic which lead a man to starve on £15 a month, when he is expected to grow rich on plunder.

The war in Crete* saddens many a household here. Sheykh Yussuf's brother, Sheykh Yooris, is serving there, and many more. People are actually beginning to say 'We hope the English and French won't fight for the Sultan if the Moscovites want to eat him—there will be no good for us till the Turks are driven out.' All the old religious devotion to the Sultan seems quite gone.

Poor Mustapha has been very unwell and I stopped his Ramadan, gave him some physic and ordered him not to fast, for which I think he is rather grateful. The Imaam and Mufti always endorse my prohibitions of fasting to my patients. Old Ismaeen is dead, aged over a hundred; he served Belzoni, and when he grew doting was always wanting me to go with him to join Belzoni at Abu Simbel. He was not at all ill—he only went out like a candle. His grandson brought me a bit of the meat cooked at his funeral, and begged me to eat it, that I might live to be very old, according to the superstition here. When they killed the buffalo for the Sheykh Abu-l-Hajjaj, the man who had a right to the feet kindly gave them to Omar, who wanted to make calves' foot jelly for me. I had a sort of profane feeling, as if I were eating a descendant of the bull Apis.

I am reading Mme. du Deffand's letters. What a repulsive picture of a woman.* I don't know which I dislike most, Horace Walpole or herself: the conflict of selfishness, vanity and *ennui* disguised as sentiment is quite hateful: to her Turgot was *un sot animal*,—so much for her great gifts.

Remember me kindly to William and tell him how much I wish I could see his 'improvements,' Omar also desires his salaam to him, having a sort of fellow feeling for your faithful henchman. I need not say he kisses your hand most dutifully.

To Sir Alexander Duff Gordon

LUXOR,
January 22, 1867.

DEAREST ALICK,

The weather has been lovely, for the last week, and I am therefore somewhat better. My boat arrived to-day, with all the men in high good-humour, and Omar tells me all is in good order, only the people in Cairo gave her the evil eye, and broke the iron part of the rudder which had to be repaired at Benisouef. Mr. Lear* has been here the last few days, and is just going up to the second cataract; he has done a little drawing of my house for you—a new view of it. He is a pleasant man and I was glad to see him.

Such a queer fellow came here the other day—a tall stalwart Holsteiner, I should think a man of fifty, who has been four years up in the Soudan and Sennaar, and being penniless, had walked all through Nubia begging his way. He was not the least 'down upon his luck' and spoke with enthusiasm of the hospitality and kindness of Sir Samuel Baker's 'tigers.' *Ja, das sind die rechten Kerls, dass ist das glückliche Leben*. His account is that if you go with an armed party, the blacks naturally show fight, as men with guns, in their eyes, are always slave hunters; but if you go alone and poor, they kill an ox for you, unless you prefer a sheep, give you a hut, and generally anything they have to offer, *merissey* (beer) to make you as drunk as a lord, and young ladies to pour it out for you—and—you need not wear any clothes. If you had heard him you would have started for the interior at once. I gave him a dinner and a bottle of common wine, which he emptied, and a few shillings, and away he trudged merrily towards Cairo. I wonder what the Nubians thought of a *howagah* begging. He said they were all kind, and that he was sure he often ate what they pinched themselves to give—dourrah bread and dates.

In the evening we were talking about this man's stories, and of 'anthropophagi and men whose heads do grow' to a prodigious height, by means of an edifice woven of their own hair, and other queer things, when Hassan told me a story which pleased me particularly. 'My father,' said he, 'Sheykh Mohammed (who was a taller and handsomer man than I am), was once travelling very far up in the black country, and he and the men he was with had very little to eat, and had killed nothing for many days; presently they heard a sort of wailing from a hole in the rock, and some of the men went in and dragged out a creature—I know not, and my father knew not, whether a child of Adam or a beast. But it was like a very foul and ill-shaped woman, and had six toes on its feet. The men wished to slay it, according to the law declaring it to be a beast and lawful food, but when it saw the knife, it cried sadly and covered its face with its hands in terror, and my father said, "By the Most High God, ye shall not slay the poor woman-beast which thus begs its life; I tell you it is unlawful to eat one so like the children of Adam." And the beast or woman clung to him and hid under his cloak; and my father carried her for some time behind him on his horse, until they saw some creatures like her, and then he sent her to them, but he had to drive her from him by force, for she clung to him. Thinkest thou oh Lady, it was really a beast, or some sort of the children of Adam?'

'God knows, and He only,' said I piously, 'but by His indulgent name, thy father, oh Sheykh, was a true nobleman.' Sheykh Yussuf chimed in and gave a decided opinion that a creature able to understand the sight of the knife and to act so, was not lawful to kill for food. You see what a real Arab Don Quixote was. It is a picture worthy of him,—the tall, noble-looking Abab'deh sheltering the poor 'woman-beast,' most likely a gorilla or chimpanzee, and carrying her *en croupe*.

To Mrs. Austin

LUXOR,
January 26, 1867.

DEAREST MUTTER,

I must betray dear Sheykh Yussuf's confidence, and tell you his love story.

A young fellow ran away with a girl he loved a short time ago, she having told him that her parents wanted to marry her to another, and that she would go to such a spot for water, and he must come on a horse, beat her and carry her off (the beating saves the maiden's blushes). Well, the lad did it, and carried her to Salamieh where they were married, and then they went to Sheykh Yussuf to get him to conciliate the family, which he did. He told me the affair, and I saw he sympathised much with the runaways. 'Ah,' he said 'Lady, it is love, and that is terrible, I can tell thee love is dreadful indeed to bear.' Then he hesitated and blushed, and went on, 'I felt it once, Lady, it was the will of God that I should love her who is now my wife. Thirteen years ago I loved her and wished to marry her, but my father, and her grandfather my uncle the Shereef, had quarrelled, and they took her and married her to another man. I never told anyone of it, but my liver was burning and my heart ready to burst for three years; but when I met her I fixed my eyes on the ground for fear she should see my love, and I said to myself, Oh Yussuf, God has afflicted thee, praise be unto Him, do thou remember thy blood (Shereef) and let thy conduct be that of the Beni Azra who when they are thus afflicted die rather than sin, for they have the strongest passion of love and the greatest honour. And I did not die but went to Cairo to the Gama el-Azhar and studied, and afterwards I married twice, as thou knowest, but I never loved any but that one, and when my last wife died the husband of this one had just divorced her to take a younger and prettier one and my father desired me then to take her, but I was half afraid not knowing whether she would love me; but, Praise be to God I consented, and behold, poor thing, she also had loved me in like manner.' I thought when I went to see her that she was unusually radiant with new-married happiness, and she talked of 'el-Sheykh' with singular pride and delight, and embraced me and called me 'mother' most affectionately. Is it not a pretty piece of regular Arab romance like Ghamem?

My boat has gone up to-day with two very nice Englishmen in her. Their young Maltese dragoman, aged twenty-four, told me his father often talked of 'the Commissioners' and all they had done, and how things were changed in the island for the better. (1) Everything spiritual and temporal has been done for the boat's safety in the Cataract—urgent letters to the Maōhn el Baudar, and him of Assouan to see to the men, and plenty of prayers and vows to Abu-l-Hajjaj on behalf of the 'property of the Lady,' or *kurzweg* 'our boat' as she is commonly called in Luxor.

Here we have the other side of the misery of the Candian business;* in Europe, of course, the obvious thing is the sufferings of the Cretans, but really I am more sorry for the poor fellah lads who are dragged away to fight in a quarrel they had no hand in raising, and with which they have no sympathy. The *Times* suggests that the Sultan should relinquish the island, and that has been said in many an Egyptian hut long before. The Sultan is worn out, and the Muslims here know it, and say it would be the best day for the Arabs if he were driven out; that after all a Turk never was the true *Ameer el-Moomeneen* (Commander of the Faithful). Only in Europe people talk and write as if it were all Muslim *versus* Christian, and the Christians were all oppressed, and the Muslims all oppressors. I wish they could see the domineering of the Greeks and Maltese as Christians. The Englishman domineers as a free man and a Briton, which is different, and that is the reason why the Arabs wish for English rule, and would dread that of Eastern Christians. Well they may; for if ever the Greeks do reign in Stamboul the sufferings of the Muslims will satisfy the most eager fanatic that ever cursed Mahound. I know nothing of Turkey, but I have seen and heard enough to know that there are plenty of other divisions besides that of Christian and Muslim. Here in Egypt it is clear enough: it is Arab *versus* Turk and the Copt siding with the stronger for his interest, while he rather sympathises with his brother fellah. At all events the Copt don't want other Christians to get power; he would far rather have a Muslim than a heretic ruler, above all the hated Greek. The Englishman he looks on as a variety of Muslim—a man who washes, has no pictures in his church, who has married bishops, and above all, who does not fast from all that has life for half the year, and this heresy is so extreme as not to give offence, unless he tries to convert.

The Pasha's sons have just been up the river: they ordered a reading of the Koran at the tomb of Abu-l-Hajjaj and gave every Alim sixpence. We have not left off chaffing (as Maurice would say) Sheykh Allah-ud-deen, the Muezzin, and sundry others on this superb backsheesh, and one old Fikee never knows whether to laugh, to cry, or to scold, when I ask to see the shawl and tarboosh he has bought with the presents of Pashas. Yussuf and the Kadee too had been called on to contribute baskets of bread to the steamer so that their sixpences were particularly absurd.

The little boy whose father died is still with the Abab'deh, who will not let him travel to Cairo till the weather is warmer and they find a safe person to be kind to him. Rachmeh says 'Please God, he will go with the Sitt, perhaps.' Hassan has consoled him with sugar-cane and indulgence, and if I lose Mabrook, and the little boy takes to me, he may fall into my hands as Achmet has done. I hear he is a good boy but a perfect savage; that however, I find makes no difference—in fact, I think they learn faster than those who have ways of their own. So I see Terence was a nigger! I would tell Rachmeh so if I could make him understand who Terence was, and that he, Rachmeh, stood in need of any encouragement, but the worthy fellow never imagines that his skin is in any way inferior to mine.

To Sir Alexander Duff Gordon

LUXOR,
February 3, 1867.

DEAREST ALICK,

The boat goes down to-morrow and I have little to add to Mutter's letter, only that I am better.

There is a man here from Girgeh, who says he is married to a Ginneeyeh (fairy) princess. I have asked to be presented to her, but I suspect there will be some hitch about it. It will be like Alexis's *Allez, Madame, vous êtes trop incrédule*. The unintelligible thing is the motive which prompts wonders and miracles here, seeing that the wonder workers do not get any money by it; and indeed, very often give, like the Indian saint I told you of who gave me four dollars. His miracles were all gratis, which was the most miraculous thing of all in a saint. I am promised that the Ginneeyeh shall come through the wall. If she should do so I shall be compelled to believe in her, as there are no mechanical contrivances in Luxor. All the Hareem here believe it, and the man's human wife swears she waits on her like a slave, and backs her husband's lie or delusion fully. I have not seen the man, but I should not wonder if it were a delusion—real *bona fide* visions and revelations are so common, and I think there is but little downright imposture. Meanwhile familiarity breeds contempt. Jinns, Afreets and Shaitans inspire far less respect than the stupidest ghost at home, and the devil (Iblees) is reduced to deplorable insignificance. He is never mentioned in the pulpit, or in religious conversation, with the respect he enjoys in Christian countries. I suppose we may console ourselves with the hope that he will pay off the Muslims for their neglect of him hereafter.

I cannot describe to you the misery here now, indeed it is wearisome even to think of: every day some new tax. Now every beast; camel, cow, sheep, donkey, horse, is made to pay. The fellaheen can no longer eat bread, they are living on barley meal, mixed with water and new green stuff, vetches etc., which to people used to good food is terrible, and I see all my acquaintances growing seedy and ragged and anxious. Yussuf is clear of debt, his religion having kept him from borrowing, but he wants to sell his little slave girl, and has sold his donkey, and he is the best off. The taxation makes life almost impossible—100 piastres per feddan, a tax on every crop, on every annual fruit, and again when it is sold in the market; on every man, on charcoal, on butter, on salt, on the dancing girls. I wonder I am not tormented for money—not above three people have tried to beg or borrow.

Thanks for the Westminster epilogue;* it always amuses me much. So Terence was a nigger. There is no trace of the negro 'boy' in his Davus. My nigger has grown huge, and has developed a voice of thunder. He is of the elephantine rather than the tiger species, a very mild young savage. I shall be sorry when Palgrave takes him. I am tempted to buy Yussuf's nice little Dinka girl to replace him, only a girl is such an impossibility where there is no regular hareem. In the boat Achmet is enough under Omar; but in this large dusty house, and with errands to run, and comers and goers to look after, pipes and coffee and the like, it takes two boys to be comfortable. Mabrook too washes very well. It is surprising how fast the boys learn, and how well they do their work. Achmet, who is quite little, would be a perfectly sufficient servant for a man alone; he can cook, wash, clean the rooms, make the beds, do all the table service, knife and plate cleaning, all fairly well, and I believe now he would get along even without Omar's orders. Mabrook is slower, but he has the same merit our poor Hassan had, he never forgets what he has been once told to do, and he is clean in his work, though hopelessly dirty as to his clothes. He cannot get used to them, and takes a roll in the dust, or leans against a dirty wall, oblivious of his clean-washed blue shirt. Achmet is quicker and more careless, but they both are good boys and very fond of Omar. 'Uncle Omar' is the form of address, though he scolds them pretty severely if they misbehave; and I observe that the high jinks take place chiefly when only I am in the way, and Omar gone to market or to the mosque. The little rogues have found out that their laughing does not 'affect my nerves,' and I am often treated to a share in the joke. How I wish Rainie could see the children: they would amuse her. Yussuf's girl, 'Meer en Nezzil,' is a charming child, and very clever; her emphatic way of explaining everything to me, and her gestures, would delight you. Her cousin and future husband, age five (she is six), broke the doll which I had given her, and her description of it was most dramatic, ending with a wheedling glance at the cupboard and 'of course there are no more dolls there; oh no, no more.' She is a fine little creature, far more Arab than fellaha; quite a *Shaitan*, her father says. She came in full of making cakes for Bairam, and offered her services; 'Oh my aunt, if thou wantest anything I can work,' said she, tucking up her sleeves.

To Mrs. Austin

LUXOR,
March 6, 1867.

DEAREST MUTTER,

The warm weather has set in, and I am already as much the better for it as usual. I had a slight attack, not nearly so bad as that at Soden, but it lingered and I kept my bed as a measure of precaution. Dear Yussuf was with me the evening I was attacked, and sat up all night to give me my medicine every hour. At the prayer of dawn, an hour and a half before sunrise, I heard his supplications for my life and health, and for you and all my family; and I thought of what I had lately read, how the Greeks massacred their own patriots because the Turks had shown them mercy—a display of temper which I hope will enlighten Western

Christendom as to what the Muslims have to expect, if they (the Western Christians) help the Eastern Christians to get the upper hand. Yussuf was asking about a lady the other day who has turned Catholic. 'Poor thing,' said he, 'the priests have drawn out her brains through her ears, no doubt: but never fear, her heart is good and her charity is great, and God will not deal hardly with those who serve Him with their hearts, though it is sad she should bow down before images. But look at thy slave Mabrook, can he understand one hundredth part of the thoughts of thy mind? Never-the-less he loves thee, and obeys thee with pleasure and alacrity; and wilt thou punish him because he knows not all thy ways? And shall God, who is so much higher above us as thou art above thy slave, be less just than thou?' I pinned him at once, and insisted on knowing the orthodox belief; but he quoted the Koran and the decisions of the Ulema to show that he stretched no point as far as Jews and Christians are concerned, and even that idolaters are not to be condemned by man. Yussuf wants me to write a short account of the faith from his dictation. Would anyone publish it? It annoys him terribly to hear the Muslims constantly accused of intolerance, and he is right—it is not true. They show their conviction that their faith is the best in the world with the same sort of naïveté that I have seen in very innocent and ignorant English women; in fact, display a sort of religious conceit; but it is not often bitter or *haineux*, however much they are in earnest.

I am going to write to Palgrave and ask him to let me send another boy or the money for Mabrook, who can't endure the notion of leaving me. Achmet, who was always hankering after the fleshpots of Alexandria, got some people belonging to the boats to promise to take him, and came home and picked a quarrel and departed. Poor little chap; the Sheykh el-Beled 'put a spoke in his wheel' by informing him he would be wanted for the Pasha's works and must stay in his own place. Since he went Mabrook has come out wonderfully and does his own work and Achmet's with the greatest satisfaction. He tells me he likes it best so; he likes to be quiet. He just suits me and I him, it is humiliating to find how much more I am to the taste of savages than of the 'polite circles.'

The old lady of the Maōhn proposed to come to me, but I would not let her leave her home, which would be quite an adventure to her. I knew she would be exclamatory, and lament over me, and say every minute, 'Oh my liver. Oh my eyes! The name of God be upon thee, and never mind! to-morrow please God, thou wilt be quite well,' and so forth. People send me such odd dishes, some very good. Yussuf's wife packed two calves' feet tight in a little black earthern pan, with a seasoning of herbs, and baked it in the bread oven, and the result was excellent. Also she made me a sort of small macaroni, extremely good. Now too we can get milk again, and Omar makes *kishta*, alias clotted cream.

Do send me a good edition of the 'Arabian Nights' in Arabic, and I should much like to give Yussuf Lane's Arabic dictionary. He is very anxious to have it. I can't read the 'Arabian Nights,' but it is a favourite amusement to make one of the party read aloud; a stray copy of 'Kamar ez-Zeman and Sitt Boodoora' went all round Luxor, and was much coveted for the village *soirées*. But its owner departed, and left us to mourn over the loss of his MSS.

I must tell you a black standard of respectability (it is quite equal to the English one of the gig, or the ham for breakfast). I was taking counsel with my friend Rachmeh, a negro, about Mabrook, and he urged me to buy him of Palgrave, because he saw that the lad really loved me. 'Moreover,' he said, 'the boy is of a respectable family, for he told me his mother wore a cow's tail down to her heels (that and a girdle to which the tail is fastened, and a tiny leathern apron in front, constituted her whole wardrobe), and that she beat him well when he told lies or stole his neighbours eggs.' Poor woman; I wish this abominable slave trade had spared her and her boy. What folly it is to stop the Circassian slave trade, if it is stopped, and to leave this. The Circassians take their own children to market, as a way of providing for them handsomely, and both boys and girls like being sold to the rich Turks; but the blacks and

Abyssinians fight hard for their own liberty and that of their cubs. Mabrook swears that there were two Europeans in the party which attacked his village and killed he knew not how many, and carried him and others off. He was not stolen by Arabs, or by Barrabias, like Hassan, but taken in war from his home by the seaside, a place called Bookee, and carried in a ship to Jedda, and thence back to Koseir and Keneh, where Palgrave bought him. I must say that once here the slaves are happy and well off, but the waste of life and the misery caused by the trade must be immense. The slaves are coming down the river by hundreds every week, and are very cheap—twelve to twenty pounds for a fine boy, and nine pounds and upwards for a girl. I heard that the last *gellab* offered a woman and baby for anything anyone would give for them, on account of the trouble of the baby. By-the-bye, Mabrook displays the negro talent for babies. Now that Achmet is gone, who scolded them and drove them out, Mohammed's children, quite babies, are for ever trotting after 'Maboo,' as they pronounce his name, and he talks incessantly to them. It reminds me so of Janet and poor Hassan, but Mabrook is not like Hassan, he is one of the sons of Anak, and already as big and strong as a man, with the most prodigious chest and limbs.

Don't be at all uneasy about me as to care. Omar knows exactly what to do as he showed the other day when I was taken ill. I had shown him the medicines and given him instructions so I had not even to speak, and if I were to be ill enough to want more help, Yussuf would always sit up alternate nights; but it is not necessary. Arabs make no grievance about broken rest; they don't 'go to bed properly,' but lie down half dressed, and have a happy faculty of sleeping at odd times and anyhow, which enables them to wait on one day and night, without distressing themselves as it distresses us.

Thursday.—A telegram has just come announcing that Janet will leave Cairo to-morrow in a steamer, and therefore be here, Inshallah, this day week. I enclose a note from a Copt boy, which will amuse you. He is 'sapping' at English, and I teach him whenever

I am able. I am a special favourite with all the young lads; they must not talk much before grown men, so they come and sit on the floor round my feet, and ask questions and advice, and enjoy themselves amazingly. Hobble-de-hoy-hood is very different here from what it is with us; they care earlier for the affairs of the grown-up world, and are more curious and more polished, but lack the fine animal gaiety of our boys. The girls are much more *gamin* than the boys, and more romping and joyous.

It is very warm now. I fear Janet will sigh terribly over the heat. They have left their voyage too late for such as do not love the Shems el-Kebeer (the big sun), which has just begun. I who worship Ammun Ra, love to feel him in his glory. It is long since I had any letters, I want so to hear how you all are.

To Sir Alexander Duff Gordon

March 7, 1867.

DEAREST ALICK,

I have written a long yarn to Mutter and am rather tired, so I only write to say I am much better. The heat has set in, and, of course with it my health has mended, but I am a little shaky and afraid to tire myself. Moreover I want to nurse up and be stronger by next Thursday when Janet and Ross are expected.

What a queer old fish your Dublin antiquary is, who wants to whitewash Miss Rhampsinitus, and to identify her with the beloved of Solomon (or Saleem); my brain spun round as I read it. Must I answer him, or will you? A dragoman gave me an old broken travelling arm-chair, and Yussuf sat in an arm-chair for the first time in his life. 'May the soul of the man who made it find a seat in Paradise,' was his exclamation, which strikes me as singularly appropriate on sitting in a very comfortable arm-chair. Yussuf was thankful for small mercies in this case.

I am afraid Janet may be bored by all the people's civility; they will insist on making great dinners and fantasias for her I am sure. I hope they will go on to Assouan and take me with them; the change will do me good, and I should like to see as much of her as I can before she leaves Egypt for good.

The state of business here is curious. The last regulations have stopped all money lending, and the prisons are full of Sheykh el-Beled whose villages can't pay the taxes. Most respectable men have offered me to go partners with them now in their wheat, which will be cut in six weeks, if only I would pay their present taxes, I to take half the crop and half the taxes, with interest out of their half—some such trifle as 30 per cent. per month. Our prison is full of men, and we send them their dinner *à tour de rôle*. The other day a woman went with a big wooden bowl on her head, full of what she had cooked for them, accompanied by her husband. One Khaleel Effendi, a new vakeel here, was there, and said, 'What dost thou ask here thou harlot?' Her husband answered, 'That is no harlot, oh Effendim, but my wife.' Whereupon he was beaten till he fainted, and then there was a lamentation; they carried him down past my house, with a crowd of women all shrieking like mad creatures, especially his wife, who yelled and beat her head and threw dust over it, *more majorum*, as you see in the tombs. The humours of tax-gathering in this country are quite *impayable* you perceive—and ought to be set forth on the escutcheon of the new Knight of the Bath whom the Queen hath delighted to honour. Cawass battant, Fellah rampant, and Fellaha pleurant would be the proper blazon. Distress in England is terrible, but, at least, it is not the result of extortion, as it is here, where everything from nature is so abundant and glorious, and yet mankind so miserable. It is not a little hunger, it is the cruel oppression which maddens the people now. They never complained before, but now whole villages are deserted. The boat goes to-morrow morning so I must say goodbye.

To Mrs. Austin

LUXOR,
April 12, 1867.

DEAREST MUTTER,

I have just received your letters, including the one for Omar which I read to him, and which he kissed and said he should keep as a *hegab* (talisman). I have given him an order on Coutts' correspondents for the money, in case I die. Omar proposes to wait till we get to Cairo and then to buy a little house, or a floor in one. I am to keep all the money till the house is found, so he will in no way be tempted to do anything foolish with it. I hope you approve?

Janet's visit was quite an *Eed* (festival), as the people said. When I got up on the morning she was expected, I found the house decked with palm branches and lemon blossoms, and the holy flags of Abu-l-Hajjaj waving over my balcony. The mosque people had brought them, saying all the people were happy to-day, because it was a fortunate day for me. I suppose if I had had a mind to *testify*, I ought to have indignantly torn down the banners which bore the declaration, 'There is no God but God, and Mohammed is His Prophet.' But it appeared to me that if Imaams and Muezzins could send their banners to decorate a Christian house, the Christian might manage to endure the kindness. Then there was fantasia on horseback, and all the notables to meet the boat, and general welcome and jubilation. Next day I went on with Henry and Janet in the steamer, and had a very pleasant time to Assouan and back, and they stayed another day here, and I hired a little dahabieh which they towed down to Keneh where they stayed a day; after which Sheykh Yussuf and I sailed back again to Luxor. As bad luck would have it we had hot weather just the week they were up here: since then it has been quite cool.

Janet has left me her little black and tan terrier, a very nice little dog, but I can't hope to rival Omar in his affections. He sleeps in

Omar's bosom, and Omar spoils and pets him all day, and boasts to the people how the dog drinks tea and coffee and eats dainty food, and the people say Mashallah! whereas I should have expected them to curse the dog's father. The other day a scrupulous person drew back with an air of alarm from Bob's approach, whereupon the dog stared at him, and forthwith plunged into Sheykh Yussuf's lap, from which stronghold he 'yapped' defiance at whoever should object to him. I never laughed more heartily, and Yussuf went into *fou rire*. The mouth of the dog only is unclean, and Yussuf declares he is a very well-educated dog, and does not attempt to lick; he pets him accordingly, and gives him tea in his own saucer, only *not* in the cup.

I am to inherit another little blackie from Ross's agency at Keneh: the funniest little chap. I cannot think why I go on expecting so-called savages to be different from other people. Mabrook's simple talk about his village, and the animals and the victuals; and how the men of a neighbouring village stole him in order to sell him for a gun (the price of a gun is a boy), but were prevented by a razzia of Turks, etc. who killed the first aggressors and took all the children—all this he tells just as an English boy might tell of bird-nesting—delights me. He has the same general notion of right and wrong; and yet his tribe know neither bread nor any sort of clothes, nor cheese nor butter, nor even drink milk, nor the African beer; and it always rains there, and is always deadly cold at night, so that without a fire they would die. They have two products of civilisation—guns and tobacco, for which they pay in boys and girls, whom they steal. I wonder where the country is, it is called Sowaghli, and the next people are Mueseh, on the sea-coast, and it is not so hot as Egypt. It must be in the southern hemisphere. The new *négrillon* is from Darfoor. Won't Maurice be amused by his attendants, the Darfoor boy will trot after him, as he can shoot and clean guns, tiny as he is Maurice seems to wish to come and I hope Alexander will let him spend the winter here, and I will take him up to the second Cataract; I really think he would enjoy it.

My boat will not return I think for another six weeks. Mr. Eaton and Mr. Baird were such nice people! their dragoman, a Maltese, appeared to hate the Italians with ferocity. He said all decent people in Malta would ten times rather belong to the Mahommedans than to the Italians—after all blood tells. He was a very respectable young man, and being a dragoman and the son of a dragoman, he has seen the world, and particularly the Muslims. I suppose it is the Pope that makes the Italians so hateful to them.

The post here is dreadful, I would not mind their reading one's letters if they would only send them on. Omar begs me to say that he and his children will pray for you all his life, please God, not for the money only but still more for the good words and the trusting him. But he says, 'I can't say much *politikeh*, Please God she shall see, only I kiss her hand now.' You will hear from Janet about her excursion. What I liked best was shooting the Cataract in a small boat; it was fine fantasia.

To Sir Alexander Duff Gordon

LUXOR,
April 19, 1867.

DEAREST ALICK,

I have been much amused lately by a new acquaintance, who, in romances of the last century, would be called an 'Arabian sage.' Sheykh Abdurrachman lives in a village half a day's journey off, and came over to visit me and to doctor me according to the science of Galen and Avicenna. Fancy a tall, thin, graceful man, with a grey beard and liquid eyes, absorbed in studies of the obsolete kind, a doctor of theology, law, medicine and astronomy. We spent three days in arguing and questioning; I consented to swallow a potion or two which he made up before me, of very innocent materials. My friend is neither a quack nor superstitious, and two hundred years ago would have been a better physician than most in Europe. Indeed I would rather swallow his physic now than that of many a M.D. I found him like all the learned theologians I have known, extremely liberal and tolerant. You can conceive nothing more interesting and curious than the conversation of a man learned and intelligent, and utterly ignorant of all our modern Western science. If I was pleased with him, he was enchanted with me, and swore by God that I was a Mufti indeed, and that a man could nowhere spend time so delightfully as in conversation with me. He said he had been acquainted with two or three Englishmen who had pleased him much, but that if all Englishwomen were like me the power must necessarily be in our hands, for that my *akl* (brain, intellect) was far above that of the men he had known. He objected to our medicine that it seemed to consist in palliatives, which he rather scorned, and aimed always at a radical cure. I told him that if he had studied anatomy he would know that radical cures were difficult of performance, and he ended by lamenting his ignorance of English or some European language, and that he had not learned our *Ilm* (science) also. Then we plunged into sympathies, mystic numbers, and the occult virtues of stones, etc., and I swallowed my mixture (consisting of liquorice, cummin and soda) just as the sun entered a particular house, and the moon was in some favourable aspect. He praised to me his friend, a learned Jew of Cairo. I could have fancied myself listening to Abu Suleyman of Cordova, in the days when we were the barbarians and the Arabs were the learned race. There is something very winning in the gentle, dignified manners of all the men of learning I have seen here, and their homely dress and habits make it still more striking. I longed to photograph my Sheykh as he sat on the divan pulling MSS. out of his bosom to read me the words of *El-Hakeem Lokman*, or to overwhelm me with the authority of some physician whose very name I had never heard.

The hand of the Government is awfully heavy upon us. All this week the people have been working night and day cutting their unripe corn, because three hundred and ten men are to go to-morrow to work on the railroad below Siout. This green corn is, of course, valueless to sell and unwholesome to eat; so the magnificent harvest of this year is turned to bitterness at the last moment. From a neighbouring village all the men are gone, and seven more are wanted to make up the *corvée*. The population of Luxor is 1,000 males of all ages, so you can guess how many strong men are left after three hundred and ten are taken.

I don't like to think too much about seeing you and Maurice next winter for fear I should be disappointed. If I am too sick and wretched I can hardly wish you to come because I know what a nuisance it is to be with one always coughing and panting, and unable to do like other people. But if I pick up tolerably this summer I shall indeed be glad to see you and him once more.

This house is falling sadly to decay, which produces snakes and scorpions. I sent for the *hawee* (snake-catcher) who caught a snake, but who can't conjure the scorpions out of their holes. One of my fat turkeys has just fallen a victim, and I am in constant fear for little Bob, only he is always in Omar's arms. I think I described to you the festival of Sheykh Gibrieel: the dinner, and the poets who improvised; this year I had a fine piece of declamation in my honour. A real calamity is the loss of our good Maōhn, Seleem Effendi. The Mudir hailed him from his steamer to go to Keneh directly, with no further notice. We hoped some good luck for him, and so it would have been to a Turk. He is made overseer over the poor people at the railway work, and only gets two pounds five shillings per month additional, he has to keep a horse and a donkey, and to buy them and to hire a sais, and he does *not* know how to squeeze the fellaheen. It is true 'however close you skin an onion, a clever man can always peel it again,' which means that even the poorest devils at the works can be beaten into giving a little more; but our dear Seleem, God bless him, will be ruined and made miserable by his promotion. I had a very woeful letter from him yesterday.

To Sir Alexander Duff Gordon

LUXOR,
May 15, 1867.

DEAREST ALICK,

All the Christendom of Upper Egypt is in a state of excitement, owing to the arrival of the Patriarch of Cairo, who is now in Luxor. My neighbour, Mikaeel, entertains him, and Omar has been busily decorating his house and arranging the illumination of his garden, and to-day is gone to cook the confectionery, he being looked upon as the person best acquainted with the customs of the great. Last night the Patriarch sent for me, and I went to kiss his hand, but I won't go again. It was a very droll caricature of the thunders of the Vatican. Poor Mikaeel had planned that I was to dine with the Patriarch, and had borrowed my silver spoons, etc., etc., in that belief. But the representative of St. Mark is furious against the American missionaries who have converted some twenty Copts at Koos, and he could not bring himself to be decently civil to a Protestant. I found a coarse-looking man seated on a raised divan smoking his chibouk, on his right were some priests on a low divan; I went up and kissed his hand and was about to sit by the priests, but he roughly ordered a cawass to put a wooden chair *off the carpet* to his left, at a distance from him, and told me to sit there. I looked round to see whether any of my neighbours were present, and I saw the consternation in their faces so, not wishing to annoy them, I did as if I did not perceive the affront, and sat down and talked for half an hour to the priests, and then took leave. I was informed that the Catholics were *naas mesakeen* (poor inoffensive people), and that the Muslims at least were of an old religion, but that the Protestants ate meat all the year round, 'like dogs'—'or Muslims,' put in Omar, who stood behind my chair and did not relish the mention of dogs and the 'English religion' in one sentence. As I went the Patriarch called for dinner, it seems he had told Mikaeel he would not eat with me. It is evidently 'a judgment' of a most signal nature that I should be snubbed for the offences of missionaries, but it has caused some ill blood; the Kadee and Sheykh Yussuf and the rest, who all intended to do the civil to the Patriarch, now won't go near him on account of his rudeness to me. He has come up in a steamer, at the Pasha's expense, with a guard of cawasses, and, of course, is loud in praise of the Government, though he failed in getting the Moudir to send all the Protestants of Koos to the public works, or the army.

From what he said before me about the Abyssinians, and still more, from what he said to others about the English prisoners up there, I am convinced that the place to put the screw on is the *Batrarchane* (Patriarch's palace) at Cairo, and that the priests are at the bottom of that affair. He boasted immensely of the obedience and piety of *El Habbesh* (the Abyssinians).

Saturday.—Yesterday I heard a little whispered grumbling about the money demanded by the 'Father.' One of my Copt neighbours was forced to sell me his whole provision of cooking butter to pay his quota. This a little damps the exultation caused by seeing him so honoured by the Effendina. One man who had heard that he had called the American missionaries 'beggars,' grumbled to me, 'Ah yes, beggars, beggars, they didn't beg of me for money.' I really do think that there must be something in this dread of the Protestant movement. Evidently the Pasha is backing up the Patriarch who keeps his church well apart from all other Christians, and well under the thumb of the Turks. It was pretty to hear the priests talk so politely of Islam, and curse the Protestants so bitterly. We were very nearly having a row about a woman, who formerly turned Moslimeh to get rid of an old blind Copt husband who had been forced upon her, and was permitted to recant, I suppose in order to get rid of the Muslim husband in his turn. However he said, 'I don't care, she is the mother of my two children, and whether she is Muslim or Christian she is my wife, and I won't divorce her, but I'll send her to church as much as she likes.' Thereupon the priests of course dropped the wrangle, much to the relief of Sheykh Yussuf, in whose house she had taken up her quarters after leaving the church, and who was afraid of being drawn into a dispute.

My new little Darfour boy is very funny and very intelligent. I hope he will turn out well, he seems well disposed, though rather lazy. Mabrook quarrelled with a boy belonging to the quarter close to us about a bird, and both boys ran away. The Arab boy is missing still I suppose, but Mabrook was brought back by force, swelling with passion, and with his clothes most scripturally 'rent.' He had regularly 'run amuck.' Sheykh Yussuf lectured him on his insolence to the people of the quarter, and I wound up by saying, 'Oh my son! whither dost thou wish to go? I cannot let thee wander about like a beggar, with torn clothes and no money, that the police may take thee and put thee in the army; but say where thou desirest to go, and we will talk about it with discretion.' It was at once borne in upon him that he did not want to go anywhere, and he said, 'I repent; I am but an ox, bring the courbash, beat me, and let me go to finish cooking the Sitt's dinner.' I remitted the beating, with a threat that if he bullied the neighbours again he would get it at the police, and not from Omar's very inefficient arm. In half an hour he was as merry as ever. It was a curious display of negro temper, and all about nothing at all. As he stood before me, he looked quite grandly tragic; and swore he only wanted to run outside and die; that was all.

I wish you could have heard (and understood) my *soirées, au clair de la lune*, with Sheykh Yussuf and Sheykh Abdurrachman. How Abdurrachman and I wrangled, and how Yussuf laughed, and egged us on. Abdurrachman was wroth at my want of faith in physic generally, as well as in particular, and said I talked like an infidel, for had not God said, 'I have made a medicine for every disease?' I said, 'Yes, but He does not say that He has told the doctors which it is; and meanwhile I say, *hekmet Allah*, (God will cure) which can't be called an infidel sentiment.' Then we got into alchemy, astrology, magic and the rest; and Yussuf vexed his friend by telling gravely stories palpably absurd. Abdurrachman intimated that he was laughing at *El-Ilm el-Muslimeen* (the science of the Muslims), but Yussuf said, 'What is the *Ilm el-Muslimeen*? God has revealed religion through His prophets, and we can learn nothing new on that point; but all other learning He has left to the intelligence of men, and the Prophet Mohammed said, "All learning is from God, even the learning of idolaters." Why then should we Muslims shut out the light, and want to remain ever like children? The learning of the Franks is as lawful as any other.' Abdurrachman was too sensible a man to be able to dispute this, but it vexed him.

I am tired of telling all the *plackereien* of our poor people, how three hundred and ten men were dragged off on Easter Monday with their bread and tools, how in four days they were all sent back from Keneh, because there were no orders about them, and made to *pay their boat hire*. Then in five days they were sent for again. Meanwhile the harvest was cut green, and the wheat is lying out unthreshed to be devoured by birds and rats, and the men's bread was wasted and spoiled with the hauling in and out of boats. I am obliged to send camels twenty miles for charcoal, because the Abab'deh won't bring it to market any more, the tax is too heavy. Butter too we have to buy secretly, none comes into the market. When I remember the lovely smiling landscape which I first beheld from my windows, swarming with beasts and men, and look at the dreary waste now, I feel the 'foot of the Turk' heavy indeed. Where there were fifty donkeys there is but one; camels, horses, all are gone; not only the horned cattle, even the dogs are more than decimated, and the hawks and vultures seem to me fewer; mankind has no food to spare for hangers-on. The donkeys are sold, the camels confiscated, and the dogs dead (the one sole advantage). Meat is cheap, as everyone must sell to pay taxes and no one has money to buy. I am implored to take sheep and poultry for what I will give.

To Mrs. Austin

LUXOR,
May 23, 1867.

DEAREST MUTTER,

I have only time for a few words by Giafar Pasha, who goes early to-morrow morning. My boat arrived all right and brought your tin box. The books and toys are very welcome. The latter threw little Darfour into ecstasies, and he got into disgrace for 'playing with the Sitt' instead of minding some business on hand. I fear I shall spoil him, he is so extremely engaging and such a baby. He is still changing his teeth, so cannot be more than eight; at first I did not like him, and feared he was sullen, but it was the usual *khoss* (fear), the word that is always in one's ears, and now that is gone, he is always coming hopping in to play with me. He is extremely intelligent and has a pretty baby nigger face. The Darfour people are, as you know, an independent and brave people, and by no means 'savages.' I can't help thinking how pleased Rainie would be with the child. He asked me to give him the picture of the English Sultaneh out of the *Illustrated London News*, and has pasted it inside the lid of his box.

I am better as usual, since the hot weather has begun, the last six days. I shall leave this in a week, I think, and Mustapha and Yussuf will go with me to Cairo. Yussuf was quite enchanted with your note to him; his eyes glistened, and he took an envelope to keep it carefully. Omar said such a letter is like a *hegab* (amulet) and Yussuf said, 'Truly it is, and I could never have one with more *baraka* (blessing) or more like the virtue which went out of Jesus, if ever I wore one at all; I will never part with it.'

We had a very pretty festival for the Sheykh, whose tomb you have a photograph of, and I spent a very pleasant evening with Sheykh Abd el-Mootooal, who used to scowl at me, but now we are 'like brothers.' I found him very clever, and better informed than any Arab I have met, who is quite apart from all Franks. I was astonished to find that he *abondait dans man sens* in my dispute with Sheykh Abdurrachman, and said that it was the duty of Muslims to learn what they could from us, and not to stick to the old routine.

On Sunday the Patriarch snubbed me, and would not eat with me, and on Monday a *Walee* (saint) picked out tit-bits for me with his own fingers, and went with me inside the tomb. The Patriarch has made a blunder with his progress. He has come ostentatiously as the *protégé* and *pronem* of the Pasha, and he has 'eaten' and beaten the fellaheen. The Copts of Luxor have had to pay fifty pounds for the honour of his presence, besides no end of sheep, poultry, butter, etc. If I were of a proselytising mind I could make converts of several whose pockets and backs are smarting, and the American missionaries will do it. Of course the Muslims sympathise with the converts to a religion which has no 'idols,' and no monks, and whose priests marry like other folk, so they are the less afraid. I hear there are now fifty Protestants at Koos, and the Patriarch was furious because he could not beat them. Omar cooked a grand dinner for him last night for our neighbour Mikaeel, and the eating was not over till two in the morning. Our Government should manage to put the screw on him about our Abyssinian prisoners. I dare not say who told me all he said, but he was a truthful man and a Christian. The Patriarch answered me sharply when I asked about the state of religion in Abyssinia that, 'they were lovers of the faith, and his obedient children.' Whenever there is mischief among the Copts, the priests are at the bottom of it. If the Patriarch chose those people would be let go; and so it would be but he hates all Europeans bitterly.

I should like to have the *Revue des Deux Mondes* of all things, but I don't know how it is to come here, or what the postage would cost. They send nothing but letters above Cairo by post, as all goes on men's backs. 'Inshallah! I am the bearer of good news,' cries the postman, as he flings the letter over the wall. I am so glad of the chance of getting news to you quick by Giafar Pasha, who came here like a gentleman, alone, without a retinue; he is on his way from two years in the Soudan, where he was absolute Pasha. He is very much liked and respected, and seems a very sensible and agreeable man, quite unlike any Turkish big-wig I have seen. Great potentate as he is, he made Yussuf Mustapha and Abdallah sit down, and was extremely civil and simple in his manners.

To Sir Alexander Duff Gordon

Benisouef,
June 30, 1867.

Dearest Alick,

I write on the chance that this may go safe by post so that you may not think me lost. I left Luxor on May 31, got to Siout (half-way) in a week, and have ever since been battling with an unceasing furious north and north-east wind. I feel like the much travelled Odysseus, and have seen 'villages and men,' unlike him, however 'my companions' have neither grumbled nor deserted, though it is a bad business for them, having received their money at the rate of about twenty days' pay, for which they must take me to Cairo. They have eaten all, and are now obliged to stop and make bread here, but they are as good-humoured as if all were well. My fleet consisted of my dahabieh, flag ship; tender, a *kyasseh* (cargo boat) for my horse and sais, wherein were packed two extremely poor shrivelled old widows, going to Cairo to see their sons, now in garrison there; lots of hard bread, wheat, flour, jars of butter, onions and lentils for all the lads of 'my family' studying at Gama'l Azhar, besides in my box queer little stores of long hoarded money for those *megowareen* (students of Gama'l Azhar). Don't you wish you could provide for Maurice with a sack of bread, a basket of onions and one pound sixteen shillings?

The handsome brown Sheykh el-Arab, Hassan, wanted me to take him, but I knew him to be a 'fast' man, and asked Yussuf how I could avoid it without breaking the laws of hospitality, so my 'father,' the old Shereef, told Hassan that he did not choose his daughter to travel with a wine-bibber and a frequenter of loose company. Under my convoy sailed two or three little boats with family parties. One of these was very pretty, whose steersman was a charming little fat girl of five years old. All these hoped to escape being caught and worried by the way, by belonging to me, and they dropped off at their several villages. I am tolerably well, better than when I started, in spite of the wind.

Poor Reis Mohammed had a very bad attack of ophthalmia, and sat all of a heap, groaning all day and night, and protesting 'I am a Muslim,' equivalent to 'God's will be done.' At one place I was known, and had a lot of sick to see, and a civil man killed a sheep and regaled us all with meat and *fateereh*. The part of the river in which we were kept by the high wind is made cheerful by the custom of the Hareem being just as free to mix with men as Europeans, and I quite enjoyed the pretty girls' faces, and the gossip with the women who came to fill their water-jars and peep in at the cabin windows, which, by the way, they always ask leave to do. The Sheykh el-Hawara gave me two sheep which are in the cargo-boat with four others—all presents—which Omar intends you to eat at Cairo. The Sheykh is very anxious to give you an entertainment at his palace, if you come up the river, with horse-riding, feasting and dancing girls. In fact I am charged with many messages to *el-Kebir* (the great master).

To Sir Alexander Duff Gordon

CAIRO,
July 8, 1867.

DEAREST ALICK,

I arrived to-day, after thirty-eight days' voyage, one month of ceaseless furious wind. My poor men had a hard pull down against it. However I am feeling better than when I left Luxor.

Omar has just brought a whole cargo of your letters, the last of the 26 June. Let me know your plans. If you can go up the river I might send the boat beforehand to Minieh, so far there is a railway now, which would break the neck of the tedious part of the voyage for you if you are pressed for time. I must send this off at once to catch early post to-morrow. Excuse haste, I write in all the bustle of arrival.

To Mrs. Austin

BOULAK,
July 28, 1867.

DEAREST MUTTER,

I know I can write nothing more sure to please you than that I am a good deal better. It has been intensely hot, and the wind very worrying, but my cough has greatly abated and I do not feel so weak as I did. I am anchored here in the river at my old quarters, and have not yet been ashore owing to the hot wind and the dust, which of course are far less troublesome here on the river. I have seen but very few people and have but one neighbour, in a boat anchored near mine, a very bewitching Circassian, the former slave of a rich Pasha, now married to a respectable dragoman, and staying in his boat for a week or two. She is young and pretty, and very amiable, and we visit each other often and get on very well indeed. She is a very religious little lady, and was much relieved when I assured her it was not part of my daily devotions to curse the Prophet, and revile the noble Koran.

I am extremely glad that the English have given a hearty welcome to the Ameer el-Moornemeen* (Commander of the Faithful); it will have an excellent effect in all Mussulman countries. A queer little Indian from Delhi who had been converted to Islam, and spent four years at Mecca acting as dragoman to his own countrymen, is now settled at Karnac. I sent for him, and he came shaking in his shoes. I asked why he was afraid? 'Oh, perhaps I was angry about something, and he was my *rayah*, and I might have him beaten.' I cried out at him, 'Ask pardon of God, O man. How could I beat thee any more than thou couldst beat me? Have we not laws? and art thou not my brother, and the *rayah* of our Queen, as I am and no more?' 'Mashallah!' exclaimed the six or eight fellaheen who were waiting for physic, in prodigious admiration and wonder; 'and did we not tell thee that the face of the Sitt brings good fortune and not calamity and stick?' I found the little Indian had been a hospital servant in Calcutta, and was practising a little physic on his own account. So I gave him a few drugs especially for bad eyes, which he knew a good deal about, and we became very good friends; he was miserable when I left and would have liked me to have taken him as a volunteer servant.

I have come to a curious honour. *Ich bin beim lebendigem Leibe besungen*. Several parties of real Arabs came with their sick on camels from the desert above Edfou. I asked at last what brought them, and they told me that a *Shaer* (bard or poet) had gone about singing my praises, as how the daughter of the English was a flower on the heads of the Arabs, and those who were sick should go and smell the perfume of the flower and rejoice in the brightness of the light (*nooreen*)—my name. Rather a highflown way of mentioning the 'exhibition' of a black dose. But we don't feel that a man makes a fool of himself here when he is romantic in his talk even about an old woman.

It is no use to talk of the state of things here; all classes are suffering terribly under the fearful taxation, the total ruin of the fellaheen, and the destruction of trade brought about by this much extolled Pasha. My grocer is half ruined by the 'improvements' made a *l'instar de Paris*—long military straight roads cut through the heart of Cairo. The owners are expropriated, and there is an end of it. Only those who have half a house left are to be pitied, because they are forced to build a new front to the street on a Frankish model which renders it uninhabitable to them and unsaleable.

The river men are excited about the crews gone to Paris, for fear they should be forcibly detained by the *Sultaneh Franzaweeh*, I assured them that they will all come home safe and happy, with a good backsheesh. Many of them think it a sort of degradation to be taken for the Parisians to stare at like an anteeka, a word which here means what our people call a 'curiosity.'

I go on very well with my two boys. Mabrook washes very well and acts as *marmiton*. Darfour is housemaid and waiter in his very tiny way. He is only troublesome as being given to dirty his clothes in an incredibly short time. His account of the school system of Darfour is curious. How when the little boy has achieved excellence he is carried home in triumph to his father's house, who makes a festival for the master and boys. I suppose you will be surprised to hear that the Darfour 'niggers' can nearly all read and write. Poor little Darfour apologised to me for his ignorance, he was stolen he said, when he had only just begun to go to school. I wish an English or French servant could hear the instructions given by an Alim here to serving men. How he would resent them! 'When thou hast tired out thy back do not put thy hand behind it (do not shirk the burden). Remember that thou art not only to obey, but to please thy master, whose bread thou eatest;' and much more of the like. In short, a standard of religious obedience and fidelity fit for the highest Catholic idea of the 'religious life.' Upon the few who seek instruction it does have an effect (I am sure that Omar looks on his service as a religious duty), but of course they are few; and those who don't seek it themselves get none. It is curious how all children here are left utterly without any religious instruction. I don't know whether it is in consequence of this that they grow up so very devout.

To Sir Alexander Duff Gordon

BOULAK,
July 29, 1867.

DEAREST ALICK,

Your letter has arrived to my great relief—only I fear you are not at all well. About Maurice. If he wishes to see the Nile let him come, but if he is only to be sent because of me, let it alone. I know I am oppressive company now, and am apt, like Mr. Wodehouse in 'Emma,' to say, 'Let us all have some gruel.'

We know nothing here of a prohibition of gunpowder, at this moment some Europeans are popping away incessantly at Embabeh just opposite. Evidently the Pasha wants to establish a right of search on the Nile. That absurd speech about slaves he made in Paris shows that. With 3,000 in his hareem, several slave regiments, and lots of gangs on all his sugar plantations, his impudence is wonderful. He is himself the greatest living slave trader as well as owner. My lads are afraid to go out alone for fear of being snapped up by cawasses and taken to the army or the sugar works. You will be sorry to hear that your stalwart friend Hassan has had fifty blows on each foot-sole, and had to pay six pounds. He was taking two donkeys to Shepheard's hotel before sunrise for a French lady and gentleman to go to the Pyramids, when a cawass met him, seized the donkeys, and on Hassan's refusal to give them up, spat on the side-saddle and reviled Hassan's own Hareem and began to beat him with his courbash. Hassan got impatient, took the cawass up in his arms and threw him on the ground, and went on. Presently four cawasses came after him, seized him and took him to the Zaptieh (police office), where they all swore he had beaten them, torn their clothes, and robbed one of an imaginary gold watch—all valued at twenty-four pounds. After the beating he was carried to prison in chains, and there sentenced to be a soldier. A friend however interfered and settled the matter for six pounds. Hassan sends you his best salaam.

Last night was very pretty—all the boats starting for the *moolid* of Seyd el-Bedawee at Tanta. Every boat had a sort of pyramid of lanterns, and the derweeshes chanted, and the worldly folks had profane music and singing, and I sat and looked and listened, and thought how many thousand years ago just the same thing was going on in honour of Bubastis.

To Sir Alexander Duff Gordon

Boulak,
August 7, 1867.

My dearest Alick,

Two sailors of mine of last year went to Paris in the dahabieh for the Empress, and are just come back. When I see them I expect I shall have some fun out of their account of their journey. Poor Adam's father died of grief at his son's going, nothing would persuade him that Adam would come back safe, and having a heart complaint, he died. And now the lad is back, well and with fine clothes, but is much cut up, I hear, by his father's death. Please send me a tremendous whistle; mine is not loud enough to wake Omar at the other end of the cabin; a boatswain's whistle or something in the line of the 'last trump' is needed to wake sleeping Arabs.

My pretty neighbour has gone back into the town. She was a nice little woman, and amused me a good deal. I see that a good respectable Turkish hareem is an excellent school of useful accomplishments—needlework, cookery, etc. But I observed that she did not care a bit for the Pasha, by whom she had a child, but was extremely fond of 'her lady,' as she politely called her, also that like every Circassian I ever knew, she regarded being sold as quite a desirable fate, and did not seem sorry for her parents, as the negroes always are.

The heat has been prodigious, but I am a good deal better. Yesterday the Nile had risen above ten cubits, and the cutting of the Kalig took place. The river is pretty full now, but they say it will go down fast this year. I don't know why. It looks very beautiful, blood-red and tossed into waves by the north wind fighting the rapid stream.

Good-bye dear Alick, I hope to hear a better account of your health soon.

To Mrs. Austin

BOULAK,
August 8, 1867.

DEAREST MUTTER,

Two of my sailors were in Paris and have just come home. I hear they are dreadfully shocked by the dancing, and by the French women of the lower class generally. They sit in the coffee-shops like *shaers* (poets), and tell of the wonders of Paris to admiring crowds. They are enthusiastic about the courtesy of the French police, who actually did not beat them when they got into a quarrel, but scolded the Frankish man instead, and accompanied them back to the boat quite politely. The novelty and triumph of not being beaten was quite intoxicating. There is such a curious sight of a crowd of men carrying huge blocks of stone up out of a boat. One sees exactly how the stones were carried in ancient times; they sway their bodies all together like one great lithe animal with many legs, and hum a low chant to keep time. It is quite unlike any carrying heavy weights in Europe.

It is getting dusk and too windy for candles, so I must say goodnight and eat the dinner which Darfour has pressed upon me two or three times, he is a pleasant little creature, so lively and so gentle. It is washing day. I wish you could see Mabrook squatting out there, lathering away at the clothes with his superb black arms. He is a capital washer and a fair cook, but an utter savage.

[The foregoing letter reached England the day after the death of my grandmother, Mrs. Austin, which was a great shock to my mother and made her ill and unhappy; so it was settled that my brother Maurice should go out and spend the winter with her on the Nile.]

To Sir Alexander Duff Gordon

BOULAK,
September 7, 1867.

DEAREST ALICK,

Many thanks for your letter and for all the trouble you have taken. I wish you were better.

There is such a group all stitching away at the big new sail; Omar, the Reis, two or three volunteers, some old sailors of mine, and little Darfour. If I die I think you must have that tiny nigger over; he is such a merry little soul, I am sure you would love him, he is quite a civilised being and has a charming temper, and he seems very small to be left alone in the world.

I hope Maurice is not of the faction of the *ennuyés* of this generation. I am more and more of Omar's opinion, who said, with a pleased sigh, as we sat on the deck under some lovely palm-trees in the bright moon-light, moored far from all human dwellings, 'how sweet are the quiet places of the world.'

I wonder when Europe will drop the absurd delusion about Christians being persecuted by Muslims. It is absolutely the other way,—here at all events. The Christians know that they will always get backed by some Consul or other, and it is the Muslims who go to the wall invariably. The brute of a Patriarch is resolved to continue his persecution of the converts, and I was urged the other day by a Sheykh to go to the Sheykh ul-Islam himself and ask him to demand equal rights for all religions, which is the law, on behalf of these Coptic Protestants. Everywhere the Ulema have done what they could to protect them, even at Siout, where the American missionaries had caused them (the Ulemas) a good deal of annoyance on a former occasion. No one in Europe can conceive how much the Copts have the upper hand in the villages. They are backed by the Government, and they know that the Europeans will always side with them.

September 13.—Omar is crazy with delight at the idea of Maurice's arrival, and Reis Mohammed is planning what men to take who can make fantasia, and not ask too much wages. Let me know what boat Maurice comes by that I may send Omar to Alexandria to meet him. Omar begs me to give you and Sitti Rainie his best salaam, and his assurance that he will take great care of the young master and 'keep him very tight.' I think Maurice will be diverted with small Darfour. Mabrook now really cooks very fairly under Omar's orders, but he is beyond belief uncouth, and utters the wildest howls now that his voice is grown big and strong like himself. Moreover he 'won't be spoken to,' as our servants say; but he is honest, clean, and careful. I should not have thought any human creature could remain so completely a savage in a civilised community. I rather respect his savage *hauteur*, especially as it is combined with truth and honesty.

To Sir Alexander Duff Gordon

BOULAK,
BOAT *MARIE LOUISE*,
October 17, 1867.

DEAREST ALICK,

You must not be wroth with me because I have not written for a long time—I have been ill, but am much better. Omar will go down to Alexandria to meet Maurice on Monday.

My boat is being painted, but is nearly finished; as soon as it is done I shall move back into her. I got out into a little cangia but it swarmed with bugs and wasps, and was too dirty, so I moved yesterday into a good boat belonging to a dragoman, and hope to be back in my own by Sunday. But oh Lord! I got hold of the Barber himself turned painter; and as the little cangia was moored alongside the *Urania* in order to hold all the mattresses, carpets, etc. I was his victim. First, it was a request for 'three pounds to buy paint.' 'None but the best of paint is fitting for a noble person like thee, and that thou knowest is costly, and I am thy servant and would do thee honour.' 'Very well,' say I, 'take the money, and see, oh man, that the paint is of the best, or thy backsheesh will be bad also.' Well, he begins and then rushes in to say: 'Come oh Bey, oh Pasha! and behold the brilliancy of the white paint, like milk, like glass, like the full moon.' I go and say, 'Mashallah! but now be so good as to work fast, for my son will be here in a few days, and nothing is ready.' Fatal remark. 'Mashallah! Bismillah! may the Lord spare him, may God prolong thy days, let me advise thee how to keep the eye from him, for doubtless thy son is beautiful as a memlook of 1,000 purses. Remember to spit in his face when he comes on board, and revile him aloud that all the people may hear thee, and compel him to wear torn and dirty clothes when he goes out:—and how many children hast thou, and our master, thy master, and is he well?' etc. etc. '*Shukr Allah!* all is well with us,' say I; 'but, by the Prophet, paint, oh *Ma-alim* (exactly the German *Meister*) and do not break my head any more.' But I was forced to take refuge at a distance from Hajj' Alee's tongue. Read the story of the Barber, and you will know exactly what Ma-alim Hajj' Alee is. Also just as I got out of my boat and he had begun, the painter whom I had last year and with whom I was dissatisfied, went to the Sheykh of the painters and persuaded him to put my man in prison for working too cheap—that was at daybreak. So I sent up my Reis to the Sheykh to inform him that if my man did not return by next day at daybreak, I would send for an European painter and force the Sheykh to pay the bill. Of course my man came.

My steersman Hassan, and a good man, Hoseyn, who can wash and is generally nice and pleasant, arrived from el-Bastowee a few days ago, and are waiting here till I want them. Poor little ugly black Hassan has had his house burnt down in his village, and lost all the clothes which he had bought with his wages; they were very good clothes, some of them, and a heavy loss. He is my Reis's brother, and a good man, clean and careful and quiet, better than my Reis even—they are a respectable family. Big stout Hazazin owes me 200 piastres which he is to work out, so I have still five men and a boy to get. I hope a nice boy, called Hederbee (the lizard), will come. They don't take pay till the day before we sail, except the Reis and Abdul Sadig, who are permanent. But Hassan and Hoseyn are working away as merrily as if they were paid. People growl at the backsheesh, but they should also remember what a quantity of service one gets for nothing here, and for which, oddly enough, no one dreams of asking backsheesh. Once a week we shift the anchors, for fear of their silting over, and six or eight men work for an hour; then the mast is lowered—twelve or fourteen men work at this—and nobody gets a farthing.

The other day Omar met in the market an 'agreeable merchant,' an Abyssinian fresh from his own country, which he had left because of the tyranny of Kassa, alias Todoros, the Sultan. The merchant had brought his wife and concubines to live here. His account is that the mass of the people are delighted to hear that the English are coming to conquer them, as they hope, and that everyone hates the King except two or three hundred scamps who form his bodyguard. He had seen the English prisoners, who, he says, are not ill-treated, but certainly in danger, as the King is with difficulty restrained from killing them by the said scamps, who fear the revenge of the English; also that there is one woman imprisoned with the native female prisoners. Hassan the donkeyboy, when he was a *marmiton* in Cairo, knew the Sultan Todoros, he was the only man who could be found to interpret between the then King of Abyssinia and Mohammed Ali Pasha, whom Todoros had come to visit. The merchant also expressed a great contempt for the Patriarch, and for their *Matraam* or Metropolitan, whom the English papers call the *Abuna*. *Abuna* is Arabic for 'our father.' The man is a Cairene Copt and was a hanger-on of two English missionaries (they were really Germans) here, and he is more than commonly a rascal and a hypocrite. I know a respectable Jew whom he had robbed of all his merchandise, only Ras Alee forced the *Matraam* to disgorge. Pray what was all that nonsense about the

Armenian Patriarch of Jerusalem writing to Todoros? what could he have to do with it? The Coptic Patriarch, whose place is Cairo, could do it if he were forced.

At last my boat is finished, so to-morrow Omar will clean the windows, and on Saturday move in the cushions, etc. and me, and on Sunday go to Alexandria. I hear the dreadful voice of Hajj' Alee, the painter, outside, and will retire before he gets to the cabin door, for fear he should want to bore me again. I do hope Maurice will enjoy his journey; everyone is anxious to please him. The Sheykh of the Hawara sent his brother to remind me to stop at his 'palace' near Girgeh, that he might make a fantasia for my son. So Maurice will see real Arab riding, and jereed, and sheep roasted whole and all the rest of it. The Sheykh is the last of the great Arab chieftains of Egypt, and has thousands of fellaheen and a large income. He did it for Lord Spencer and for the Duke of Rutland and I shall get as good a fantasia, I have no doubt. Perhaps at Keneh Maurice had better not see the dancing, for Zeyneb and Latefeeh are terribly fascinating, they are such pleasant jolly girls as well as pretty and graceful, but old Oum ez-Zeyn (mother of beauty), so-called on account of his hideousness, will want us to eat his good dinner.

To Sir Alexander Duff Gordon

Urania, Boulak,
October 21, 1867.

Dearest Alick,

So many thanks for the boxes and their contents. My slaves are enchanted with all that the 'great master' has sent. Darfour hugged the horsecloth in ecstasy that he should never again be cold at night. The waistcoats of printed stuff, and the red flannel shirts are gone to be made up, so my boys will be like Pashas this winter, as they told the Reis. He is awfully perturbed about the evil eye. 'Thy boat, *Mashallah*, is such as to cause envy from all beholders; and now when they see a son with thee, *Bismillah! Mashallah!* like a flower, verily. I fear, I fear greatly from the eye of the people.' We have bought a tambourine and a tarabouka, and are on the look-out for a man who can sing well, so as to have fantasia on board.

October 22.—I hear to-day that the Pasha sent a telegram *hochst eigenhändig* to Koos, in consequence whereof one Stefanos, an old Copt of high character, many years in Government employ, was put in chains and hurried off within twenty minutes to Fazoghlou with two of his friends, for no other crime than having turned Presbyterian. This is quite a new idea in Egypt, and we all wonder why the Pasha is so anxious to 'brush the coat' of the Copt Patriarch. We also hear that the people up in the Saaed are running away by wholesale, utterly unable to pay the new taxes and to do the work exacted. Even here the beating is fearful. My Reis has had to send all his month's wages to save his aunt and his sister-in-law, both widows, from the courbash. He did not think so much of the blows, but of the 'shame'; 'those are women, lone women, from whence can they get the money?'

To Mrs. Ross

BOULAK,
November 3, 1867.

DEAREST JANET,

Maurice arrived on Friday week, and is as happy as can be, he says he never felt so well and never had such good snipe shooting. Little Darfour's amusement at Maurice is boundless; he grins at him all the time he waits at table, he marvels at his dirty boots, at his bathing, at his much walking out shooting, at his knowing no Arabic. The dyke burst the other day up at Bahr Yussuf, and we were nearly all swept away by the furious rush of water. My little boat was upset while three men in her were securing the anchor, and two of them were nearly drowned, though they swim like fish; all the dahabiehs were rattled and pounded awfully; and in the middle of the *fracas*, at noonday, a steamer ran into us quite deliberately. I was rather frightened when the steamer bumped us, and carried away the iron supports of the awning; and they cursed our fathers into the bargain, which I thought needless. The English have fallen into such contempt here that one no longer gets decent civility from anything in the *Miri* (Government).

Olagnier has lent us a lovely little skiff, and I have had her repaired and painted, so Maurice is set up for shooting and boating. Darfour calls him the 'son of a crocodile' because he loves the water, and generally delights in him hugely, and all my men are enchanted with him.

To Sir Alexander Duff Gordon

LUXOR,
December 20, 1867.

DEAREST ALICK,

We arrived here all safe three days ago. I think of starting for Nubia directly after Christmas Day, which we must keep here. We have lovely weather. Maurice is going with a friend of my friends, a Bedawee, to shoot, I hope among the Abab'deh he will get some gazelle shooting. I shall stop at Syaleh to visit the Sheykh's mother, and with them Maurice could go for some days into the desert. As to crocodiles, Inshallah, we will eat their hearts, and not they ours. You may rely on it that Maurice is 'on the head and in the eye' of all my crew, and will not be allowed to bathe in 'unclean places.' Reis Mohammed stopped him at Gebel Abu'l Foda. You would be delighted to see how different he looks; all his clothes are too tight now. He says he is thoroughly happy, and that he was never more amused than when with me, which I think very flattering.

Half of the old house at Luxor fell down into the temple beneath six days before I arrived; so there is an end of the *Maison de France*, I suppose. It might be made very nice again at a small expense, but I suppose the Consul will not do it, and certainly I shall not unless I want it again. Nothing now remains solid but the three small front rooms and the big hall with two rooms off it. All the part I lived in is gone, and the steps, so one cannot get in. Luckily Yussuf had told Mohammed to move my little furniture to the part which is solid, having a misgiving of the rest. He has the most exquisite baby, an exact minature of himself. He is in a manner my godson, being named Noor ed-Deen Hishan Abu-l-Hajjaj, to be called *Noor* like me.

To Sir Alexander Duff Gordon

On Board the Urania,
January, 1868.

Dearest Alick,

Your letter of the 10 December most luckily came on to Edfoo by the American Consul-General, who overtook us there in his steamer and gave me a lunch. Maurice was as usual up to his knees in a distant swamp trying to shoot wild geese. Now we are up close to Assouan, and there are no more marshes; but *en revanche* there are quails and *kata*, the beautiful little sand grouse. I eat all that Maurice shoots, which I find very good for me; and as for Maurice he has got back his old round boyish face; he eats like an ogre, walks all day, sleeps like a top, bathes in the morning and has laid on flesh so that his clothes won't button. At Esneh we fell in with handsome Hassan, who is now Sheykh of the Abab'deh, as his elder brother died. He gave us a letter to his brother at Syaleh, up in Nubia; ordering him to get up a gazelle hunt for Maurice, and I am to visit his wife. I think it will be pleasant, as the Bedaween women don't veil or shut up, and to judge by the men ought to be very handsome.

Both Hassan and Abu Goord, who was with him, preached the same sermon as my learned friend Abdurrachman had done at Luxor. 'Why, in God's name, I left my son without a wife?' They are sincerely shocked at such indifference to a son's happiness.

ASSOUAN,
10 *Ramadan*.

I have no almanach, but you will be able to know the date by your own red pocketbook, which determined the beginning of Ramadan at Luxor this year. They received a telegram fixing it for Thursday, but Sheykh Yussuf said that he was sure the astronomers in London knew best, and made it Friday. To-morrow we shall make our bargain, and next day go up the Cataract—Inshallah, in safety. The water is very good, as Jesus the black pilot tells me. He goes to the second Cataract and back, as I intend to stay nearly two months in Nubia. The weather here is perfect now, we have been lucky in having a lovely mild winter hitherto. We are very comfortable with a capital crew, who are all devoted to Maurice. The Sheykh of the Abab'deh has promised to join us if he can, when he has convoyed some 400 Bashibazouks up to Wady Halfa, who are being sent up because the English are in Abyssinia.

To Sir Alexander Duff Gordon

LUXOR,
April, 1868.

DEAREST ALICK,

I have been too weak to write, but the heat set in three days ago and took away my cough, and I feel much better. Maurice also flourishes in the broil, and protests against moving yet. He speaks a good deal of Arabic and is friends with everyone. It is *Salaam aleykoum ya maris* on all sides. A Belgian has died here, and his two slaves, a very nice black boy and an Abyssinian girl, got my little varlet, Darfour, to coax me to take them under my protection, which I have done, as there appeared a strong probability that they would be 'annexed' by a rascally Copt who is a Consular agent at Keneh. I believe the Belgian has left money for them, which of course they would never get without someone to look after it, and so I have Ramadan, the boy, with me, and shall take the girl when I go, and carry them both to Cairo, settle their little business, and let them present a sealed-up book which they have to their Consul there, according to their master's desire, and then marry the girl to some decent man. I have left her in Mustapha's hareem till I go.

I enjoyed Nubia immensely, and long to go and live with the descendants of a great *Ras* (head, chief,) who entertained me at Ibreem, and who said, like Ravenswood, 'Thou art come to a fallen house, and there is none to serve thee left save me.' It was a paradise of a place, and the Nubian had the grand manners of a very old, proud nobleman. I had a letter to him from Sheykh Yussuf.

Since I wrote the above it has turned quite chilly again, so we agreed to stay till the heat really begins. Maurice is so charmed with Luxor that he does not want to go, and we mean to let the boat and live here next winter. I think another week will see us start down stream. Janet talks of coming up the Nile with me next year, which would be pleasant. I am a little better than I have been the last two months. I was best in Nubia but I got a cold at Esneh, second hand from Maurice, which made me very seedy. I cannot go about at all for want of breath. Could you send me a chair such as people are carried in by two men? A common chair is awkward for the men when the banks are steep, and I am nervous, so I never go out. I wish you could see your son bare-legged and footed, in a shirt and a pair of white Arab drawers, rushing about with the fellaheen. He is everybody's 'brother' or 'son.'

To Sir Alexander Duff Gordon

MINIEH,
May, 1868.

DEAREST ALICK,

We are just arriving at Minieh whence the railway will take letters quickly. We dined at Keneh and at Siout with some friends, and had fantasia at Keneh. Omar desires his dutiful salaams to you and hopes you will be satisfied with the care he has taken of 'the child.' How you would have been amused to hear the girl who came to dance for us at Esneh lecture Maurice about evil ways, but she was an old friend of mine, and gave good and sound advice.

Everyone is delighted about Abyssinia. 'Thank God our Pasha will fear the English more than before, and the Sultan also,' and when I lamented the expense, they all exclaimed, 'Never mind the expense, it is worth more than ten millions to you; your faces are whitened and your power enlarged before all the world; but why don't you take us on your way back.'

I saw a very interesting man at Keneh, one Faam, a Copt, who has turned Presbyterian, and has induced a hundred others at Koos to do likewise: an American missionary is their minister. Faam was sent off to the Soudan by the Patriarch, but brought back. He is a splendid old fellow, and I felt I looked on the face of a Christian martyr, a curious sight in the nineteenth century: the calm, fearless, rapt expression was like what you see in noble old Italian pictures, and he had the perfect absence of 'doing pious' which shows the undoubting faith. He and the Mufti, also a noble fellow, sparred about religion in a jocose and friendly tone which would be quite unintelligible in Exeter Hall. When he was gone the Mufti said, 'Ah! we thank them, for though they know not the truth of Islam, they are good men, and walk straight, and would die for their religion: their example is excellent; praise be to God for them.'

To Sir Alexander Duff Gordon

Boulak,
June 14, 1868.

Dearest Alick,

The climate has been odious for Egypt—to shiver in cold winds of June on the Nile seems hard. Maurice inherits my faculty for getting on with 'd—d niggers'; all the crew kissed him on both cheeks and swore to come back again in the winter; and up the country he was hand and glove with all the fellaheen, eating a good deal of what he called 'muck' with great enjoyment, walking arm in arm with a crazy derweesh, fetching home a bride at night and swearing lustily by the Prophet. The good manners of the Arab *canaille*, have rubbed off the very disagreeable varnish which he got at Brussels.

Dr. Patterson wants me to go to Beyrout or one of the Greek isles for a change. I am very feeble and short of breath—but I will try the experiment. Would you be shocked if a nigger taught Maurice? One Hajjee Daboos I know to be a capital Arabic scholar and he speaks French like a Parisian, and Italian also, only he is a real nigger and so is the best music-master in Cairo. *Que faire?* it's not catching, as Lady Morley said, and I won't present you with a young mulatto any more than with a young *brave Belge*. I may however find someone at Beyrout. Cairo is in such a state of beggary that all educated young men have fled. Maurice has no sort of idea why a nigger should not be as good as anyone else, but thinks perhaps you might not approve.

You would have stared to see old Achmet Agha Abd el-Sadig, a very good friend of ours at Assouan, coaxing and patting the *weled* (boy) when he dined here the other day, and laughing immoderately at Maurice's nonsense. He is one of the M.P.'s for Assouan, and a wealthy and much respected man in the Saeed. The Abyssinian affair is an awful disappointment to the Pasha; he had laid his calculations for something altogether different, and is furious. The Coptic clergy are ready to murder us. The Arabs are all in raptures. 'God bless the English general, he has frightened our Pasha.'

Giafar Pasha backsheeshed me an *abbayeh* of crimson silk and gold, also a basket of coffee. I was obliged to accept them as he sent his son with them, and to refuse would have been an insult, and as he is the one Turk I do think highly of I did not wish to affront him. It was at Luxor on his way to Khartoum. He also invited Maurice to Khartoum, and proposed to send a party to fetch him from Korosko, on the Nile. Giafar is Viceroy of the Soudan, and a very quiet man, who does not 'eat the people.'

My best love to Janet, I'll write soon to her, but I am lazy and Maurice is worse. Omar nearly cried when Maurice went to Alexandria for a week. 'I seem to feel how dull we shall be without him when he goes away for good,' said he, and Darfour expresses his intention of going with Maurice. 'Thou must give me to the young man backsheesh,' as he puts it, 'because I have plenty of sense and shall tell him what to do.' That is the little rascal's sauce. Terence's slaves are true to the life here.

To Sir Alexander Duff Gordon

BOULAK,
October 22, 1868.

DEAREST ALICK,

The unlucky journey to Syria almost cost me my life. The climate is absolute poison to consumptive people. In ten days after I arrived the doctor told me to settle my affairs, for I had probably only a few days to live, and certainly should never recover. However I got better, and was carried on board the steamer, but am too weak for anything. We were nearly shipwrecked coming back owing to the Russian captain having his bride on board and not minding his ship. We bumped and scraped and rolled very unpleasantly. At

Beyrout the Sisters of Charity wouldn't nurse a Protestant, nor the Prussians a non-Lutheran. But Omar and Darfour nursed me better than Europeans ever do. Little Blackie was as sharp about the physic as a born doctor's boy when Omar was taking his turn of sleep. I did not like the few Syrians I saw at all.

To Sir Alexander Duff Gordon

BOULAK,
November 6, 1868.

DEAREST ALICK,

I am sure you will rejoice to hear that I am really better. I now feel so much like living on a bit longer that I will ask you to send me a cargo of medicines. I didn't think it worth while before to ask for anything to be sent to me that could not be forwarded to Hades, but my old body seems very tough and I fancy I have still one or two of my nine lives left.

I hope to sail in a very few days, Maurice is going up to Cairo so I send this by him. Yesterday was little Rainie's birthday, and I thought very longingly of her. The photo, of Leighton's sketch of Janet I like very much.

To Sir Alexander Duff Gordon

ASSOUAN,
January 25, 1869.

DEAREST ALICK,

We have been here ten days, and I find the air quite the best for me. I cough much less, only I am weak and short of breath. I have got a most excellent young Reis for my boat, and a sailor who sings like a nightingale, indeed he is not a sailor at all, but a professional Cairo singer who came up with me for fun. He draws crowds to hear him, and at Esneh the congregation prayed for me in the mosque that God might reward me for the pleasure I had provided for them. Fancy desiring the prayers of this congregation for the welfare of the lady who gave me her opera-box last Saturday. If prayers could avail to cure I ought to get well rapidly. At Luxor Omar killed the sheep he had vowed, and Mustapha and Mohammed each killed two, as thank-offerings for my life, and all the derweeshes held two great *Zikrs* in a tent pitched behind the boat, and drummed and chanted and called on the Lord for two whole nights; and every man in my boat fasted Ramadan severely, from Omar and the crew to the little boys. I think Darfour was the most meritorious of all, because he has such a Gargantuan appetite, but he fasted his thirty days bravely and rubbed his little nose in the dust energetically in prayer.

On Christmas day I was at Esneh, it was warm and fine, and I made fantasia and had the girls to dance. Zeyneb and Hillaleah claim to be my own special *Ghazawee*, so to speak my *Ballerine da camera*, and they did their best. How I did long to transport the whole scene before your eyes—Ramadan warbling intense lovesongs, and beating on a tiny tambourine, while Zeyneb danced before him and gave the pantomime to his song; and the sailors, and girls, and respectable merchants sat *pêle-mêle* all round on the deck, and the player on the rabab drew from it a wail like that of Isis for dead Osiris. I never quite know whether it is now or four thousand years ago, or even ten thousand, when I am in the dreamy intoxication of a real Egyptian fantasia; nothing is so antique as the Ghazawee—the *real* dancing girls. They are still subject to religious ecstasies of a very curious kind, no doubt inherited from the remotest antiquity. Ask any learned pundit to explain to you the *Zar*—it is really curious.

Now that I am too ill to write I feel sorry that I did not persist and write on the beliefs of Egypt in spite of your fear that the learned would cut me up, for I honestly believe that knowledge will die with me which few others possess. You must recollect that the learned know books, and I know men, and what is still more difficult, women.

The Cataract is very bad this year, owing to want of water in the Nile, and to the shameful conduct of the Maōhn here. The cataract men came to me, and prayed me to 'give them my voice' before the Mudir, which I will do. Allah ed-deen Bey seems a decent man and will perhaps remove the rascal, whose robberies on travellers are notorious, and his oppression of the poor savages who pull the boats up odious. Two boats have been severely damaged, and my friend the Reis of the Cataract (the one I threatened to shoot last year, and who has believed in me ever since) does not advise me to go up, though he would take me for nothing, he swears, if I wished. So as the air is good here and Maurice is happy with his companions, I will stay here.

I meant to have discharged my men, but I have grown so fond of them (having so good a set), that I can't bring myself to save £20 by turning them adrift when we are all so happy and comfortable, and the poor fellows are just marrying new wives with their wages. Good-bye dearest Alick, forgive a scrawl, for I am very weak all over, fingers and all. Best love to my darling Rainie. Three boats have little girls of five to eight on board, and I do envy them so. I think Maurice had better go home to you, when we get to Cairo. He ought to be doing something.

To Sir Alexander Duff Gordon

BOULAK,
June 15, 1869.

DEAREST ALICK,

Do not think of coming here. Indeed it would be almost too painful to me to part from you again; and as it is, I can patiently wait for the end among people who are kind and loving enough to be comfortable, without too much feeling of the pain of parting. The leaving Luxor was rather a distressing scene, as they did not think to see me again.

The kindness of all the people was really touching, from the Kadee who made ready my tomb among his own family, to the poorest fellaheen. Omar sends you his most heartfelt thanks, and begs that the boat may remain registered at the Consulate in your name for his use and benefit. The Prince has appointed him his own dragoman. But he is sad enough, poor fellow, all his prosperity does not console him for the loss of 'the mother he found in the world.' Mohammed at Luxor wept bitterly and said, 'poor I, my poor children, poor all the people,' and kissed my hand passionately, and the people at Esneh, asked leave to touch me 'for a blessing,' and everyone sent delicate bread, and their best butter, and vegetables and lambs. They are kinder than ever now that I can no longer be of any use to them.

If I live till September I will go up to Esneh, where the air is softest and I cough less. I would rather die among my own people in the Saeed than here.

You must forgive this scrawl, dearest. Don't think please of sending Maurice out again, he must begin to work now or he will never be good for anything.

Can you thank the Prince of Wales for Omar,* or shall I write? He was most pleasant and kind, and the Princess too. She is the most perfectly simple-mannered girl I ever saw. She does not even try to be civil like other great people, but asks blunt questions, and looks at one so heartily with her clear, honest eyes, that she must win all hearts. They were more considerate than any people I have seen, and the Prince, instead of being gracious, was, if I may say so, quite respectful in his manner: he is very well bred and pleasant, and has the honest eyes that makes one sure he has a kind heart.

My sailors were so proud at having the honour of rowing him *in our own boat*, and of singing to him. I had a very good singer in the boat. Please send some little present for my Reis: he is such a good man; he will be pleased at some little thing from you. He is half Turk, and seems like whole one. Maurice will have told you all about us. Good-bye for the present, dearest Alick.

To Sir Alexander Duff Gordon

HELWAN,
OPPOSITE BEDRESHAYN,
July 9, 1869.

DEAREST ALICK,

Don't make yourself unhappy, and don't send out a nurse. And above all don't think of coming. I am nursed as well as possible. My two Reises, Ramadan and Yussuf, are strong and tender and Omar is admirable as ever. The worst is I am so strong.

I repeat I could not be better cared for anywhere than by my good and loving crew. Tell Maurice how they all cried and how Abd el-Haleem forswore drink and hasheesh. He is very good too. But my Reises are incomparable. God bless you. I wish I had seen your dear face once more—but not now. I would not have you here now on any account.

Biographical Afterword

IT IS IMPOSSIBLE to read Lucie Duff Gordon's letters home to her family without falling a little in love with her poignant joy at life in the face of her imminent death and with her open-minded care for and curiosity about her Egyptian neighbours. It is clear that they, in their turn, both respected and admired her, taking her to themselves in the absence of her own family. What was it that bred such a natural nobility and sense of equality and service in her, when British colonial administrators of a very different stripe were already lining up to exploit the desperate poverty of the Egyptians while trumpeting their own superiority?

Lucie was the only child born to John and Sarah Austin, on 24 June 1821. Despite her parents' close connections to radical political circles in London, hers was an erratic and unconventional childhood, shaped by her father's constitutional anxiety and her mother's strength of character. Her father trained for the Bar, but his nerves forced him from the profession and from a series of jobs in academia, where lecturing proved too much for him. Her mother was the stable centre of the household, turning to writing and translation herself to help the family finances, but so preoccupied with supporting her delicate husband that she appears to have paid little attention to Lucie in infancy. Left to her own devices, the young girl apparently invented elaborate fantasy fairy worlds in Jeremy Bentham's garden and kept a menagerie of pet mice, canaries, newts and turtles, the beginning of a lifelong love of animals. It wasn't until the little family travelled to Bonn in Germany in 1827, that six-year-old Lucie finally made some friends of her own at a local German school.

Back in London, Lucie furthered her education in Latin and German with her mother. She also read voraciously, including books such as *The Odyssey*, *Don Quixote* and *Robinson Crusoe*. Sarah, writing to her sister, described Lucie as 'a monstrous, great girl, but though she has admirable qualities, I am not satisfied with her. She is too wild, undisciplined and independent; and though she knows a great deal it is in a strange, wild way. She reads everything; composes German verses, has imagined and put together a fairy world, dress, language, music, everything, and talks to them in the garden; but she is sadly negligent of her own appearance'. Yet far from encouraging more decorum and femininity, she sent Lucie to an all-boys school in Hampstead run by a German man called Dr Biber. Her own mother had been a firm advocate of the importance of female education, and perhaps Sarah's letter to her sister conceals a secret glee at her self-willed daughter. As her mother put it, 'beside the intrinsic pleasure to be derived from solid knowledge, a woman ought to consider it her best resource against poverty.' And so it turned out to be. When John Austin quit his professorship in 1832, Sarah took it upon herself to turn his lectures into a book and negotiated with John Murray (the publisher of all her translations thus far) to have them published at the end of 1832 as *The Province of Jurisprudence*, which though not popular at the time, continued to sell for many years.

At around this time, young Lucie finally made a female friend close to her age, Alice Spring-Rice, daughter of a secretary to the Treasury. Their friendship seems to have been intense, bordering on romantic (although this may have been because she was Lucie's *only* real friend). Many of Lucie's letters opened with, 'My own darling wife' and ended, 'Your faithful husband, Roger Austin'. The eleven-year-old once wrote to Alice, 'How is it, how can it be that you love me so much? When I think of it I feel bewildered and wonder whether I am really that Lucy Austin whom the Spring-Rices are fond of… No one else loves me or ever did love me, how is it, what is it in me that you above all others see to love?'

After another nervous turn, in 1833 John Austin took his family to live in Boulogne, at that time a simple fishing village popular with financially beleaguered English families. While her father rested, and her mother worked on a volume of selections from the Old Testament, Lucie seems to have thrived, foreshadowing her later pleasure at living abroad in Luxor. She became fluent in French, befriended a sailor called Pierre Henin who taught her to swim, and a French family called Fleuret with six children, who lived and worked in a one-room cottage. Here, too, Lucie was exposed to her mother's radical liberal sensibilities and politics. During a stormy night at the end of August, a female convict transport ship headed for New South Wales, the *Amphitrite*, sunk off the coast of Boulogne. Sarah cleared a ground-floor room at the local inn which she used as a first-aid station and, with Lucie in tow, attempted to resuscitate the women and children washed up on the beach. Of the 131 on board, only four crew members survived but Sarah was later awarded a medal for her actions by the Royal Humane Society. Sarah was enraged by what had taken place, writing to *The Times*, 'These 120 women and children … were more kindly treated by the raging elements than by the Society that corrupted and then cast them forth. My poor offending sisters! It is not in your death that I weep for you, terrible as it was, it is in the bitter hours of shame and guilt that preceded it – the cruelty and injustice of man to you'.

Shortly after their return to London, and their move to ever smaller lodgings, Sarah took Lucie to stay with her brother in Hastings for a month, where she made her second bosom friend, Janet North, whose father was a Whig MP. A family visitor at the time described Lucie as 'handsome, very striking, with a stern determined expression of countenance which might qualify her to sit for a picture of Cassandra or Clytemnestra… She speaks German and French like a native, and knows as much of Greek and Latin as most boys… She is pleasant when she is pleased but I cannot help thinking that if anyone were to inconvenience her and there were to be a dagger, a pair of scissors, or any other sharp, pointed instrument, she would be hasty and inconsiderate; … in other words … I see her as a potential homicide', or as her mother put it 'un peu unmanageable'.

Strong as the women of the household seem to have been however, it did not rub off on John, whose panic attacks became ever more frequent, feverish and violent. In further straitened financial circumstances, they moved back to Boulogne in 1835, but without sunny future prospects, this stay was less enjoyable. Although Lucie characteristically carried on back with her old French friends, unlike other English exiles who seemed to avoid fraternising with locals, surrounded by the misery of her father and mother, Lucie wrote to her friend Alice, 'I am in a most unsatisfactory state of

Lucie Austin, aged 15

existence. I am not absolutely idle, yet I do nothing… I am not absolutely miserable and yet I am far from being happy'. At times of great distress her young fourteen-year-old mind seems to have turned to religion and again she wrote to Alice, 'I cannot say I belong to any particular sect… if it were necessary to choose… I should hesitate between the Catholics and the Unitarians, for I am lothe [sic] to part with our Lady, it is so delightful to pray to a woman… besides which one person worships God under one form, one under another, each choosing the form or image most congenial to his or her imagination, but it is the same Creator and Preserver everywhere.'

In the late spring of 1836, thanks to the Austins' various friends and connections in the Colonial Office and parliament, John was appointed to head a two-person commission into colonial grievances in Malta. Afraid of the foreign climate and diseases, Sarah arranged for Lucie to be put in a boarding school run by a Miss Shepherd in Bromley, a choice deeply unpopular with Lucie. The strict schedule of prayers, lessons, meals, bells and on Sunday, full day services at the parish church with a picnic in the graveyard, were a complete antithesis to how the 'unmanageable' Lucie had lived thus far. A month into the school her friend Janet came to visit with her mother, Mrs North, and afterwards wrote in her diary 'we found [Lucie] … looking ill and wretched and Miss Shepherd cross and not amiable to her. Harriet Stone … said Lucie had been crying violently. I, who know her pride, know full well how very miserable she must have been to have cried … she is a splendid creature, full of genius, of talent and honesty, simplicity and confidence in others and herself. I suspect Lucie has shocked Miss Shepherd's conventionalism'. To make matters worse, she had barely any contact from her mother in Malta, with messages infrequent and letters often rushed, talking mainly of how busy they were.

In Malta, the Austins were indeed busy. While John set about restructuring the constitution and legal system, Sarah got involved in the local community. She started village schools, sorted out Maltese crafts to be sold in England to raise revenue, and in the midst of a cholera epidemic, nursed the sick and dying. To her friends she wrote of her aversion to colonial society and her horror at the plight of the Maltese. Inevitably, John's health eventually broke down and they returned to London in July 1838.

Lucie, now seventeen, left Miss Shepherd's without a backwards glance and moved back with her parents, ready to be introduced to London society. Although Miss Shepherd's had been a disturbing experience for her, its 'taming' influence may have been a boon when it came to her new, adult social life. In early 1939, while Lucie was still eighteen, she met Sir Alexander Duff Gordon, twenty-eight, at a ball at Lord Lansdowne's. The two seemed immediately suited, with Alexander being much that her father was not: cheerful, strong, sturdy, of good temperament, socially adept and artlessly genuine. He was also a

Lucie Duff Gordon

lover of German literature and politically liberal – a Whig. Lucie's mother wrote that he possessed 'nothing but a small salary, his handsome person, excellent and sweet character and his title (a great misfortune!).' Their courtship was short and within months, on one of their walks, Alexander asked, 'Do you know people say we are going to be married? Shall we make it true?' Although there were a couple of reasons against their union (Lucie was still only eighteen, Alexander did not have a great financial fortune and Lady Duff Gordon, his mother, seemed very against one of her boys marrying a girl of such social obscurity), John Austin's initial reaction to the news was extreme. We have no account of what happened in the meeting, but both Alexander and Lucie sent letters to John promising to delay their engagement and in the meantime not to see one another. However, by the autumn

Sir Alexander Duff Gordon (Alick)

of 1939 they were formally engaged. In the ensuing months they paid visits to relatives to introduce one another, including a very tense stay with Lady Duff Gordon. When they visited her, Mrs North described the couple out walking in the hills wrapped in a single blanket, and smoking cigarettes together on her roof. On 16 May 1840, they were married in Kensington Old Church, with Lucie's cousin Henry Reeve standing in for her father, who was unsurprisingly prevented from attending by his health.

They spent their honeymoon in Germany, visiting galleries and libraries, and calling on philosophers. Back in London, they moved into 8 Queen Square, Westminster and maintained a happy and uniquely equal married life. They soon became a golden couple, with Lucie a delightful, if bohemian, literary hostess. Their house boasted an eclectic mix of family and friends, Italian refugees, German philosophers and a host of literary figures – including Richard Monckton Milnes, Dickens, Thackeray, Carlyle and Tennyson. The latter remarked to Alexander, 'I never loved a dear gazelle, but some damned brute, that's you, Gordon, had married her first'. Even her mother-in-law conceded to her 'powers of conversation and clearness of intellect'.

The couple seemed uniquely and perhaps wilfully ignorant of social convention, with Lucie often wearing men's jackets and remaining at the dinner table at the end of their meals to smoke cigars with the gentlemen. William Brookfield, after dining with them, remarked of the pair that 'The Gordons are peculiarly far from "fine". He is most gentlemanly … and would seem perfectly unconscious that such and such things were considered vulgar; she, on the other hand, would seem rather as if she gloried in their very commonness: but not so much – I don't mean to malign her… Lady Gordon had dressed the salad herself in the kitchen. But the difference with which he would mention such a thing as a simple matter of fact, and she with the least little tinge of bravado, would strike an acute observer.'

Nor would the Duff Gordons stand for the conventional judgements of society in matters of morals. Lucie was great friends with the author and divorcee Caroline Norton, who had been much maligned in British society after her husband accused her, unfairly, of a love affair with the Prime Minister, Lord Melbourne. The couple made a point of not attending any party that Caroline was not also invited to. When they took in a servant girl called Mary, who had had a child out of wedlock, Lucie warned the other servants that anyone who spoke out against the new maid would be dismissed.

Lucie discovered she was pregnant in June 1841, at the age of twenty, and gave birth to Janet Anne Duff Gordon on 24 February 1842. Although they had hoped for a boy, the entire family was infatuated by the new child, Lucie writing that 'children are delicious, the naïveté with which they display every human vice is indescribably charming' and Sarah commenting that she had become 'the most foolish of grandmothers … and never so happy when all my schemes are disconcerted and all my things thrown into confusion by this little creature'. It was around this time that Lucie, aided by her mother, began to do some translating work herself (both French and German). Beginning with children's stories and books about witches, she was soon inspired by her friend Alexander Kinglake (who had just published a successful account of his travels in the Middle East, *Eothen*) to work on the Islamic world. She translated two books by Frenchmen about Algeria *The Prisoners of Abd el-Kader* (in which she removed many racist passages in favour of those which reflected well on the character of Abd el-Kader himself) and *The Soldier of the Foreign Legion.*

In 1844, a twelve-year-old Sudanese servant boy named Hassan el-Bakkeet turned up on the Duff Gordons' doorstep. Lucie had met him while visiting a friend in a boarding house where the boy's master was also staying. Hassan had been turned out after going blind and as a last resort turned up at Lucie's home. The Duff Gordons took him in, had his eyes cured and Hassan (nicknamed 'Hatty' by the young Janet) became a kind of child to Alexander and Lucie. Although technically a servant, he was mainly Janet's playmate, and family trips and holidays automatically included him.

The following year, in February 1845, just before Janet's third birthday, Lucie gave birth to a second baby, this time a boy. They named him Maurice and baptised him on 30 July with Lord Lansdowne and Caroline Norton as godparents. Tragically, soon after Maurice caught an awful fever, and though Lucie nursed him sleeplessly, he died in her arms on 4 August. The loss was felt greatly by both parents, and writing to Lord Lansdowne on the evening of the fifth Lucie said, 'Of course, none but ourselves can see in the death of so young a creature any very great grief, but to me it seems a terrible loss. The child was so strong and so handsome that I had indulged hopes of so much happiness from what he would one day be to me, and now I find it hard to bear the destruction of them… My poor husband is so cut up that I am forced to do all that has to be done… I feel I have no right to lament, for all has gone so well with us some misfortune was due… [But] you will be sorry for my grief … and able to imagine that blank left in my life by the loss of a creature who had never been absent from me one night or day since its birth.'

In an attempt to restart herself, in late October Lucie began to translate a German work that she had put off at the birth of Maurice. It would eventually be called *Narratives of Remarkable Criminal Trials* and contained lurid depictions of crimes and their trials, at a time when thrillers and crime novels were not yet widely popular. She was certain the book would do well, and condensed its thirteen hundred pages into four hundred, selecting just fourteen representative cases. Using her husband to negotiate on her behalf, she quadrupled her usual payment of £50 from John Murray to £200. The book was very popular, not only in literary circles but also among the wider press and public, earning her a more prominent reputation as a translator.

Three years after their first son died, Lucie gave birth to another baby boy on 15 March 1849. He was once more called Maurice and Lord Lansdowne and Caroline Norton made his godparents. In July that year (with Maurice at four months) the whole family visited Lucie's parents, the Austins, now moved to Weybridge. They remained there until October, with the smiling happy baby Maurice becoming completely enamoured by his dour and grumpy grandfather. However, in the autumn the entire family, excluding Alexander, caught terrible colds and retreated to London, with Hatty faring the worse. Alexander sat up night after night with him, nursing him and calling for doctors. However it soon became clear that the boy had caught consumption, and he died in Alexander's arms on Christmas Day. Once more the entire family, this time with Janet old enough to be aware, mourned the loss of another member.

Lucie Duff Gordon in 1851

They remained in London until 1851, when finances (Alexander remained an underpaid senior clerk in the Treasury) forced them to relocate to Esher in Surrey, close enough to London that Alexander could travel in every day. Throughout this time Lucie suffered a series of colds and bronchitis, and in January 1851 was lucky to escape death herself. Although she recovered, she wrote to a friend that her illnesses had made her 'preternaturally weak, languid and nervous. Today I ought to be dining in London with Lord Lansdowne ... but my eyes are weak and painful, and myself low and seedy and exactly what is called "not up" to anything'. This was perhaps the first sign that it was not only Hatty who had contracted tuberculosis on their trip to Weybridge. The move did little to dampen their social lives, however, with friends coming to visit so frequently that their home was nicknamed 'The Gordon Arms'. Luckily Alexander's unexpected promotion to Commissioner of Inland Revenue finally brought them an income which kept up with their expenditure.

Somewhat like her mother, it was only when Janet was eleven that her parents realised her want of a formal education. She was described by Tennyson as 'a clever girl, but extremely badly brought up' and by her grandmother (on her father's side) as wanting 'manners and breeding and all feminine graces (as her mother did before her), and respect for God and man'. In 1853, Janet was sent to Dresden for a year with a German governess to study in a German school. Janet's independent spirit was clearly picked up from her mother, who continued to espouse controversial political views. Writing in 1857 after the Indian Mutiny, Lucie said, 'I am singular ... in giving ... my sympathy to the natives who are between two millstones – first tyrannised by the sepoys ... and then harried by the English... The English victims at least will have vengeance and subscriptions, but who will pity the poor helpless mass of the people guilty of the offence of a dark skin and a religion of their own?'

As she had remained frail and sickly in the intervening years, Lucie was surprised and delighted to discover in April 1858, nine years after the birth of Maurice and at the age of thirty seven, that she was once again pregnant. On 5 November, Urania Duff

Gordon was born. By all accounts she was a *wunderkind* and Urania's mother was besotted. Sarah Austin, coming to visit after she was born, wrote, 'the Heaven has sent me a new grandchild – a granddaughter, a prodigy of beauty and vigour. This little creature come late to us all – the "last rose of summer" to her parents – "the last flower of autumn" to us. I am full of thankfulness for [her]'.

However, in late autumn of that year disaster struck. John Austin contracted bronchitis and seemed unlikely to recover. Lucie rushed to be with her dying father and the ordeal that followed, as described by Janet, was heartbreaking, with Lucie sitting night after night 'white as marble, her face set and stern … her large eyes fixed on his face'. When he died on 17 December, Lucie immediately had a severe attack of haemorrhaging from her lungs, revealing that she did indeed have tuberculosis.

Lucie was rushed back to Esher, and Sarah also moved in. Early 1860 seemed hellish for the family. Sarah was deep in grief, and Lucie confined to bed. She was moved with her mother and Urania to the Isle of Wight to convalesce, eventually joined by Alexander and Maurice. The attacks were terrifying ordeals, described by Lucie as 'sudden, and utterly annihilating while they last' with 'the real evil … the feeling of being a trouble and expense to my husband, and unable to contribute to his comfort'.

Back in Esher the headstrong Janet, newly out in society, made use of her empty house. Inviting her great aunt Charlotte to stay as a chaperone, she invited Henry Ross down to better get to know him. Henry was a director of a Bank in Alexandria, Egypt and 'a wonderfully vivid raconteur'. He also had an income of £5,000 a year and was a year older than Janet's mother Lucie. Janet reported, 'I took Mr Ross out with the Duc d'Aumale's harriers, and was much impressed by his admirable riding, his pleasant conversation, and his kindly ways. The result was that I promised to marry him'. This took all members of the family by surprise; Alexander, for whom Janet was 'the sunbeam in … life made so dreary by Lucie's illness', was distraught and Sarah commented that there was 'a little too much difference in their ages, but Janet never liked young men'.

Her other grandmother, Lady Duff Gordon, suspecting Ross's income as an ulterior motive to Janet's keenness, wrote to her parents saying, 'I trust that there will be no marriage unless Janet *from her heart* wishes it!' However, it is Lucie's response that is perhaps revealing of an understanding of Janet's situation. She said that Ross was 'everything I could wish … he is so excellent and agreeable; and there is quite enough money and a new country to see, and an interesting life' and was 'heartily glad to get [Janet] away from the depressing influence of illness and anxiety, and to know her enjoying her youth'. She of all people knew the corrupting influence of the chronic illness of a parent and seemed painfully aware of the effect of her tuberculosis on her family. Janet and Ross were married on 5 December 1860, in Ventnor, the Isle of Wight, so as to be close to Lucie, who in an echo of her own marriage was too ill to attend on the day. The newly-weds set off almost immediately for Paris, en route for Alexandria.

Although slowly recovering, another haemorrhage attack in May 1861 sealed Lucie's fate. If she wanted to survive the winter, she had to move to a warmer climate. The 'Gordon Arms' was let, Lucie moving in with the family of her Esher doctor Dr Izod. Maurice went to Eton, Alexander to his mother's in London, and Urania, after a lot of agonising, to live with Lucie's maiden aunt, Charlotte Austin. In late July, Lucie and her maid Sally Naldrett boarded the *St Lawrence* to South Africa. 'A most sad, anxious business!' she wrote in her diary.

For a woman in the throes of tuberculosis, Lucie took surprisingly well to the somewhat dangerous voyage to the Cape. The intrepid young traveller she once was reappears. Writing one day to Alexander she described how 'the sea struck us on the weather side … nurse and four children in fits. Mrs Taylor and babies afloat, but good-humoured. Army surgeon and I picked up children and bullied nurse, and helped to bale. Went to bed at 9, couldn't undress, it pitched so. Slept sound but seedy next day.' Her maid Sally seems to have been an intrepid and perfectly matched travelling companion. When the ship almost sank after crashing into another larger one, Lucie wrote that 'Sally was cool as an icicle, offered me my pea jacket which I declined as I preferred going down comfortably in my cot'.

Lucie took to South Africa, loving the country itself and taking well to travelling, making good of her medical exile. Much like her younger self in France and her mother in Malta, she intensely disliked colonial society and preferred the company of locals. She made good friends with a couple called Adbul Jermaalee and his wife Betsy, 'a couple of old folks who were slaves to Dutch owners, and now keep a fruit shop of a rough sort', after Abdul bought back their freedom. They had a son studying in Cairo and the three would often commiserate over missing their children; 'We were not afraid of boring each other, and pious old Abdul sat and nodded, and said, "may Allah protect them all!" as a refrain – "Allah-il-Allah!"' She was incredibly critical of the way the Dutch treated the locals, like many of her compatriots at the time, however she was also deeply critical of the English; 'As Sally says, "The English here think the coloured people ought to do the work and they to get the wages; nothing less would satisfy them." Few of the English will do anything but lounge, while they abuse the Dutch as lazy and the Malays as thieves, and feel their fingers itch to be at the blacks.'

Around this time Alexander suggested that her letters home, mainly to him and her mother, should be published. Lucie seemed alarmed by the suggestion, writing 'My dear Alick, you must have fallen into second childhood to think of *printing* such rambling hasty scrawls as I write. I never could write a good letter; and unless I gallop as hard as I can and don't stop to think, I can say nothing; so all is confused and unconnected; only I fancy *you* will be amused by some of my impressions'. However she changed her mind at the suggestion that it might help finance her trip. Alexander showed them to their friend George Meredith who was very encouraging, and Sarah went about beginning to collate and edit them. These letters became her first original publication, *Letters from the Cape*, and were extremely popular.

Sarah Austin, c. 1867 when she was editing Lucie's letters

She eagerly returned to her family in July 1962, finding Urania a large three-year-old, Maurice tall and lanky and Janet eight months pregnant, visiting from Egypt. However, the stay was short-lived; two days after her arrival she was informed by doctors that she must leave again as soon as possible. This was another huge wrench. Looking for a dryer climate, and hoping to stay closer to her family, she decided on Egypt, arriving in Alexandria on 26 October. At first she seemed to hate it. Alone apart from Sally, the land and the language were utterly alien. She stayed in Janet's home, though Janet and Henry were still in England. Luckily, she met two friends of the Rosses: Hekekyan Bey (a civil engineer) and William Thayer, the American Consul-General in Cairo. They invited her and Sally to stay with them in Cairo and organised for Lucie to hire Omar Abu Halaweh as her dragoman for £3 a month. This decision transformed Lucie's life in Egypt, and it is at this point that Lucie's letters take up the story.

The one incident which is remarkably edited from the letters is an event which sits oddly with all that we know of their author. Just as we find it hard to square it with the woman we feel we have met through her letters, so too did her editors, her mother and her daughter. On Christmas Day 1864, Sally gave birth to Omar's child. She had kept the pregnancy, and the relationship with the married Omar, a complete secret, and Lucie was incandescent with rage. Unable to acknowledge, perhaps, her jealousy at the intimate relationship which had grown in the bosom of her small Egyptian 'family' and afraid of the impact it would have on her household just as her need for Omar was growing, she painted Sally as 'a regular old roué' and 'a common adulterer' and refused to acknowledge their marriage, though polygamy was not illegal in Egypt. Under the circumstances, she forbade Omar from divorcing his Egyptian wife to marry Sally in a lawful English fashion. She allowed Sally to stay until Abdullah was four months old, when she demanded the baby be given to Omar's wife and Sally, her long-time dedicated travelling companion, be sent back to Europe with a small amount of money and a reference. Why Lucie, the champion of fallen women, should have taken such an unforgiving attitude to the faithful Sally is a mystery that she took with her to the grave. She may have simply been jealous, but also cross with herself for being so. In the event, her daughter Janet had a less emotional reaction and took Sally into her own Alexandria household.

Lucie lasted for a further five days after her final, heart-wrenching letter to her beloved husband Alick on 9 July 1869. Waited on by Omar and her new maid Emma Matthews on her boat in Cairo, she died at dawn on 14 July. The Koran was recited outside her cabin within the hour, as she was prepared for burial later that day in the Muslim tradition. Hekekyan Bey, who had done so much to make Lucie's time in Egypt the profound experience it was, found an American missionary to preside over the funeral in the Christian cemetery. She lies there to this day, an honoured English guest in a city which came to have good cause to hate her fellow countrymen. Though the whereabouts of her grave is unknown, the innocent enchantment that characterised the relationship between Lucie and Egypt is preserved in these letters and lives on.

Hannah Rogerson
London, 2021

Notes

Page 13, line 5. 'this horrid Shepheard's Hotel': Lucie almost certainly despised the hotel for its grandeur and aloofness from Egyptian society. It had already established itself as the social centre of the British community in Cairo, which it remained for another hundred years until burnt down by rioters on Black Saturday, 26 January 1952. It had been founded by an odd pair of entrepreneurs, Samuel Shepheard who described himself as an 'undistinguished apprentice pastry chef from Nottingham' and Mr Hill, the Khedive Muhammad Ali's head coachman. The food was never good, the service at the long bar notoriously slow, and Mr Shepheard had sold up in 1861 so was no longer running the show when Lucie stayed.

Hekekian Bey was a distinguished and affable man who had trained as an engineer in England as a young man. He was a member of a prominent Armenian family and one of his brothers-in-law had even served as Prime Minister to Muhammad Ali (1805–49). They lost their position during the reign of Abbas I (1848–54) a traditionalist who tried to halt the intense westernisation of Egypt begun by his grandfather. Said Pasha then presided over a boom period (1854–63) fuelled by the rise in the price of cotton. By the time Lucie was in Egypt, Ismail Pasha (Khedive from 1863–79) was pushing forward an aggressive campaign of modernisation and imperial expansion.

Page 13, line 9. 'like Rachel': this is not a learned Biblical reference but refers to the stage name of a popular French actress, Elizabeth Felix.

Page 14, paragraph 3, line 1. 'Omar took Sally sightseeing': Sally was Lucie's maid. They had already travelled to South Africa and the South of France together. Sally's sister Ellen was employed in Alexandria by Janet Ross, Lucie's eldest daughter.

Page 14, paragraph 4, line 6. 'Arab Grisi' is another stage reference, to the Italian singers, Judith and Julia Grisi.

Page 15, line 6. 'Wallah!': I swear to God

Page 16, line 1. 'like Hagar': the beautiful Arab wife of Abraham.

Page 16, line 2. 'There is Boaz': another happy reference from the Old Testament. Boaz was a wealthy landowner from Bethlehem, Judea who fell in love with Ruth and broke the prohibition on marrying a Moabite (an Arab).

Page 16, paragraph 2, line 6. 'my Reis': my captain and helmsman.

Page 16, paragraph 3, line 1. Hekekian (God bless him) took Lucie to the two greatest buildings in Cairo, the 14th-century medersa-mosque of Sultan Hassan and that of Ibn Tulun. The vast courtyard mosque of Ibn Tulun was finished in 879 AD for the Turkic governor of Egypt who broke away from the Abbasid Caliphate. It was designed to be the centre of a new city (which later decayed into a suburb of Cairo) and has always been somewhat neglected and romantic.

Page 17, paragraph 2, line 3. 'Kibleh' is the apsidal niche which indicates the direction of prayer in a mosque.

Page 17, paragraph 2, line 9. 'tombs of the Khalifah': One of the great sites of Islamic Cairo is the City of the Dead, a vast medieval necropolis of ornate tombs and chantry chapels built by the Mameluke Sultans (1250–1517). The Mamelukes were Sultans and never claimed to be Caliphs (Khalifah) but maintained a dynasty of titular Abbasid Caliphs like captive songbirds in a gilded cage. The Fatimid dynasty (909–1170) ruled from Cairo and did claim to be Caliphs (Khalifah) but their monumental tombs were flattened by the Mamelukes.

Page 18, paragraph 2, line 3. 'Zint el Bachreyn': Zint is not an immediately recognisable but makes more sense as an incorrect spelling of either 'Bint' – daughter or 'Zinat' – adornment. So the boat was called 'Daughter of the Two Seas' or 'The Adornment of the Two Rivers' or some such thing.

Page 25, paragraph 2, line 3. Lucie's first testimony to the suffering inflicted on the poor farmers of Egypt by the compulsory labour service used to excavate the Suez Canal for Said Pasha and later Ismail Pasha, to the designs of de Lesseps. The canal had been surveyed in 1854 but British influence deliberately frustrated the scheme for two years. Over a million men laboured on it for a period of ten years, with labour battalions from the different provinces, variously estimated at between 30,000 and 100,000 men, working at any one time, usually for periods of 60 or 90 days.

Page 27, line 19. 'Thebes' is wonderfully evocative but can be confusing, as there is an ancient city in central Greece with the same name. The ancient Egyptian city of Waset was known to the Greeks as Thebes – the city of a hundred gates – while Greek Thebes had just seven. It is now known as Luxor, derived from the Arabic *El-Uksur* – the castles – after the old temple complexes of Karnak and Luxor had been turned into fortresses in the late Roman Empire.

Page 30, paragraph 2, line 23. 'Prince Pückler Muskau' was a famous German traveller (1785-1871) who wrote up his adventures in four volumes. Lucie would probably have liked to kick him more than once, as he was a famous womaniser and had bewitched her mother.

Page 30, paragraph 2, line 26. 'that august and pathetic giant who sits at Abou Simbel' is of course a reference to Rameses II, who had himself carved into the living rock, of equal size to a trinity of deities. In this period the temple was romantically covered in windblown desert sand.

Page 31, paragraph 2, line 1. 'we met a Rifae darweesh': The Koranic scholar from southern Iraq, Ahmad al-Rifai (1118–82) is the founder of the Rifai Sufi brotherhood, which spread all over the Arab Middle East and throughout the Ottoman Empire. It was one of the most popular of the mystical brotherhoods within Islam, and one which allowed its members, known as dervishes (darweesh), to incorporate local spiritual practices. Lucie kept pet snakes as a child, so is amused rather than fearful.

Page 37, paragraph 3, line 2. 'telling me of dear Lord Lansdowne's death': Lansdowne (1780-1863) was loved for many things. He was a gallant but moderate leader of the Whig (reform) party in England, who campaigned long and hard against slavery and the oppression of Catholics in Ireland. He was also a personal friend of Lucie and her husband. Indeed they had first met, and fallen in love, at a ball in his London residence, Lansdowne House, in 1840. He died from a fall whilst at Bowood, his stately home in Wiltshire.

Page 42, line 40. 'the Sultan and his doings': The visit to Egypt of the ruling Ottoman Sultan Abdel Aziz created a buzz of speculation. The rulers of Egypt, though in all ways politically independent of the Ottoman Empire, were in theory just viceroys, or Khedives. The two nations had fought each other twice over the rule of Syria (in 1831–33 and 1839–41) but had been allies against the Greeks during the Greek War of Independence (1821–32) and during the recent Crimean War (1853–56). The Ottoman Sultan certainly entertained a number of projects, which included the re-annexation of the independent Beylik of Libya back into the Ottoman Empire, which happened in a bloodless coup the following year, 1864.

Page 42, line 10. 'tomorrow the Mahmaal goes': This was indeed a sight not to miss. The sacred caravan left Cairo once a year taking offerings to the holy city of Mecca, including a new silk cover for the Kaaba, carried in an ornate pavilion on the back of a camel.

Page 42, paragraph 2, line 1. 'I have a black slave – a real one': Lucie perhaps contrasts this 'real one' with Hassan el Bakkeet, whom she had rescued from the streets of London. Hassan had been the Nubian servant of an Italian, who abandoned him fearing that his eye disease was infectious. Lucie took Hassan in, cured him and adopted him into her family, where he was affectionately known as Hatty.

Page 45, paragraph 2, line 1. 'the khamseen is blowing': literally the 'fifty days', when a hot, dry wind blows from the south and east, bringing the dust of the Sahara. It also means the season of the wind, which is between Easter and Whitsun, April to May.

Page 56, paragraph 2, line 5. 'to the tomb of Sittina Zeyneb': Al-Sayeda Zeynab (599–629) is one of the heroic female figures of early Islam, adored by both Sunni and Shia. She was the daughter of Imam Ali (nephew and son-in-law of the Prophet) and Fatimah (the Prophet Muhammad's youngest daughter). After the death of her brother Husayn at the Battle of Kerbala, leadership of the surviving members of the Prophet's family fell on Zeynab's shoulders. Her nobility and dignity were revealed in adversity, as the column of dejected female prisoners and one or two surviving infants, were marched from Kerbala to Syria. Her grave is also venerated in Damascus. She was named after her aunt, who was one of the four daughters of the Prophet.

Page 59, line 4. 'the only gentleman was a poor Moor': Lucie had translated two accounts of the brutal French conquest of Algeria, so her sympathies are not with the Europeans.

Page 66, paragraph 2, line 4. 'I asked if Abdel Kader': The heroic leader of Algerian resistance to the French conquest had been allowed to go into exile in Syria, where he astonished the world again by protecting thousands of native Christians against the 1860 massacres. He was fêted, thanked and honoured when he visited London and Paris in 1865.

Page 77, line 4. 'Sultan of Darfoor': Darfur was an independent Muslim Sultanate (1603-1874) in the southern Sahel, whose borders expanded and contracted in the region between Lake Chad and the banks of the Nile – the eastern half of what is now Sudan.

Page 77, line 10. 'the Pasha's Arnouts were too bad company': These Albanian highlanders were customarily employed as a sort of freelance militia throughout the Ottoman Empire. They were glamorous figures but not always very well behaved. Two paragraphs later Lucie mentions 'the Illyrian Arnouts' – probably picking up on a distinction between the Gheg of the northern highlands (bordering Serbia) and the more Mediterranean culture of the southern Tosk.

Page 83, paragraph 3, line 1. 'new even to Lane I think': This is a reference to Edward William Lane (1801–76) author of *Manners and Customs of Modern Egyptians*, first published in 1836.

Page 89, paragraph 2, line 14. 'the tombs if Abu-l-Hajjaj and his three sons' are in a magnificent position, built above the colonnade of an ancient pharaonic temple. Abu-l-Hajjaj was a Sufi sheikh, who was born around 1150 and died in 1244. He was a disciple of a disciple of Abu Madyan, the great mystic of the Maghreb whose tomb is in western Algeria.

Page 92, line 3. 'gave me Miss Martineau's book': *Eastern Life Present and Past* by Harriet Martineau, a prominent female writer and early sociologist, was published in 1848 and described her Egyptian and Levantine travels in 1846–47.

Page 95, paragraph 3, line 9. Karsten Niebuhr (1733–1815) was sent by the King of Denmark to explore the Middle East in 1761, a hundred years before Lucie's travels. Captain Cook's several voyages of exploration within the Pacific happened between 1769–80.

Page 96, paragraph 4, line 2. 'shooting their pigeons': If only British travellers and residents in Egypt had read Lucie, we would have been spared the deaths and judicial murders of the 13 June 1906 Denshawi incident. The villagers of Denshawi chased off a group of British officers who were shooting their pigeons as if they were wild game. The British were unaware that in Egypt all pigeons are a treasured resource that contribute to the livelihood of the village. There were shots fired in panic by the 'sportsmen', one of whom wounded a female villager, so the shouting got worse. One of the sportsmen then bolted for safety and would later die of sunstroke. The British officers were clearly at fault but nevertheless the Egyptian villagers were summarily punished with a mass arrest, while a trumped-up trial led to four men being publicly hung and eight flogged. Denshawi is widely considered to be a turning point from which British rule in Egypt never recovered its moral authority, possibly on a par with their actions in Dublin, in 1916 and in Amritsar, in 1919.

Page 101, line 8. 'Layard' refers to Sir Henry Layard, who knew all about being a hard-working and overlooked young consul, from his period as attaché in Istanbul. Now, however, he was in his prime – excavator and author of books about the archaeological discoveries at Nimrud and Nineveh and an MP who had risen to be Under Secretary for Foreign Affairs, 1861–66. He would not have overlooked any communication from Lucie as he was a cherished old family friend and had been Henry Ross's first choice for best man at his wedding to Janet Duff Gordon.

Page 116, line 1. 'I often hear of Lady Ellenborough': better known as Jane Digby (1807–81) a society beauty with a taste for reckless men, until, at the age of 46, she met Medjuel, the love of her life, in the Syrian desert. We do not need to worry about her being 'cut' by English travellers. In Damascus she struck up a great friendship with Richard and Isobel Burton and Abdel Kader.

Page 146, paragraph 2, line 12. 'Simoom' is literally 'the poisonous wind'. In Lucie's case that means touched by damp, but it is usually associated with a brief, half-hour-long sandstorm with a sudden rise in temperature and atmospheric pressure.

Page 166, paragraph 2, line 4. 'some of the Anglo-Indian travellers passed and gazed with fierce disgust': Lucie's invincible humanity was part of a universal tradition of humanism that was about to be eclipsed by racism which was a brand new evil that was leeching out into the world. The Indian Mutiny/Struggle for Independence of 1857 was a key turning point in British racial attitudes, which coincided with the rise of the pseudo-science of racism. Arthur Gobineau's *Essay on the Inequality of the Human Races* was translated in America within a year of its first publication, in 1855 in Paris. Darwin cannot be blamed for his *Origin of the Species* in 1859, but racist minds were attracted to his concept of the survival of the fittest.

Page 178, paragraph 3, line 12. 'he knows Madlle. Tiné': Alexandrine Tiné (1835–69) was a famously wealthy and intrepid Danish-Dutch traveller. She had explored the Sudan and the White Nile between 1861–64, and though her mother and aunt died during this expedition she determined to continue. She spent the next three years on the coast of North Africa, made a failed attempt to cross the Sahara from Algiers, but determined to try again in January 1869, setting off from Tripoli on a journey to Lake Chad. She was murdered on 1st August, on the caravan trail between Murzuk and Ghat, probably the victim of a feud amongst the Tuareg clans who escorted her.

Page 181, line 6. 'Prévost Paradol': liberal minded French journalist, editor and philosopher, 1829–70, who was sent to the USA as a French envoy and took his life there, depressed by the Franco-Prussian War.

Page 213, line 2. 'Sir Bartle Frere': An exceptional colonial administrator, enlightened, interested and imaginative, who ruled as governor of Bombay from 1862–67. He came a cropper in South Africa, aspiring to create a confederation of states that might become an independent Dominion in something of the manner of Canada and Australia. There is a fine statue of him in London's Victoria Embankment gardens.

Page 226, paragraph 2, line 1. 'Mr. and Miss North': Lucie knew the North family of old, having spent much time with them as a teenager (when both her parents were in Malta). The genial and hospitable Frederick North was M.P. for Hastings and Lucie was a friend to his daughters, one of whom was the redoubtable traveller and botanical artist Marianne North (1830–90), who has a gallery devoted to her works in Kew Gardens. As Lucie observes in a later letter, her sketches 'were absolutely true in colour'.

Page 240, paragraph 2, line 1. 'till Mr. Palgrave arrived': William Gifford Palgrave (1826–88) was one of the greatest British travellers in Arabia. He was a brilliant classics scholar at Charterhouse and Oxford, going on to serve in the army of the East India Company which he left to become a Jesuit. Living in Syria, he improved his Arabic to a standard that allowed him to travel across Arabia in the guise of a Syrian physician in 1862–63. *A Narrative of a Year's Journey through Central and Eastern Arabia* had been published in 1865, after which he left the ranks of the Jesuits and joined the British Foreign Office. His three brothers were also formidable characters. The Palgrave *Golden Treasury of English Songs and Lyrics* was created by his brother Francis.

Page 252, paragraph 2, line 1. This letter is full of book talk with four intriguing literary references: 'Miss Berry *is* dull' refers to the three-volume memoir of Mary Berry (1763–1852) which had been published in 1866. Mary had been the trusted friend of the waspish Horace Walpole, whose letters and diaries she prepared for the press in 1798.

Three lines later, Lucie rightly does not need to be sent a copy of Emily Eden's book of Indian travels, *Up the Country*, published in 1866. Emily Eden (1797–1869) was the snobbish and disdainful sister of the British Governor-General of India, Lord Auckland.

Sir Samuel Baker (1821–93) was of much greater interest. He was not the classic lone male British adventurer but travelled in comfort and in the agreeable company of his Levantine wife. Together they explored the Nile from the Egyptian end. They met Speke and Grant (who had been exploring East Africa) at the island of Gondokoro (in southernmost Sudan, 750 miles south of Khartoum). Speke and Grant arrived all exhausted from their travels at this exotically isolated island, deep in darkest Africa, to be greeted by the Bakers who were able to offer them a cup of tea in their well-appointed encampment. Baker's book on their Nile explorations also came out in 1866.

A French translation of Abdel Kader's philosophical treatise had been published in 1858, *Rappel a l'Intelligent*.

Page 254, paragraph 3, line 3. The Saadiya Sufi brotherhood of Cairo showed their devotion by forming a living carpet over which their sheikh rode on a horse – the ceremony of 'Doseh' (treading).

Page 254, paragraph 3, line 7. 'Mrs Lott's most extraordinary book': Miss Emmeline Lott spent two years looking after a young son of Ismail Pasha, and published her memoir of court gossip, *English Governess in Egypt: Harem Life in Egypt and Constantinople*, in 1866.

Page 254, paragraph 4, line 2. 'the cutting of the canal' does not refer to the Suez Canal but a canal that branched off the Nile to enter the city of Cairo during the annual flooding, or rise in river level. Every year it was dammed with a hymen of earth that was known as the Bride of the Nile.

Page 283, paragraph 2, line 1. 'The war in Crete': The Khedive sent 16,000 Egyptian soldiers to reinforce the Ottoman army in 1866, to quell the Cretan rebellion which ended with the dramatic siege of Arkadi monastery. The Egyptians were often involved in the affairs of Crete. It was an Egyptian army that in 1828 finally quashed the Greek Revolt that had begun in 1821 and stayed on as a ruling garrison until they formally handed the island back to the Ottoman Empire in 1840 – though the popular Egyptian governor was left in power until 1852. There had been another Cretan revolt in 1858, which had been settled with some reforms which were never quite actioned. Hence the revolt of 1866.

Page 283, paragraph 4, line 2. 'What a repulsive picture of a woman': The Marquise du Deffand (1697–1780) was one of those disdainful intellectual aristocrats who you should read in order to understand why the French invented the guillotine. She ran a literary salon in Paris and wrote letters to Horace Walpole, which had been collected together in four volumes by Mary Berry and published in 1810. A bigger collection had just come out in 1865.

Page 284, paragraph 3, line 5. Edward Lear (1812–88) is now worshipped for his *Book of Nonsense* but was an indefatigable traveller in the Eastern Mediterranean, and paid his way by making the most beautiful landscape sketches and watercolours.

Page 287, paragraph 3, line 2. 'the Candian business': Candia is an old name for Crete, which was then still part of the Ottoman Empire. Cretan politics has always been complex. The island had been part of the Ottoman Empire since the 1645–69 war, before which it had been ruled by Venice. What is often forgotten is that a majority of the islanders had converted to Islam in the 17th century

– probably for no greater spiritual cause than tax avoidance – but in the 19th century many of the highland Cretan clans were flocking back to the Orthodox Church which was passionately nationalist. Greece obviously had its sights on the island, but knew it could only achieve this with the support of either France, Britain or Russia, or ideally (such as at the Battle of Navarino forty years before) all these powers.

Page 290, paragraph 2, line 1. 'Thanks for the Westminster epilogue': Lucie refers to the annual Latin play performed by Westminster School, which seems to have had some reference to the fact that the famous Latin playwright, Terence, had been born in North Africa and brought to Rome as a slave.

Page 310, paragraph 3, line 2. 'a hearty welcome to the Ameer' – In 1867, the Ottoman Sultan Abdel Aziz, accompanied by Khedive Ismail Pasha, undertook state visits to Paris then London.

Page 332, paragraph 5, line 1. 'can you thank the Prince of Wales for Omar': Edward Prince of Wales (the future King Edward VII) took his young Danish wife (Princess Alexandra) on a six-month tour of the Eastern Mediterranean over the winter of 1868–69. They first visited Alexandra's brother, who had been made King of Greece, and then moved on to Istanbul before finishing their tour in Egypt. Alexandra visited the ladies of the harem of Khedive Ismail Pasha and they both rode camels out to the pyramids in February but also spent some time on the Nile. Princess Alexandria had read the first edition of Lucie's *Letters from Egypt* and wanted to visit the author, but this meeting was probably postponed at the request of Khedive Ismail who knew that Lucie strongly disapproved of his autocratic use of Egyptian labour to dig the Suez Canal. Lucie was removed from the official itinerary, but Omar seems to have been employed by the royal party which could not have been easy for Lucie who knew her end was now very close. But right at the end of their Egyptian tour the royal couple did manage to visit Lucie, albeit briefly, for her boat, the *Urania*, was then moored at Aswan. Prince Edward appointed Omar his official Dragoman (interpreter) as a mark of favour for that young man, conscious of how much that would please Lucie.

It was Prince Edward's second visit to Egypt. He had been sent on a four-month-long tour of the Eastern Mediterranean in 1862, accompanied by a dull group of elderly and worthy companions assembled for his continuing education by his parents. This trip is well chronicled for he was accompanied by the pioneer photographer Francis Bedford. Prince Edward's second visit to Egypt was the start of a very busy year for the Khedive and had its own diplomatic context. The waters of the Red Sea and the Mediterranean were married that summer when the Suez Canal was opened. In November 1869 the canal was officially inaugurated with a monumental gala in the presence of the Khedive, the Empress Eugenie of France and dozens of other European monarchs. *Rigoletto* was performed in the Egyptian Opera House for these distinguished foreign guests, to be followed two years later by the first performance of *Aida*. The British were not well represented at the canal ceremonies, for they had been opposed to the creation of the canal right from the start. This adds a further element of farcical hypocrisy to the 'protectorate' they later imposed over Egypt but also gives even greater interest to Prince Edward's visit.

ELAND

61 Exmouth Market, London EC1R 4QL
Email: info@travelbooks.co.uk

Eland was started in 1982 to revive great travel books which had fallen out of print. Although the list soon diversified into biography and fiction, all the titles are chosen for their interest in spirit of place. One of our readers explained that for him reading an Eland is like listening to an experienced anthropologist at the bar – she's let her hair down and is telling all the stories that were just too good to go into the textbook.

Eland books are for travellers, and for those who are content to travel in their own minds. We can never quite define what we are looking for, but they need to be observant of others, to catch the moment and place on the wing and to have a page-turning gift for storytelling. And they might do that while being, by turns, funny, wry, intelligent, humane, universal, self-deprecating and idiosyncratic. We take immense trouble to select only the most readable books and therefore many people collect the entire series.

Extracts from each and every one of our books can be read on our website, at www.travelbooks.co.uk. If you would like a free copy of our catalogue, please order it from the website, email us or send a postcard.